New Party Politics

*From Jefferson
and Hamilton to the
Information Age*

John Kenneth White
Catholic University of America

Daniel M. Shea
Allegheny College

BEDFORD/ST. MARTIN'S   Boston ♦ New York

For Bedford/St. Martin's

Political Science Editor: James R. Headley
Senior Editor, Publishing Services: Douglas Bell
Production Supervisor: Joseph Volpe
Project Management: Stratford Publishing Services, Inc.
Marketing Manager: Charles Cavaliere
Cover Design: Lucy Krikorian
Composition: Stratford Publishing Services, Inc.
Printing and Binding: Haddon Craftsman, an R. R. Donnelley & Sons Company

President: Charles H. Christensen
Editorial Director: Joan E. Feinberg
Director of Editing, Design, and Production: Marcia Cohen
Manager, Publishing Services: Emily Berleth

Library of Congress Catalog Card Number: 99–62371

Manufactured in the United States of America.

5   4   3   2   1   0
f   e   d   c   b   a

For information, write: Bedford/St. Martin's, 75 Arlington Street, Boston, MA 02116 (617–399–4000)

ISBN: 0–312–15254–X (paperback)
        0–312–23255–1 (hardcover)

Acknowledgments

Acknowledgments and copyrights appear at the back of the book on pages 316–318, which constitute an extension of the copyright page.

This book is dedicated to

Jeannette Brigitte Prevost White, who is too young to know
the real meaning of donkeys and elephants

and to

Dennis M. Shea, a dedicated student and teacher of party politics.

Preface

In the *Federalist Papers*, Alexander Hamilton wrote: "Every vital question of state will be merged in the question, 'Who will be the next president?'"[1] Hamilton's query was on the minds of his fellow citizens at the end of the eighteenth century. It is on our minds once more as we approach the twenty-first century. In the presidential contest that is already underway as we write this in the fall of 1999, no incumbent president will be listed on the ballot—the first time that has happened since 1988. Since the ratification of the Twenty-Second Amendment in 1951, no president has been allowed to serve more than two terms in office. Thus, Bill Clinton will retire to his New York estate, and his wife, Hillary, is poised to run for a vacancy created by the retirement of New York's senior U.S. Senator Daniel Patrick Moynihan. A prospective presidential contest between Republican George W. Bush and Democrat Al Gore, not to mention Hillary Clinton's all-but-announced campaign for the Senate, ensures that 2000 will not be a run-of-the-mill election year.

Open-seat contests for the presidency are rare. Since 1952, there have only been three times when voters were asked to select a newcomer: 1960, 1968, and 1988. But the significance of these elections has varied. The 1960 John F. Kennedy–Richard M. Nixon contest was a struggle between former junior military officers who served during World War II over which one would replace President Dwight D. Eisenhower, who had been a leading Army general during the war. The 1968 Richard M. Nixon–Hubert H. Humphrey–George C. Wallace election marked the introduction of social and cultural issues (including crime and the 1960s sexual revolution) that Republicans used to their advantage in the elections that followed. The 1988 George Bush–Michael S. Dukakis race was markedly less important—marred by debates about whether the Pledge of Allegiance should be said in public schools, and Dukakis's poor judgment in giving a weekend furlough pass to convicted criminal Willie Horton. Bush won, but his ideas ("read my lips, no new taxes") proved insufficient for governing.

The 2000 election promises to be much more important. Democratic and Republican operatives see this presidential contest as one that gives each party a unique opportunity to reposition itself for the new century. Hamilton's query notwithstanding, the next election is about much more than who will be the next president. It takes place in a new context: the infancy of the Information Age. Of course, the Information Age has been with us for some time. Computers, once commonplace in our offices, have moved into our homes. The Internet, with its capacity to take us places on the World Wide Web heretofore unimaginable, has altered the terms upon which voters and politicians interact. Web users can read the speeches of their favorite candidates; volunteers can sign up on-line; and e-precincts have added a new dimension to political organizing. Political parties have had to adapt to these technological changes. The national Democratic and Republican parties have established their own Web pages, as have most of their state counterparts. Third parties have also found the World Wide Web to be an important resource. The Reform Party, Green Party, and Libertarian Party—just to name a few—have their own sophisticated Web sites that invite browsers to come aboard.

In one sense, this story of party change and adaptation is not new. Ever since their inception at the end of the eighteenth century, political parties have struggled to adapt to new conditions on the peculiar soil we call the United States. Their ability to conform to their environment has varied over time. During their heyday, extending from immediately after the Civil War until the 1930s, Democrats and Republicans built machines which were powerful instruments that organized elections and the administrations of government that followed. The demise of those machines has led many to bemoan the decline of parties—a "fact" much written about since the mid-twentieth century.

This book tells the story of political parties in America. It is a story of adaptation and renewal. We began this work with a bias toward strong parties—seeing them as necessary instruments for governance in such a large, diverse country as the United States. We conclude with this viewpoint intact. Unlike many of our colleagues, we are impressed with the ability of American parties to find new strengths in altered environments. To be sure, political parties "ain't what they used to be." The old urban machines have withered away, lingering in only a few places. Strong voter loyalties toward the Democrats and Republicans have also ebbed, as issues and candidates dominate how Americans act inside the privacy of the voting booth. But the Information Age is forcing parties to become more interactive—to use the wizardry of technology to communicate with a generation of new voters already comfortable with the tools of the Information Age.

But this text is more than a story about party evolution. Each of the chapters says much about who we are as Americans. Some years ago, Ronald Reagan declared: "A political party isn't a fraternity. It isn't something like the old school tie you wear. You band together in a political party because of certain beliefs of what government should be."[2] For nearly two centuries, Democrats and Republicans have battled over such large ideas as Alexander Hamilton's concept of a national family of Americans inextricably tied to one another (which meant a strong role for the federal government) and Thomas Jefferson's preference for lightly governed local communities (which meant a less dominant role for the federal government). Our varied answers over time to this dispute says much about who we are and what kind of government (and society) we want.

This, then, is our story. Both of us have told it to our graduate and undergraduate students over the years. It seemed especially fitting to put our ideas into a larger parties textbook, a daunting task that many of our colleagues have wanted us to do for years. In this enterprise we have been supported by now former editors at Bedford/St. Martin's, Beth Gillett and James Headley. Both provided words of encouragement when they were needed. We would like to thank those who have commented on all or parts of this book in its various stages: Cheryl L. Brown,

UNC–Charlotte; Greg Hager, University of Kentucky; Douglas Koopman, Calvin College; Penny Miller, University of Kentucky; J. P. Monroe, University of Miami; Mark Petracca, University of California–Irvine; Gerald Pomper, Rutgers University; Gary L. Rose, Sacred Heart University; Hanes Walton, Jr., University of Michigan and anonymous reviewers.

We also owe a great debt to our wives, Yvonne and Christine, whose love and support sustained us every step of the way.

Finally, we dedicate this book to our children, Jeannette White and Abigail and Daniel Shea. They are too young to appreciate political parties—being much more interested in donkeys and elephants, instead of Democrats and Republicans. But they are destined to live out their lives in the new century, and the answers they give to the question, "What does it mean to be an American?" will say much about how parties will fare in the next millennium.

John Kenneth White

Daniel M. Shea

NOTES

1. Quoted in Emmet John Hughes, *The Living Presidency* (New York: Coward, McCann, and Geoghegan, 1973), 40.
2. Hugh Sidey, "A Conversation with Reagan," *Time*, September 3, 1984.

Contents

PREFACE   v

ABOUT THE AUTHORS   xvii

**Introduction: Rethinking
Political Parties in the Information Age   1**
NOTES   11

1 **Political Parties in an American Setting   13**
POLITICAL PARTIES: INSTITUTIONS
AMERICANS LOVE TO HATE   14

Praise from the Ivory Tower   16
Politics without Parties   16

The Parties Speak: Gejdenson versus
White on the Importance of Political Parties   17

THREE IMPORTANT PARTY DISTINCTIONS   18

How Parties Differ from Other Organizations   18
The Components of American Political Parties   19
Does the Tripod Work in the Information Age?   21
What Do Political Parties Seek to Accomplish?   23

THE BATTLE OF THE TITANS: HAMILTON
VERSUS JEFFERSON   27

LIKE GOD, PARTIES ARE NOT DEAD   30

FURTHER READING   30

NOTES   31

2 **The Ascendance of Party Politics   33**
THE PRE-PARTY ERA   33

THE COLONIAL EXPERIENCE   34

NASCENT PARTIES: FEDERALISTS VERSUS REPUBLICANS   37

ix

PARTY RULE: 1824–1912   40

Breakdown and Renewal: The Election of 1824   41

The Jackson-Van Buren Alliance   42

The Rise of Mass-Based Politics and the Emergence of the Spoils System   44

The Interregnum: Parties and the Civil War   45

The Coming of the Machine   48

The Parties Speak: A Day in the Life of
Party Boss George Washington Plunkitt   49

The Parties Speak: Lyndon B. Johnson and
Richard J. Daley on Patronage   51

PARTIES "AMERICAN STYLE"   52

FURTHER READING   53

NOTES   53

3   The Decline of Party Politics   55

"CLEAN IT UP!": THE PROGRESSIVE MOVEMENT   56

Enter the Progressives   57

The Parties Speak: Robert M. LaFollette, Sr.,
"The Menace of the Machine" (1897)   61

Why the Progressive Movement Was Successful   65

An End to Party Politics?   68

FRANKLIN D. ROOSEVELT AND THE NEW DEAL   70

The New Deal and Party Politics   71

POLITICAL PARTIES AND THE COLD WAR   72

THE RISE OF INTEREST GROUPS   74

The Interest Group Explosion   74

THE RISE OF CANDIDATE-CENTERED POLITICS   76

Party Activist versus Professional Consultant   76

Party Member versus Nonpartisan Candidate   77

The Parties Speak: Ed Rollins and the "Campaign from Hell"   78

Party Affiliation versus Voting Choice   79

The Parties Speak: Louis LaPolla, "The Pothole Mayor,"
A Case Study in Ambition   80

A PARTYLESS AGE?   81

FURTHER READING   82

NOTES   82

4   Party Organizations in the Twenty-First Century   84

ORGANIZATIONAL ADJUSTMENT AND GROWTH   86

The Rebirth of the Republican National Committee   87

The Democratic National Committee Plays Catch-Up   89

New Technologies in the Information Age   89

Summary   90

THE EMERGENCE OF LEGISLATIVE
CAMPAIGN COMMITTEES   93

The Hill Committees   93

The Parties Speak: Congressman David Price on the Role of Party in
Campaigns   96

State Legislative Campaign Committees   97

The Parties Speak: Party Leaders Voice Concerns about Legislative
Campaign Committees   98

WITHER THE LOCAL PARTIES?   99

Evidence of Local Party Renewal   99

Evidence of Local Party Decline   102

REVITALISTS VERSUS DECLINISTS   103

CONCLUSION   105

FURTHER READING   105

NOTES   106

**5   Nominating Presidents
in the Information Age   108**

WHAT KIND OF PRESIDENT?   108

From John Adams to Bill Clinton: The Problem of Presidential Selection   113

The Parties Speak: Alexander Hamilton on Choosing an American
President   114

HAMILTON'S FAMILY VERSUS
JEFFERSON'S COMMUNITY   116

The Rise of Nominating Conventions   117

THE RISE OF HAMILTONIAN NATIONALISM   120

The McGovern-Fraser Commission   121

The Parties Speak: The *New Republic's* Reflections on the Assassination of
Robert F. Kennedy and the Democratic Party of 1968   122

Are Primaries and Caucuses Representative?   128

Republicans Follow the McGovern-Fraser Lead   130

The Unintended Consequences of the McGovern-Fraser Reforms   *132*
The Mikulski and Winograd Commissions   *133*
Enter the Superdelegates   *134*

LOOKING TO 2000   135

FURTHER READING   137

NOTES   137

6   **Party Brand Loyalty and the American Voter   140**

THE IMPORTANCE OF PARTY IDENTIFICATION   142

Measuring Party Identification   *145*
Is Party Identification Obsolete?   *147*

THE MAKING OF AN IDEA: PARTY REALIGNMENT   147

V. O. Key and Party Realignment   *148*
The Parties Speak: V. O. Key and the Theory of Party Realignment   149
Party Realignment: The Death of a Concept?   *152*
The Parties Speak: Everett C. Ladd, Like
Waiting for Godot, the Uselessness of Party Realignment   154

WHERE ARE THE VOTERS GOING?   157

The End of the New Deal Coalition   *157*
Here Come the Ticket-Splitters   *157*

PARTY COALITIONS IN THE CLINTON ERA   160

The Gender Gap   *163*
Divided Government   *166*

WHAT'S LEFT FOR PARTIES?   169

FURTHER READING   170

NOTES   171

7   **State and Local Parties: Mom-and-Pop Shops in the
Information Age   174**

STATE AND LOCAL PARTIES
IN THE INFORMATION AGE   175

Regulating State Parties   *176*
Party Structure   *177*
A Network of Allied Party Groups   *180*
The Parties Speak: David Rehr on the National
Beer Wholesalers Association and the GOP   182

WHO BELONGS? 184

Primary Voters 184
Officials in the Party Organization 189
Activists 191
Summary 192

LOCAL POLITICAL CULTURE 192

The Parties Speak: The "Amateur Democrats" 194

WHAT STATE AND LOCAL PARTIES DO 195

Manifest Party Functions 195
Nassau County Republicans: A Machine That Keeps on Ticking 197
The Kings County Republican Committee: Fighting the Nonpartisan Tide 198
The Loudoun County Democrats: An Information Age Revival Story 199
Dare County Democratic Committee: Hoping for a Policy Makeover 200
Summary 200

STATE AND LOCAL PARTIES, COMPUTERS, AND THE INTERNET 201

Desktop Tools 201
State Parties on the Net 201

COMPUTERS TO THE RESCUE? 203

APPENDIX A: REPUBLICAN STATE COMMITTEE WEB SITES AS OF 1998 204

APPENDIX B: DEMOCRATIC STATE COMMITTEE WEB SITES AS OF 1998 205

FURTHER READING 206

NOTES 206

8   Campaign Finance and Information Age Political Parties 208

A BRIEF LOOK AT MONEY IN ELECTIONS 210

Phase 1: Money as a Supplement to Party Activities (1790s to 1880s) 210
Phase 2: The Rise of Corporate Politics (1880s to 1950s) 211
Phase 3: Media-Centered Elections (1960s to the Present) 213

EFFORTS TO REGULATE THE FLOW OF MONEY IN ELECTIONS 214

Meaningful Reform: Watergate and Federal Reforms 216
A Challenge in the Courts: Buckley v. Valeo 218
The Rise of PACs 220

**CREATIVE PARTY FINANCES
IN THE INFORMATION AGE**   222

Issue Advocacy   223

    The Parties Speak: Ten Myths about Money in Politics   224

Independent Expenditures   227

Hard and Soft Money   229

Transfers to State Party Committees   231

Bundling   232

Funding Nominating Conventions   233

THE FUTURE OF PARTY FINANCE IN AMERICA   233

FURTHER READING   235

NOTES   235

**9   Elected Officials: The Reluctant
Sales Force of the Party System   237**

    The Parties Speak: The 1994 House Republicans'
Contract with America   238

THE PRESIDENT AS PARTY LEADER   240

THE PARTY IN CONGRESS   241

    The Parties Speak: Toward a More Responsible Two-Party System   245

THE CONTRACT WITH AMERICA   247

    The Parties Speak: The House Judiciary
Committee on the Question of Impeachment   252

THE RISE OF THE PUBLIC SPEAKERSHIP   252

HAMILTON'S CONGRESS?   255

FURTHER READING   261

NOTES   261

**10   Third Parties and the Information Age:
The Orphans of American Politics   264**

THE THIRD-PARTY PARADOX   265

Institutional Barriers   267

American Political Culture   273

The Momentum of History   276

    The Parties Speak: Benjamin C. Bubar, 1976 and
1980 Prohibition Party Presidential Nominee   278

SIGNIFICANT THIRD PARTIES IN AMERICAN HISTORY   280

The Anti-Mason Party   281
The Free-Soil Party   281
The American (Know-Nothing) Party   282
The Greenback and Populists (People's) Parties   283
The Progressives: 1912–1924   285

   The Parties Speak: William Jennings Bryan's
   "Cross of Gold" Speech Presented to the Democratic
   National Convention, Chicago, Illinois, July 8, 1896   286
Henry Wallace and the Progressive Party of 1948   287
State's Rights Party (1948) and the American Independent Party (1968)   289
The Reform Party   290

THIRD PARTIES IN THE INFORMATION AGE   291

An Explosion of Minor Parties   291
Changes in Voter Attitudes toward Minor Parties   293
Minor Parties and the Internet   294

**JEFFERSON, HAMILTON, AND
THE FUTURE OF THIRD PARTIES IN AMERICA   296**

   The Parties Speak: Ventura Win Marks Dawn of New Era:
   Age of Digital Politics   297

FURTHER READING   299

NOTES   300

**Conclusion: Hamilton's Triumph and
the Advent of the "Base-Less" Party System   302**

**THE 1998 ELECTION AND THE
"BASE-LESS" PARTY SYSTEM   307**

PARTY POLITICS IN THE NEXT MILLENNIUM   312

Voter Trends   312
Organizational Developments   312
Legislative Politics   313
New Laws   313
Minor Parties   314

NOTES   314

INDEX   319

About the Authors

John Kenneth White (Ph.D., University of Connecticut, 1980) is professor of politics at the Catholic University of America. His previous books include *Political Parties and the Collapse of the Old Orders*, (edited with Philip J. Davies); *Still Seeing Red: How the Cold War Shapes the New American Politics; The Politics of Ideas: Intellectual Challenges to the Parties after 1992* (edited with John C. Green); *Challenges to Party Government* (edited with Jerome M. Mileur); *The New Politics of Old Values;* and *The Fractured Electorate: Political Parties and Social Change in Southern New England.*

Daniel M. Shea (Ph.D., State University of New York at Albany, 1993) is associate professor of political science at Allegheny College. Before receiving his doctorate, Shea was a campaign operative for the New York State Democratic Assembly Campaign Committee. His research interests include campaign management, political parties, Congress and state legislatures, and the politics of the media. He has written or edited several books, including *Mass Politics: The Politics of Popular Culture* (St. Martin's/Worth, 1999); *Transforming Democracy; Campaign Craft; The State of the Parties;* and *Contemplating the People's Branch.* His articles have appeared in many leading journals, including the *American Politics Quarterly,* the *Harvard Journal of Press/Politics, American Review of Politics,* and *Campaigns and Elections.*

Rethinking Political Parties in the Information Age

On his first day as national chairman of the Democratic Party back in 1985, Paul Kirk received a large bouquet of flowers from his friend, Paul Sarbanes, a U.S. senator from Maryland. Kirk was delighted until he glanced at the enclosed card that read, "Rest in Peace." He promptly placed an angry telephone call to the Baltimore florist who had delivered the flowers. The man was profusely apologetic, saying a grievous mistake had been made. It seems that at a Greek Orthodox cemetery somewhere in Maryland there was a large floral arrangement on a fresh grave with a card that read, "Congratulations. You have a tough job ahead. Best of luck in your new position. Paul Sarbanes."[1]

Some might say that misplaced bouquet is one sardonic indicator, among many, that political parties "ain't what they used to be." Indeed, as we enter the Information Age, most things ain't what they used to be. Change is the order of the day, and it affects how we live, work, and communicate. At home, family life is vastly different from *Ozzie and Harriet, Leave It to Beaver,* and *The Cosby Show,* once popular television programs that depicted "all-American" households barely recognizable now. Today, divorce, remarriage, blended families, and even gay couples challenge once-conventional standards. Relations between the sexes have also changed dramatically, as fathers *and* mothers frequently work outside the home. In some families, "househusbands" cook, clean, and care for the children—a reversal from stay-at-home moms Harriet Nelson and June Cleaver.

Our work habits have also changed—from the introduction of the home computer that has revolutionized the way information is organized to the Internet that has vastly altered the way we process and receive information. More and more people are staying at home to work on full-time jobs, or come home from work to surf the Internet and correspond around the world via e-mail with friends, acquaintances, and even people they don't know. Almost without warning, the Information Age has arrived, with its plethora of Internet resources and wired computers. Little more than a decade ago, the Internet connected approximately 600 computers; by the mid-1990s, that figure had expanded to more than 1 million computers which were linked to approximately 50,000 networks around the world. At this rate of growth, by the year 2005, the Internet will be in nearly 300 million homes with access to 3 million worldwide networks.[2]

The Internet has made access to political leaders more readily available, as evidenced by the use of e-mails during the impeachment inquiry into President

Clinton's conduct during the Monica Lewinsky affair. Immediately after the release of Independent Counsel Kenneth Starr's report calling for Clinton's impeachment, Massachusetts Senator John Kerry received more than 7,000 e-mails. New Jersey Democratic Representative Steve Rothman was likewise inundated, getting 763 e-mails during one eighteen-hour period. Responses varied from "IMPEACH" (followed by 97 exclamation points), to a Virginia woman who complained that "the Internet dumping of a one-sided prosecutor's 'report' was the most egregious affront to democratic principles in my lifetime."[3] After Clinton was impeached by the House and the trial began in the Senate, the flood of e-mails rose to as many as 1 million per day.[4]

As the two parties begin the 2000 presidential campaign, the Internet has become an indispensable tool that no Information Age candidate can afford to ignore. Estimates place the number of Internet users in 1999 at 76 million, with 1 million new users logging on to the World Wide Web each month. One survey estimates that 70 percent of voting-age Americans will be on-line by election day 2000. Given these astounding figures, it is not surprising to learn that in the first days of Campaign 2000, presidential candidates were hastily investing large sums of cash into Web site development. On the Republican side, Steve Forbes has created one of the most sophisticated Web sites ever developed. Forbes, son of the wealthy publisher Malcolm Forbes, announced his candidacy on the Internet. His Web site includes new technologies such as the e-precinct, which encourages participants to enroll friends, forming "e-blocks," "e-neighborhoods," and even an "e-national committee." Forbes used his Web site to speak live to a town hall meeting in New Hampshire. In its first six weeks of operation, <Forbes2000.com> enrolled 12,720 volunteers and 1,620 e-precinct leaders, while racking up 20.3 million hits in 377,000 separate visits to the site. Rick Segal, who heads Web site development for Forbes, says: "We're reconstructing the old-fashioned ward and precinct system. I may not be the first person to invent a political machine, but I may be the first to create a political machine that's really a machine."[5] Other Republican contenders have also developed their 2000 Web sites. Dan Quayle shelled out $26,000 to get his Web page up and running—one of the biggest checks he wrote—before ending his candidacy. Pat Buchanan hired a webmaster at $50,000 a year to develop his Web page. Lamar Alexander spent an initial $20,000 on his Web site.[6] Frontrunner, Texas Governor George W. Bush raised an astounding $60 million in 1999, but initially spent a measly $15,000 to get his Web site up and running.[7] (See Figure I.1.)

Democrats also have been avid users of Information Age technologies. Democratic National Chairman Joe Andrew, himself a true believer, has noted, "All politics is local, but local has been redefined."[8] In the Information Age, people often associate with fellow enthusiasts on the Internet. Andrew applied this knowledge to Internet politics. Prior to becoming Democratic national chairman, in 1996 and again in 1998, Andrew blended Indiana's voter files with data about age, race, income, religion, magazine subscriptions, and the like to gather detailed information on the state's voters. He gave CD-ROM disks with that information to local organizers, who used it for calls, mailings, and door-to-door canvassing. They in turn enhanced the database with new, more personalized information gathered

FIGURE I.1 ▪ Republican presidential candidate George W. Bush is one of several GOP candidates to have his own Web site.

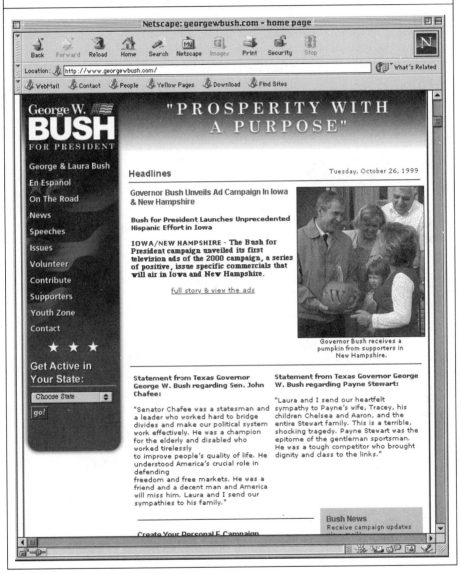

along the way. That information was credited with boosting voter turnout, and Democrats elected more new officeholders in Indiana during these two elections than in any year since 1932. Vice President Al Gore selected Andrew to be Democratic National Chairman and instructed him to apply the same technologies to the 2000 presidential race. Andrew sees his job this way: "There are fifty counties in America who may determine who's the next president."[9] By targeting individuals in each of these counties with coordinated, personalized mail, e-mail, calls, and visits, Andrew believes his party will retain the presidency.

Not surprisingly, Al Gore and his Democratic opponent Bill Bradley have invested heavily in their own Web sites. Gore has been widely praised for his sophisticated Web page that allows young children to follow his campaign activities. Long known for his advocacy of the Information Superhighway, Gore checks on his Web site at least twice a day. (See Figure I.2.) Democrat Bill Bradley has also

FIGURE I.2 ▪ **Democratic presidential candidate Al Gore has one of the most sophisticated Web sites.**

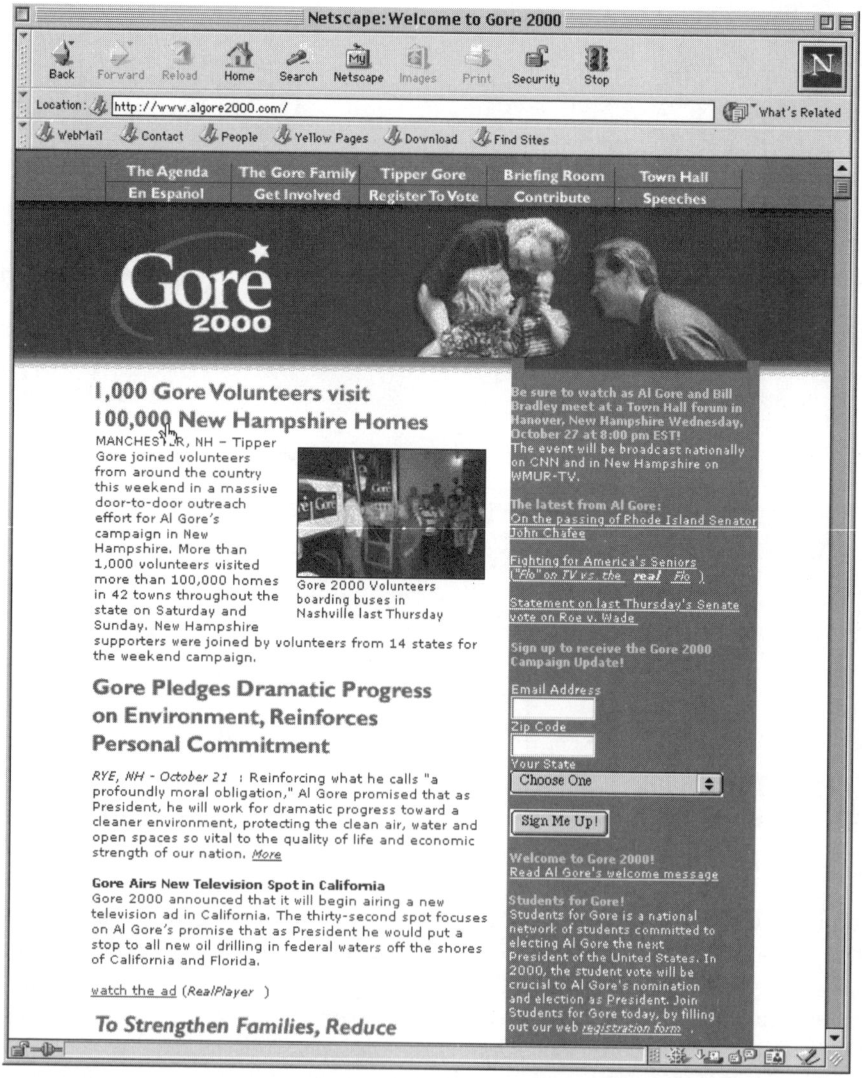

used his Web site to maximum political advantage. In 1999, the former New Jersey senator became the first presidential candidate in history to raise more than $1 million from donors using his Internet address to send in their contributions.

The situation was radically different in 1996. Far fewer Americans were online, and Web sites were generally considered a novelty rather than a sophisticated campaign tool. Steve Forbes's polling shows that in 1996 only 14 percent of New Hampshire Republicans were on-line; today, 68 percent are—and most use the Internet regularly.[10] Thus, in just four short years, the Internet has gone from a mere campaign curiosity to an indispensable instrument for reaching potential supporters.

The Internet explosion and the vast transformations it has created, to date, have not prompted political scientists to reexamine the principles they apply to the study of political parties. For decades, scholars have extolled political parties as vital transmission agents between the voters and those who hold public office. E. E. Schattschneider set the tone nearly sixty years ago when he wrote these words in a book titled *Party Government:* "Without parties there can be no organized and coherent politics. When politics lacks coherence, there can be no accountable democracy. The stakes are no less than that."[11] Clinton Rossiter reiterated Schattschneider's axiom in 1960: "No America without democracy, no democracy without politics, and no politics without parties."[12] In the decades since these glowing words were written, political scientists— including the authors of this text— have celebrated parties as vital instruments that make American democracy work. In 1983, John Kenneth White penned these words: "The survival of the political system is jeopardized. The political system is not self-supporting. Rather, it is sustained by four distinct pillars that share responsibility: the parties, the executive branch, the legislative branch, and the judiciary."[13] Daniel M. Shea, coauthor of this volume, shares this perspective. In 1995, he wrote: "Parties organize and oversee elections, encourage political participation, and educate voters. . . . [They] are the channels through which demands of participation can be accommodated and new groups of citizens brought into the political system."[14]

The idea that parties are important indicators of democratic development has been applied to nearly every nation around the globe. For example, in the once communist-controlled "captive nations" of Eastern Europe, the emergence of party competition is used to measure the varying progress of these countries toward democracy. Likewise, in the former Soviet Union, the beginnings of a fledgling party system win accolades from the vast majority of scholars. The range of parties in these countries varies from the Beer-Lovers party in Russia to the Bread-Lovers party in Poland. In the Western Hemisphere, the march toward democracy in South America is celebrated, as one country after another has discarded dictatorship in favor of democratic party rule.

The only place that political parties are not celebrated is in the United States. For quite some time, Americans have harbored a wellspring of anger and distrust toward the Democratic and Republican parties and their leadership. During the 1960s, a majority believed that parties "do more to confuse the issues than to provide a clear choice on the issues" and often "create conflict where none exists."[15] In 1982, 40 percent of Massachusetts residents told one pollster: "Instead of being the servants of the people, elected officials in Massachusetts are really *the enemy of the people* [emphasis added]."[16] By the 1990s, the hostility expressed by so many Bay Staters had spread to the rest of the country. In 1992, independent candidate Ross Perot castigated elected Democrats and Republicans alike as ineffectual trouble-makers: "Everybody has detailed positions. Nobody implements them."[17] Four years later a CNN/*Time* poll found 57 percent agreed with the statement, "If the two parties agree on anything, it will not work to my advantage."[18]

Today, more than half of Americans believe parties make the country's system of government less efficient, often saying in effect: "It would be better if, in all elections, we put no party labels on the ballot." As they have on so many other occasions, Californians have become trendsetters by taking nonpartisanship to new heights. In 1998, they were allowed to vote for candidates from different parties in what is called a **blanket primary.** Party affiliation did not matter, as Democrats, Republicans, and even independents could support the candidates of their choice whatever their party listing. According to one exit poll, 58 percent liked this new method of choosing party candidates; only 9 percent found it confusing.[19] But the result has been to make party membership so casual that it has virtually no relevance. The same is true in several other states where independents can vote in either the Democratic or Republican primaries, and upon leaving the polling booth immediately reclaim their independent status. In 1986, Connecticut Republicans defied state law to allow independents to participate in selecting their candidates for office. This is a long way from the nineteenth century when voters were given no choice but to publicly select a brightly colored party ballot and drop it into the ballot box.

The Information Age has changed the way voters receive and process information. With a flick of a button, television viewers can channel surf and check out the latest candidate sound bites. For their part, broadcast correspondents have become the equivalent of old-fashioned party bosses. In calculating which presidential candidates to cover, the press often accedes to what is called "horse-race journalism"—meaning that reporters use polls and campaign finance reports to show which candidates have collected the most money and predict who might have the greatest public following. Press coverage to those deemed serious contenders is allocated accordingly. After a credible showing in the 1976 Iowa caucuses, former Oklahoma Senator Fred Harris enthused that while some candidates had been winnowed out by the press, he had been "winnowed in" thanks to his 9.9 percent tally.[20] In 1982, Massachusetts Republican State Chairman Andrew Natsios told John Kenneth White that parties were losing their "raison d'être":

> It used to be that political parties were intermediaries between the voters and the politicians; they used to nominate people for office at conventions; they used to dole out patronage; they used to raise money for candidates. They don't do those things anymore. Patronage has declined, the media [have] become the link between the voter and the politician; and the convention has given way to the direct primary. The functions of the old party structures are gone.[21]

Natsios's lament is even more true today than it was sixteen years ago. Television remains the most direct means of communication between those who exercise power and the voters. Beginning in the 1950s, television began to replace radio as the primary source of broadcast news. According to statistics compiled in 1986, 30 million people watched one of the three network (ABC, CBS, and NBC) evening newscasts each evening. In contrast, not quite 1 million read the *New York Times* each day.[22] Only the Internet looms as a potential rival to television as a primary source of information. The Democratic and Republican parties have entered the Information Age by creating homepages that anyone can visit. But they compete with thousands of other politically oriented Web sites (e.g., CNN and *Time* magazine's sponsored "AllPolitics," the *Washington Post, Congressional Quarterly, National Journal,* and MSNBC) and interest groups (e.g., the National Organization for Women, National Rifle Association, and the AFL-CIO). The competition for the voters' attention has become so intense that some see parties as being in danger of extinction. Pollster Dick Morris believes that the Internet will result in the death of political parties, since voters will interact directly with their elected officials: "Political parties are kept alive now by two things. They don't control elections anymore, but they control Congress and they control fund-raising. Congress is going to be controlled by voters and referenda and direct points of view. Congressmen are going to tell the Republican and Democratic leadership, go fly a kite. I'm going to vote the way my voters voted on the Internet."[23]

Other once seemingly invulnerable party provinces are also under attack. In 1990, the U.S. Supreme Court voted to strip the parties of one of their last vestiges of power—patronage. In *Rutan, et al. v. Republican Party of Illinois,* Justice William Brennan articulated the court's preference for nonpartisanship in filling state jobs: "To the victor belong only those spoils that may be constitutionally obtained."[24] Only deficient work, not one's party affiliation, were valid grounds for dismissal. Issuing a strong dissent in this case, Justice Antonin Scalia wondered aloud: "Political parties have assuredly survived—but as what? As the forges upon which many of the essential compromises of American political life are hammered out? Or merely as convenient vehicles for the conducting of national presidential elections?"[25]

The answer seems to be neither. Instead, parties may be morphing into large cash registers. The Democratic and Republican national committees and their congressional counterparts have never raised and spent such vast sums of money as they have during the Clinton era. In 1996, Democratic campaign committees raised $332.3 million, while Republicans garnered an even larger $548.7 million.[26] In 1998, the U.S. Senate debated whether parties should continue to receive "soft money"—a reference to monies given to national party committees that are, in turn, distributed to state parties and individual candidates. Republican John McCain and Democrat Russ Feingold sponsored a bipartisan bill aimed at reducing party influence in national elections by eliminating political action committees—a major source of party money.

Political scientists are aware of the array of forces aligned against resurrecting the political parties of yesteryear. Still, the discipline clings fast to its first principle that parties equal democracy (and democracy equals parties) uttered by Schattschneider and Rossiter so long ago. Building on this axiomatic formula, many party scholars assign to parties several "intermediary functions" that, they say, are crucial to forging a successful democracy. These include:

1. Promoting agreement between different interests and groups. *Explanation:* In our individualistic, pluralistic, sometimes fractured country, unifying forces are needed. Ergo, because parties want to win elections most of all, they compromise their differences in pursuit of the common good.

2. Promoting discussion of major issues. *Explanation:* A party seeks support for a program, not only for individuals. By presenting a platform—or a legislative agenda such as the Contract with America, the New Deal, or the Great Society—a party organizes the choices facing the electorate and helps voters make informed decisions.

3. Fostering effective government. *Explanation:* Deadlock and gridlock threaten the functioning of government because they complicate the existing constitutional divisions of power among the three federal branches, as well as the separation of powers created by the Tenth Amendment between national and state governments. Parties create unity within government, and are important vehicles to link competing power centers in Washington, D.C., and the various state capitals.

4. Providing responsibility and accountability. *Explanation:* When parties decide public issues, they accept a collective obligation to further the public interest as they see it. Voters consequently know whom to praise or blame for the results of government action. This so-called "responsible parties" argument places parties at the crux of the voting decision and at the heart of formulating a governing agenda.

5. Promoting participation. *Explanation:* Parties work hard to enroll voters. They combat cynicism about politics by giving citizens a way to join with others, to contribute time and money, and to become involved in exciting and effective political action.

But when each of these intermediary functions is subjected to a reality check, the results are often quite different from those expected. As to the first point, Democratic and Republican activists seem less interested in compromise and winning elections, and more concerned with hijacking their respective party organizations to further their personal agendas. In 1998, for example, members of the Republican-oriented Christian Coalition sponsored a resolution that would prohibit GOP money from going to candidates who supported partial-birth abortion. The resolution was defeated at a Republican gathering in Palm Springs, but it symbolized the growing frustration of the Religious Right. Randy Tate, the executive director of the Christian Coalition, said his group didn't want "to be given crumbs off the table and taken for granted."[27] Pro-choice Democrats have also made the abortion issue a litmus test for party loyalty. In 1992, Pennsylvania Governor Robert P. Casey was not allowed to speak from the podium at the Democratic National Convention because of his pro-life abortion stance.

As to the second intermediary function, parties can prompt discussion of major issues. But such discussions are rare. Instead, it is the candidates who often establish an agenda for governing. Thus, while individuals may receive "personal mandates," parties are rarely given similar license. This is quite different from past years when parties were relatively strong. For example, the New Deal and Great Society were Democratic programs. Franklin Roosevelt and Lyndon Johnson were dynamic leaders who pushed for enactment of key provisions of each, such as Social Security and Medicare. Most Democrats were in full support of their efforts, and ran promising to help their presidents win congressional approval for these popular programs. Voters gave these presidents, *and their parties*, a mandate for governing. This rarely happens in the Information Age. The Contract with America is a case in point. The contract was signed by nearly all Republican congressional candidates in 1994. It promised that if the GOP won control of the House, votes would be held within the first hundred days of the new Congress on such items as requiring Congress to live under the laws it applies to everyone else, providing the president with a line-item veto, term limits for members of Congress, and a balanced budget amendment to the U.S. Constitution. Though much-touted, shortly before the election, only one voter in eight knew much about the contract, and seven in ten had never heard of it.[28] In the end, it prompted only a handful of voters to support the GOP that year.

As to the third point, parties *do* foster effective government—meaning that effective government is an *active* government. The Contract with America, for example, may not have meant much to voters, but it certainly meant a great deal to the Republican candidates who signed it. During the first hundred days of the 104th Congress, every item listed in the ten-point contract had been put to a vote on the House floor. Moreover, voting scores compiled by such respected nonpartisan organizations as the *National Journal* and *Congressional Quarterly*, showed that congressional party voting—with Democrats voting one way and Republicans another—increased markedly to 71 percent in 1995.[29] During the presidencies of Richard Nixon and Gerald R. Ford, only 35 percent of roll calls in the House of Representatives had produced a partisan split.[30]

The increase in party voting was especially evident during the first two years of the Clinton presidency when Congress approved his 1993 economic program (Clinton's supposed "mandate" from the 1992 elections). Not surprisingly, Clinton lost a few Democratic members in each house, but *no* Republican supported him. On issues ranging from the economy, crime, and gun control, Clinton had to fashion a party-based coalition. The major exception was the North American Free Trade Agreement (NAFTA) which won approval on a bipartisan vote. But NAFTA, which symbolized the once bipartisan, go-along, get-along folkways of the Congress, has been the exception, not the rule. According to former Senate Majority Leader Mike Mansfield, the present ideological polarization means that the two parties no longer truly listen to each other: "I've always felt that the true strength of the Senate lay in the center, not on the right and not on the left, but with those people who could see both sides and were not so convicted of their own assumptions that they wouldn't listen to the other side."[31] Today, instead of listening and deliberating, Democrats and Republicans are busy declaring war on each other—either by negative campaigning while seeking an office or claiming ethical violations while in office.

The fourth defense of parties has been labeled the "responsible parties" argument. This position gained credence with the 1950 publication of an American Political Science Association report titled *Toward a More Responsible Two-Party System*. The essence of the report's themes was expressed in this sentence: "An effective party system requires, first, that the parties are able to bring forth programs to which they commit themselves and second, that the parties possess sufficient internal cohesion to carry out these programs."[32] Though some political scientists have criticized the report from time to time, most have accepted it as a central tenet in making the case for parties.[33] By elevating the "responsible party" argument from dogma to theory, a host of other theoretical conceptualizations have emerged. Foremost among these is party realignment—which depends on the voters' understanding of party positions on issues and making a party-centered decision that lasts for many years.[34] But as voters are drawn away from policy-based assessments to image-based themes as presented on television, realignment no longer seems possible. Indeed, many suggest that in light of the persistent division of party control at the federal and state level, realignment should be scrapped as an analytic tool.

Finally, political scientists have created a tautology: Parties promote participation; ergo, when parties decline, turnout must inevitably fall. In fact, voter turnout decreased markedly from 1960 to 1988, only to rise somewhat in 1992, and then fall back to near-record lows in 1996—much as the pro-party advocates predicted. What was not foreseen was that much of the 1992 increase in voter turnout was due to the antiparty candidacy of Texas billionaire Ross Perot.

In sum, the precise nexus between the advantages parties afford and their actual behavior has never been clear. Surely, parties help make democracy work, but how? This question seems especially relevant in the change-oriented Information Age. Parties are adapting to new communication methods, as evidenced by the sophisticated use of new technologies that allow them to raise money and communicate with voters. But to what purpose are these monies and tools being put? And do they enhance the prospects for democracy? Former British Prime Minister Benjamin Disraeli once said, "In times of great political change and rapid political transition, it will generally be observed that political parties find it convenient to re-baptize themselves."[35] A recent study of European parties found that nearly one-quarter had disappeared, while one in five had undergone major structural revisions in order to survive.[36]

But what about parties in the United States? Certainly, it is true that in a *post-*modern, *post-*Cold War, *post-*Industrial era, it is fair to say that Americans have entered a *post-*party era that challenges most conventional understandings of how political parties operate. But, to paraphrase Disraeli, what sort of baptism awaits the parties in the twenty-first century? Clearly, they are no longer the indispensable units of government, as political scientists from another era once envisioned. But this does not mean that parties are irrelevant. They continue to afford the American polity with significant advantages, even as they compete with a host of new players, including presidential candidates (who may not wish to be identified with their ostensible political party), political action committees (which compete with the parties newfound brokerage role), special interest groups (which some put on a par with parties, or even elevate above them in importance), and an omnipotent media (which feeds citizens nearly all their information about politics). Rather than simply accepting a list of party functions applicable to the days of yore and then detailing how contemporary parties fall short (as most other texts do), it is time to rethink what we expect parties to accomplish in the Information Age. From Washington, D.C., to the state capitals, to local precincts, those working in the party organizations are attempting to do just that. So far, the journey has been an interesting one—with many unexpected twists and turns. We invite you, the student, to join us in continuing that journey.

NOTES

1. Cited in John Kenneth White, *The New Politics of Old Values* (Hanover, N.H.: University Press of New England, 1990), 74.

2. Cited in Edward Sidlow and Beth Henschen, *America at Odds: An Introduction to American Government* (Belmont, Calif.: West/Wadsworth, 1998), 309.

3. Laurence Arnold, "Impeachment E-Mail Floods Capitol," Associated Press, September 17, 1998, <http://cnn.allpolitics.com>.

4. Roberta Fusaro, "Congress Sees E-Mail Flood During Trial," *Computerworld*, February 3, 1999.

5. Dana Milbank, "Virtual Politics: Candidates' Consultants Create the Customized Campaign," *New Republic*, July 5, 1999, 22, 27.

6. "Presidential Campaigns Take to the Internet," May 7, 1999, <http://cnn.allpolitics.com>.

7. Milbank, "Virtual Politics," 24.

8. Ibid., 25.

9. Ibid.

10. Ibid., 22.

11. E. E. Schattschneider, *Party Government* (New York: Rinehart, 1942), 1.

12. Clinton Rossiter, *Parties and Politics in America* (Ithaca, N.Y.: Cornell University Press, 1960), 1.

13. John Kenneth White, *The Fractured Electorate: Political Parties and Social Change in Southern New England* (Hanover, N.H.: University Press of New England, 1983), 101.

14. Daniel M. Shea, *Transforming Democracy: Legislative Campaign Committees and Political Parties* (Albany, N.Y.: State University of New York Press, 1995), 10–11.

15. Jack Dennis, "Support for the Party System by the Mass Public," *American Political Science Review* 60 (September 1966): 605.

16. Ibid., 103.

17. E. J. Dionne, Jr., "Voters' Attraction to Perot May Signal that Party Labels Are Now Liabilities," *Washington Post*, May 21, 1992, A17.

18. CNN/*Time*, survey, February 23–25, 1996.

19. CNN, exit poll, June 2, 1998.

20. See Jules Witcover, *Marathon: The Pursuit of the Presidency, 1972–1976* (New York: Viking Press, 1977), 214. The final results were uncommitted, 37 percent; Jimmy Carter, 27.6 percent; Birch Bayh, 13.1 percent; Fred Harris, 9.9 percent; Morris Udall, 5.9 percent; Sargent Shriver, 3.3 percent.

21. Quoted in White, *The Fractured Electorate*, 99.

22. Cited in Thomas E. Patterson, *The American Democracy* (New York: McGraw-Hill, 1990), 350.

23. Dick Morris, interview, *Larry King Live*, CNN, November 18, 1999.

24. *Rutan, et al. v. Republican Party of Illinois*, in *Supreme Court Reporter* (1990: 1).

25. Ibid., 15.

26. Cited in Regina Dougherty, Everett C. Ladd, David Wilber, and Lynn Zayachkiwsky, *America at the Polls, 1996* (Storrs, Conn.: Roper Center for Public Opinion Research, 1997), 154.

27. Quoted in Christopher Caldwell, "The Southern Captivity of the GOP," *Atlantic Monthly*, June 1998, 62.

28. Cited in Guy Molyneux, "The Big Lie," *Rolling Stone*, December 1994, 154.

29. See Alan Greenblatt, "Despite Drop in Partisan Votes, Bickering Continued in 1997," *Congressional Quarterly*, January 3, 1998, 18.

30. Cited in Norman J. Ornstein, Thomas E. Mann, and Michael J. Malbin, *Vital Statistics on Congress, 1995–1996* (Washington, D.C.: Congressional Quarterly, Inc., 1996), 198–199.

31. Quoted in David E. Rosenbaum, "A Senator's Old Speech Holds Truths for Today," *New York Times*, March 22, 1998, 20.

32. Committee on Political Parties, *Toward a More Responsible Two-Party System* (New York: Rinehart, 1950), 1.

33. See especially Julius Turner, "Responsible Parties: A Dissent from the Floor," *American Political Science Review* (March 1951): 143–152; and Evron Kirkpatrick, "Toward a More Responsible Two-Party System: Political Science, Policy Science, or Pseudo Science?" *American Political Science Review* (December 1971): 965–990.

34. See especially V. O. Key, Jr., "A Theory of Critical Elections," *Journal of Politics* 17 (February 1955): 3–18; and Walter Dean Burnham, *Critical Elections and the Mainsprings of American Politics* (New York: Norton, 1970).

35. Quoted in Ronald P. Formisano, *The Transformation of Political Culture: Massachusetts Parties, 1790s–1840s* (New York: Oxford University Press, 1983), 18.

36. Richard Rose and Thomas T. Mackie, "Do Parties Persist or Fail? The Big Trade-Off Facing Organizations," in Kay Lawson and Peter H. Merkl, *When Parties Fail* (Princeton, N.J.: Princeton University Press, 1988), 543.

CHAPTER 1

Political Parties
in an American Setting

The framers of the U.S. Constitution were well versed in the writings of Aristotle, John Locke, Montesquieu, and other democratic thinkers. From their extensive reading of history, they understood the dangers of unchecked ambition and the necessities of free speech and minority protections so vital in creating a representative democracy. The tripartite system of government they created—consisting of a president, Congress, and judiciary—has endured with only modest revisions to their original work. In the two centuries since the U.S. Constitution was ratified, those who have inhabited the presidential offices have sung its praises. For example, upon leaving the presidency in 1796, George Washington urged that the Constitution "be sacredly maintained—that its administration in every department may be stamped with wisdom and virtue."[1] Forty-two years later, Abraham Lincoln told the Springfield's Young Men's Lyceum that the Constitution should become "the *political religion* of the nation."[2]

Despite Lincoln's plea, it was in creating a political system that the Framers were less than successful. One of the first problems they confronted was how to organize elections. Popular, democratic elections were a novel experiment that many believed could not happen without widespread turmoil and violence. One Massachusetts delegate to the Constitutional Convention in Philadelphia contended that the "evils we experience flow from the excess of democracy."[3] Alexander Hamilton agreed: "The people are turbulent and changing; they seldom judge or determine right."[4] By the late twentieth century, however, the "excess of democracy" had become universal. According to the U.S. Census Bureau, in 1992 there were 511,039 popularly elected officials. Of these, 491,669 held local positions; 18,828 were state officeholders, with half of them serving as administrative officials and judges.

To the astonishment of the Constitution's Framers, political parties proved to be the agents that made the document and the complex system of elections work. Parties afforded a way of organizing elections, legitimizing opposition, and guaranteeing peaceful transitions of power. Once in office, they helped elected officials work together and bridged the gaps among the various segments of government. One might assume, therefore, that political parties would be welcome instruments of governance. Quite the contrary. For more than two hundred years, Americans have steadfastly refused to embrace party-led government—preferring instead that their leaders act in a nonpartisan manner. In 1956, John F. Kennedy wrote the

13

Pulitzer-prizewinning *Profiles in Courage*, which extolled those who placed conscience above party.[5] Three decades later, one public opinion poll found 92 percent
of Americans agreed with the statement, "I always vote for the person who I think is
best, regardless of what party they belong to."[6]

Given the widespread public ambivalence directed at all political parties since
the country's founding, it should come as no surprise that American parties have
struggled to find their rightful place. The "solutions" to this dilemma have varied
from place to place and time to time. For example, parties acquired a degree of public
approval at the end of the nineteenth century as America entered the Industrial Age.
But near the close of the twentieth century, parties have resumed their search for their
proper place in the new, postindustrial, computer-generated Information Age.

This chapter sets the foundation for the rest of the book. We start with a discussion of the love-hate relationship Americans have with parties and how this has
influenced party development. Next, we address what roles parties play and how
they differ from other players in the political system. The chapter ends with a discussion of the theoretical models used to help structure the remainder of the book—
what we have dubbed the Hamiltonian and Jeffersonian models of political parties.

POLITICAL PARTIES: INSTITUTIONS
AMERICANS LOVE TO HATE

The Founding Fathers were elitists who wanted to minimize the role citizens would
play in choosing their officeholders. They were especially fearful of political parties,
arguing that it was necessary, in Madison's words, to "break and control the violence of faction [meaning parties and other special interest groups]."[7] James Madison, George Washington, Alexander Hamilton, and Thomas Jefferson all believed
that an enlightened citizenry would have no use for parties. Instead of parties,
Madison hoped that other mediating institutions would "refine and enlarge the
public views by passing them through the medium of a chosen body of citizens,
whose wisdom may best discern the true interest of their country and whose patriotism and love of justice will be least likely to sacrifice it to temporary or partial conditions."[8] But Madison's idea of mediating institutions that would consider public
sentiments and translate them into public policies whenever it was deemed timely
and appropriate did not include political parties. In his view, continental expansion
meant that a multitude of interests would proliferate, thus making the development
of large, mass-based parties virtually inconceivable: "You make it less probable that
a majority of the whole will have a common motive to invade the rights of other citizens; or if such a common motive exists, it will be more difficult for all who feel it
to discover their own strength and to act in unison with each other."[9]

Madison's belief that parties were unsuited filters for mass expressions of public opinion was based on his reading of history. He thought that human beings were
emotional creatures, embracing different religions and political leaders with a
zealotry that usually resulted in chaos and violence. Most of Madison's contempo-
raries agreed, and they scorned political parties as vehicles that would, inevitably,
ignite uncontrollable political passions. George Washington, for example, was

especially critical of partisan demagogues whose objective, he claimed, was not to give people the facts from which they could make up their own minds, but to make them followers instead of thinkers. In an early draft of a speech renouncing a second term (not used in 1792), Washington maintained that "we are *all* children of the same country . . . [and] that our interest, however diversified in local and smaller matters, is the same in all the great and essential concerns of the nation."[10] Determined to make good on his intention to leave office in 1796, Washington issued his famous farewell address, in which he admonished his fellow citizens to avoid partisanship at any cost:

> Let me . . . warn you in the most solemn manner against the baneful effects of the spirit of party. . . . It exists under different shapes in all governments, more or less stifled, controlled, or repressed; but, in those of the popular form, it is seen in its greatest rankness and is truly their worst enemy. The alternate domination of one faction over another, sharpened by the spirit of revenge natural to party dissension, which in different ages and countries has perpetrated the most horrid enormities, is itself a frightful despotism . . . [The spirit of party] agitates the community with ill-founded jealousies and false alarms; kindles the animosity of one part against another; ferments occasional riot and insurrection. It opens the door to foreign influence and corruption, which finds a facilitated access to the government through the channels of party passions.[11]

As the eighteenth century gave way to the nineteenth, American attitudes toward parties remained largely unchanged. Observing the effects of partisan attacks on her husband, John Adams, during his presidency, Abigail Adams wrote: "Party spirit is blind, malevolent, un-candid, ungenerous, unjust, and unforgiving."[12] James Monroe, who would become the nation's fifth chief executive, urged his backers to obliterate all party divisions. Other presidents have voiced similar sentiments. When Abraham Lincoln sought reelection in 1864 under the newly created National Union banner, half a million pamphlets were published bearing titles such as "No Party Now but All for Our Country."[13] Campaigning for president in 1992, then-Governor Bill Clinton denounced the "brain-dead politics" of both political parties.

The danger of faction against which the Framers warned still resonates with most Americans. During the 1992 presidential campaign, when ten registered voters were asked what the two parties meant to them, two shouted "Corruption!" Others used words like "rich," "self-serving," "good-old-boy networks," "special interests," "bunch of lost causes," "lost sheep," "immorality," "going whatever way is on top," and "liars."[14] Other polls confirm the public scorn for party politics. In 1996, the National Opinion Research Center found that 85 percent believed that political action committee (PAC) money had more influence on the parties than the public did; and 82 percent thought "both parties are pretty much out of touch with the American people."[15]

Even party leaders seem skeptical about a place for parties in the American setting. Seeking reelection in 1972, Richard Nixon instructed his staff not to include the word *Republican* in any of his television advertisements or campaign brochures. Four years later Gerald R. Ford was bluntly told by his advisors not to campaign for Republican candidates lest his support erode among independents and ticket-splitters: "Any *support* given to a GOP candidate must be done in a manner to *avoid* national media attention."[16] Jimmy Carter once described the Democratic Party as "an albatross around my neck." In 1996, Bill Clinton devoted one line in his acceptance speech to making a case for Democratic control of the presidency and the Congress.

Praise from the Ivory Tower

The idea that political parties have become the proverbial scarlet letter of American politics is not shared by the vast majority of political scientists. In his book *The American Commonwealth* published in 1888, James Bryce began a tradition of scholarly investigation of political parties devoting more than two hundred pages to the subject. His treatment was laudatory: "Parties are inevitable. No free large country has been without them. No-one has shown how representative government could be worked without them. They bring order out of chaos to a multitude of voters."[17] More than a century later, scores of other academicians agree with Bryce. In a 1996 amicus curiae (friend-of-the-court) brief filed with the U.S. Supreme Court, the Committee for Party Renewal, a bipartisan group of political scientists, summarized the views held by most party scholars:

> Political parties play a unique and crucial role in our democratic system of government. Parties enable citizens to participate coherently in a system of government allowing for a substantial number of popularly elected offices. They bring fractured and diverse groups together as a unified force, provide a necessary link between the distinct branches and levels of government; and provide continuity that lasts beyond terms of office. Parties also play an important role in encouraging active participation in politics, holding politicians accountable for their actions, and encouraging debate and discussion of important issues.[18]

Without parties, the Committee for Party Renewal claimed that civic life would be reduced to "a politics of celebrities, of excessive media influence, of political fad-of-the-month clubs, of massive private financing by various 'fat cats' of state and congressional campaigns, of gun-for-hire campaign managers, of heightened interest in 'personalities' and lowered concern for policy, of manipulation and maneuver and management by self-chosen political elites."[19] Such statements buttressed the consensus that strong, vital parties are a prerequisite for a healthy democracy. Thus, political scientists measure the march toward democracy in such diverse nations as Haiti, Bosnia, and the former Soviet Union, in terms of those countries' capacities to develop strong party organizations that are the foundations for free, democratic elections—even as average Americans deplore what they see as the scourge of parties in their own country.

Politics without Parties

It seems apparent that the Framers intended to create a system where liberty (freedom) could be safeguarded. Only one dilemma confronted the Framers: how to protect liberty and still prevent the formation of political parties. Their solution was to devise an elaborate system of government spreading over an extended republic. In such a setting, parties would find their existence frustrating and thus would fade away. The Framers' complicated scheme of translating public opinion into public policy quickly fell of its own weight. Parties soon burst on the scene and have been part of American politics ever since.

The uniqueness of the American party system lies not only in the unhappy marriage between parties and the Constitution, but also between parties and the thousands of politicians who have used them as vehicles to win elections. Elected officials often pitch themselves to voters as independent thinkers, yet nearly all are listed on the ballot under a party label. One Massachusetts Republican officeholder famously observed, "The Republican party is a Hertz car we all rent around election time."[20] Congressman Sam Gejdenson (D-Conn.) told one of the authors of this text, John Kenneth White, that he could care less about his own party (see "The Parties Speak: Gejdenson versus White on the Importance of Political Parties").

The Parties Speak: *Gejdenson versus White on the Importance of Political Parties*

In 1991, John Kenneth White had the following exchange with Representative Sam Gejdenson, a Connecticut Democrat and then chairman of the House Task Force on Campaign Finance Reform.

Gejdenson: Why would it be our responsibility to help these parties move forward? It seems to me, if parties stood for something, or if they did things, they on their own would do fine. . . . Why should we rig the [campaign finance] rules to strengthen the parties? Isn't that the parties' own business? The problem gets to be, as a lot of us here, both Democrat and Republican, know, is that the parties want to be nurtured. Should we also be nurturing the Communist Party? . . . If the parties stand for something, they'll survive; if they don't stand for anything, maybe they shouldn't survive.

White: Well, I believe that political parties will survive, largely because they are so ingrained in the minds of Americans. After all, millions vote for only the Democratic or Republican candidate, not for a third-party candidate. I think there is a larger purpose involved generically with political parties, period, which is that they mobilize people to act. No other single interest group does that the way the parties do.

Gejdenson: Maybe they should. I don't know if they do. But why should they do it with taxpayer dollars?

White: Let me just say—You know, you mentioned what your obligation was to political parties. Let me just offer that the Democratic Party in Connecticut tendered you their nomination, as did the Democratic—

Gejdenson: No, no. That's not how it happened. They tendered the nomination to somebody else. I went out and got the people's support, and then I . . . won the nomination in a primary. . . . But why should the taxpayers, or why should the government, give [the parties] free television time to strengthen or weaken their hold? Why should it be their business?

SOURCE: Testimony of John Kenneth White before the House Task Force on Campaign Finance Reform, May 28, 1991.

Like Sam Gejdenson, millions of Americans loathe the idea of partisanship, seeing political parties as irrelevant to their everyday lives. Yet, most continue to link their civic activities, like voting, to a party. In fact, party affiliation remains a reliable predictor of how voters will behave in the polling booth. Thus, parties have been an integral thread in the fabric of American politics since its inception, but oddly enough they have never achieved full acceptance.

In this light, our study of the American party system will be structured by the conflict between the necessity for party-like organizations, and the scorn heaped on them by the public and most elected officials. If anything, it is conceivable that parties will confront even greater public relations challenges in the twenty-first century given that citizens have quicker access to information and modes of communication.

THREE IMPORTANT PARTY DISTINCTIONS

One topic that bedevils any examination of parties in America is how one goes about defining them. What is a political party? What makes one organization more "party like" than another? What are the differences between interest groups, campaign consulting firms, political action committees, and political parties? What are the various components of political parties? Are parties member-oriented or are they simply tools for an office-seeking elite?

Scholars have wrestled with these and other related questions for some time. Many of these topics are discussed in the chapters that follow, but a few clarifications are in order. They center around three questions:

1. How do political parties differ from other organizations, particularly those concerned with the outcome of government activity?
2. What are the various elements that comprise American political parties?
3. What do parties seek to accomplish and how are their activities related to these goals?

How Parties Differ from Other Organizations

At first glance, strangers to the American party system might find little distinction between parties and interest groups. Indeed, Madison's own discussion of "faction" is vague, and scholars have tangled with this issue for nearly two centuries. In the 1940s, for example, it was suggested that special interest groups "promote their interests by attempting to influence the *government* rather than by nominating candidates and seeking the responsibility for the management of government [as political parties do]."[21] Others disagreed, noting that interest groups do influence nominations, elect favorite candidates, and manage the government by influencing the appointment of officials and actual decisions being made. So what, if anything, distinguishes a political party from, say, the American Association of Retired Persons, the Environmental Defense Fund, or the National Association of Manufacturers? There are three important distinctions between political parties and special interest groups:

1. Parties run candidates for office under their own label. While interest groups may consistently back candidates of one party, such as the AFL-CIO's support of Democrats or the National Association of Manufacturers' for Republicans, they do not have a party label and they do not officially nominate candidates for office.
2. When it comes to determining policy, parties have a broad range of concerns. A cursory reading of the 1996 Democratic and Republican party platforms shows that both had something to say about nearly every issue. Democrats, for example, addressed the importance of bringing high technology into the nation's classrooms, community policing, upholding the Brady Bill (which required a mandatory waiting period before the purchase of a handgun), the assault weapons ban, and *Roe v. Wade*. In the wake of the O. J. Simpson trial, Democrats denounced domestic violence and even included a toll-free phone number in their platform should anyone reading it need help. Republicans cited the need for tax relief, creating a balanced budget and reducing spending, reforming immigration policy, sexual abstinence, and voluntary school prayer. Interest groups have a much narrower set of concerns. The American Association of Retired Persons, for example, is keenly interested in policies affecting older Americans, but pays scant attention to environmental legislation. The Environmental Defense Fund makes its views plain on modifications to the Endangered Species Act, but offers little input on a constitutional amendment banning the burning of the American flag.
3. Political parties are subject to state and local laws and the relationship between parties and the state is an intimate one. Interest groups, on the other hand, are private organizations operating under minimal state or federal regulations and with the aid of constitutional protections of free speech, assembly, and petition.

There have been numerous occasions in American history when interest groups and parties have worked together. The merging of business interests with the Republican Party during the Industrial Revolution is one example. Likewise, the close ties forged by Franklin D. Roosevelt between the Democratic Party and organized labor to win important backing for the New Deal is another. Today, there are so many overlapping activities between political parties and interest groups that the competition between the two has become especially intense—a development that is discussed in greater detail in Chapter 3.

The Components of American Political Parties

In ancient Greece, when the priestess of Apollo at Delphi made ready to deliver a prophesy, she positioned herself on a special seat supported by three legs, the tripod.[22] The tripod gave the priestess a clear view of the past, present, and future. In much the same fashion, political scientists in the early 1950s likened political parties to the famous tripod of so long ago. From their perch, they saw parties supported by three legs: party-in-the electorate, party organization, and the party-in-government.[23]

Party-in-the-electorate (PIE) refers to those who attach themselves to a particular party. When voters say they are "Republican" or "Democrat," they are acknowledging their membership in a party-in-the-electorate, although they might not think of themselves in these terms. Sometimes this affiliation is a casual one, such as when a person in the privacy of the voting booth splits his or her vote between Democratic and Republican candidates. At other times the relationship is more formal—such as when a prospective party member travels to the local town hall to register as a member of a particular political party. Other formalized party activities include participation in a party primary, raising money at a party fund-raiser, or making telephone calls to help get out the vote. In some countries, party organizations require active participation in order to be considered a member, which often means paying a membership fee. In the United States, however, party membership is not nearly as well-defined. Here the party-in-the-electorate denotes a person's psychological attachment to a particular party. Some root for a political party, just as others cheer the victories of their favorite sports teams.

Party organization (PO) refers to the formal apparatus of the party, including the party headquarters, conventions, regulations activities, leaders and rank-and-file workers. One way of thinking about party organization is that it is the official bureaucracy of the party. When party meetings are held, members of the organization show up. When party officials make statements to the media, it is the top brass of the organization doing all the talking. And when the party passes out literature during a campaign, it is the organization that delivers the pamphlets. The Republican National Committee (RNC) and the Democratic National Committee (DNC) each have headquarters in Washington, D.C., and Democratic and Republican state party committees can be found in every state capital. If one is interested in chatting with a local party official, they need only look up the number in a telephone directory.

Party-in-government (PIG) refers to those who have captured office under a party label. For example, Republicans in the Senate comprise one segment of the GOP party-in-government led by Majority Leader Trent Lott (R-Miss.). For Democrats, the head of their party-in-government is President Bill Clinton. In addition to these officials, there are many sub-branches of the party-in-government at the state, county, and municipal levels. All the Democrats of the Miami City Council, for instance, belong to the same party division.

When it was first advanced, the tripod seemed both accurate and parsimonious. Partisanship was broad and fixed—no less so than one's religion. The public was divided between Democrats and Republicans and they voted accordingly. What few "independents" there were generally did not vote and were seen as outside the system. Legislative leaders, including powerful Democrats such as Senate Majority Leader Lyndon B. Johnson and Speaker of the House Sam Rayburn, were important figures. Party organizations were fixtures in nearly every community and controlled nominations for most elective offices. Citizens were active in party organizations not just for material gain, such as postelection patronage jobs, but for ideological reasons and a sense of belonging to the larger community. Elected officials carried the party banner because partisan voters back home expected no less. In short, the tripod provided a clear view of the supporting roles political parties played.

Does the Tripod Work in the Information Age?

At the close of the twentieth century, the tripod has outlived its usefulness. Voters have turned away from both the Democratic and Republican parties, as evidenced by the growing numbers of independents. The party-in-the-electorate has given way to candidates making their case to individual voters over the television airwaves. But while the party-in-the-electorate has withered away, party organizations have demonstrated a surprising resilience and are more powerful than at any time in this century. Surely the technological revolution has changed how party organizations operate, how issues are communicated, and what citizens think about when they contemplate "politics." As for the party-in-government, contradictory trends exist. Party-line voting in the Congress and state legislatures has been on the rise, but **divided government**—that is, split partisan control of the executive and the legislative branches of government—has become commonplace in Washington, D.C., and in most state capitals. Moreover, even though elected officials are prone to adhere to the party line while in office, they seem increasingly willing to abandon their party when seeking office. Thus, questions abound. Are parties doing well or are they withering away? Do parties remain an important part of our political system? The lack of consistent answers suggests that the tripod has become obsolete.

One reason why the tripod is no longer a useful organizing concept is that the climate in which political parties operate has changed dramatically. During the agricultural era, the key to production was land; in the industrial era, human labor; today it is trained intelligence. In the 1970s, sociologist Daniel Bell heralded the coming of a new "post-industrial" society which placed a premium on the gathering and dissemination of information.[24] In the years since, American life has been transformed by several interrelated developments:

- Ours is a wealthier and more affluent society compared to earlier eras. Most workers are salaried white collars, whereas in the Industrial Era most employees wore blue collars and were paid by the hour.
- Knowledge is especially important in the Information Age. Just as hands were a measure of production in the Industrial Era, brainpower is an important productive tool today. A college degree, often followed by a postgraduate degree, has become the "union card" for employment in the Information Age.
- A technological revolution has made mass communication between individuals across vast corners of the globe possible. That technological revolution now fuels the Internet which makes instantaneous communication, however impersonal, a new reality.
- New occupational structures, and with them new lifestyles and social classes, are creating new elites in the Information Age.

- Modes of recreation have changed. More people find recreational outlets in their living rooms (e.g., television and the Internet). Internet chat rooms, for example, are as commonplace as the coffee socials of a bygone era.

The Information Age affects the way most Americans live, work, and communicate with each other. To take but one example, in 1997 the number of e-mail messages sent totaled 2.6 trillion. By 2000, it is estimated that 6.6 trillion e-mails will travel on the Information Superhighway.[25] In 1998, the online division of the Republican National Committee sought to obtain the e-mail addresses of 50,000 party activists by election day. E-mails were sent by the Republicans with a message to forward it to their friends. By the year 2000, Republicans hope to have the e-mail addresses of more than two million party loyalists.[26]

The magnitude of the changes wrought by the Information Age is so vast that sometimes it is hard to comprehend. President Clinton, for example, likes to tell Generation Xers that unlike their parents they will work for several companies during their professional careers. Parental loyalties to corporations such as IBM, Sears, or AT&T—industrial giants in their heyday—has become passe. Leaving behind what was once familiar to so many Americans is profoundly unsettling for some. Robert Reich, secretary of labor during Clinton's first term, described the effect on the public psyche: "All the old bargains, it seems, have been breached. The economic bargain was that if you worked hard and your company prospered, you would share the fruits of success. There was a cultural bargain, too, echoing the same themes of responsibility and its rewards: live by the norms of your community—take care of your family, obey the law, treat your neighbors with respect, love your country—and you'll feel secure in the certainty that everyone else would behave that way."[27] One by one, the old bargains have been ripped asunder.

Not surprisingly, political parties are caught in the swirling winds of change. But academic thinking about parties—as symbolized by the party-in-the-electorate, party organization, and party-in-government model—has failed to keep pace with the times. This text suggests that a better way of thinking about political parties is to use a **business firm analogy**.[28] From this perspective, political parties are firms that work to win elections, while voters are the consumers that the firms attempt to attract each election. A firm's profit is measured by the market share it receives in each election, that is, how many votes they garner. Using this model, elections are high production times for the firms, as parties put additional suppliers (e.g., consultants, pollsters, contributors, and candidates) to work during these temporary spurts in production.

Applying the business firm analogy to present-day politics, one finds a drop in the number of those who call themselves Democrats or Republicans. That decline is evident in the rise of independent voters and those who split their ballots, meaning they vote for candidates without regard to their party label. This is akin to a decline in brand loyalty, as voters prefer a generic product to that offered by the Democratic or Republican parties (see Chapter 6). The business firm analogy also helps explain why so few third-party candidates win elections. Electoral laws also make it difficult for new firms to enter the market which is regulated by federal, state, and local authorities. Democratic and Republican legislators like to write election laws that favor the two-party system. Thus, in the United States it is fair to say that there are Democrats and Republicans—and no other parties of any real consequence (see Chapter 10).

This business firm analogy holds that elected officials are quite unique. Elected officials belong to a political party, sometimes as both a candidate and as officials of the party organization. During Bill Clinton's second term, for example, Roy Romer of Colorado was both governor of that state and general chair of the Democratic National Committee. But there is no "in-government" branch of the party. Rather, there exists a group of successful candidates whom the party wishes to control. Put differently, during the campaign candidates are the products being marketed; but after the election they are prompted by the party to be members of their sales force. There is a connection to the parent corporation, the party, but also a great deal of autonomy. This suggests a mutually beneficial relationship: elected officials use the party during elections, and the party seeks help from them after they win. Thus, although there are connections between elected officials and the party organizations, each remains a distinct entity.

The business firm analogy better describes the realities of American party politics. For example, the tight grasp that party machines had on elected officials during much of the nineteenth century derived from their ability to generate brand loyalty. Elected officials sold the party's goods after the election because their autonomy was restricted. Later, they broke ranks, rebelled against the firm, and started their own independent franchises. Back in the 1950s, there was little need for innovation as brand loyalty was rather fixed. During the 1970s, the rebirth of aggressive party organizations represented an effort to recapture the loyalty of consumers in an increasingly competitive market. In the 1990s, voters have been bombarded with political information compelling parties to sharpen their organizational prowess. The same sort of analogy can be helpful in understanding changes in the presidential nomination process, the interaction between parties and the media, and nearly every topic confronted in this text. We spend a good deal of time discussing the role voters and elected officials play in the party system because they represent strong variables in the market. But it is important that we see them as external forces—something that affects the activities and well-being of parties—rather than components of these organizations.

What Do Political Parties Seek to Accomplish?

A final clarification relates to what political parties seek to accomplish—that is, what would suggest a "year-end profit." To some, a party is simply a team of candidates seeking to win control of government through competitive elections. The profit motive is straightforward: to win elections in order to control government and collect the material benefits of a party's success (i.e., the "spoils" of office). This view has been dubbed the *rational-efficient* or *minimalist* perspective. A few often-repeated definitions of party along these lines include:

- Joseph Schlesinger: A political party is a group organized to gain control of government in the name of the group by winning election to public office.[29]
- Leon Epstein: [What] is meant by a political party [is] any group, however loosely organized, seeking to elect government officeholders under a given label.[30]
- John Aldrich: Political parties can be seen as coalitions of elites to capture and use political office. [But] a political party is more than a coalition. A political party is an institutionalized coalition, one that has adopted rules, norms, and procedures.[31]

Others would argue that a party's true objective is to implement its ideology by adopting a particular set of policies. Winning elections and controlling the government are means to larger ends—changing the course of government. This perspective is often termed the *responsible party* model. Definitions of party along these lines include:

- Edmund Burke: [A] party is a body of men [sic] united, for promoting by their joint endeavors, the national interest, upon some particular principle in which they all agree.
- Jay M. Shafritz: Political party [is] an organization that seeks to achieve political power by electing members to public office so that their political philosophies can be reflected in public policies.[32]

Beyond these definitions, the two models suggest a number of important differences relating to objectives, functions, and structure as outlined in Table 1.1. From a rational-efficient perspective, parties are just one of many actors in the pluralist system. Relying on our business analogy, the emphasis is on the competitive struggle to gain office in the free market, that is, fair and open elections. Party platforms are continually shifted to solicit the support of consumers—voters. The representative function performed by parties parallels other groups; interest groups articulate interests and parties aggregate them. Conflict is seen as disruptive and plays no role in governing.

Rather than viewing parties as one of many actors in a pluralist system, responsible party advocates see them as goal-definers. Parties develop platforms based on purposive criteria related to activists' values and policy preferences. Adherents to the responsible party model want to win elections so they can implement their program. In their view, parties serve as the primary link between the citizens and government and play a dominant role in government. Moreover, parties control elites by structuring competition, selecting and supporting office-seeking individuals, and using actual and perceived threats of electoral retribution. Finally, parties are said to peacefully articulate and mediate conflict, as well as make agreement and consensus possible.

With regard to specific functions, rational-efficient proponents emphasize only the parties' electoral activities—all other functions are subordinate to winning elections. In their view, winning is not simply a nice thing to have—it's the only

TABLE 1.1 ▪ **Contrasting Attributes of Rational-Efficient and Responsible Party Models**

Attribute	Rational-Efficient	Responsible
View of democracy	Pluralist view Conflict avoided	Party goal definers Conflict part of change
Functions	Election activities	Linkage Aggregation Articulation Participation Community service
Goal(s)	Win elections/Control office Efficiency	Implement their policy Ideological unity
Structure	Professional	Mass membership Amateur
Role in government	None—Members granted autonomy	Interdependence between member and party
View of intraparty democracy	Hinders efficiency	Essential
Incentives for activists	Material (power/money)	Mix of ideological and social

SOURCE: Daniel M. Shea, *Transforming Democracy: Legislative Campaign Committees and Political Parties* (Albany: State University of New York Press, 1995), 61.

thing worth having. As a victorious Richard Nixon told cheering supporters in 1968, "Winning's a lot more fun." Parties exist to win elections and all party-related projects are designed to make that happen. Incentives to participate in the process come from the patronage jobs that are to be had once victory is ensured. Responsible parties, on the other hand, have ideological, electoral, and governing functions. They operate throughout the calendar year. Winning elections is simply a means to an end, not an end in itself.

The organizational structure of rational-efficient parties consists of a cadre of political entrepreneurs. There is a large degree of centralization and no formal party membership. The organizational style is professional where workers, leaders, and candidates are often recruited from outside the organization or are self-recruited. Efficiency is stressed above all else. There is little, if any, organizational continuity after the election. On the other hand, responsible parties maintain a highly integrated structure. Formal membership is critical and grass-roots committees play an important role. Volunteers rise through the ranks as loyal, hard-working activists.

Candidates who receive support from the party organization are recruited from within its ranks and must be programmatically and ideologically in agreement. In the responsible party model, a candidate's ability to win is subordinate to ideological and policy considerations.

Lastly, the two models are at odds regarding their role in government. In the rational-efficient model, elected officials are allowed to do as they wish once elected, as long as their activities help to win the next election. This is not the case with the responsible party model. Here, there is a high degree of interdependence between the party and elected officials, as voters must make judgements as to what the party stands for.

Where do American-style parties in the Information Age fit into these theoretical perspectives? Most scholars would place the Democrats and Republicans toward the rational-efficient end of the spectrum. Party membership in the United States is very porous. Few, if any, party organizations require their followers to pay dues or attend specific meetings. A small set of party elites make decisions for the entire organization and voters are best viewed as consumers. Ideological diversity is tolerated and party-line voting is far from the norm. The parties want elected officials to stick to the platform, but most stray at least somewhat. Also, there are numerous other linkage structures, such as special interest groups, that play an equal or greater role in the democratic process than parties do. The rise of candidate-centered campaigns is seen as a further push toward rational-efficient parties.

Yet, one must be cautious not to go too far in the rational-efficient direction. A number of points can be raised from the opposite perspective. Numerous reforms during the early 1970s opened party organizations to greater involvement by rank-and-file party followers, and while ideological diversity is generally tolerated, this is not always the case. In some areas of the United States, politicians who refuse to toe the party line are encouraged to switch parties, and many local party organizations perform activities in nonelection periods—including those not directly related to winning office. The overall party structure is less centralized and more diffuse. Most who are involved in party activities are amateurs who give their own time for purposive and social incentives; for them, any economic (patronage) rewards are secondary.

The foremost problems with using the election-policy dimension to define the essence of parties is that it is static, incomplete, and discounts the diversity of party structures in the United States. The history of parties is continually evolving as new conditions arise. Suggestions that American parties are "election driven," "policy oriented," or searching for the "vital center" assume that it has always been so, and that all party organizations scattered throughout the nation follow a similar pattern. A close reading of American history suggests that party goals and activities have changed and are a function of where the party is located. As the next four chapters suggest, sometimes parties have leaned toward the election-centered pole, while at other times they have been closer to the policy-driven perspective. Therefore, instead of defining party goals in any sort of concrete way, conceivably the best approach is to remain mindful of the dichotomy between responsible and rational-efficient parties models. Sometimes and in some places the profit motive has been to merely win elections, whereas at other times and in other places it was to enact certain policies. The chore for the student of political parties is, of course, to discern when each perspective best fits and why.

THE BATTLE OF THE TITANS: HAMILTON VERSUS JEFFERSON

After traveling what was then the breadth of the United States in 1831 and 1832, Alexis de Tocqueville remarked, "All the domestic controversies of the Americans at first appear to a stranger to be incomprehensible or puerile, and he is at a loss whether to pity a people who take such arrant trifles in good earnest or to envy that happiness which enables a community to discuss them."[33] Today, Tocqueville's complaint is echoed in the oft-heard line: "There's not a dime's worth of difference between the Democratic and Republican parties."

Such ideological homogeneity has given rise to a belief that the United States is a special country set apart from its European origins. Bill Clinton, for instance, has stated: "America is far more than a place. It is an idea, the most powerful idea in the history of nations."[34] Such expressions constitute what some have called **American Exceptionalism.**[35] The ideological consensus in the United States remains so pervasive that it even influences how Americans speak. Expressions such as the "American Dream" and "the American Way of Life" (along with the damning phrase "un-American") easily escape the lips, a reflection of the extraordinary self-confidence most Americans have in the experiment devised by the Framers. Historians have been struck by the rigidity of the American mind. As one has observed, "Who would think of using the word 'un-Italian' or 'un-French' as we use the word 'un-American?'"[36]

But such ideological rigidity does not mean that disagreements are lacking either in the history books or in contemporary news accounts about politics. After the Constitution was ratified and George Washington took his place as the nation's first president, Alexander Hamilton and Thomas Jefferson began to act, as Jefferson recalled, "like two cocks."[37] The raging battle between these two stubborn and forceful men was not only personal, but political. Both were staunchly committed to individualism, freedom, and equality of opportunity. Yet they had a strong difference of opinion as to how these values could be translated into an effective form of governance.

Those disagreements came from the vastly different solutions each man devised to a vexing problem—namely, how liberty could be restrained such that it could be enjoyed. For his part, Hamilton preferred that liberty be coupled with authority: "In every civil society, there must be a supreme power, to which all members of that society are subject; for, otherwise, there could be no supremacy, or subordination, that is no government at all."[38] Jefferson, meanwhile, preferred that liberty be paired with local civic responsibility. It was on that basis that the enduring struggle between **Hamiltonian Nationalism** and **Jeffersonian Localism** began.

Hamiltonian Nationalism envisions the United States as one "family," with a strong central government and an energetic president acting on its behalf. Addressing the delegates to the New York State convention called to ratify the Constitution, Hamilton noted: "The confidence of the people will easily be gained by good administration. This is the true touchstone." To him, good administration meant a strong central government acting on behalf of the national—or family—interest. Thus, any expression of a special interest was, to use Hamilton's word, "mischievous."[39] But Hamilton had his own partialities, favoring the development of the nation's urban centers and an unfettered capitalism. His espousal of a strong central government aroused considerable controversy.

Unlike Hamilton, Jefferson had a nearly limitless faith in the ordinary citizen. To a nation largely composed of farmers, he declared, "Those who labor in the earth are the chosen people of God, if ever He had a chosen people."[40] Jefferson's devotion to liberty made him distrust most attempts to restrain it, particularly those of the federal government: "Were we directed from Washington when to sow, and when to reap, we should soon want bread."[41] In 1825, Jefferson warned of the expanding power of government and wrote that the "salvation of the republic" rested on the regeneration and spread of the New England town meeting.[42] The best guarantee of liberty in Jefferson's view was to restrain the mighty hand of government.

Table 1.2 highlights several additional differences between Hamilton and Jefferson's views of government, with a special focus on how these differences might relate to the party system.

TABLE 1.2 ▪ The Hamiltonian and Jeffersonian Models of American Governance

Hamiltonian Nationalism	*Jeffersonian Localism*
Views the United States as one national "family."	Sees the United States as a series of diverse communities.
Prefers a concentration of power in the federal government so that it may act in the interest of the national family.	Prefers to give power to state and local governments so that they can act in deference to local customs.
More inclined to constrain liberty for the sake of national unity by marrying liberty with a strong central authority.	More inclined to favor liberty and wary of national authority. Prefers to concentrate governmental power at the state and local levels.
Trusts in elites to run the government.	Trusts in the common sense of average Americans to run their government.
Prefers a hierarchal party structure populated by "professional" party politicians.	Prefers a decentralized party structure populated by so-called amateur politicians, who often are local party activists.
Sees parties as vehicles whose primary purpose is to win elections and control the government.	Views parties as more ideologically based. Commitment to principles is viewed as even more important than winning elections.

It is this debate between the political descendants of Alexander Hamilton and Thomas Jefferson that forms the various settings for partisan conflict—and, indeed, the nature of party politics in America. Martin Van Buren, among many others, traces the evolution of parties to the factional disputes between Hamilton and Jefferson:

> The two great parties of this country, with occasional changes in name only, have for the principal part of a century, occupied antagonistic positions upon all important political questions. They have maintained an unbroken succession, and have, throughout, been composed respectively of men agreeing in their party passion, and preferences, and entertaining, with rare exceptions, similar views on the subject of government and its administration.[43]

Over time the two parties, with changing names and roles, recast Hamiltonian Nationalism and Jeffersonian Localism to suit the present and provide greater definition of political thought to the growing number of citizens permitted to cast a ballot. For example, during the Civil War and the Industrial Era that followed, Republicans stood with Hamilton, while Democrats claimed Jefferson as one of their own and promoted states rights. Since the days of Franklin D. Roosevelt's New Deal, Democrats have consistently aligned themselves with Hamilton, likening the nation to a family. As former New York Governor Mario M. Cuomo once put it: "The recognition that at the heart of the matter we are bound inextricably to one another; that the layoff of a steel worker in Buffalo is our problem; the pain and struggle of a handicapped mother in Houston is our struggle; the fight of a retired school teacher in Chicago to live in dignity is our fight."[44]

While Cuomo and his fellow Democrats espouse Hamiltonian Nationalism, today's Republican party has immersed itself in the values cherished by Jeffersonian Localism. Listen to Ronald Reagan: "Through lower taxes and smaller government, government has its ways of freeing people's spirits."[45] Reagan and likeminded Republicans see the country not as a family, but as a collection of diverse communities for whom liberty means the right to be left alone. During the 1960s, Senate Majority Leader Trent Lott, then a student at the University of Mississippi, was caught in the maelstrom surrounding school integration with the admission of James Meredith as the school's first black student. As Lott recalled: "Yes, you could say that I favored segregation then. I don't now. The main thing was, I felt the federal government had no business sending in troops to tell the state what to do." In the Senate, Lott has vowed to restore Jeffersonian Localism by opposing any effort to concentrate more power in Washington.[46]

Many historians believe that since the nation's founding the character of the American people has not changed greatly. Our values may be constant, but the circumstances in which they are applied are not. The whiff of civil war, the onset of a depression, or the ravages of inflation inevitably cause Americans to take stock of the situation, alter their expectations of government, and choose a political party and a course of action in a manner consistent with the cherished values of freedom, individualism, and equality of opportunity. At critical junctures, Americans have shifted from Hamiltonian Nationalism to Jeffersonian Localism. Such shifts in public attitudes have usually been influenced by a dominant personality. Abraham

Lincoln, for example, reasserted Hamilton's vision of a national family in order to save the Union. Three score and ten years later, Franklin Roosevelt redefined Hamiltonian Nationalism to meet the challenges of the Great Depression. At other times, Jeffersonian Localism has thrived. Ronald Reagan, a towering figure during the late twentieth century, promised to restore the idea of community.

Often, Americans do not want to choose between Hamiltonian Nationalism and Jeffersonian Localism. Instead, they want to enjoy the fruits of both. Thus, it is the inevitable perversion of Hamiltonian Nationalism and Jeffersonian Localism that ensures periodic swings from one faction to the other. At each juncture, Americans experience a "sense of return" when the old battles start up again on new, but seemingly familiar, territory. Hamilton would be astonished to learn that his concept of a national family is being used to promote the interests of have-nots, especially women and minorities. And Ronald Reagan's espousal of Jeffersonian Localism is premised on a welfare state first erected by Franklin Roosevelt's New Deal. But as this book suggests, political parties have developed and continue to evolve in the vineyards tilled by Hamilton and Jefferson. Simply put, political parties thrive in an American setting; they give expression to American ideological impulses; and they serve as instruments used by Americans to implement the constitutional designs of the Framers.

LIKE GOD, PARTIES ARE NOT DEAD

A couple of decades ago, *Time* magazine ran a cover story with the title "God is Dead." Today, death and political parties are often found in the same sentence. Admittedly, we are not neutral observers of the debate about political parties. We do not share the sentiment that parties are dying. Contradicting that famous *Time* magazine cover, God has made a comeback. So, too, have the political parties—albeit to a more limited extent. Political parties are not God, of course. Yet, it is hard to envision a twenty-first century America without them. Should they die, there would be significant costs to the democratic process. We believe that democracy—the will of the people—is best served through the party system. For all their deficiencies, parties still afford average Americans the best avenue for speaking their minds and being heard. In fact, it is precisely because the Information Age is already here that political parties will continue to play an important role in the next century.

This is not to say the reader will share these sentiments at the beginning or end of the book. You are invited to decide for yourself what role, if any, parties perform in our system. Will parties in the United States find their place in the twenty-first century? Come join the debate.

FURTHER READING

Boorstin, Daniel. *The Genius of American Politics*. Chicago: University of Chicago Press, 1953.
Lipset, Seymour Martin. *American Exceptionalism: A Double-Edged Sword*. New York: Norton, 1996.

Madison, James. "Federalist 10." In *The Federalist,* edited by Edward Meade Earle. New York: Modern Library, 1937.

Tocqueville, Alexis. *Democracy in America.* Richard D. Heffner, ed. New York: New American Library, 1956.

Washington, George. "Farewell Address," September 17, 1796. Reprinted as Senate Document Number 3, 102nd Cong., 1st sess., Washington, D.C., 1991.

NOTES

1. George Washington, "Farewell Address," September 17, 1796. Reprinted as Senate Document Number 3, 102nd Cong., 1st sess., 1991.

2. Abraham Lincoln, "Address to the Young Men's Lyceum of Springfield, Illinois," *Abraham Lincoln: Speeches and Writings, 1832–1858* (New York: Library of America), 32–33.

3. Quoted in James MacGregor Burns, *Cobblestone Leadership: Majority Rule, Minority Power* (Norman: University of Oklahoma Press, 1990), 5.

4. Ibid.

5. John F. Kennedy, *Profiles in Courage* (New York: Harper, 1956).

6. Cited in Martin P. Wattenberg, *The Rise of Candidate-Centered Politics* (Cambridge: Harvard University Press, 1991), 34.

7. James Madison, "Federalist 10," in Edward Meade Earle, ed., *The Federalist* (New York: Modern Library, 1937), 77.

8. Ibid., 59.

9. Ibid., 61.

10. Quoted in James Thomas Flexner, *Washington: The Indispensable Man* (New York: New American Library, 1974), 263.

11. Washington, "Farewell Address."

12. Quoted in A. James Reichley, *The Life of the Parties: A History of American Political Parties* (New York: Free Press, 1992), 29.

13. David Herbert Donald, *Lincoln* (New York: Touchstone Books, 1995), 537.

14. See Richard Morin and E. J. Dionne, Jr., "Majority of Voters Say Parties Have Lost Touch," *Washington Post,* July 8, 1992, 1.

15. National Opinion Research Center, General Social Surveys, 1996.

16. President Ford Committee, "Ford Campaign Strategy Plan," August 1976. Courtesy of Gerald R. Ford Library.

17. Quoted in Leon D. Epstein, *Political Parties in the American Mold* (Madison: University of Wisconsin Press, 1986), 18.

18. Amicus curiae brief filed by the Committee for Party Renewal in *Colorado Republican Federal Campaign Committee v. Federal Election Commission,* February 1996, 3.

19. Committee for Party Renewal, "Statement of Principles," September 1977.

20. Quoted in "Brooke Is Safe, But, . . ." *Boston Globe,* October 31, 1971, A5.

21. V. O. Key, Jr., *Politics, Parties, and Pressure Groups* (New York: Crowell, 1958), 23.

22. See Everett Carll Ladd with Charles D. Hadley, *Transformations of the American Party System* (New York: Norton, 1975), 1.

23. The PIE, PO, PIG model was first developed by Ralph M. Goldman in 1951. See Ralph M. Goldman, *Party Chairmen and Party Faction, 1789–1900* (Ph.D. diss., University of Chicago, 1951), introduction; and Ralph M. Goldman, *The National Party Chairmen and Committees: Factionalism at the Top* (New York: M.E. Sharpe, 1990).

24. Daniel Bell, *The Coming of Post-Industrial Society* (New York: Basic Books, 1973).

25. S. C. Gwynne and J. E. Dickerson, "Lost in the E-Mail," *Time,* April 21, 1997, 89.

26. "On Capitol Hill, GOP E-Mail Bumps into Legal Dead End," *Washington Post,* September 25, 1998, A19.

27. Quoted in E. J. Dionne, *They Only Look Dead* (New York: Simon & Schuster, 1996), 90.

28. See John Frendries, "Voters, Government Officials, and Party Organizations: Connections and Disconnections," in John C. Green and Daniel M. Shea, eds., *The State of the Parties: The Changing Role of Contemporary American Parties* (Lanham, Md.: Rowman and Littlefield, 1996); and Joseph A. Schlesinger, *Political Parties and the Winning of Office* (Ann Arbor: University of Michigan Press, 1991).

29. Joseph A. Schlesinger, *Political Parties and the Winning of Office* (Ann Arbor: University of Michigan Press, 1991).

30. Leon D. Epstein, *Political Parties in Western Democracies* (New Brunswick, N.J.: Transaction Books, 1980).

31. John H. Aldrich, *Why Parties?* (Chicago: University of Chicago Press, 1995).

32. Jay M. Shafritz, *The Dorsey Dictionary of American Government and Politics* (Chicago: Dorsey Press, 1988).

33. Alexis de Tocqueville, *Democracy in America*, Richard D. Heffner, ed. (New York: New American Library, 1956), 90.

34. Bill Clinton, State of the Union Address, Washington, D.C., February 3, 1997.

35. Seymour Martin Lipset, *American Exceptionalism: A Double-Edged Sword* (New York: Norton, 1996).

36. Daniel Boorstin, *The Genius of American Politics* (Chicago: University of Chicago Press, 1953), 14.

37. See William Nisbet Chambers, "Party Development and the American Mainstream," in William Nisbet Chambers and Walter Dean Burnham, eds., *The American Party Systems* (New York: Oxford University Press, 1975), 6.

38. Quoted in Reichley, *The Life of the Parties*, 40.

39. See Morton J. Frisch, ed., *Selected Writings and Speeches of Alexander Hamilton* (Washington, D.C.: American Enterprise Institute, 1985), 316.

40. Quoted in Ted Morgan, *FDR: A Biography* (New York: Simon & Schuster, 1985), 38.

41. Quoted in Richard Reeves, *The Reagan Detour* (New York: Simon & Schuster, 1985), 19.

42. Quoted in Robert F. Kennedy, *To Seek a Newer World* (New York: Doubleday, 1967), 56.

43. Quoted in A. James Reichley, "Party Politics in a Federal Polity," in John Kenneth White and Jerome M. Mileur, eds., *Challenges to Party Government* (Carbondale: Southern Illinois University Press, 1992), 43.

44. "The Themes of 1984 with Governors Mario Cuomo and George Deukmejian," *Public Opinion* (December/January 1984): 20.

45. Ronald Reagan, State of the Union Address, Washington, D.C., January 27, 1987.

46. Quoted in Dan Goodgame, "A Lott Like Clinton?" *Time*, March 10, 1997.

CHAPTER 2

The Ascendance of Party Politics

The most frequently quoted lines in the study of political parties were penned in 1942: "It should be flatly stated," wrote E. E. Schattschneider, "that the political parties created democracy and that modern democracy is unthinkable save in terms of parties."[1] Schattschneider's proclamation is found in nearly every text on political parties written since the 1940s, and most political scientists still accept his assertion as a fact. Yet, to the average citizen, political parties are synonymous with corruption, gridlock, and elitism. Americans relish bashing parties and confounding the experts by splitting our votes among them. Concentrating power in one party has become so suspect that some voters have taken an odd pleasure in choosing presidents of one party and Congresses of another. This process of cohabitation (the French term for divided government) is often an uneasy one for party leaders, but voters don't care much about the discomfiture: 56 percent of those leaving the polls in 1996 said they wanted control of the White House and the Congress split between Democrats and Republicans.[2] The pervasive trend of split-ticket voting and partisan cohabitation even extends to most state capitals. After the 1996 results were tallied, only eighteen states had their state legislative and executive branches held by the same party: twelve Republican; six Democratic.

Given such cavalier treatment by the voters, it should come as no surprise that political parties have had a tortured and tormented history. Although Americans, along with the British, can stake their claim toward the invention of the modern political party, few take pride in having such an important historical legacy. But it is this unique soil—a vineyard in which parties were sown amidst widespread public disdain—that has influenced the party progression from the earliest days of the republic. For more than two hundred years, political parties have searched for their rightful place in the American polity without ever, given the peculiar acidity of the American vineyard, quite finding it. But we are getting ahead of our story.

THE PRE-PARTY ERA

The origins of American political parties have their roots in seventeenth century England. Between 1640 and 1660, a period known as the Puritan Revolution, controversy swirled over the concept of a parliamentary prerogative—namely, whether authority should rest solely with the crown or whether parliament should have some say in the affairs of the day. Those loyal to the monarch were dubbed **Tories** (or members of the Court Party), whereas those preferring a greater parliamentary role became known as **Whigs** (members of the Country Party). Tories were for the country aristocracy, the small group of landowners, and they were jealous of the growing commercial middle class. Whigs, on the other hand, promoted commercial interests and, because of this, they were dubbed "radicals."

The Glorious Revolution of 1688–1689 transformed the monarchy from a nearly despotic institution (a process begun by the Magna Carta in 1215) to one that increasingly yielded to an assertive parliament, which had new authority and convened on a regular basis. Tories and Whigs continued to divide the parliament, with control switching from one party to another. These contests were tawdry affairs involving only a small portion of citizens as voters, and were rife with corruption. But the shift from an authoritarian monarchy to a somewhat more democratic parliament was a significant one. By the eighteenth century, historians would hail the British for ushering in an "age of legislatures"—a fact of which the Framers of the U.S. Constitution were very much aware.

But these "proto-parties" were a far cry from their modern-day counterparts—especially in their exclusion of the mass public. Divisions between Tories and Whigs were often based on the skills of persuasive individuals, tradition, and family connections rather than any split on policy questions. Moreover, there were no formal party organizations as such. Neither party had official leaders, meeting places, lines of authority, or resources. Yet, in their own way, they were a beginning.

THE COLONIAL EXPERIENCE

To a significant degree, American politics during the Colonial Era mirrored that of mother England, because the New World was largely under English domination and the predominantly English colonists held to the political customs and traditions of their homeland. Political parties before the Revolutionary War were not much more than extensions of rival family clans such as the Wards and Hopkins in Rhode Island and the DeLanceys and Livingstons in New York. As in England, the contests between these various clans often involved an ideological dispute over the extent to which royal authority should be exercised in the colonies. As John Adams recalled: "In every colony, divisions always prevailed. In New York, Pennsylvania, Virginia, Massachusetts, and all the rest, a court and country party have always contended."[3] Indeed, the dispute began almost as soon as the British ships carrying the settlers to Jamestown left port in 1607. On one side were those loyal to the Crown and the appointed royal governors—the Court; those opposed were faithful to the elected colonial assemblies—the Country. Those supporting the Crown were often wealthy, having received immense land grants from the King, whereas those who did not share these special privileges were tradesmen, small shop owners, and those who tilled the soil and had become accustomed to the hardships of the New World.

These poor, adventurous outcasts were deeply suspicious of authority figures, especially the king, and their political cynicism was deep-seated.

While parliamentary prerogative did much to structure colonial politics, it did not foster real parties as we know them today due to several obstacles. In pre-Revolutionary America, localism was a much greater force than nationalism, as each colony had its own customs, history, and political identity. Moreover, there was a great diversity of individual interests among small-freehold farmers, plantation slave-holders, merchants, shipowners and builders, emerging manufacturers, and others. In addition, there were numerous ethnic and religious groups, the most influential being those who wanted an aristocratic and consolidated republic versus those who preferred a more democratic regime with power concentrated in the states.

During the American Revolution, the old cleavages engendered by parliamentary prerogative were transformed into a debate about self-governance. Country followers despised King George III and favored severing ties with Britian. Dubbed **patriots,** many advocated violence to end what they saw as British subjugation. British exports to the colonies, which accounted for one-twelfth of that country's exports in 1704, had mushroomed to one-third by 1772. Edmund Burke, a member of the House of Commons at the time, noted that "the state of America has been kept in continual agitation. Everything administered as [a] remedy to the public complaint, if it did not produce, was at least followed by, a heightening of the distemper." Burke observed that the colonists "owe little or nothing to any care of ours" thanks to "a wise and salutary neglect" from their British overseers.[4]

The increased trade, with accompanying taxes, and British neglect prompted a number of high-profile protests, such as the Boston Tea Party of 1773 and sinking of the *Gaspee* off the Rhode Island coast one year earlier. The Court group, or **loyalists,** remained faithful to the Crown, and they likened the patriots to rabble-rousers and ne'er-do-wells. With the uprisings at Lexington and Concord in 1775, the contest between the patriots and loyalists became an outright civil war, with patriots winning control of state governments in all the colonies. In most states, the patriots were well-organized, establishing societies like the Sons of Liberty. They held rallies, sponsored "committees of correspondence" to spread their views, and recruited important community leaders to their cause. Patriot leader Thomas Paine espoused the virtues of self-rule in his 1776 pamphlet *Common Sense*, and John Adams organized the Boston Junta to fight against foreign influence in colonial affairs. Their activities were less focused on winning elections (there were few voters at the time) than on the larger battle of changing public opinion.

An opportunity for party formation presented itself with the collapse of the Articles of Confederation in 1787, but was never fully realized. For a brief time after the Revolution, a short-lived boom in imports from England pushed the cost of agricultural and manufactured goods downward. Money became scarce, especially specie or "hard money" (silver and gold). The result was a severe economic depression that began in the late 1770s and lasted nearly a decade. Among the hardest hit were working-class citizens and small farmers. Because farmers had little specie, bank foreclosures skyrocketed. The problem was further complicated when most states levied heavy taxes in a largely unsuccessful attempt to eliminate their wartime debts. By the mid-1780s, the demands for action grew louder.

To avoid bloodshed, so-called *stay laws* were passed in some states to postpone foreclosures. New "*tender laws*" allowed farmers to use agricultural products to help pay loans, and paper money became more widespread, easing debt payment. But none of these actions eased the governing crisis which came to a head when former army captain Daniel Shays led a mob of farmers against the state government of Massachusetts in 1787. Shays and his comrades unsuccessfully tried to capture the federal arsenal in Springfield. Their purpose was to prevent foreclosures on their debt-ridden land by keeping the country courts of western Massachusetts from sitting until the next election. The state militia eventually dispersed the mob, but the uprising, which became known as **Shays's Rebellion,** left its mark. George Washington captured the sentiments of most American elites: "I am mortified beyond expression that in the moment of our acknowledged independence we should by our conduct verify the predictions of our transatlantic foe, and render ourselves ridiculous and contemptible in the eyes of all Europe."[5] Alexander Hamilton agreed, noting that the rebellion prompted "the question, whether societies of men are really capable or not of establishing good government from reflection and choice, or whether they are forever destined to depend for their political constitutions on accident and force."[6] Many feared the latter was the answer. As Publius later wrote in the *Federalist Papers,* "A NATION without a NATIONAL GOVERNMENT is, in my view, an awful spectacle."[7]

It was Shays's Rebellion that galvanized the states to convene delegates in Philadelphia for the purpose of drafting a new governing document. The Constitution's supporters, who became known as **Federalists,** and those who opposed its ratification, dubbed **Anti-Federalists,** carried their dispute from Independence Hall in Philadelphia to the various state capitals. Anti-Federalists contended that representatives in any national government must reflect a true picture of the people, possessing an intimate knowledge of their circumstances and needs. This could only be achieved, they argued, through small, relatively homogeneous republics such as those already constructed in the existing states. One prominent Anti-Federalist spokesperson asked: "Is it practicable for a country so large and so numerous . . . to elect a representation that will speak their sentiments? . . . It certainly is not."[8] Federalists believed that a representative republic was possible and desirable—especially if populated by those "who possess [the] most wisdom to discern, and [the] most virtue to pursue, the common good of society."[9]

The adoption of the Constitution did not end the disputes between the Federalists and Anti-Federalists. Soon after the Constitution went into effect came the first signs of party activity. Although the Framers disliked parties, they made them more likely to prosper by adopting the Bill of Rights—a concession given to the Anti-Federalists. The Bill of Rights was a boon to party development because it (1) guaranteed that Congress could make no law abridging freedom of speech; (2) gave ordinary citizens the right to assemble and petition their government for a redress of grievances; and (3) created a free press.

NASCENT PARTIES: FEDERALISTS VERSUS REPUBLICANS

George Washington assumed the presidency in 1789 believing that parties were unnecessary, and that he could bypass them by creating an "enlightened administration." To that end, Washington took into his Cabinet the leading political antagonists of his time: Alexander Hamilton as treasury secretary and Thomas Jefferson as secretary of state. Less than a year after becoming president, Washington's experiment of having a government without parties faltered. Hamilton and Jefferson vehemently disagreed in the Cabinet councils over how to manage the growing economic crisis. Hamilton offered a sweeping plan to revive the sagging economy—the most controversial portion of which involved the complete assumption of debts incurred by the states during the Revolutionary War. To Hamilton and his Federalist followers, this policy was not only sound economics but good politics. By helping those who backed the revolt against King George III, confidence in the national government would be restored and nearly $80 million would be put in the pockets of those most likely to reinvest in the nation's tiny infrastructure. The result would be an increase in the flow of goods and services accompanied by a general rise in living standards.

To pay for full assumption, Hamilton proposed an excise tax on distilled spirits which became known as the Whiskey Tax. Because most whiskey producers were farmers in the South and West, this measure shifted the tax burden from northeastern business owners to small farmers—in effect, punishing those most likely to support Jefferson's Republicans. Hamilton's tax of eight cents per gallon of whiskey seems small by today's standards. But at the time, whiskey cost thirty-two cents per gallon—thus, Hamilton was suggesting a tax of 25 percent! Yet, even this hefty tax was not enough to set the economy aright. To ensure that enough money would fill the federal coffers, Hamilton advocated establishing a Bank of the United States that would make loans and collect interest payments while it curbed the diverse practices of state-chartered banks. The idea of a national bank, not one of the powers specifically given to the Congress in the Constitution, created enormous animosity between advocates of states' rights and those seeking a more powerful national government—a dispute that would not be resolved until 1819 by the Supreme Court in the case of *McCulloch v. Maryland*.

Jefferson and the Republicans believed that federal assumption of state debts would create immense profits for the monied class, especially those living in New England. Opposition to Hamilton's scheme was led in the House of Representatives by James Madison. Madison agreed with Hamilton that the economy needed strengthening, but fretted about the shift of capital from the agricultural states (including his native Virginia) to a few northeastern manufacturing states. Moreover, Madison thought that the Whiskey Tax would be a financial disaster for small farmers. His prediction came true in 1794 when farmers in western Pennsylvania caused an uprising that became popularly known as the **Whiskey Insurrection.** Madison corralled seventeen House members to his side—about one-quarter of the chamber. Opposing him were about the same number of legislators. At the conclusion of the First Congress, an exasperated Hamilton exclaimed: "It was not till the last session that I became unequivocally convinced that Mr. Madison, cooperating with Mr. Jefferson, is at the head of a faction decidedly hostile to me and my administration; and actuated by views, in my judgment, subversive to the principles of good government and dangerous to the union, peace, and happiness of the country."[10]

The battle between Hamilton and Madison extended beyond the halls of Congress to the newspapers. In a move that foreshadowed the inextricable link that would develop between political parties and the mass media (especially in the Information Age), Hamilton forged a close alliance with John Ward Fenno, publisher of the *Gazette of the United States*. Madison, not willing to let Fenno's editorials go unanswered, persuaded Philip Freneau to edit a rival newspaper, the *National Gazette*. These party-controlled newspapers, although having a small number of subscribers (the *Gazette of the United States* had only 1,500), quickly became the most popular method of communicating with the party faithful.[11] Together, they helped clarify this first battle between Hamiltonian Nationalism and Jeffersonian Localism; even as they exacerbated the animosity between these two leaders. The battle of epithets made it clear that not only within the Washington administration were there leaders of two rival parties, but that much of American society was caught in the maelstrom of partisan politics.

Despite the intense opposition to Hamilton's economic plan, it won congressional approval after some wily backroom maneuvering. Jefferson played a key behind-the-scenes role, endorsing the bill in exchange for assurances that the federal capital would be moved south from New York City to the District of Columbia. But Jefferson's support for Hamilton's economic rescue plan alienated his agrarian constituents. Seeking to mend political fences, Jefferson embarked on a tour with his ally James Madison during the spring of 1791 that was to have profound consequences for party development. Ostensibly, the duo set out to "observe the vegetation and wildlife in the region," but their real purpose was to sample public opinion. In effect, they were testing the waters for the formation of a new political party. In New York City, Jefferson and Madison met with Robert Livingston and George Clinton—two longtime rivals of Hamilton—as well as Senator Aaron Burr who was attempting to broaden his political influence.

Two years later, in 1793, Jefferson and Hamilton renewed their struggle. This time, the issue was how to respond to the French Revolution. To Jefferson and his followers, the French cry for "liberty, equality, and fraternity" was an extension of the American Revolution. Thomas Paine was so moved by the French revolutionaries that he journeyed to France to help the cause. The German Republican Society was formed in Philadelphia. Its members sympathized with the French revolutionaries, and believed that the American Revolution was losing momentum thanks to Hamilton, who, they claimed, was endangering the promise of democracy contained in the Declaration of Independence. By 1798, there were forty-three of these popular societies in every state except New Hampshire and Georgia.

To Hamilton and his Federalist backers, the French Revolution signaled the emergence of anarchy and a rejection of traditional Christian values. They were horrified by the mob violence, and feared that the emerging republican movement could lead America down the same path. Jefferson remarked that these different reactions to the French Revolution "kindled and brought forth the two [political] parties with an ardor which our own interests merely could never incite."[12] Jefferson dubbed Hamilton's party the "monocrats." For his part, Jefferson never referred to his party as the Democrats, since the term conjured visions of mob rule, preferring the name Republicans to describe his emerging political organization.

When the bloody beheadings of the Terror of 1793 became known, reservations about the French experiment became widespread. Seeking to cool the growing political passions in his own country, President Washington sent James Monroe to Paris and John Jay to London to obtain treaties that would protect American shipping interests and keep the United States out of the European political thicket. But when Jay returned with an agreement that many believed was partial to the British, a political firestorm erupted. The treaty was so controversial that Washington waited six months before submitting it to the Senate for ratification in 1795, where it passed by a twenty–to-ten margin—the bare two-thirds required.

By 1796, Hamilton's controversial economic policies and the Jay Treaty divided public opinion and led to the creation of the nation's first official political parties. The **Federalists** took their name to signal their intention of creating a strong, centralized government (It is important to note here that this group of Federalists does not refer to the defenders of the Constitution crafted in Philadelphia in 1787.). The opposing **Republicans** wished to make clear that they were devoted to the people—thus the phrase "the republican principle" was coined. (It is important to note here that this group later changed their name to the Democratic Party.) Most Federalists were affluent businessmen from the northeastern states, while Republicans won backing from small farmers in the mid-Atlantic and southern states. The division proved so powerful that in 1796 a presidential election was hotly contested for the first time. Thomas Jefferson was so opposed to the Jay Treaty that he accepted the Republican call to lend his name as a presidential candidate. The battle between Federalist John Adams and Jefferson was a close one, with Adams winning seventy-one electoral votes to Jefferson's sixty-eight. Under the peculiar constitutional arrangements of the time, runner-up Jefferson became vice president.

The 1796 Adams-Jefferson contest was more than a struggle between two men—it was a battle between two political organizations. But although there were scores of local groups, some even using the term *parties* before 1796, it was the election of 1800 that saw the emergence of political organizations as we know them today. Propelled by a strong conviction that the Federalist-controlled U.S. government was abandoning sacred "republican principles," Jefferson and the Republicans formed a party replete with grassroots groups, slates of candidates, and a united platform of issues that appealed to the American sense of limited government and a prevailing fear of placing too much authority in one individual.

In what proved to be a futile attempt to stem the growing Republican tide, John Adams and his Federalist followers in Congress sought to emulate Jefferson's organizational skills. But since they had less grassroots support—there were no Federalist clubs to speak of—organizing proved difficult. Yet, by virtue of the fact that they ran the government, they could use their positions to press their advantage. Thus, the Federalist-controlled Congress passed the 1798 Sedition Act which made it a misdemeanor to publish false or malicious information and provided that anyone convicted of conspiring to hinder the operations of the federal government would be subject to heavy fines and possible imprisonment. The Alien Acts, which became law the same year, made it easier to deport political adversaries who were not citizens—especially the growing Irish population, which was pro-Republican as well as any migrating French revolutionaries. Fourteen indictments were issued between 1798 and 1800. One Republican was jailed because he carried a placard protesting the acts; another was sentenced for six months for attempting, in the words of a Federalist-appointed judge, to "mislead the ignorant and inflame their minds against the President."[13]

Jefferson worried that these new laws might make it possible for the Federalists to install one of their own as a president-for-life. Thus, the organizing efforts of Jefferson and Madison became a whirlwind of activity as the election of 1800 approached. Republican members of Congress met in Philadelphia and formally endorsed Jefferson for president and Aaron Burr for vice president. The Federalists responded by nominating a ticket consisting of John Adams of Massachusetts and Thomas Pinckney of South Carolina—the first of many North-South pairings.

As in 1796, the Adams-Jefferson contest was hard fought. Hamilton warned his Federalist followers that no defections would be tolerated in the Electoral College. But Hamilton's admonition notwithstanding, Jefferson prevailed. Like the first Adams-Jefferson race, the South backed Jefferson while most of the Northeast sided with Adams. But the switch of New York from Adams to Jefferson—the culmination of Jefferson's courting of New Yorkers that began with his 1793 "bird-watching" trip—paid off. Clinton and Livingston, together with Burr's New York City organization, rallied the troops on Jefferson's behalf. New York's electoral votes gave Jefferson an eight–vote plurality in the Electoral College. The Republican victory, which had to be ratified in the House of Representatives, extended to both houses of Congress. As Jefferson later recalled, "The Revolution of 1800 was as real a revolution in the principles of our government as that of 1776 was in its forms."[14] Despite the strenuous efforts of the Framers to stop them, political parties were here to stay.

PARTY RULE: 1824–1912

In the two decades following Jefferson's election, Republicans strengthened their hold on the government and overcame an abortive attempt by the Federalists to lengthen their stay. On the eve of his leaving the presidency in March 1801, John Adams issued several "midnight appointments" of loyal Federalists to judicial posts. The Federalists hoped that by making these appointments they could limit the damage done by the Republicans until the next election in 1804.

One of those appointed by Adams was William Marbury who was slated to become a justice of the peace. The incoming secretary of state, James Madison, refused to deliver Marbury's nominating papers. Marbury and seven others sued the government, claiming that Madison had defaulted on his duty to serve his appointment papers. The case of *Marbury v. Madison* was heard by the Supreme Court in 1803. In a landmark ruling, Chief Justice John Marshall (another last-minute Adams appointee whose papers were prepared in time) wrote that the court had no power to order Madison to surrender the papers since a portion of the Judiciary Act of 1789 itself was unconstitutional. In declaring that it is "the province and duty of the judicial department to say what the law is," Marshall wormed his way out of a difficult political thicket while giving the Supreme Court the vital authority known as **judicial review**.[15] With the Federalists in full retreat, and Jefferson quite willing to accept Marshall's ruling, the Republicans set about the task of running the government.

The next twenty years saw what many historians have described as the Era of Good Feelings. The trio of Jefferson, Madison, and Monroe established a Virginia dynasty that controlled the White House. In the five elections held between 1804 and 1820, Republicans won between 53 and 92 percent of the Electoral College votes, and held between 61 and 85 percent of the seats in Congress. The Republicans were so powerful that for the only time in American history there was essentially a one-party government in that there was virtually no serious electoral competition from another major party.

Meanwhile, the Federalists started down a path that led to political obscurity. The War of 1812 virtually sealed the party's fate. Federalists, who retained a strong base of support in the New England states, vehemently opposed the war believing that it would seriously impede vital trade with England. They dubbed the conflict "Mr. Madison's War," and New Englanders continued to illicitly trade with the British, sometimes even withholding money and militia from the war effort. Republicans seethed at the British impressment of sailors—the removal of British-born sailors from American vessels and forcing them into the British navy—because the practice included the taking of many native-born Americans by mistake. Americans were repulsed by the British aggression, and Republicans believed that the rampant nationalism would unify their already diverse party. When Congress declared war on Great Britain in 1812, the war of words escalated as well. The *National Intelligencer* declared: "This is no time for debating the propriety of war. WAR IS DECLARED, and every patriot heart must unite in its support."[16] When the *Federal Republican*, a Federalist newspaper located in Baltimore, editorialized against the war, an angry mob razed the building where it was printed. Elsewhere, Federalist sympathizers were beaten, stabbed, and even tarred and feathered. Two years later the Federalists met in Hartford, Connecticut, and proposed generous peace terms. Rumors persisted that the Federalists favored the seccession of the New England states from the Union, and the party, already weakened by its antiwar stance, fell into disrepute. By 1820, the Federalists had become political dinosaurs, not even bothering to nominate a token candidate to oppose James Monroe in that year's presidential contest. Hamilton's party faded into the history books, although Hamilton's ideas did not.

Breakdown and Renewal: The Election of 1824

The strength of the Republicans ultimately was their undoing. By 1810, the House of Representatives was filled with a variety of Republicans. Some were traditional states' rights advocates; others wanted an enlarged role for the federal government to enhance westward expansion. Thus, while most elected officials were Republicans, the label became increasingly ambiguous. By 1824, the divisions within the party had widened into a chasm. Five candidates, each representing a different Republican faction, aggressively sought the presidency: Henry Clay, the powerful Speaker of the House and champion of westward expansion; John C. Calhoun, secretary of war and supporter of states' rights; Andrew Jackson, the hero of the Battle of New Orleans; John Quincy Adams, son of the former president and secretary of state under Monroe; and William Crawford, former treasury secretary and, like Calhoun, a doctrinaire states' rights advocate. The Congressional Caucus (the means by which Republican nominees had been chosen since 1800) convened in Washington, D.C., in February and selected Crawford to be the party's standard-bearer with Calhoun as his running mate. Just 66 of 231 eligible Republicans attended, and the remaining three candidates boycotted the caucus. They then persuaded their respective state legislatures to place their names in contention.

On Election Day, Jackson led in the popular votes cast, winning 153,000, more than the combined votes cast for Adams and Crawford. But Jackson failed to win an electoral majority. The all-important Electoral College vote split, with Jackson receiving 99 votes; Adams, 84; Crawford, 41; and Clay, 37. Under such conditions, the Constitution turns the matter over to the House of Representatives for a final decision among the top three contenders. Clay, who finished last and was excluded from consideration, backed Adams, telling him in January 1825 that after "a decent time for his own funeral solemnities as a candidate . . . he had no hesitation in saying that his preference would be for me."[17] Adams reciprocated by promising to make Clay secretary of state in the new administration. Since he was the powerful Speaker of the House, the deal clinched the presidency for Adams who won the votes of thirteen state delegations in the House to Jackson's seven and Crawford's four. Two days after the House confirmed Adams as the next president, Clay was offered the position of secretary of state. Adams expressed his hope that he could "bring the whole people of the Union to harmonize together" without regard to partisan affiliation.[18] But an embittered Jackson denounced what he saw as a quid pro quo between Adams and Clay: "So you see the Judas of the West has closed the contract and will receive the thirty pieces of silver."[19] Indeed, Jackson and his followers considered Adams a usurper in the White House, and in several state capitals they plotted a comeback.

The Jackson-Van Buren Alliance

The history of American politics is filled with characters who, in the words of famed party leader, George Washington Plunkitt, "have seen their opportunities and took 'em." Such was the case with Martin Van Buren following the 1824 debacle. At the time, Van Buren was a U.S. senator representing New York. For years, he had fought to win control of the Republican New York City political machine headed by then-governor DeWitt Clinton. Yet, whenever Van Buren seemed on the verge of controlling the Bucktails (the name given to the New York City organization), Clinton would mount an offensive and regain power. Frustrated with his inability to become a local kingmaker, Van Buren turned his prodigious skills to presidential politics. Knowing that the New York State vote in 1828 would be decisive, Van Buren reckoned he could determine the next president.

By 1826, his hunch was paying off. A strong grassroots movement led by the Anti-Masonic orders in New York and Pennsylvania wanted to strip elite politicians from their kingmaker role. At the same time, several states changed their laws allowing voters to choose delegates to the Electoral College rather than leaving the task to the various state legislatures. A general loosening of voter qualifications also greatly enlarged the size of the potential electorate. Meanwhile, the Republican party was fracturing. On one side were the Adams-Clay followers who were determined to implement internal improvements to the nation's infrastructure. Like the Federalists of two decades earlier, they were convinced that national prosperity necessitated an active government. On the other side were the so-called traditional Republicans whose ranks included Van Buren. They opposed internal improvements, including road and canal construction, because they believed such projects would violate state sovereignty. Keeping his distance from these two factions was Andrew Jackson, who remained a popular figure but lacked an official party organization until Van Buren took charge of his campaign.

Van Buren's first step toward involvement in national politics was to solidify his following in the Congress. He quickly became leader of the Democratic-Republicans, a name chosen to express solidarity with the more egalitarian agrarian wing of the Republican Party. Van Buren undertook scores of trips to various states, campaigning for Jackson wherever he went. His goals were to arouse public indignation against the Adams-Clay deal, conduct door-to-door canvasses in every town, and make sure that Jackson supporters went to the polls on Election Day. Adams's forces derided Jackson as a military butcher, and even called the chastity of his wife into question. Nonetheless, Jackson handily beat Adams winning all of the South and the new western states. Jackson also took New York thanks to Van Buren's efforts. Just as significantly, voter turnout doubled from 25 percent in 1824 to 50 percent in 1828. Van Buren was the first to understand the power of mass-based party politics. Political parties were now firmly established as a primary vehicle for translating public sentiments into governing policies. Henceforth, parties became a mainstay of American politics.

After Jackson's victory, the Democratic-Republican Party shortened its name to **Democrats.** Maintaining its advocacy of states rights, lower taxes, and individual freedom, the new Democrats were opposed by Henry Clay, John C. Calhoun, and others who banded together as the **Whigs.** Their name was intended to summon up the spirits of those who comprised the patriot party during the heyday of the American Revolution and the British Whigs of the eighteenth century. Whigs stood for restrained executive powers, western expansion, and protective tariffs. Thus, by the mid-1830s, a two-party system had taken root on American soil. But unlike the earlier political skirmishes between Hamilton and Jefferson, ideological differences were gradually supplanted by a "politics of personality," as people decided they either loved or hated Jackson. In addition, by raiding the federal treasury Van Buren purchased an additional degree of party unity. The bargain was straightforward: state and local Democrats would be given dollars from the national treasury so long as they called themselves Democrats, supported Jackson on most matters, and took no controversial policy stands. As for issues of local concerns, they were free to do as they saw fit. This move established a pattern of **reciprocal deference** where there are important linkages between levels of the party system, but also autonomy at each level. In this case, local party organizations would be linked to the state and national organizations, but they were also free to run their own shows.

By forming a political machine capable of winning elections, Van Buren won the grudging admiration of his opponents. Parties had moved beyond a collection of like-minded followers to organizations seeking the control of government. Indeed, *organization* has been a watchword in party politics ever since. As will be seen in subsequent chapters, the resource-driven nature of party organizations and policy independence has defined much of contemporary politics in the Information Age and is likely to determine what role parties will play in the next century.

The Rise of Mass-Based Politics and the Emergence of the Spoils System

During Jackson's presidency, the nation witnessed a democratization known as **Jacksonian Democracy** in which power shifted from the affluent to the common citizen. Jacksonian Democracy had a number of consequences—the most significant of which was an immense increase in both the number of elected officials and those allowed to participate in electoral politics. Between 1824 and 1848, voter turnout increased from 26 percent to 79 percent—and in some states was as high as 92 percent. State and national party conventions emerged as important decision-making bodies in selecting candidates for office. A partisan press developed, as parties used newspapers to communicate with their expanding ranks of followers—a precursor to the late twentieth century's Information Age. Added to the mix was a huge influx of immigrants whose political activities became a means of assimilation into the American way of life.

To Van Buren, this new political environment posed both challenges and opportunities. Could the ever-increasing range of political voices be harmonized into consistently supporting one political party? Could issues attract new backers, or would appealing personalities be the key to winning new supporters? Van Buren maintained that the answers to these questions lay in building a party organization that was committed to principles even as it dispensed political favors. But it was jobs, not principles, that formed much of the basis of politics in the 1830s and 1840s. The emergence of the **spoils system** (so-named for the phrase "to the victor belong the spoils of the enemy"[20]) had a single purpose: to fill government jobs with loyal party workers. Even the mailman was a party loyalist. Van Buren believed that the thousands of jobs doled out through the spoils system enhanced public accountability. If a party failed to run the government properly (i.e., maintain clean streets and parks, and provide adequate police and fire protection), voters could dismiss these partisans and replace them with others at the next election. Thus, the "rotation of office" would give every person an opportunity to serve one's fellow citizens.

The spoils system meant that those filling these so-called patronage jobs would work diligently for the party or risk being bounced from the payroll. Since a job was based on one's party activity, giving time and money to the party became a means of ensuring economic security. The opposition Whig party denounced the spoils system, but emulated it on the rare occasions they won the White House. When Whig Zachary Taylor assumed the presidency in 1849, Abraham Lincoln requested that Taylor appoint a replacement for the postmaster's job in Springfield, Illinois: "J. R. Diller, the present incumbent, I cannot say has failed in the proper discharge of any of the duties of the office. He, however, has been an active partizan [sic] in opposition to us . . . [and] he has been a member of the Democratic State Central Committee."[21]

Deciding who would be the next president often determined whether one was gainfully employed or not. This made for contentious, hard-fought elections. In the nine largest states between 1838 and 1854, the average Democratic vote equaled 48.0 percent while the Whigs averaged 48.4 percent. Over time, the spoils system changed the essence of politics. Elections were no longer solitary affairs confined to the affluent. Instead, they were community events, as issues and candidates were debated over the "cider barrel." Party organizations sponsored picnics, socials, and dinners, and held rallies, demonstrations, and conventions. By immersing themselves in the social fabric of civic life, parties kept citizens involved and inspired their loyalty on election day. Many voters proudly displayed their party affiliation by wearing political buttons on their lapels. Party devotion affected more people and reached more deeply than ever considered possible. The result was a stable pattern of voting, and true independents and vote-switching between elections were rarities.

Parties reached their zenith by the late nineteenth century. They organized politics by affording social outlets, presenting tickets of candidates, drafting platforms, and initiating meaningful cues and symbols to voters. In short, American politics was party politics. Parties provided coherence to political thought, even as they created new social organizations and, on occasion, divided families—creating a politics of us versus them.

The Interregnum: Parties and the Civil War

Us versus them politics reached its zenith during and in the years following the Civil War, the most bitter, bloody conflict ever fought on American soil. Although sectionalism had been a factor in American politics since 1796, the growing economic disparities between North and South during the first decades of the nineteenth century heightened those regional differences. The North was increasingly urban and ethnically pluralistic as it developed a strong industrial-based economy, while the South remained mostly agricultural. This economic gulf led each region to see its political interests differently. So completely separate were the two regions that it was common among ordinary citizens of the day to say, "The United States *are* . . ." But the difference between an increasingly industrial society and an agricultural one paled in comparison to the animosities aroused by the slavery issue. Northerners disdained the "peculiar institution" of slavery that had taken root in the South. Northern abolitionists were often uncomfortably seated next to slaveholders in presidential cabinets and in the halls of Congress, but this delicate balance was upset in 1846 when the **Wilmot Proviso** became a hotly contested issue.

Introduced by Democratic Congressman David Wilmot from Pennsylvania, the proviso prohibited slavery in any territory acquired from the Mexican War. It passed the House where representatives from states prohibiting slavery were in the majority, but failed in the Senate where pro-slavery Southerners blocked it. Bitter animosities ensued. The Whig party split into two factions: Conscience Whigs claimed that the party had to represent both the conscience and the cotton interests of a given state. Cotton Whigs opposed the Wilmot Proviso and believed that the federal government had no business outlawing slavery.

The Wilmot Proviso also tore the Democratic party in two. In 1848, Democrats chose Senator Louis Cass as their standard-bearer. Cass tried to restore the status quo ante by advocating popular sovereignty—a concept that would allow each state to decide whether it would be slave or free. But instead of uniting the Democrats, Cass's nomination divided them. Several southern delegations boycotted the Democratic Convention, while many northerners contemplated establishing a new abolitionist party. Hundreds of abolitionist societies sprouted up in the North. Meanwhile, the Whigs fudged their internal divisions by selecting Zachary Taylor, a slaveholder from Louisiana, as their standard-bearer. The Whig party refused to consider the Wilmot Proviso, and many of the Conscience Whigs left the party in disgust.

By 1854, all semblance of party unity was shattered when the **Kansas-Nebraska Bill** became law. The bill annulled the provisions of the Missouri Compromise of 1820 by permitting slavery in these two states if voters so approved. The Kansas-Nebraska Bill created a political firestorm, and ignited violence between supporters and opponents in the two states. Pro-slavery Democrats backed the new law, and excluded abolitionist Democrats from party councils. Opposition to the new law was widespread in the North, resulting in protests that led to the creation of the **Republican Party.** After an 1854 Republican gathering in Ripon, Wisconsin, one participant observed: "We came into the little meeting held in a schoolhouse Whigs, Free Soilers, and Democrats. We came out of it Republicans."[22] Four years later the Republicans attained major party status when Democrats lost 40 percent of their northern seats in the House of Representatives allowing the Republicans to win control—an extraordinary achievement. In 1860, Republicans nominated Abraham Lincoln for president who, in a four-way race, won every free state except New Jersey. Democrats had become the party of the South; Republicans, the party of the North.

The rise of the Republican party came at the expense of the Whigs. Like the Democrats, Whigs were not immune from the taint of slavery. A large number of northern Whigs were morally opposed to its extension into the new western territories—placing them at odds with their southern brethren. Henry Clay's 1850 attempt at compromise only led to further schisms. The dilemma the Whigs faced proved insurmountable. Caught between the need to survive as a national party, which meant compromise on the question of slavery, and the demand for strength in the northern states, which meant a rejection of slavery, the Whig party collapsed.

Slavery sealed the Whig's fate, but the question of immigration also contributed to their demise. Northern Whigs were buffeted by powerful nativist, anti-Catholic sentiments following the huge influx of new Irish citizens. The failure of the Irish potato crop in 1840 and the death from famine of over a million people prompted more than 750,000 Irish to emigrate to the United States from 1841 to 1850. These numbers were so massive that the 1855 Massachusetts census reported that if the children of foreign-born parents were considered aliens, then 62 percent of Bostonians were foreigners, most of them Irish. A person visiting the nation's metropolitan areas found them radically changed by the new wave of immigrants. Returning in 1869 to his native Hartford, Connecticut, after serving eight years in Washington, D.C., as secretary of the navy, Gideon Welles found that city "greatly altered. . . . A new and different people seem to move in the streets. Few, comparatively, are known to me."[23] As Welles intimated, white Anglo-Saxon Protestant domination was being eroded by a growing Catholic, predominently Irish, constituency. That transformation sometimes was accompanied by violence. Anti-Catholic riots erupted in Boston, Philadelphia, and New York. For example, in 1854, a Roman Catholic church in Boston was destroyed by gunpowder by Protestant militants.

As the anti-immigrant fervor spread, an organization called the **Know-Nothings,** a name derived from members' statements that they "kn[e]w nothing" about this secret society's existence, gained influence. Adopting the name American Party, the Know-Nothings believed that "foreigners ha[d] no right to dictate our laws, and therefore ha[d] no just ground to complain if Americans see proper to exclude them from offices of trust."[24] Their contempt for the foreign-born was directed at Roman Catholics who, they believed, owed their primary allegiance to the pope rather than the Constitution—a prejudice that was not fully expunged until John F. Kennedy became the first Catholic president in 1961. The Know-Nothings enjoyed their greatest success in 1854 when they successfully fielded candidates in Massachusetts, New York, Maryland, Kentucky, and California. In Massachusetts, where Irish Catholic immigrants had been pouring into the state at a rate of more than 100,000 per year, the Know-Nothings won all but 3 seats in the more than 350-seat State House of Representatives, every congressional seat, and all statewide offices including the governorship. One despondent Whig declared, "This election has demonstrated that, by a majority, Roman Catholicism is feared more than American slavery."[25]

In 1856, the Know-Nothings attempted to capitalize on their victories by selecting former President Millard Fillmore to be their presidential candidate. Fillmore won considerable public backing, including that of Mary Todd Lincoln, wife of Abraham, who wrote that her "weak woman's heart" compelled her to favor Fillmore, who understood "the *necessity* of keeping foreigners, within bounds." Fillmore and Republican candidate John C. Fremont split the anti-slavery vote, resulting in Democrat James Buchanan's victory. As Abraham Lincoln predicted, "With the Fremont and Fillmore men united, here in Illinois, we have Mr. Buchanan in the hollow of our hand; but with us divided, . . . he has us."[26] Buchanan carried Illinois and with it a majority in the Electoral College. The schism was eventually repaired as the Know-Nothings became subsumed into the ranks of an insurgent Republican party.

The Republican Party retained its popular majority from its inception until the Great Depression of the 1930s. Republicans benefitted from having been the party that saved the Union and emancipated the slaves. Civil War veterans were reminded by GOP leaders to "vote as you shot," and their partisan loyalties were reinforced by generous benefits allocated by Republican-controlled Congresses. Later, Republicans became associated with industrialism and the economic prosperity that followed. They appealed to farmers by supporting the Homestead Act which offered cheap land in the West, and won support from business and labor by advocating high protective tariffs and land grants designed to develop transcontinental railroads. Only when the Republicans were divided, or nominated weak candidates, were Democrats able to win the presidency—as happened with Grover Cleveland in 1884 and 1892 and Woodrow Wilson in 1912 and 1916.

The Coming of the Machine

With the conclusion of the Civil War and Lincoln's promised "new birth of freedom," came a reinvigoration of political parties. Just as the Irish immigration crested in 1890, a massive wave of immigrants began arriving from central, eastern, and southern Europe, jettisoned by poor soil and overpopulation in their homelands. From 1890 to 1930, more than 15 million left Europe—roughly the same number who had emigrated to the United States from all countries during 1820 to 1890. By 1926, the transformation of New England from a once-homogeneous enclave to an ethnic polyglot was so complete that one writer spoke of "the conquest of New England by the immigrant."[27]

For those stepping from the steerage ships, confusion about where to stay and employment predominated. The Industrial Revolution provided jobs, but at low wages and under insufferable conditions. Few services existed to help the downtrodden, and a controversial debate as to whether the federal government should impose restraints on child labor began. In this make-it-on-your-own atmosphere, party machines helped ease the transition for many immigrants. In exchange for a job, food, and occasional help with the law, party bosses only asked for votes on election day. As Richard Croker, one-time head of Tammany Hall, put it: "Think of what New York is and what the people of New York are. One-half are of foreign birth. . . . They do not speak our language, they do not know our laws. . . . There is no denying the service which Tammany has rendered to the Republic, there is no such organization for taking hold of the untrained, friendless man and converting him into a citizen. Who else would do it if we did not?"[28] George Washington Plunkitt, one of Croker's successors at Tammany Hall, became infamous for his candid portrayal of how the machine worked, and won the undying loyalty of those who benefitted from it (see "The Parties Speak: A Day in the Life of Party Boss George Washington Plunkitt").

The more people the machine helped, the greater was its grasp of the reins of power. State political leaders, mayors, and other ward leaders doled out thousands of patronage jobs to loyal party workers. Jobs were the fuel that ran the party machine, and astute bosses knew it. In Pennsylvania, the Quay Machine had a

---

The Parties Speak: *A Day in the Life of Party Boss*
George Washington Plunkitt

---

*George Washington Plunkitt was an influential New York City Democratic Party
leader of the infamous Tammany Hall machine whose daily comings and goings were
chronicled by journalist William Riordan.*

2:00 A.M.: Aroused from sleep by the ringing of his doorbell; went to the door and
found a bartender, who asked him to go to the police station and bail out a saloon-
keeper who had been arrested for violating the excise law. Furnished bail and
returned to bed at three o'clock.

6:00 A.M.: Awakened by fire engines passing his house. Hastened to the scene of the
fire, according to the custom of the Tammany district leaders, to give assistance to
the fire sufferers, if needed. Met several of his election district captains who are
always under orders to look out for fires, which are considered great vote-getters.
Found several tenants who had been burned out, took them to a hotel, supplied
them with clothes, fed them, and arranged temporary quarters for them until they
could rent and furnish new apartments.

8:30 A.M.: Went to the police court to look after his constituents. Found six
"drunks." Secured the discharge of four by a timely word with the judge, and paid
the fines of two.

9:00 A.M.: Appeared in the Municipal District Court. Directed one of his district
captains to act as counsel for a widow against whom dispossess proceedings had
been instituted and obtained an extension of time. Paid the rent of a poor family
about to be dispossessed and gave them a dollar for food.

11:00 A.M.: At home again. Found four men waiting for him. One had been dis-
charged by the Metropolitan Railway Company for neglect of duty, and wanted the
district leader to fix things. Another wanted a job on the road. The third sought a
place on the Subway and the fourth, a plumber, was looking for work with the Consolidated Gas Company. The district leader spent nearly three hours fixing things
for the four men, and succeeded in each case.

3:00 P.M.: Attended the funeral of an Italian as far as the ferry. Hurried back to make
his appearance at the funeral of a Hebrew constituent. Went conspicuously to the
front both in the Catholic church and the synagogue, and later attended the
Hebrew confirmation ceremonies in the synagogue.

7:00 P.M.: Went to district headquarters and presided over a meeting of election district captains. Each captain submitted a list of all the voters in his district, reported
on their attitude toward Tammany, suggested who might be won over and how
they could be won, told who were in need, and who were in trouble of any kind and
the best way to reach them. District leaders took notes and gave orders.

8:00 P.M.: Went to a church fair. Took chances on everything, bought ice cream for
the young girls and the children. Kissed the little ones, flattered their mothers and
took their fathers out for something down at the corner.

continued

The Parties Speak: *A Day in the Life of Party Boss*
George Washington Plunkitt (continued)

9:00 P.M.: At the clubhouse again. Spent $10 on tickets for a church excursion and promised a subscription for a new church bell. Bought tickets for a baseball game to be played by two nines from his district. Listened to the complaints of a dozen pushcart peddlers who said they were persecuted by the police and assured them he would go to Police Headquarters in the morning and see about it.

10:30 P.M.: Attended a Hebrew wedding reception and dance. Had previously sent a handsome wedding present to the bride.

12:00 P.M.: In bed.

SOURCE: William L. Riordan, *Plunkitt of Tammany Hall* (New York: Dutton, 1963), 91–93.

---

workforce of 20,000 at an annual cost of $24 million; New York's Platt machine employed 10,000 at a cost of $20 million. Every year, employees in these states would receive a letter from the Republican State Committee reading: "Two percent of your salary is _____. Please remit promptly. At the close of the campaign we shall place a list of those who have not paid in the hands of the head of the department you are in." Awarding jobs after a campaign was a top priority. One party leader reputedly met with his director of patronage every week to pursue every application for every city job down to the lowliest ditch digger's. Patronage was an important party tool that continued to be widely used until the dawn of the Information Age. President Lyndon B. Johnson and Chicago Mayor Richard J. Daley, for example, routinely consulted about who would get what job—with Johnson often deferring to Daley (see "The Parties Speak: Lyndon B. Johnson and Richard J. Daley on Patronage").

The machines were also aided by local election laws which ensured that voting was not a private matter. Prior to 1888, each party printed its own ballot usually in a distinctive color. Voters chose a party ballot and placed it in the ballot box. Split-ticket voting was not possible under this system, and the public selection of a ballot made it no secret whom the voter preferred. Moreover, election "inspectors" were appointed by the party machine to view the proceedings, sometimes even getting their supporters to vote more than once, or to vote under the name of a deceased person. A common joke had it that the machine politicians were devout Christians because they so firmly believed in the resurrection of the dead. As recently as 1960, Chicago Mayor Richard J. Daley told John F. Kennedy's brother Bobby on election night that he would see to it that Illinois was safe for Kennedy.

By 1900, robust machines ruled in New York, Chicago, St. Louis, Boston, Pittsburgh, Philadelphia, Kansas City, and Minneapolis. At the state level, machines controlled Pennsylvania, New York, Ohio, Illinois, Michigan, and Wisconsin. Whether city or state, the party machines were powerful, and often corrupt, organizations. Characteristically, the bosses required firms doing government

---

The Parties Speak: *Lyndon B. Johnson and Richard J. Daley on Patronage*

The following is a transcription of a telephone conversation between President Lyndon B. Johnson and Chicago Mayor Richard J. Daley on January 20, 1964. Johnson tape-recorded nearly all of his telephone conversations while he was in the White House.

Daley: And I wanted you to know we're very much interested in the appointment of Ed Hanrahan as District Attorney.

Johnson: Is that what you want?

Daley: He's got a family and he's got integrity and decency.

Johnson: Is he your man?

Daley: Yes, he is.

Johnson: Do you want him?

Daley: We surely do.

Johnson: You got him, you got him. . . .

Daley: You're doing a great job and don't let them tell you any differently. And the people are with you—the fellow on the bottom rung—and the people that elect Presidents [here Daley is referring to himself and other Democratic Party bosses] are with you.

Johnson: Will you call me when I need to know otherwise?

Daley: I surely will. You know that.

Johnson: This will be done today [referring to his appointment of Hanrahan]. We'll send it up in the morning, and you just get me good men because I want your kind.

SOURCE: Excerpted from Michael R. Beschloss, *Taking Charge: The Johnson White House Tapes, 1963–1964* (New York: Simon & Schuster, 1997), 168–69.

---

business to pay a kickback fee. After all, they reasoned, there were other companies waiting for the same lucrative contracts. The same held true to secure favorable health and safety inspections, and zoning regulations. Overt corruption was tolerated because party leaders had such a devoted following. If someone's house burned, a child was arrested, or there was no food in the pantry, it was the boss who came to the rescue. As Chicago resident Jane Anderson wrote in 1898:

> If the Boss's friend gets drunk, he takes care of him; if he is evicted for rent, arrested for crime, loses wife or child, the Boss stands by him and helps him out. . . . The Boss gives presents at weddings and christenings; buys tickets wholesale for benefits; provides a helping hand at funerals, furnishing carriages for the poor and a decent burial for the destitute when they are dead, keeping his account with the undertaker and never allows a county burial. To ask where the money comes from which the Boss uses this way would be sinister. He gets it from the rich, of course; and so long as he distributes it to the poor, what if he is the leader of the gang of "gray wolves" in the city council selling franchises and betraying the most important interests of the city? What if he is a successful boodler? This is the way political business is run, and it is fortunate that a kind-hearted man so close to the people gets so large a share of the boodle.[29]

The "boodle" to which Anderson referred was the large sum of monies party leaders got to feather their own nests. Of course, some of the money was obtained dishonestly, often from blackmailing and gambling. But Tammany Hall leader George Washington Plunkitt claimed to have "made a big fortune" from what he called "honest graft." According to Plunkitt, the game went something like this:

> My party's in power in the city, and its goin' to undertake a lot of public improvements. Well, I'm tipped off, say, that they're going to lay out a new park at a certain place.
>
> I see my opportunity and I take it. I go to that place and I buy up all the land I can in the neighborhood. Then the board of this or that makes the plan public, and there is a rush to get my land, which nobody cared particular for before.
>
> Ain't it perfectly honest to charge a good price and make a profit on my investment and foresight? Of course, it is. Well, that's honest graft.[30]

PARTIES "AMERICAN STYLE"

At a shoe shine stand in the streets of Manhattan early in the twentieth century, George Washington Plunkitt offered an impassioned defense of political parties: "First, this great and glorious country was built up by political parties; second, parties can't hold together if their workers don't get offices when they win; third, if the parties go to pieces, the government they built up must go to pieces; fourth, then there'll be hell to pay."[31] From their fledgling beginnings in the early nineteenth century, to their heyday as election-seeking machines in the early twentieth, political parties have been viewed by scholars as vital to understanding how the American polity works. As James Bryce wrote in *The American Commonwealth* in 1888, parties had become "to the organs of government almost what the motor nerves are to the muscles, sinews, and bones of the human body."[32]

Parties were also viewed, at least once upon a time, by the voters as indispensable aids in casting a ballot. A tale is told among Irish Americans of a Mrs. O'Reilly being driven to the polls one election day by her son, James. Mrs. O'Reilly, who is seventy years old, has always sided with Democratic candidates. James, who is forty-five and has obtained some financial success, votes Democratic more often than not but, sometimes, will vote Republican. James asks his mother how she plans to vote and is given the predictable reply, "Straight Democratic."

"Mom," says a frustrated son, "If Jesus Christ came back to earth and ran as a Republican, you'd vote against Him."

"Hush," replies Mrs. O'Reilly. "Why should He change His party after all these years?"[33]

Such reverence for parties seems strange today (see Chapter 3). But the period from the 1830s to the 1890s can accurately be described as America's true party period; parties shaped the government and the way average citizens thought about politics. Some have even described this period as the "cult of parties," meaning that voters had an obsessive lifelong commitment to a particular party. Wearing party buttons, attending party socials, and making friends with those who belonged to the same party were commonplace. Some remnants of the party cult persist, as we will see in subsequent chapters. But the heyday of parties lasted for about sixty years—little more than one-third of our nation's total history.

During the twentieth century, the party tale took a number of interesting twists and turns—once again, peculiarly American ones. But the state of the parties today is quite different from that envisioned by most scholars.

FURTHER READING

Chambers, William Nisbet and Walter Dean Burnham, eds. *The American Party Systems.* New York: Oxford University Press, 1975.

Hofstadter, Richard. *The Idea of a Party System: The Rise of Legitimate Opposition in the United States, 1780–1840.* Berkeley: University of California Press, 1969.

Polakoff, Keith Ian. *Political Parties in American History.* New York: Wiley, 1981.

Reichley, A. James. *The Life of the Parties: A History of American Political Parties.* New York: Free Press, 1992.

Riordan, William L. *Plunkitt of Tammany Hall.* New York: Dutton, 1963.

Van Buren, Martin. *Inquiry into the Origin and Course of Political Parties in the United States.* New York: Augustus M. Kelley Publishers, 1967. First edition published by Hurd and Houghton, 1867.

NOTES

1. E. E. Schattschneider, *Party Government* (New York: Rinehart, 1942), 1.

2. *Los Angeles Times*, exit poll, November 5, 1996. Text of question: "Do you think it is better when one political party controls both the White House and Congress, or the White House and Congress are divided between the two political parties?" One-party control, 44 percent; divided government, 56 percent.

3. Quoted in A. James Reichley, "Party Politics in a Federal Polity," in John Kenneth White and Jerome M. Mileur, eds, *Challenges to Party Government* (Carbondale: Southern Illinois University Press, 1992), 42.

4. Howard Bement, ed., *Burke's Speech on Conciliation with America* (Norwood, Mass.: Ambrose and Company, 1922), 45, 54–55, 61.

5. Quoted in Samuel E. Morrison, Henry Steele Commager, and William Leuchtenberg, *The Growth of the American Republic*, vol. 1 (New York: Oxford University Press, 1969), 244.

6. Quoted in James MacGregor Burns, *The Vineyard of Liberty* (New York: Knopf, 1982), 21.

7. Quoted in Herbert J. Storing, *What the Anti-Federalists Were For* (Chicago: University of Chicago Press, 1981), 10.

8. "Essays of Brutus," in Herbert Storing, ed., *The Complete Anti-Federalist* (Chicago: University of Chicago Press, 1981).

9. Alexander Hamilton, James Madison, and John Jay, "Federalist 57," in Edward Mead Earle, ed. *The Federalist*, (New York: Modern Library, 1937), 370.

10. Quoted in A. James Reichley, *The Life of the Parties: A History of American Political Parties* (New York: Free Press, 1992), 42.

11. Cited in Thomas E. Patterson, *The American Democracy* (New York: McGraw-Hill, 1990), 350.

12. Quoted in James Thomas Flexner, *Washington: The Indispensable Man* (New York: New American Library, 1974), 276.

13. Quoted in Reichley, *The Life of the Parties*, 52.

14. Ibid., 64.

15. *Marbury v. Madison*, 1 Cr. 137 (1803).

16. Michael Farquhar, "America's Second War with Britain," *Washington Post*, June 11, 1997, H6.

17. John Quincy Adams, *Memoirs of John Quincy Adams: His Diary from 1795 to 1848* (Freeport, N.Y.: Books for Libraries Press, 1969 reprint), 464–65.

18. Ibid., 493.

19. Quoted in Burns, *The Vineyard of Liberty*, 267.

20. See Reichley, "Party Politics in a Federal Polity," 44. The originator of the phrase was New York Governor William Marcy, a close Van Buren ally.

21. Quoted in David Herbert Donald, *Lincoln* (New York: Touchstone Books, 1995), 138.

22. Quoted in Reichley, *The Life of the Parties*, 120.

23. Quoted in John Kenneth White, *The Fractured Electorate: Political Parties and Social Change in Southern New England* (Hanover, N.H.: University Press of New England, 1983), 7.

24. Quoted in Elinor C. Hartshorn, "Know-Nothings," in *Political Parties and Elections in the United States: An Encyclopedia*, L. Sandy Maisel, ed. (New York: Garland, 1991), 549.

25. Quoted in William E. Gienapp, "Formation of the Republican Party," in Maisel, *Political Parties and Elections in the United States*, 399.

26. Quoted in Donald, *Lincoln*, 192, 194.

27. Daniel Chauncey Brewer, *The Conquest of New England by the Immigrant* (New York: Putnam, 1926).

28. Quoted in Reichley, "Party Politics in a Federal Polity," 48.

29. Quoted in James Albert Woodburn, *Political Parties and Party Problems in the United States* (New York: Putnam, 1903), 416–17.

30. Riordan, *Plunkitt of Tammany Hall*, 3.

31. Ibid., 13.

32. Quoted in Reichley, *The Life of the Parties*, 140.

33. The story is told in E. J. Dionne, Jr., "Catholics and the Democrats: Engagement but not Desertion," in Seymour Martin Lipset, ed., *Party Coalitions in the 1980s* (San Francisco: Institute for Contemporary Studies, 1981), 308.

CHAPTER 3

The Decline of Party Politics

One hundred years ago, a puzzled expression would have been the response from anyone asked whether the two-party system was necessary. It was an odd question because Democrats and Republicans had dominated the political system for nearly all of the previous century. Americans forged connections to public officials through parties, and they spent much of their leisure time involved in party-related activities. "How could politics, much less government, be separate from party politics?" surely would have been the answer. Or, to paraphrase James Madison, "Eliminating parties from politics would be like separating air from fire; how could the latter exist without the former?"

At the close of the twentieth century, parties no longer matter much to most Americans. By 1992, most wanted a third party to join the fray: 58 percent said the country needed "a new political party to compete with the Democratic and Republican parties in offering the best candidates for political office"—including majorities of self-described Democrats and Republicans.[1] Not since the Republican Party grew from a minor party to a major one back in the 1850s had there been such demand for a new party. Survey data show an ever-shrinking portion of respondents believe political parties can solve important problems. A 1995 Gallup poll found only one-quarter of the respondents said the two-party system was appropriate for solving the nation's problems.[2]

Even if the public wanted the Democratic and Republican parties to resume their once-prominent positions, it is doubtful they could. Americans are busy doing other things. A 1995 poll found 54 percent engaged in charity or social service activities such as helping the poor, sick, or elderly. Even young Americans have abandoned party activity for volunteerism: 57 percent of Generation Xers belong to one or more volunteer organizations.[3] This is a far cry from their heyday when social activities were an important part of party life, and political parties could entice young people, as described by Tammany Hall leader George Washington Plunkitt:

> Here's how I gather in the young men. I hear of a young feller that's proud of his voice, thinks that he can sing fine. I ask him to come around to Washington Hall and join our Glee Club. He comes and sings, and he's a follower of Plunkitt for life. Another young feller gains a reputation as a baseball player in a vacant lot. I bring him into our baseball club. That fixes him. You'll find him workin' for my ticket at the polls next election day. Then there's the feller that likes rowin' on the river, the young feller that makes a

name as a waltzer on his block, the young feller that's handy with his dukes—I rope them all in by givin' them opportunities to show themselves off. I don't trouble them with political arguments. I just study human nature and act accordin'.[4]

This chapter confronts a number of issues related to the decline of parties in America. What caused parties, once vital players in politics at the close of the nineteenth century, to become minor actors by the late twentieth? When did these changes occur? Were they intentional or the byproducts of other developments unrelated to politics? Most importantly, have these transformations shifted what remains of the party system in a Jeffersonian or Hamiltonian direction?

"CLEAN IT UP!": THE PROGRESSIVE MOVEMENT

America was not an idyllic place around the turn of the century. The rise of corporations and the Industrial Revolution produced a whirlwind of change. Colossal fortunes were made by John D. Rockefeller, Cornelius Vanderbilt, and J. P. Morgan, industrial giants who controlled the production and delivery of everything from oil to sugar, copper to beef, tobacco to rubber, and candy to locomotives. But not everyone was so well off. Most urban residents found themselves huddling in tiny tenements after working long hours in unsightly factories and sweatshops. Calls for reform abounded but went largely unheeded. For example, the Connecticut Democratic Party in 1920 advocated health and social insurance, an eight-hour day for women and children, and funds beyond those already provided by the Workmen's Compensation Act. In 1924, the party supported a constitutional amendment prohibiting child labor.

But for years these reforms languished as the U.S. government and most states pursued a laissez-faire policy on economic matters. Many Republicans, who were the majority party at the time, believed the federal government should confine itself to those explicit powers given the president and the Congress in the Constitution. That meant virtually no government intervention in ending child labor, alleviating horrendous working conditions, and improving the poverty-level wages paid by the industrial giants. Whenever the states attempted to do something, the courts blocked their path. In 1905, the U.S. Supreme Court in *Lochner v. New York* ruled that New York State could not limit the number of hours bakers worked in their overheated environments to ten hours per day and sixty hours a week. A Court majority wrote that such laws "limiting the hours in which grown and intelligent men may labor to earn their living are mere meddlesome interferences with the rights of the individual."[5] Justice John Marshall Harlan issued a strongly worded dissent that would later be used to overturn the Court's decision: "I take it to be firmly established that what is called the liberty of contract may, within certain limits, be subjected to regulations designed and calculated to promote the general welfare, or to guard the public health, the public morals, or the public safety."[6] But Harlan notwithstanding, Abraham Lincoln's trilogy of a government of, by, and for the people had been twisted into a government of, by, and for big business.

Frustrated by government inaction and gridlock, the working class mobilized. Labor unions, such as the Federation of Labor and the Knights of Labor, quickly expanded. But they were no match for the corporate-government tag team. When the unions decided to strike, government injunctions were issued to summon workers back to the factories. Union leaders were jailed for conspiracy and contempt for not obeying the injunctions. Labor riots ensued—notably the Pullman Car Strike in May 1894 following a cut in workers' wages. The American Railway Union, led by Eugene Debs, authorized a sympathy strike which spread from Chicago to the Northwest. After several frequent outbursts of violence, President Grover Cleveland sent thousands of federal troops and marshals into Chicago in August 1894 under the pretense of protecting mail deliveries. With that, the strike came to a screeching halt.

Factory workers were not the only Americans suffering. Farmers were upset over the falling prices of their goods, low inflation, and the private ownership of railroads. Appalachian coal miners were forced to accept insufferable working conditions because the government did little to help and there was no other work available. Poverty-stricken twelve- and thirteen-year-old children were often pressed into work because their small bodies could fit more easily into the tiny mine shafts. After working more than a sixty-hour week, instead of U.S. dollars, miners would be paid in scrip, a form of paper money issued by the mining company. The scrip was redeemable only at the company store where prices were exorbitantly inflated. Even well-to-do urban residents were irritated with the poor services provided by city governments. Sewer and garbage collections, for instance, were wholly inadequate. Social workers, clergymen, teachers, and doctors tried to improve conditions in their neighborhoods, but local officials often turned a blind eye toward the problems. Moreover, utility companies were privately owned. Gas, water, and electric companies faced little competition and gouged customers at every turn. Residents could either pay the prices set by the company or go without lights, heat, or fresh water.

It was of no small consequence that many upper-class citizens were angry with such inefficiency and corruption. Graft and kickbacks were costly party tools. By the early 1880s, the reformers banded together calling themselves **mugwumps**—a name which became synonymous with independent or nonpartisan voters. They were less concerned with the substance of public policy than with the allegedly corrupt manner in which it was made. The winds of change were blowing and the party machines were about to confront a storm.

Enter the Progressives

Ending corruption was easier said than done. During the early years of the twentieth century, local government was party government. The spoils system meant that by controlling city jobs and contracts, the party machines could retain legions of loyal workers. Tammany Hall Democratic chief George Washington Plunkitt was among the first to compare politics to a business: "Politics is as much a regular business as the grocery or the dry-goods or the drug business. You've got to be trained up to it or you're sure to fail."[7]

Reformers also liked the business analogy, but they wanted the party machines to put up signs reading, "Going Out of Business." These crusaders for reform, now called **Progressives,** maintained that the reason why ordinary citizens had not taken back their government was because the Plunkitts and other party bosses stood in the way. The Progressive Party platform of 1912 described how the party machines controlled by both the Democrats and the Republicans had become a threat to liberty:

> Political parties exist to secure responsible government and to execute the will of the people. From these great tasks both of the old parties have turned aside. Instead of instruments to promote the general welfare, they have become the tools of corrupt interests which use them impartially to serve their selfish purposes. Behind the ostensible government sits enthroned an invisible government owing no allegiance and acknowledging no responsibility to the people.
>
> To destroy this invisible government, to dissolve the unholy alliance between corrupt business and corrupt politics is the first task of the statesmanship of the day.[8]

In contrast to the Progressives, the Republican Party platform of 1912 sought refuge in the Constitution: "The principles of constitutional government, which make provisions for orderly and effective expression of the popular will, . . . have proved themselves capable of sustaining the structure of a government which, after more than a century of development, embraces one-hundred millions of people, scattered over a wide and diverse territory, but bound by common purpose, common ideals, and common affection to the Constitution of the United States."[9] In sum, neither the Republicans nor the Democrats were going to yield to the Progressives without a fight.

But how could the reformers succeed given the tight grasp machines had on public policy? Help eventually arrived from the media, charismatic individuals, a third-party movement, and most of all the voters. In the end, the legal reforms engendered by the progressive movement not only changed the character of party politics but the nature of government itself.

The Australian Ballot.   The central target of the Progressives were the rules of electoral politics. One of the first vestiges of tight party control to disappear was the way voters selected candidates for office. During the heyday of parties, voters were forced to choose a ballot produced by one of the parties and drop it into the voting box in full public view. Because each party printed its ballot on different colored paper, it was no secret how a person voted. People either supported the party in power or risked retribution. Bribery, or vote buying, was also easy. The Australian ballot, named after its country of origin, curbed these abuses (see Figure 3.1). It required that election ballots be prepared by the states, not party organizations. Ballots were to be identical and include the names of all candidates seeking office, thereby allowing voters to cast a secret ballot. It did not eliminate intimidation and bribery, but party henchmen could now lose an election and never know who to blame. The new ballot also allowed citizens to split their tickets—that is, to vote for candidates of opposing parties running in the same election. For example, a voter might place an X next to a Republican congressional candidate and then place

FIGURE 3.1 ▪ The "Australian" or Secret Ballot (still used today)

RESOLUTION 1998-1	RESOLUTION 1998-2
Shall the Pennsylvania Constitution be amended to disallow bail when the proof is evident or presumption great that the accused committed an offense for which the maximum penalty is life imprisonment or that no condition or combination of conditions other than imprisonment of the accused will reasonably assure the safety of any person or the community?	Shall the Pennsylvania Constitution be amended to provide that the Commonwealth shall have the same right to trial by jury in criminal cases as does the accused?

	YES	NO		YES	NO		

1	2 3	4 5	6	7 8	
UNITED STATES SENATOR	GOVERNOR AND Lt. GOVERNOR	REPRESENTATIVE U.S. CONGRESS 21st DISTRICT	SENATOR GEN. ASSEMBLY 50th DISTRICT	REPRESENTATIVE GENERAL ASSEMBLY 6th DISTRICT	
Vote for One (Six Year Term)	Vote for Candidates of One Party (Four Year Term)	Vote for One (Two Year Term)	Vote for One (Four Year Term)	Vote for One (Two Year Term)	
1A Republican **Arlan SPECTER**	2A Republican **Tom RIDGE (Gov.) Mark SCHWEIKER (Lt. Gov.)**	4A Republican **Phil ENGLISH**	6A Republican **Robert D. ROBBINS**	7A Republican **Teresa FORCIER**	
1B Democratic **Bill LLOYD**	2B Democratic **Ivan ITKIN (Gov.) Marjorie MARGOLIES-MEZVINSKY (Lt. Gov.)**	4B Democratic **Larry CLEMENS**	6B Democratic **Mary Ann McDANNIELS-KULESA**	7B Democratic	
1C Constitutional **Dean SNYDER**	2C Constitutional **Peg LUKSIK (Gov.) Jim CLYMER (Lt. Gov.)**				
1D Libertarian **Jack IANNANTUONO**	2D Libertarian **Ken KRAWCHUK (Gov.) Henry E. HALLER (Lt. Gov.)**				

an X next to a Democratic state legislative candidate. Thus, the Australian ballot loosened the machine's grip on public policy. The Australian ballot was first introduced in Kentucky in 1880; by 1896 most states had followed suit.

The Direct Primary. Reforming party machines was difficult because under the existing election laws even if a reformer was willing to challenge the party machine, voters never got a chance to consider that person on election day. Bosses controlled party nominations, and to qualify for the ballot a candidate had to receive the party's nomination. (Write-in candidacies, where the voters write the name of the candidate on the ballot, are almost never successful.) Nominations were cleared by party leaders in private and subsequently ratified at local or state party conventions. An ambitious, civic-minded reformer might consider running for office under a third-party label, but most state election laws were written with the consent of both Democrats and Republicans, thereby prohibiting insurgent candidates and parties from participating in the election process. Even if an outsider was to overcome this hurdle, chances of victory were slim. As long as the two major parties dominated the nomination process, they controlled whom the voters selected to run the government.

Given this dilemma, the Progressives realized reform had to come from *within* the two-party system. The **direct primary** provided a remedy. The idea was simple: Instead of a small group of party leaders choosing a nominee, *all* party supporters would be given the opportunity. Nominations would be made through elections, called primaries, where the entire party membership had a say.

The direct primary movement began in Wisconsin. Its champion was Robert M. LaFollette, Sr., an ardent Progressive reformer and one-time governor, U.S. senator, and presidential candidate. In a widely acclaimed speech, dubbed "The Menace of the Machine" (1897), LaFollette described how dangerous the mixing of corporate influence was with party corruption (see "The Parties Speak: Robert M. LaFollette, Sr., 'The Menace of the Machine' (1897)").

LaFollette's home state of Wisconsin adopted the direct primary in 1904 and others soon followed. But unfortunately for the Progressives, most states enacted laws with stringent requirements to get on the primary ballots—often requiring thousands of valid signatures to obtain ballot access. The organizations best able to conduct these labor-intensive projects were the party machines. Thus, the direct primary was a step in the right direction, but only a step.

The Merit System.   The Australian ballot and direct primary wounded the parties. Yet the fuel propelling the machines was the spoils system—that is, the ability to give patronage jobs to loyal party workers. As long as local governments had jobs cleaning roads, fixing sewers, building parks, and inspecting buildings among other tasks, parties would provide loyal workers to fill them. Supporters of the merit system were generally well-to-do urban mugwumps. They believed that attacking the patronage system would accomplish two key objectives: (1) no longer would the party machines have hundreds of jobs available to faithful subordinates; and (2) government positions would be filled with qualified people—a novel idea at the time. Thus, the merit system (later termed the civil service) became a pillar of the Progressive platform, favored by reformers weary of lackluster government services. The idea was not well received by party leaders who thought the idea of a civil service was foolish and would further remove government and the political parties from any sense of public accountability.

By 1881, party patronage had become so rampant that President James Garfield wrote that "my day is frittered away with the personal seeking of people when it ought to be given to the great problems which concern the whole country."[10] Following Garfield's assassination by a disappointed job seeker in 1881, Congress established the Civil Service Commission to set standards for employment by the federal government and create thousands of permanent jobs that would continue in each Cabinet-level department regardless of which party controlled the White House. By the turn of the twentieth century, most states followed the federal government's example. In

The Parties Speak: *Robert M. LaFollette, Sr., "The Menace of the Machine" (1897)*

This speech was delivered at the University of Chicago on February 22, 1897, and became a rallying call for Progressives. Robert M. LaFollette, Sr., a leading Progressive and the 1924 Progressive Party presidential candidate, urged that nominations be removed from the control of party bosses and be settled by a direct primary.

"The government of the people, by the people, and for the people".... How dear to us then were those words! How deeply they laid hold of our national life! What sacrifices we were freely making for that kind [of] government! How ready were we to give our fortunes, mortgage our future, march our brave men to battle, blot out our individual homes and hopes, clothe the dead in glory and the living in mourning—all to preserve a government of the people, by the people, and for the people! Who then would have believed that before a generation of time should pass this would gradually become a government of the people, by the machine, and for the machine? ...

Again and again, season after season, the majority went out blindly to defeat the practical politicians, but always with the same result. For a long time the business of manipulating the caucuses and conventions had been left to the practical politician, and he had become very expert. He matured and perfected a system. It produced results with mathematical certainty. It was always in operation. It had acquired the trick of perpetual motion.

This is the modern political machine. It is impersonal, irresponsible, extralegal. The courts offer no redress for the rights it violates, the wrongs it inflicts. It is without conscience and without remorse. It has come to be enthroned in American politics. It rules caucuses, names delegates, appoints committees, dominates the councils of the party, dictates nominations, makes platforms, dispenses patronage, directs state administrations, controls legislatures, stifles opposition, punishes independence, and elects United States Senators. In the states where it is supreme, the edict of the machine is the only sound heard, and outside it is easily mistaken for the voice of the people. If some particular platform pledge is necessary to the triumph of the hour, the platform is so written and the pledge violated without offering excuse or justification. If public opinion be roused to indignant protest, some scapegoat is put forward to suffer vicariously for the sins of the machine, and subsequently rewarded for his service by the emoluments of machine spoils. If popular revolt against the machine sweeps over the state on rare occasions and the machine finds itself hard pressed to maintain its hold on party organization, control conventions, and nominate its candidates—when threats and promises fail—the "barrel" is not wanting until the way is cleared.

What, then, shall we do to be saved? ... If we provide the same safeguards, the same certainty, the same facility for expressing and executing the will of the people at the primaries as now prevail at the elections, we shall have the same general interest, the same general participation in the one as in the other.... The reformation effected in our elections by the Australian voting system should inspire us with confidence in advancing the lines of attack.... Beginning the work in the state, put aside the caucus and the convention. They have been and will continue to be prostituted to the service

continued

The Parties Speak: *Robert M. LaFollette, Sr., "The Menace of the Machine" (1897) (continued)*

of a corrupt organization. They answer no purpose further than to give respectable form to political robbery. Abolish the caucus and the convention. Go back to the first principles of democracy. Go back to the people. Substitute for both the caucus and the convention a primary election—held under all the sanctions of law which prevail at the general elections—where the citizen may cast his vote directly to nominate the candidate of the party with which he affiliates, and have it canvassed and returned just as he cast it.

To every generation some important work is committed. If this generation will destroy the political machine, will emancipate the majority from its enslavement, will again place the destinies of this nation in the hands of its citizens, then, "Under God, this government of the people, by the people, and for the people shall not perish from the earth."

SOURCE: Excerpted from Carl R. Burgchardt, *Robert M. LaFollette, Sr., The Voice of Conscience* (Westport, Conn.: Greenwood Press, 1992), 171–83.

New York, for instance, a comprehensive civil service bill was pushed through the legislature in 1899 by newly elected Governor Theodore Roosevelt. While the parties attempted to devise various ways to maintain some of their patronage, the merit system dealt a decisive blow to their organizational brawn.

Municipal Ownership of Utilities. At the turn of the twentieth century, utility companies that had been awarded their franchises by the party machines charged exorbitant rates even as they continued to provide poor service. The companies were guaranteed huge profits, raising the cost to customers who had no choice but to pay. Party leaders kept profits high because they were receiving huge kickbacks from the companies in exchange for franchise rights.

Reformers realized that breaking this cozy relationship meant that public regulation of utility companies was necessary, and pushed measures to do so through state and local governments. Many of these businesses remained privately owned, but in exchange for the franchise they agreed to allow a public board or commission to set rates. Other services, such as garbage collection, sewage removal, and transportation, would be assumed by government under new agencies administered by employees who got their jobs through the merit system.

Ballot Initiative, Referendum, and Recall. One way to link voters to their government is to give average citizens a direct say in what government does. Another would be to dismiss elected officials should they lose voter confidence. These were not widely accepted ideas during the nineteenth century. But in an era of partisan corruption, Progressives championed these reforms. The **ballot initiative** requires a legislature to consider a specific measure. The **referendum** gives voters a voice on a policy matter by gathering enough signatures to place a measure on a ballot. The **recall** allows voters to remove elected officials in a special election before their term of office is over. These reforms were championed by Progressives to restore representative government. Woodrow Wilson, then governor of New Jersey and a strong supporter of these changes, declared: "Bills that the machine and its backers do not desire are smothered in committee. Measures which they do desire are brought out and hurried through their passage. It happens again and again that great groups of such bills are rushed through in the hurried hours that mark the close of the legislative sessions, when everyone is withheld from vigilance by fatigue and when it is possible to do secret things."[11]

Several western states adopted the initiative, referendum, and recall as the nineteenth century gave way to the twentieth. South Dakota was first to authorize ballot initiatives in 1898; Oregon was first with referenda in 1902 and with recalls in 1908. But it was not until Republican Hiram Johnson was elected governor of California in 1910 that these measures earned national attention. Johnson, an outspoken Progressive, got the California State Legislature to pass the initiative. Several states followed suit, and by the 1920s about three-fourths allowed initiatives, referenda, and recalls.

Today, many states and localities permit these forms of direct popular participation. Twenty-six states and the District of Columbia use the initiative. In 1996, voters in twenty states determined the outcome of ninety citizen-initiated ballot measures including term limits, campaign finance reform, and gambling. Frequently, these initiatives were controversial. California voters were asked to decide the future of that state's affirmative action programs. Voters in Arizona and California approved the medical use of marijuana, provoking a storm of protest. In 1997, Oregon voters permitted that state's doctors to assist in the suicides of terminally ill patients. Table 3.1 provides a sampling of some of the more controversial questions voters were asked to settle in 1996.

Nonpartisan Municipal Elections. Generally, Progressives believed that the problems facing most municipalities were technical, and could be solved by a combination of professional administration and scientific principles. A common phrase heard among Progressives was, "There is no Republican, no Democratic, way to clean streets."[12] Adopting that adage, several large cities instituted the nonpartisan form of election. Boston was first in 1909; two decades later twenty-six of the nation's largest cities had local elections in which candidates were listed on the ballot without reference to their party affiliations. Like the direct primary, however, this reform has been only modestly successful. While the party labels of these mayoral candidates are not printed on the ballot, it is generally no mystery which candidates are sponsored by a particular political party. Thus, these "nonpartisan" elections have become a symbolic gesture rather than a real alternative to party politics.

Two variations of this trend have been the development of the commission form of government and the employment of city managers. Believing that professionally trained public administrators could best administer growing municipalities, cities scrapped the mayor-council form of government and elected a small board of commissioners, each responsible for a single area of municipal administration. Voters could easily identify those commissioners who were responsible for a particular function and either reward or punish them at the polls. But the commission plan did not provide for a single executive to coordinate the commissioners' actions, and the city manager form of government began to take hold. In those cities that have such

TABLE 3.1 ▪ 1996 Ballot Initiatives, Selected States

State	Question	Outcome
Alaska	Instructs elected officials to support congressional term limits.	Yes: 55 percent No: 45 percent
Wyoming	Repeals 1995 legislative act that extended legislative service from six to twelve years.	Yes: 54 percent No: 46 percent
Colorado	Limits individual contributions to legislators, statewide candidates, and political parties and committees.	Yes: 66 percent No: 34 percent
Arizona	Revises statute for controlled substances; allows medical use of marijuana	Yes: 65 percent No: 35 percent
California	Exempts from criminal laws patients and caregivers who possess or cultivate marijuana for medical treatments as recommended by a doctor.	Yes: 56 percent No: 44 percent
California	Prohibits discrimination or preferential treatment by state and other public entities.	Yes: 55 percent No: 45 percent
Massachusetts	Prohibits use of traps for hunting bear and bobcat.	Yes: 64 percent No: 36 percent
Michigan	Permits casino gambling in qualified cities.	Yes: 52 percent No: 48 percent
Nebraska	Makes "quality education" a fundamental right.	Yes: 22 percent No: 78 percent
Washington	Provides vouchers for K–12 students to attend public schools of their choice.	Yes: 35 percent No: 65 percent

SOURCE: Regina Dougherty, Everett C. Ladd, David Wilber, and Lynn Zayachkiwsky, eds., *America at the Polls, 1996* (Storrs, Conn.: Roper Center for Public Opinion Research, 1997), 127, 135–38.

an arrangement, an elected city council hires a manager to run the day-to-day operations. Today, most cities with a population of more than 10,000 have such a council-manager form of government.

The Direct Election of U.S. Senators and Women's Suffrage. Finally, two additional progressive measures helped reduce the influence of party machines: the direct election of U.S. senators and extending the vote to women. Under Article I of the Constitution, the election of senators was left to state legislatures. Progressives argued that this provision, combined with a six-year term and staggered elections, insulated the upper chamber from public opinion. They provided the impetus for the **Seventeenth Amendment** (ratified in 1913) that allowed citizens to cast a ballot for individual senatorial candidates. As one congressman observed, "What with our daily newspapers and our telegraph facilities we need not delegate our powers."[13]

Women's suffrage was another Progressive cause. In 1890, Wyoming was the first state to grant women the right to vote, followed by Utah and Idaho in 1896. Even though the women's suffrage movement was centered in the East (primarily New York and Massachusetts), change did not come to that region until 1919—the year the **Nineteenth Amendment** to the Constitution was ratified, giving women the right to vote. Credit for passage of the amendment lies with the grit and determination of women demanding equality, especially Susan B. Anthony and Elizabeth Cady Stanton. But the Progressive reformers also lent their voices to the cause, because they believed that by enfranchising women corrupt party machines would suffer at the polls.

Why the Progressive Movement Was Successful

If the machines had such a tight grip on public policy and the flow of information to voters, how could Progressive reforms have succeeded? The answer lies in a number of factors: (1) the slow but steady pace of the Progressive movement; (2) the rise of muckraking journalism; (3) Teddy Roosevelt and the election of 1912; and (4) the parties eventually yielding to public demands for reform.

A Progressive Glacier.   The reform movement advanced slowly like a glacier over many decades. Reform initiatives began in 1870, shifted into high gear during the 1890s, and finally slowed after the 1912 elections. In some states, the merit system did not take hold until the 1900s, and the direct primary not until a few years later. Nonpartisan local elections began in some cities around 1910; others, a decade later. One reason why the Progressive movement was successful was due to this slow forward movement. Once a state or city was "cleaned up," residents elsewhere took notice and demanded reform in their communities. Almost like an ice cap, the Progressive movement gathered more followers as it pushed ahead, until nearly all in its path were engulfed.

Muckraking.   The Progressives found an invaluable ally in the news media. By the 1890s, a new form of entertainment medium had emerged—magazines. Initially focusing on "polite interest" themes such as travel, nature, and biographies, a handful of magazines led by *McClure's* shifted their attention to public and corporate corruption. The idea proved immensely popular with readers and other publications soon followed. The new brand of journalism was termed *muckraking* and its practioners were dubbed **muckrakers.** The expression was coined by Teddy Roosevelt, himself both a reformer and media target, after a muckrake which was a tool used to clean out stables.

We now take it for granted that the media will expose blatant corruption, but this was not always true. Our nation's history is filled with tales of corruption, but investigative journalism, per se, began during the muckraking period. Reporters and writers around the turn of the century vigorously pursued corporate and government wrongdoing. Newspapers, magazines, and books exposed evidence of abuse—from entire police departments in partnership with gangsters, to churches owning whole blocks of foul-smelling slums, to an entire U.S. Senate "on the take." Muckrakers provided a startling new view of business and government. It was not a pretty picture.

Lincoln Steffens is credited with being the first and most prominent of the muckrakers. He began his career as an investigative reporter with the *Saturday Evening Post* in 1892, but joined *McClure's* shortly thereafter. Together with a team of reporters, Steffens exposed corruption among the highest ranks in cities including New York, St. Louis, Minneapolis, Chicago, Pittsburgh, and Philadelphia. In 1904, Steffens compiled several articles he had written for *McClure's* into the best-selling book *The Shame of the Cities*. In it, he wrote: "Our political failures are not complete; they are simply ridiculous"; adding, "If we would leave parties to the politicians, and would not vote for the party, not even for men, but for the city, and the State, and the nation, we should rule parties, and cities, and states, and nation."[14]

Reporters were not the only muckrakers; novelists also joined the movement. One of the most powerful books written during this period was Upton Sinclair's *The Jungle*, published in 1906. Sinclair chronicled the appalling conditions in Chicago's meatpacking industry, and the difficulties immigrants faced in the New World. As he recalled, "I aimed at the public's heart, and by accident I hit it in the stomach."[15] The story Sinclair told was simple—a tale of immigrants longing for a better life in the promised land called America. But it is also an indignant story of newcomers being exploited by employers and left to survive in impoverished conditions. Sinclair's work ignited public outrage, and governments reacted. Ironically, however, instead of reforming working conditions as Sinclair had hoped, the federal government imposed new regulations on the sanitary conditions of the meatpacking industry.

Muckraking covered nearly every aspect of American life, but two areas stand out: corporate greed and the corruption of the party machines. As for the latter, one disreputable machine after another was exposed, often resulting in the local institution of Progressive reforms. In 1904, for example, it was revealed that Cincinnati Party Boss George Cox developed a perfect lock on *both* the Democratic and Republican parties, thus controlling everything that happened in that city. Because local businesses cooperated with Cox, shopkeepers broke city ordinances, banks received public deposits, financiers got canals, utility companies won franchises, and property owners were awarded low assessments. Much the same occurred elsewhere. In California, it was discovered that the Southern Pacific Railroad controlled both political parties, and used its extensive personnel and huge war chest to dominate the state legislature.

Teddy Roosevelt and the Bull Moose Party.   It is ironic that the very person who disparaged muckraking journalists became one of the leading players in the reform movement. Teddy Roosevelt carried the Progressive Party banner despite his early association with the Republican Party establishment. Roosevelt began his political career after returning as a hero from the Spanish-American War in 1898. He was elected governor of New York thanks to the backing of GOP boss, Senator Thomas C. Platt. Roosevelt was quickly sickened by the graft of both the honest and dishonest variety that characterized New York politics. Rather than abandoning party politics, however, Roosevelt attempted to remake the Republican Party into an agent of reform. His efforts did not sit well with the party chiefs, and they vowed to get rid of their nemesis. Although some worried about Roosevelt's passion for reform, Platt sponsored Roosevelt as the Republican vice presidential candidate in 1900, where he believed the obscurity of the vice presidency would surely bury Roosevelt. Even Roosevelt sensed that he was being pushed aside, but he accepted when William McKinley prevailed upon him, and the duo won with ease. Within a few months McKinley was assassinated and Roosevelt became the twenty-sixth president of the United States. Almost overnight, Vice President Roosevelt was catapulted from obscurity to prominence.

Roosevelt's reform agenda was modest. Besieged by conservative, business-minded congressional Republicans on the one hand, and reform-minded Progressives on the other, Roosevelt chose a middle-of-the-road course. This explains why he derided his media critics as "muckrakers." He declined to seek reelection in 1908, opting to support his longtime friend, Secretary of War William Howard Taft, who easily defeated Democrat William Jennings Bryan.

Frustrated by Taft's lackluster performance as president, and his failure to espouse Progressive reforms, Roosevelt once again sought the presidency in 1912. But wresting the Republican nomination from an incumbent president whom he had virtually anointed proved impossible. Roosevelt was backed by progressive Republicans, but they were no match for the more conservative, pro-business elements that controlled the party machinery and staunchly supported Taft. At a contentious convention in Chicago, the establishment prevailed and Taft accepted renomination.

But that was not the end of the story. Dissatisfied with Taft and their party's antireform stance, several Republican delegates staged their own rump convention at a nearby hotel. They decided that a new party would be formed, and seven weeks later the Progressive Party nominated Theodore Roosevelt for president. The convention that chose Roosevelt was not a gathering of the party faithful; instead, it was an assembly of crusaders determined to change the country forever. Delegates were so caught up in the revival-like atmosphere that the nickname "Bull Moose" (following Roosevelt's declaration that he was "as strong as a bull moose") stuck to the new party. The Bull Moose platform called for the direct election of U.S. senators, women's suffrage, restricting the president to a single six-year term, a constitutional amendment allowing an income tax, institution of a minimum wage, prohibiting child labor, creating a Department of Labor, and even the recall of some judicial decisions.

On election day, Roosevelt finished second, winning more votes than the hapless Taft—the best performance on record for a third-party presidential candidate in the twentieth century. But, as Roosevelt had predicted, the Republican split allowed Democrat Woodrow Wilson to enter the White House. Wilson received 41.8 percent of the popular vote (435 electoral votes), Roosevelt netted 27.4 percent (88 electoral votes), and Taft received just 23.2 percent (8 electoral votes).

Democrats also captured both houses of Congress. These results, though disastrous for the Republicans, proved to be a high-water mark for the Progressives and marked only an interlude in GOP control of the White House.

The Progressive Party faded from the scene in 1916 after Roosevelt refused its nomination, and most of its followers returned to the Republican ranks. Robert M. LaFollette, Sr. was the Progressive Party's presidential nominee in 1924 and attracted 16 percent of the popular vote, but won only his home state of Wisconsin. In retrospect, though, the 1912 election had a decisive impact on the Progressive struggle. Democrats, as well as conservative Republicans, could no longer withstand the power of the reform wave. Unless serious changes were made, both parties were vulnerable to insurgent candidacies. President Wilson won enactment of several Progressive planks, as did most state and local governments. By attacking political parties so vehemently and scoring so solidly with the voters, the Progressives ensured that what remained of the twentieth century would be labeled as an antiparty age.

The Parties Reform Themselves.   Finally, the bosses yielded to the inevitable and accepted reform. Placed on the defensive by disclosures of corruption and a growing sense of public outrage, change was certain. But this did not mean that they were willing to commit suicide. In fact, many reform measures reduced corruption even as they guaranteed the continuation of the two-party system.

An End to Party Politics?

The Progressive movement was about curtailing corruption. Reformers quickly found that the path to true reform began with changing the way government operated by allowing ordinary citizens a say in making public policy. This meant eliminating most "mediating institutions," especially the party machines. The **direct primary** stripped party leaders of their ability to completely control nominations; the **secret ballot** reduced voter intimidation and election fraud; the **merit system** lessened patronage opportunities; and **public control of utility companies** drained party coffers. The **direct election of U.S. senators** and **women's suffrage** were the icing on the cake.

The Progressive reforms created several challenges for leaders of both parties, though initially, they were able to forestall some of the reforms' effects. For instance, while the direct primary precluded complete control over nominations by party leaders, a candidate's ability to get on state primary ballots required a massive number of signatures. This labor-intensive process was something parties were well-suited to accomplish. Senators were subject to direct popular election, but they needed a party nomination to win a place on the ballot and initially relied on party organizations to run their campaigns. The merit system reduced patronage, yet there remained scores of "exempt" and "temporary" positions to be filled. Utilities might be controlled by boards and commissions, but the city government-corporate nexus was far from broken. Party war chests continued to overflow with contributions from businesses.

Over time, however, the Progressives fundamentally altered the party system changing politics from a private affair to a public concern. During the 1800s, parties conducted their business free from government interference, operating as private organizations. Progressives demanded public oversight and regulation of most party activities, transforming the parties into quasi-public agencies subject to legislative control. The most obvious change was the use of government-printed ballots, but others included the creation of nonpartisan boards of elections, regulations defining what constitutes a party, state-regulated primary dates, laws governing how often party committees must meet, and in some states regulations on how parties can raise and spend money.

Ironically, some of these reforms strengthened the parties' legal standing. The new laws curtailed the worst abuses of the machine era, but also made independent and minor-party candidacies more difficult. Instead of adhering to the Australian practice of omitting party designation, most states adopted a general election ballot that required party labels be placed alongside a candidate's name. It was easy for the two major parties to keep this official ballot recognition because state law reserved a place for whichever two parties received the most votes in the last election. Any remaining parties would have to circulate petitions before the next election to gain ballot access—a difficult and extremely time-consuming chore.

Some have argued that the persistence of the two-party system long after the Progressive reforms were instituted demonstrates their continued importance to making the system work. Others disagree. In a harshly worded attack denouncing "the high priests of the two-party system," Theodore Lowi, a former president of the American Political Science Association (APSA), wrote: "One of the best kept secrets of American politics is that the two-party system has long been brain-dead—kept alive by support systems like state electoral laws that protect the established parties from rivals and by public subsidies and so-called campaign reform. The two-party system would collapse in an instant if the tubes were pulled and the IVs were cut."[16]

Lowi's attack may be new to academicians long accustomed to praising the "genius" of having a stable, two-party system. But the Progressive hostility toward parties has had an enduring impact on voters. At the turn of the century, most Americans voted the party line all the way down from president, governor, member of the House or Senate to local county coroner, railroad assessor, or university trustee. Today, few consistently support candidates of one party. According to a 1996 Roper Center poll, 65 percent typically split their tickets; 58 percent say they have voted for different parties in previous presidential elections; 37 percent have supported an independent or third-party candidate; and 19 percent said they were currently registered as an independent.[17]

Finally, the Progressive movement directly attacked the Jeffersonian-style of local governance. By opposing corruption at the local level, two methods evolved for cleaning things up: (1) shifting governing responsibilities to nonpartisan administrative agencies; and (2) looking to the national government for greater involvement in protecting its citizens. The Progressive movement did the former; Franklin D. Roosevelt's New Deal accomplished the latter.

FRANKLIN D. ROOSEVELT AND THE NEW DEAL

Other than Wilson's upset victory in 1912 and his narrow reelection victory four years later, Republicans controlled the federal government during the first third of the twentieth century. By decisive margins, Warren Harding won in 1920, Calvin Coolidge in 1924, and Herbert Hoover in 1928. This Republican trio profited from a strong national economy. As long as the economy prospered, Republicans would retain their natural majority. But the economy faltered badly. On October 24, 1929, the stock market crashed and the Great Depression began. Stock values dropped nearly 75 percent overnight, and two years later unemployment reached 25 percent. Farmers were especially hard hit, seeing prices for commodities drop to their lowest levels since 1910. Thousands of children were unable to attend school due to a lack of shoes. Things were so bleak that in May of 1934 Eleanor Roosevelt warned her husband, "I have moments of real terror when I think we may be losing this generation."[18]

The Democrats were poised to win the White House in 1932. They had done well in the congressional elections two years earlier, taking control of the House and falling one seat short of capturing the Senate. Hoover was viewed by the vast majority of the voters as a weak and ineffectual leader. Democrats chose Franklin Delano Roosevelt, the popular governor of New York and cousin to Teddy, as their candidate. On election day, Roosevelt won nearly 23 million votes to Hoover's 16 million, and forty-two states to Hoover's mere six. Roosevelt's landslide resulted in overwhelming Democratic control of both houses of Congress. In the Senate, Democrats won 59 seats to the Republicans' 37; in the House, Democrats had 312 members to the Republicans' 123.

Given these overwhelming majorities, Roosevelt proposed a flurry of legislation designed to provide immediate relief to those he described as "ill-nourished, ill-clad, and ill-housed." During his first term, Congress approved the Tennessee Valley Authority (TVA), the National Recovery Administration (NRA), the Works Progress Administration (WPA), the Public Works Administration (PWA), the Civilian Conservation Corps (CCC), and the Social Security Act. The first hundred days of Roosevelt's administration, during which many of the so-called alphabet soup agencies of the New Deal were created, set a standard against which Roosevelt's successors have been measured ever since.

Roosevelt's New Deal drastically transformed both the national government and the political parties. Abandoning its laissez-faire posture, the federal government became an active player whose primary responsibility was to ensure the economic well-being of the people. The New Deal signaled the emergence of a system where the federal government regulated some elements of the economy; elevated the cause of organized labor, farmers, and the elderly; and redistributed wealth through a progressive income tax. It also transformed the relationship between citizens and government. Prior to Roosevelt, a rugged individualism prevailed. But the Great Depression made it possible for Roosevelt to construct a foundation for economic security. The inalienable rights secured by the Constitution—speech, press, worship, due process—were supplemented by a new bill of rights "under which a new basis of security and prosperity can be established for all—regardless of station, race, or creed."[19] It was Roosevelt's hope that this second bill of rights would become so widely accepted that no future president would dare rip the social safety net he had so carefully constructed. Indeed, when Ronald Reagan attempted to modify Social Security in 1981, public opposition was so strong that he had to abandon his proposals and appoint a commission to study the program. Later, when the Republican-controlled Congress tried to trim proposed increases in Medicare and shut down the government in 1995, voter opposition was so powerful that President Clinton successfully painted the GOP Congress as extremist. Today, most Americans recognize the need for reforms in Social Security and Medicare, but the issue is so "hot" that most politicians are reluctant to touch it.

The New Deal and Party Politics

The New Deal affected political parties in a profoundly negative way. The rise of the welfare state, coupled with the reconstitution of rights, created an **executive-centered government** and the removal of partisan politics from its administration. The president became the center of the governing process—in effect, a guarantor of economic rights granted by the New Deal. To ensure a more efficient and enlightened administration, Roosevelt proposed the 1939 Executive Reorganization Act, which gave the president extraordinary powers and created a personalized White House bureaucracy known as the Executive Office of the President—an agency that has epitomized the personalization of presidential power.

The rise of executive-centered government was a serious blow to local party organizations. As Americans looked to the federal government, especially the president, for leadership, local and state powers diminished. Surprisingly, the two parties had not established ongoing national party organizations until the late 1920s. Under Roosevelt, Democrats established a permanent national headquarters in 1932, and Republicans quickly followed suit. Since then, the Democratic National Committee and the Republican National Committee (and their congressional counterparts) have vastly expanded their money-gathering abilities even as local party organizations have withered. Together, they constitute the focal points of what remains of the two-party system.

Nationalization of politics did more than transfer power, it altered political parties forever. Prior to Roosevelt, parties were agents that exercised responsibility by developing platforms and transforming them into law. But in an executive-centered system, presidents do not depend on parties—instead, they boast of their independence from them. In 1950, the Committee on Political Parties, a group sponsored by APSA, warned that an overextended presidency presented a grave danger to democracy:

> When the President's program actually is the sole program, either his party becomes a flock of sheep or the party falls apart. This concept of the presidency disposes of the party system by making the President reach directly for the support of a majority of the voters. It favors a president who exploits skillfully the arts of demagoguery, who

uses the whole country as his political backyard, and who does not mind turning into the embodiment of personal government.[20]

The effects of the progressive and New Deal reforms were apparent by the 1950s. A premium was placed on nonpartisan administration, which meant the removal of the spoils system and party-centered politics, and a concentration of power at the federal level. Jeffersonian-style parties, which placed a premium on local governance, became passé. By 1964, any resurrection of Jeffersonian Localism—which concentrated power at the state and local level, instead of the federal government and especially the presidency—was viewed as a radical departure. Presidential nominee Barry Goldwater bowed to this new reality, telling the Republican Convention: "Extremism in the defense of liberty is no vice. Moderation in the pursuit of justice is no virtue."[21]

POLITICAL PARTIES AND THE COLD WAR

Aside from progressivism and the New Deal, another transforming event that deeply affected party politics was the Cold War. Initially, the rise of communism was a boon to the Republicans who had been shut out of the White House in five consecutive elections from 1932 through 1948. Though Republicans attacked the New Deal as "socialistic," such disparaging remarks had little effect on a country reeling from the effects of the Great Depression. Roosevelt dismissed the GOP charges, claiming it was the Republican Party that had encouraged the spread of domestic communism: "In their speeches they deplored [communism], but by their actions they encouraged it. The injustices, the inequalities, the downright suffering out of which revolutions come—what did they do about these things? Lacking courage, they evaded. When the [economic] crisis came—as these wrongs made it sure to come—America was unprepared."[22]

But after the close of World War II, communism was on the march in Eastern Europe and Asia. Poland and Czechoslovakia were among its first victims. China fell to Mao Zedong's rebels in 1949. In 1950, communists from North Korea overran South Korea, prompting the immediate U.S. intervention in that war. At home, Americans were scared. Whittaker Chambers, a senior editor at *Time* magazine, accused Alger Hiss, a veteran State Department employee who played a key role in forming the UN, of belonging to the U.S. Communist Party and handing over government documents to Soviet spies. The House Committee on Un-American Activities investigated the charges led by California freshman Republican Richard M. Nixon. After Hiss was found guilty of lying about his communist connections, Republicans raised the specter of widespread communist infiltration of the federal government. Wisconsin Senator Joseph R. McCarthy charged that a nest of communist spies had infiltrated the State Department. Others were equally vehement. The Democrats were so burned by the accusation that they were "soft on communism" that years later Lyndon Johnson would escalate the Vietnam War partly because he feared Republican attacks that if he did not, he, too, would be labeled "soft on communism."

From 1952 to 1988, Republican presidential candidates benefitted from the increased Cold War tensions between the United States and the Soviet Union. Touting their stance of "peace through strength," Dwight Eisenhower, Richard Nixon, Ronald Reagan, and George Bush won the presidency because they projected the right combination of military might with a hard-headed negotiation stance in superpower summits. Since much of the U.S. economy was tied to defense and defense-related industries, Republicans were able to negate the Democratic party's New Deal legacy as "the party best able to keep the nation prosperous." In the ten presidential elections held between 1952 and 1988, Republicans won seven. The Republican Party had come a long way since the debacles of the 1930s.

Although voters generally liked tough-minded Republican presidents when it came to dealing with the communists, the Republican Party paid a high price for its presidential victories. Instead of adding more supporters to its ranks, Eisenhower, Nixon, Reagan, and Bush were "plebiscitary presidents"—winning personal victories at the expense of partisan ones. Moreover, as the Cold War droned on, Republican White Houses became staffed by people whose own party credentials were less than sterling. Most Cabinet officers, for example, had never held elective office. Rather, their expertise lay in managing bureaucracies (Henry Kissinger, Alexander Haig, Caspar Weinberger, and James Baker are examples). Democratic presidents followed a similar pattern (see Dean Rusk, Robert McNamara, Cyrus Vance, Harold Brown, Warren Christopher, Madeleine Albright). These White House staffers were presidential loyalists rather than partisans.

The plebiscitary presidency reached its zenith during the Nixon administration. Presidential aides H. R. Haldeman, John Ehrlichman, and the ubiquitous Chuck Colson (who declared he would run over his grandmother, if necessary, to reelect his boss in 1972) erected a political Berlin Wall separating the president from his party. They were so effective that the word *Republican* was banished from Nixon's television advertisements and campaign brochures. Instead, Nixon touted his "new American majority" as an alignment without the party-as-midwife. Accepting renomination in 1972, Nixon told the Republican delegates: "I ask everyone listening to me tonight—Democrats, Republicans, independents, to join our new majority—not on the basis of the party label you wear in your lapel, but on the basis of what you believe in your hearts."[23] Thus, while the Cold War served the Republican Party's immediate political interests, it actually weakened both parties. Republicans won the presidency more often than not. But the party lost most congressional races, and failed to add many new partisans to their ranks—despite having some very popular presidents (e.g., Dwight Eisenhower and Ronald Reagan). According to Gallup polls, Republican Party identifiers held steady at 32 percent in 1937 and 30 percent in 1993. Democrats also grew weaker. Their congressional incumbents ran increasingly personal campaigns, often stressing their own local accomplishments rather than broad party themes. Democrats continued to lose support from their New Deal heights. According to the Gallup polls, the number of people calling themselves Democrats dropped from 53 percent to 36 percent.[24] By the time Bill Clinton became president in 1993, both parties were in precarious positions.

THE RISE OF INTEREST GROUPS

The 1960s and 1970s were difficult years for parties. During this time, hundreds of state and national special interest groups entered the political fray. There have always been factions in American politics, but the nature and volume of the interest groups represented drastically changed. Groups representing consumers, environmentalists, professionals, women, the elderly, business, and labor, among others, mushroomed. For example, the National Organization for Women was founded in 1966; today it has more than 600 local chapters and 250,000 members. Environmental groups have experienced similar growth. Membership in the Sierra Club which hovered at 114,336 in 1970 ballooned to more than 550,000 in 1996. Likewise, the environmental organization Greenpeace had a roster of just 250 members in 1971; today, almost 1.7 million belong. Many of these organizations have usurped the parties by articulating policy demands and engendering fierce loyalties among their members.

In addition, the 1960s marked a change in how elections were conducted. Using many of the time-honored techniques of consumer marketing specialists, professional consultants have replaced party leaders as campaign tacticians. John Kennedy was the first presidential candidate to employ a professional pollster, Lou Harris, in 1960. Today, the presidential pollster has become a valued strategist, as Bill Clinton's close relationship with Dick Morris illustrates. In his memoir, Morris recalled Clinton's reaction to learning about the polling process at their first encounter in 1978: "He was fascinated by the process. Here was a tool he could use, a process that could reduce the mysterious ways of politics to scientific testing and evaluation. Implicit in his and my calculation was the idea the elections are won by issues, not by images, a thought that would shape our collaboration for nearly two decades."[25]

In the years since, candidates and would-be candidates have acquired the assistance of specialists, such as pollsters, media relations people, and other professional consultants to enhance their communication with voters in the Information Age. In so doing, they do not often present themselves as partisans—instead, they appeal to a strong streak of independence that voters like in their candidates. Even activities once dominated by the political parties, such as get-out-the-vote drives, are services now offered by professional consultants.

The Interest Group Explosion

As noted in Chapter 1, there are three important distinctions between political parties and interest groups:

1. Parties run candidates under a label. Although interest groups might consistently support candidates of one party, they do not have a label, nor do they officially nominate candidates.
2. When it comes to policy matters, parties are inclusive organizations. Interest groups, on the other hand, concentrate on a narrower range of concerns.

3. Finally, parties are regulated by scores of state and local regulations, making them akin to public utility corporations. Interest groups, on the other hand, operate under minimal regulations and with the constitutional protections of free speech, assembly, and petition.

Both parties and interest groups affect each other's standing in the political system. Although parties have clearly been the dominant force during most of our nation's history, this too is changing.

The number of issue advocacy groups in Washington has risen exponentially since 1960. Back then, there were approximately 5,000 associations; that number doubled by 1965, tripled by 1975, and by 1996 had reached roughly 25,000. These organizations include a wide-ranging list of business, labor, racial, religious, consumer-oriented, and environmental groups. Their involvement is often far-reaching and the political coalitions they assemble vary dramatically from issue to issue. In 1989 for example, when the Supreme Court heard the *Webster v. Reproductive Health Services* that permitted states to place restrictions on abortion, seventy-four interest groups submitted briefs to the justices (twenty-four supporting restrictions on abortion; fifty opposed). These included the American Family Association, the Knights of Columbus, the National Association of Evangelicals, and the National Right-to-Life Committee in favor of restrictions, and the American Civil Liberties Union, American Medical Association, American Nurses Association, Brooklyn Women's Martial Arts, Gay Men's Health Crisis, YWCA of the U.S.A., and the United Electrical, Radio, and Machine Workers of America against restrictions. A similar interest group explosion has occurred in each of the fifty state capitals, with equally wide-ranging interest group involvement in a variety of local issues.

There are numerous and conflicting accounts as to why this change occurred. Leading explanations include:

- As the whir of government activity increased with Franklin Roosevelt's New Deal and Johnson's Great Society, interest groups organized to get a larger slice of the pie. Often, they were created in response to new government initiatives.
- By the 1960s, Americans had become increasingly dissatisfied with their government. A growing public alienation—accentuated by the Vietnam War and Watergate—prompted many to look for alternative avenues of public service. Trust in government fell from 73 percent in 1958 to 32 percent in 1997.[26] The distrust of government extended to most large institutions, including political parties. Interest groups seemed a less partisan and more acceptable way to alter public policies. Moreover, the legacy of the civil rights and anti–Vietnam War movements suggested that citizens could change the course of government without the aid of parties, as long as they worked together.
- A third explanation has been dubbed the "post-materialist" perspective. This view suggests that as Americans entered into a post-industrial society they were so prosperous that a broader set of issues such as environmental protection and consumer affairs emerged. The parties, historically preoccupied

with economic concerns, seemed a poor choice to advance these "post-materialist" issues.

- Sociological changes, including increased levels of education following World War II and the exodus from the cities to the suburbs, resulted in an issue-oriented politics that did not include a role for traditional parties in the new Information Age.

Perhaps the greatest impetus to the interest group explosion were changes in the Federal Election Acts of the early 1970s which permitted **political action committees (PACs).** PACs are the money-raising arms of interest groups. Their growth gave candidates new sources of campaign funds and reduced the need for party money (see Chapter 8).

The growth of organized groups vying for power and influence in the political system stunned both Democrats and Republicans and shocked students of American government. Prior to this period, many believed that parties best served the public interest because they set their sights on winning elections and consequently drew ordinary citizens into the political process. Interest groups, concerned with changing policy and not the outcome of elections per se, have no reason to bring average folks into the fray. In fact, it is to their advantage to keep politics private. One thing is certain, though, most Americans see interest groups as their best vehicle for articulating changes in public policy.

THE RISE OF CANDIDATE-CENTERED POLITICS

Candidate-centered elections involve a number of interrelated concepts. Three of the most important include:

1. The people planning and conducting campaigns are no longer party activists, but instead are a personal team assembled by the candidate and are beholden to that candidate.
2. Candidates are often "marketed" not as party members, but as individuals free from the constraints of partisan politics.
3. Consequently, voters view politics in terms of individuals, not as one party against the other.

Party Activist versus Professional Consultant

Throughout most of American history, campaigns were conducted by party activists. They were, after all, the most experienced and had access to legions of party workers who could knock on doors and distribute pamphlets. Things began to change in the Information Age with the arrival of professional campaign consultants and their broad-based voter contact techniques—radio, television, and direct mail. These people learned their craft not in the trenches of partisan political warfare, but in marketing firms and university communications departments. They pushed electioneering from a party-centered sphere to a nonpartisan, professional contest between strategists and handlers. Today, nearly every congressional candidate, most state legislators, and a growing number of municipal officials hire campaign consulting firms. The breadth of their services is staggering: polling, fund-raising, direct mail, radio and television production, planning events, demographic research, message development, etc. Volunteer-based and party-run campaigns are a rarity, as candidates prefer to delegate the running of their campaigns to the so-called professionals.

Most of these professionals are "partisans" in the sense that they usually work for candidates of one party. But that is about as far as the relationship goes. An increasing number of consultants are willing to hop from one side of the political fence to another in order to run campaigns and make money. In 1992, longtime GOP consultant Ed Rollins decided to lend a hand to Ross Perot's presidential bid. As Rollins later recalled: "Lust for payback was central to my motivation. I was bitter about my treatment by the [George] Bush crowd, and wanted to stick it to them, pure and simple, to show them they'd been fools to spurn my talents."[27] Rollins's defection shocked many Republicans, but of course the $1 million Perot paid surely explains part of the story (see "The Parties Speak: Ed Rollins and the 'Campaign from Hell'"). In 1995, Dick Morris, who had polled for such prominent Republicans as Senate Majority Leader Trent Lott and North Carolina Senator Jesse Helms, became a key strategist in the Clinton reelection campaign.

Party Member versus Nonpartisan Candidate

Until the 1970s, most candidates ran for office as part of a party ticket. In 1960, for example, many Democratic candidates portrayed themselves as part of the team headed by John F. Kennedy. In those areas where Kennedy was popular, he touted the candidacies of state and local Democrats who could ride to victory on his coattails. In the South, where Kennedy was less popular, vice presidential candidate Lyndon Johnson stood in for him.

The idea of acquiring a party's nomination, and then all but abandoning the party began in the 1950s. Dwight Eisenhower was the first of several "citizen politicians" to seek the presidency. On February 2, 1952, Citizens for Eisenhower opened its doors. Instead of Republican partisans, the organization was staffed by those who adhered to the corporate ethos: Walter Williams, head of Citizens for Eisenhower, was a mortgage banker; his assistant, Paul Hoffman, was president of the Ford Foundation. By placing himself above the mere politics-as-usual, Eisenhower presented himself to the voters as a nonpartisan office seeker who was simply renting the top slot on the Republican ticket. For their part, voters could support Eisenhower without making a partisan commitment. It was a marriage of convenience.

Richard Nixon emulated Eisenhower's approach in 1968. In *The Selling of the President, 1968*, author Joe McGinniss described how Nixon's campaign handlers transformed their man from a stiff partisan into a compassionate leader acting on behalf of "average Americans." The nonpartisan approach was given its greatest boost in the 1970s when both parties, starting with the Democrats, allowed greater

The Parties Speak: *Ed Rollins and the "Campaign from Hell"*

Ed Rollins was a influential Republican operative who managed Ronald Reagan's 1984 reelection campaign and briefly served as executive director of the National Republican Congressional Committee under President Bush.

In mid-June [1992], [Ross Perot cochair Hamilton] Jordan and I had put together a message strategy with three distinct planks. The first would emphasize a little-known aspect of Perot's persona: his humanitarianism. Over the years, he has done hundreds of good deeds, most of them for fellow citizens he's never met. Only a few of them, like his efforts on behalf of Vietnam POWs and MIAs, have ever been publicly disclosed. He's sent money to strangers. He's paid tens of thousands of dollars for special surgeries the Veterans Administration wouldn't perform on injured veterans because of the cost. Beneath that flinty exterior beats the heart of a Good Samaritan. We aimed to tell this good and real story.

Our second theme would stress Perot's can-do spirit. The rags-to-riches story of his rise from IBM salesman to megabillionaire was the stuff of American folklore. Because of his strong work ethic and self-made success, Perot's wealth was actually a powerful draw for the blue-collar voters he needed to attract.

Once we persuaded voters that this was a guy they should like and admire, we'd hammer home the theme that Ross Perot was no traditional politician. The country was sick of politics as usual. Perot was the prescription for a cynical electorate precisely because he hadn't spent a day of his career in Washington.

While Perot was riding high, we'd come in with a heavy wave of national media buys to define this image. While we reinforced his positives and softened his negatives, we'd let Bush and Clinton chew each other up. It all seemed perfectly sensible to me. What I didn't count on was Perot's bullheadedness.

Most candidates think they're smarter about politics than their handlers. Sometimes they're right, but most of the time they're not. One of the little appreciated but most demanding skills of the campaign consultant is being able to convince your principal that he may not be as brilliant as he thinks.

This is arduous duty; the disdain most office seekers feel for their operatives is crystallized in one of George Bush's favorite lines: "If you're so smart, why aren't you president?" (In Bush's case, the answer today is, "Because Ronald Reagan didn't hand it to me on a silver platter.")

But at least most candidates know the territory. The great emotional struggle of the entire Perot campaign was trying to find a way to tell the candidate he simply didn't know what the hell he was doing.

Given his Napoleon complex, I couldn't say what all of us were thinking: "Ross, sit down and shut up. This is how you run a campaign, and this is your role. This is not like anything else you've ever done in your life. That's understandable, but you don't have a clue. If you'll let us, we can save you from yourself."

SOURCE: Excerpted from Ed Rollins with Tom DeFrank, *Bare Knuckles and Back Rooms: My Life in American Politics* (New York: Broadway Books, 1996), 240–41.

participation by rank-and-file party followers in selecting their presidential candidates. No longer did presidential aspirants need the blessing of party leaders in order to capture the party's nomination. In fact, it quickly became a hindrance to become known as the choice of the party bosses. George McGovern was the first to capitalize on this change, and every successful candidate since has done the same (see Chapter 4).

Today, candidates for all offices build personal organizations devoted exclusively to their own electoral needs. These "instant parties" hire consultants, recruit volunteers, conduct media campaigns, and develop their own set of policy positions. They align themselves to other members of the ticket when such a move is expedient, and distance themselves when the opposite seems to be the case. In 1992, Democratic candidates were generally supportive of Bill Clinton and were often at his side while he campaigned for president. Two years later many Democrats distanced themselves from the unpopular Clinton—especially when their Republican opponents used a high-technology television technique called "morphing" to alter the Democratic candidate into Clinton's image. Such behavior is not limited to Democrats. Republicans flocked to the popular Ronald Reagan in 1984, but distanced themselves from a besieged Bob Dole in 1996. Instead of running a party-centered campaign, most Democrats and Republicans abandon their party from the time they enter politics. They often are self-recruited, ambitious political players as is evident in "The Parties Speak: Louis LaPolla, 'The Pothole Mayor,' A Case Study in Ambition."

Party Affiliation versus Voting Choice

The final component of the shift toward candidate-centered politics is the declining use of party as a voting cue (see Chapter 6). Just a few decades ago, most voters adhered to their party line when deciding whom to support in a given election—particularly if they did not know much about the candidates. Straight-ticket voting was common, with many considering themselves "yellow dog" Democrats or Republicans. In other words, they would rather vote for a yellow dog than a member of the other party—even for low-level offices like county coroner, sheriff, or village trustee.

Today, things have changed. The number of those for whom partisanship is a voting cue has dropped steadily during the last three decades. One reason why voters no longer use partisan cues is because it is no longer rational to do so, since candidates themselves do not adhere to a party ticket or platform. Candidates say they are forced to depart from the party framework because voters are now independent-minded, thereby rendering party-centered appeals ineffective. Following Bill Clinton's 1996 victory, political scientist Everett Carll Ladd declared: "Americans [are] remarkably unanchored in partisan terms. . . . Regular party identifiers are now too small a proportion for anyone to win the presidency largely on party terms. In this setting presidential elections, especially when an incumbent is running, hinge more than ever on short-term factors such as the perceived state of the economy, together with the comparative personal standing of the main contenders."[28]

The Parties Speak: *Louis LaPolla, "The Pothole Mayor," A Case Study in Ambition*

Louis LaPolla was a Republican mayor of Utica, New York, during the 1980s. Prior to becoming mayor, he was a sixth-grade schoolteacher and a member of the City Council. Previously, Utica had been governed by a Democratic machine founded by Rufus P. Elefante during the 1950s. The following excerpt is adapted from Allen Ehrenhalt's The United States of Ambition.

At a time when political organization had ceased to count for much in Utica campaigns, [Louis] LaPolla had made himself mayor largely by wanting it more than anything else in the world. Raised in a public housing project by a mother who was employed as a maid, LaPolla worked his way through Utica College, then became a sixth-grade teacher in the city schools. But he began running for office almost as soon as he could vote. . . .

He ran for the [Utica City] Council at age twenty-three, pledging to work for the demolition of an abandoned bridge he and other residents of his ward considered a safety hazard. He won the election and never stopped agitating until the bridge was torn down, several years later. Over more than fifteen years as a city councilman, LaPolla proved to be a loner. He rarely disclosed how he planned to vote until it was absolutely necessary. "My best and only friend," he says, "is my wife." What he excelled at was campaigning. La Polla never developed much skill as a public speaker, but he was fantastic as a one-on-one campaigner. "I'm a workhorse," he says. "I'm a door-to-door guy. I ring 8,000 to 10,000 doorbells every time I run." He has a memory for detail that has to be seen to be believed. If a Utica resident tells LaPolla his name and the street he lives on, the mayor can nearly always come up with the exact address.

During three terms in office, LaPolla has not made many changes in the routine that got him elected. He shows up everywhere. "We have five senior citizens' centers. I go to their birthday parties every month. I serve the food. I go to 90 percent of the wakes. If I know one person in the family, I go. I'll get invited to three weddings on a Saturday night. I go to all of them. I'm not selective."

In the office LaPolla spends a good deal of time talking to constituents about the most routine problems of urban life. "They call me for potholes, they call me for garbage." He does not go home at night until he has personally answered every phone call he has received during the day. He pretty much has to return them himself, since he has reduced his office staff from [former mayor Stephen J.] Pawlinga's six mayoral aides, some of them deputized to make important decisions, to three routine clerical positions. When LaPolla wants to show a visitor a report or a document, he goes into a storage room and looks for it in the files.

In many ways LaPolla is the reincarnation of the old-fashioned urban politician: favors, personal contact, and personal service. He takes pride in what he says is his reputation as the "pothole mayor." But in the days of machine control, personal service translated into both votes and governmental power. The success at the polls that placed [Rufus P.] Elefante's loyalists in office created a network of obligation and loyalty that enabled them to function as a team once they got there. In the LaPolla era personal service translates only into votes, and into votes for one candidate. Popular as he is, LaPolla is not much help to any of the council candidates, and rarely do they need to vote with him out of political indebtedness. "They are an independent group of people," says planning director Steve DiMeo. "They don't defer to any type of leadership."

SOURCE: Excerpted from Allen Ehrenhalt, *The United States of Ambition: Politics, Power and the Pursuit of Office* (New York: Times Books, 1991), 118–20.

A PARTYLESS AGE?

Americans have never fully embraced political parties. As we have seen, public distaste for parties lingered throughout the nineteenth and twentieth centuries, even as they became more deeply rooted in the political system. Parties were tolerated because they helped create an efficient means of organizing mass-based politics. They also organized elites by merging the disparate executive, congressional, and judicial branches of government established by the Framers in the U.S. Constitution. In addition, parties molded diverse interests into an agenda for unified action and provided voters rational cost-saving cues on election day. In short, they dominated the American political system throughout much of the last century because they performed necessary and desirable functions.

Yet the heyday of parties was remarkably short-lived. Just when they reached their zenith, a reform wave swept the nation and systematically dismantled much of the leverage party machines held on the system. Parties had, it was argued, overstepped their assigned charge and had become corrupt institutions. Progressives stripped party organizations of their institutional strengths, and helped change public attitudes toward them. Direct primaries reduced the capacity of party leaders to control who got on the ballot. Referenda allowed average citizens to go over the heads of elected officials to change public policy. Franklin D. Roosevelt continued the movement away from parties by shifting the locus of governance from local to national, and from the legislature to the executive. The Cold War accelerated the emphasis toward a personalized president alone at the top rung of the political ladder. The brisk rise of interest groups and the emergence of candidate-centered campaigning during the 1960s were the final nails in the party coffins. As we near the end of the twentieth century, the state of the parties is remarkably different than it was at the beginning.

But as noted in Chapter 1, proclamations of the demise of political parties have been greatly exaggerated. Indeed, it would be a mistake to assume the party system has collapsed completely or that we now live in a "party-less" era. As will be seen in subsequent chapters, political parties are resilient creatures. In some ways, they are stronger now than they were in Boss Tweed's day. The principal difference between the major parties at the onset of the twenty-first century from their predecessors lies not in their relative standing, but in their characters as players in the process. The Progressive movement and other phenomena that have contributed to party decline might best be described as a shift from the Jeffersonian-style local parties to more nationally based parties in the Hamiltonian tradition.

At the start of the century, party activity was centered at the community level. Parties aided candidates, organized campaigns and local government, recruited grassroots workers, to some extent provided a safety net for the underclass, and even afforded a social outlet for community activities. True, many party machines were corrupt. But like a quarrelsome adolescent, unscrupulous party organizations were generally tolerated because they were, after all, "ours." Steadily, the Progressives tightened the reins on political parties and curtailed their activities. Muckrakers uncovered the breadth of machine corruption and, in turn, changed public attitudes about them. Franklin Roosevelt's New Deal compelled many political activists to leave home and head for Washington. The rise of interest groups and candidate-centered elections gave voters intermediaries other than parties. Today, the once-troubled adolescent has matured, but the mischievous behavior has not been forgotten. Parties have been given new powers and much authority at the national and state level, but have forged little attachment with citizens back home. Candidates seek office using a party label, elected officials of the same party caucus together, and some voters still rely on partisanship when voting. But these Hamiltonian-style organizations are entirely different than the local, community-based organizations of the last century. They remain part of the family of American politics—though very much the black sheep. To use another analogy, parties are still invited to dinner, but only at holidays.

FURTHER READING

Ehrenhalt, Alen. *The United States of Ambition: Politics, Power and the Pursuit of Office*. New York: Times Books, 1991.

Lowi, Theodore J. *The Personal President: Power Invested, Promise Unfulfilled*. Ithaca: Cornell University Press, 1985.

McCormick, Richard L. *The Party Period and Public Policy: American Politics for the Age of Jackson to the Progressive Era*. New York: Oxford University Press, 1986.

Shea, Daniel M. *The Campaign Craft: The Strategists, Tactics, and Art of Modern Political Campaigning*. Lanham, Md.: Praeger, 1996.

Wattenberg, Martin P. *The Rise of Candidate-Centered Politics*. Cambridge: Harvard University Press, 1991.

White, John Kenneth. *Still Seeing Red: How the Cold War Shapes the New American Politics*. Boulder, Colo.: Westview Press, 1997.

NOTES

1. CBS News/*New York Times*, survey, June 17–20, 1992. Text of question: "Some people think the country needs a new political party to compete with the Democratic and Republican parties in offering the best candidates for political office. Do you agree or disagree?" Agree, 58 percent; disagree, 36 percent; don't know, 6 percent. Democrats: agree, 54 percent; disagree, 40 percent; don't know, 6 percent. Republicans: agree, 53 percent; disagree, 25 percent; don't know, 8 percent.

2. George Gallup, Jr., *The Gallup Poll: Public Opinion, 1995* (Wilmington, Del.: Scholarly Resources, Inc., 1996), 263.

3. Princeton Survey Research Associates, survey, June 19–25, 1995. Text of question: "Do you, yourself, happen to be involved in any charity or social service activities, such as helping the poor, the sick, or the elderly?" Gallup Organization for the Independent Sector, 1992. Text of question: "By volunteer activity I mean not just belonging to a service organization, but actually working in some way to help others for no monetary pay. In which, if any, of the areas listed . . . have you done some volunteer work in the past twelve months? Did you work for only one organization or more than one?" One or more, 57 percent; none, 43 percent. The data in this section were taken from the *Public Perspective* (June/July 1996).

4. William L. Riordan, *Plunkitt of Tammany Hall* (New York: Dutton, 1963), 25–26.

5. *Lochner v. New York* in *U.S. Supreme Court Reports* (Washington, D.C.: Lawyer's Co-Operative Publishing, 1905), 943, 944.

6. Ibid, 946.

7. Riordan, *Plunkitt of Tammany Hall*, 17.

8. "Progressive Platform, 1912," in Kirk H. Porter and Donald Bruce Johnson, *National Party Platforms, 1840–1968* (Urbana: University of Illinois Press, 1970), 175.

9. "Republican Platform, 1912," in Porter and Johnson, *National Party Platforms*, 183.

10. Quoted in Leonard D. White, *The Republican Era* (New York: Free Press, 1958), 6.

11. Quoted in Thomas E. Cronin, *Direct Democracy: The Politics of Initiative, Referendum, and Recall* (Cambridge, Mass.: Harvard University Press, 1989), 1.

12. A. James Reichley, *The Life of the Parties: A History of American Political Parties* (New York: Fress Press, 1992), 207.

13. Quoted in C. H. Hoebeke, "Democratizing the Constitution: The Failure of the Seventeenth Amendment," *Humanitas* IX, no. 2 (1996): 25.

14. Lincoln Steffens, *The Shame of the Cities* (1904; New York: Sagamore Press, 1957), 2, 6.

15. Quoted in Greg Mitchell, *The Campaign of the Century: Upton Sinclair's Race for Governor of California and the Birth of Media Politics* (New York: Random House, 1992), xv.

16. See Theodore J. Lowi, "Toward a Responsible Three-Party System: Prospects and Obstacles," in John C. Green and Daniel M. Shea, eds., *The State of the Parties* (Lanham, Md.: Rowman and Littlefield, 1996).

17. Media Studies Center/Roper Center, survey, February 1996. Text of question: "When voting in elections do you typically vote a straight ticket—that is for candidates of the same party, or do you typically split your ticket—that is vote for candidates from different parties? Have you always voted for the same party for president or have you voted for different parties for president? In 1996, how likely is it that you would vote for an independent candidate for president? Is it very likely, somewhat likely, not too likely, or not at all likely?"

18. Quoted in Robert Caro, *The Years of Lyndon Johnson: The Path to Power* (New York: Knopf, 1983), 341.

19. Franklin D. Roosevelt, Address to the Commonwealth Club, 1932. Quoted in Sidney M. Milkis, "Programmatic Liberalism and Party," in John Kenneth White and Jerome M. Mileur, eds., *Challenges to Party Government* (Carbondale: Southern Illinois University Press, 1992), 111.

20. Committee on Political Parties, *Toward a More Responsible Two-Party System* (New York: Rinehart, 1950). Reprinted in White and Mileur, *Challenges to Party Government*, 250.

21. Barry M. Goldwater, "Acceptance Speech," Republican National Convention, San Francisco, July 16, 1964.

22. Franklin D. Roosevelt, "Address at the Democratic State Convention," Syracuse, New York, September 29, 1936.

23. Richard M. Nixon, "Acceptance Speech," Republican National Convention, Miami Beach, August 23, 1972.

24. Cited in John Kenneth White, *Still Seeing Red: How the Cold War Shapes the New American Politics* (Boulder, Colo.: Westview Press, 1998), 148.

25. Dick Morris, *Behind the Oval Office: Winning the Presidency in the Nineties* (New York: Random House, 1997), 47.

26. Cited in William Schneider, "A Crime that Made Cynicism the Rule," *National Journal*, June 21, 1997, 1306.

27. Ed Rollins with Tom DeFrank, *Bare Knuckles and Back Rooms: My Life in American Politics* (New York: Broadway Books, 1996), 234–35.

28. Everett Carll Ladd, "1996 Vote: The 'No Majority' Realignment Continues," *Political Science Quarterly* (Spring 1997): 23.

CHAPTER 4

Party Organizations in the Twenty-First Century

The 1996 election produced a number of notable outcomes. It marked the first time since 1928 that Republicans captured both houses of Congress in two consecutive elections (1994 and 1996), while Democrats held the White House in back-to-back elections (1992 and 1996) for the first time since 1964. It was the most expensive campaign in American history, with presidential and congressional candidates spending more than $2 billion—$650 million more than in 1992. Justice Department investigations into phone solicitations made by President Bill Clinton and Vice President Al Gore also grabbed the headlines. It was the first time in American history that both of the presidential candidate's wives gave important televised speeches at the national party conventions. Most significantly, 1996 saw new technologies become a staple in presidential campaigns. All three of the major party candidates—Bill Clinton, Bob Dole, and Ross Perot—had homepages on the World Wide Web, as did several contestants for the Republican presidential nomination.

The 1996 election also illustrates how the American party system appears to be heading in two contradictory directions at once: Both the Democratic and Republican parties are thriving and declining at the same time. To paraphrase Charles Dickens, 1996 was the best of times and the worst of times. The best of times was evident in the resurgence of parties as organizational entities. On the Democratic side, Bill Clinton owed his political comeback in part to the Democratic National Committee (DNC) which implemented an aggressive fund-raising plan and engineered a novel way of spending money. From July 1995 until election day 1996, Clinton bombarded the television airwaves with thousands of commercials advocating his reelection. Most were sponsored by the DNC. Although the Democratic party's "issue advocacy" commercials did not explicitly ask people to vote for Clinton, they derided the Republican budget proposals and the federal government shutdown. These same ads showed a hard-working Clinton in the serenity of the Oval Office acting as a necessary barrier against these Republican excesses. Voters in a dozen key states saw these DNC advertisements about once every three days for a year-and-a-half.[1] Republicans tried to copy Clinton with their own "issue advocacy" advertisements, but their efforts were too little, too late. By the time Dole won the Republican presidential nomination, his campaign coffers were empty. The DNC's innovative strategy boasted Clinton's popularity ratings, making him a cinch for reelection. Republicans took these lessons to heart, and no doubt the Republican National Committee (RNC) will try to duplicate the Democratic effort in 2000.

The capacity of the parties to raise large sums of money does not mean that they are the beneficiaries of the sort of attention you would expect candidates to give them. Bill Clinton profited from the commercials put on by the DNC, but paid scant attention to the party in public appearances. Accepting renomination at the Democratic National Convention in July 1996, Clinton referred to the Democratic Party just once in a sixty-six-minute speech. By contrast, Harry Truman made twenty-seven direct references to the Democratic Party in a 1948 acceptance speech that lasted just twenty-four minutes. Bob Dole adopted a similar approach, mentioning the Republican Party just twice (and the Democrats not at all) during his fifty-seven minute acceptance speech. Thus, while both party organizations were important behind-the-scenes operators, both candidates had little difficulty shunning their respective party labels.

This same paradox is evident in many congressional and state elections. Republicans collected and disbursed record amounts of cash in 1996 into the party's congressional coffers. But that did not stop scores of candidates from breaking ranks with the Republican leadership, especially House Speaker Newt Gingrich, casting themselves as "independent-minded" Republicans. Even the National Republican Congressional Committee (NRCC) encouraged voters to split their ballots once it was evident that Dole was doomed. On election night, Republicans cobbled together a television advertisement for viewing on the West Coast that abandoned Dole: "Remember the last time Democrats ran everything? The largest tax increase in history. Government-run health care. More wasteful spending. Who wants that again? Don't let the media stop you from voting. And don't hand Bill Clinton a blank check."[2]

Scores of books written during the last three decades have chronicled the demise of parties with titles like *The Party's Over*, *The Decline of American Political Parties*, and *Party Decline in America*.[3] The common threads running through these and other related works are: (1) voters no longer adhere to party labels; (2) scores of reforms have made party organizations infirm and irrelevant; and (3) elected officials hold less allegiance to party than ever before. One of the leading advocates of party decline, *Washington Post* columnist David S. Broder, paints a grim portrait of just how irrelevant the political parties have become:

> Parties are almost invisible in the public dialogue today—especially on television. On the tube, conflicts are always personal, not institutional—Clarence Thomas versus Anita Hill, not a Republican president against a Democratic Senate. Individualistic office-seekers ignore or camouflage their party labels. Federal and state laws impede the parties' operations.[4]

Despite such dire warnings, a new chorus of voices has challenged the evidence of party decay saying in effect, "Not so fast." As a new century draws near, it has become clear that American parties are resilient creatures. Both the Democratic and Republican parties have developed unique branch organizations, revamped their internal operations, and devised innovative ways to influence elections. In each case, the number of full-time party employees, the size of their operating budgets, their average financial contribution to individual candidates, and the range of services provided has vastly increased. Those in this emerging revivalist camp have written books with titles like *The Party Goes On, The Party's Just Begun, Party Renewal in America,* and *The Parties Respond.*[5] The authors developed the following themes:

1. In the face of a changing and often unfriendly environment, state parties have demonstrated an unusual degree of adaptability and resilience.
2. Thanks to a heightened sense of close electoral competition, parties have become more nationalized and more active.
3. National party organizations have successfully adapted to contemporary politics. They are wealthier, more stable, better organized, and better staffed than ever before.

This chapter, which concludes our discussion of the history of parties in America, explores both sides of the revivalist versus decline debate. We review evidence from all sides. Revivalists assert that parties are far from dead and that a phoenix has arisen from the ashes. Those saying parties are still in decline have assembled reams of data to support their arguments. As before, the Hamiltonian and Jeffersonian models provide an important glimpse into the health of the party system.

ORGANIZATIONAL ADJUSTMENT AND GROWTH

Precisely how a party adjusts its structures and modes of operation to fit changing conditions has puzzled observers. In some instances, it adapts and thrives; in others, it founders and dies. Several rival explanations attempt to answer the question, "What does change look like?" Two stand out: the contextual approach and the functionalist model. The **contextual approach** studies the historical antecedents, economic conditions, cultural traditions, and other societal factors that either inhibit future development or cause a party to change.[6] If conditions are right, organizations adjust. Several urban party machines at the turn of the century weathered the storm of Progressive criticism because the waves of new immigrants added a contextual element that allowed them to linger a while longer.

The **functionalist model** studies change from a different perspective. It suggests that when a gap exists between the functions provided by a party organization and the needs of its members, change is inevitable. This approach puts a premium on member involvement and the vigor of organizational leaders. The most famous champions of this approach have been sociologist Robert Merton and political scientist John Aldrich.[7] Aldrich argues that parties emerged in the United States by 1800 because Thomas Jefferson and Alexander Hamilton believed they could best achieve their political aims by creating them.

While each approach has its merits, a mixture of both best describes the party situation in the Information Age. The signs of change are everywhere. New technologies have made personal contact unnecessary, interest groups dominate the policy process, and professional campaign consultants sell their services for cash.

Couple this with unpredictable electorates and skyrocketing campaign costs, and one has all the ingredients needed for highly competitive elections. As a result, party adjustments are being made because candidates desperately need parties to help them win. Because many voters have abandoned their once firmly held party allegiances, politicians want stronger party organizations. Decline in one sphere has triggered growth in another.

The Rebirth of the Republican National Committee

Republicans were first to adapt to the new political environment. From the ashes of defeat in 1964, the GOP organizationally resurrected itself. That year, Barry M. Goldwater, a conservative Republican U.S. senator from Arizona, won just six states and 52 electoral votes compared to Democrat Lyndon B. Johnson's forty-four states and 486 electoral votes. Johnson's coattails produced a Democratic landslide that saw the Republican ranks in the House of Representatives fall to their lowest level since the Great Depression. The few Republicans who remained were engaged in a bitter struggle between eastern upper-class business interests and western middle-class activists.

Although Republican prospects improved when Richard M. Nixon won the presidency in 1968, Democrats maintained their control of both houses of Congress and most state and local offices. By 1973, the GOP was in serious trouble as the economy soured; then, in 1974, the Watergate scandal forced Nixon's resignation. The 1974 midterm elections proved disastrous for Republicans, when a large class of Democratic freshmen, dubbed "Watergate babies," were elected in heretofore safe Republican districts. Following Jimmy Carter's 1976 victory, some prognosticators predicted that the GOP was headed for extinction. Don Roch, a former state chairman of the Rhode Island Republican Party, told John K. White in October 1979:

> I am a salesman. I know how to sell. I know what I can't sell. When I first ran for election in the town of West Warwick, Rhode Island, I had to sell Don Roch. That was enough. That was all the people could take. . . . Yet, I lost. In 1970, I ran for the State Senate. I ran once again selling Don Roch. The third week before the election I added the tag "Republican." Now, if I've sold Don Roch, they can accept the word *Republican*. It's the soft sell.[8]

Given the prevailing pessimism, leaders in the RNC decided to reconfigure the party. The task fell to the newly appointed chair, William Brock, a former U.S. senator from Tennessee who had been defeated for reelection in 1976. To enhance the party's electoral prospects, Brock opted to centralize power within the RNC. He initiated a four-part strategy to accomplish this goal: (1) aggressive fund-raising, (2) organizational improvements, (3) better candidate recruitment, and (4) changing the party's image.

Fund-raising. Believing that Republicans needed more money to win more elections, Brock decided to solicit it from ordinary voters. Large computerized lists of potential prospects were sent letters asking for small contributions. While the response rate to these direct mail solicitations was low, those who gave were placed on a donor list and asked every six months or so to contribute more money. Brock argued that direct mail had two advantages: (1) by seeking small individual contributions, the party could shatter its image of catering to the rich; and (2) if successful, direct mail could raise large sums. Brock's bet paid off. In 1977, the RNC expanded its base of contributors from 250,000 to 350,000. Three years later a phenomenal 1.2 million Republicans were sending in checks payable to the RNC. While the average contribution was small—just $25—total receipts grew from $12.7 million in 1976 to more than $26 million in 1980.[9]

Organizational Improvements.   Brock also revamped the organizational structure of the national committee by installing fifteen regional directors to help plan strategy and bolster the state parties; establishing task forces to encourage states to develop long-range plans; providing regional finance directors to help raise money; and sending one organizational expert to help each state committee. Brock also initiated a program whereby state and local party organizations could use RNC-owned equipment and sophisticated technologies at a minimal cost. A massive computer network allowed the state and local Republican parties to download a variety of software programs to expedite accounting, word processing, direct-mail, get-out-the-vote drives, mailing list maintenance, and political targeting. Finally, the RNC provided GOP candidates with low-cost polling services. In 1980, it supplied 130 campaigns with discounted polling, sometimes for as little as $250.[10] Thus, Brock reconfigured the RNC to meet the demands of modern-day campaigns where high technology, survey research, computer driven targeting, television advertisements, and direct mail are essential Information Age tools.

Candidate Recruitment.   Brock also realized that these tools meant nothing without good candidates. He instituted a "farm-team" approach to candidate development by recruiting prospective Republicans to seek lesser offices. Once these rising stars got a taste for public life, Brock reasoned, they would seek higher office and, thanks to their previous political experience, they would win. Toward that end, the RNC created the Concord Conferences that permitted young professionals, party leaders, and prospective candidates to discuss strategy, tactics, and the importance of political involvement. In 1980, more than 600 men and women attended these events. Brock also developed other forums for would-be candidates that included training seminars on issue development, public speaking, managing the inevitable stresses of a campaign, and media relations. Between 1977 and 1980, more than 10,000 Republicans, mostly state and local candidates, attended these sessions.[11]

Image Repair.   Finally, Brock sought to refurbish the Republican party's tattered image. Prior to his tenure, the Republican Party was likened to a country club inhabited by older, white, well-to-do men. Brock wanted these "country club Republicans" to make way for more women and minorities. To accomplish this, he spent $640,000 in 1977 to attract more African Americans to the Republican ranks, largely without success. A few years later Brock organized a similar effort to recruit women. To help these efforts along, Brock began publication of a lively opinion journal entitled *Commonsense*. *Commonsense* included articles from prominent Democrats (such as Jeane Kirkpatrick), independents, and Republicans—providing an intellectual breath of fresh air to replace what had become stale party doctrine. By 1980, new ideas had become the hallmark of the GOP.

Finally, Republican spending grew at a rate of four times that of the Democrats. Brock's checkbook activism allowed for a centralization of power in Washington because Republican state leaders readily accepted the money and expertise Brock was providing.

The Democratic National Committee Plays Catch-Up

The Democratic reaction to the Brock reforms was to say, in effect, "Stop until we can catch up!" Disgruntled Democrats pointed to Brock's success at fund-raising, and wondered how they could match it. In 1978, for example, the RNC disbursed more than $2.7 million to state and local candidates while the DNC contributed just $107,000.[12] After the drubbing at the polls that the Democrats took in 1978 and 1980, the grumbling grew louder. The head of the Association of State Democratic Chairs complained: "The 1980 election was a referendum on national party structure. We were outspent, out-targeted, and out-polled. The RNC did a superlative job. The Democratic Party should hold its head in shame."[13]

The search was on to find someone who could revive the Democratic National Committee. After much intraparty bickering, Charles Manatt was chosen in 1981 to serve as party chair. Manatt had previously been the DNC's finance chair and California state chair. Upon taking the helm, Manatt set about reorganizing the DNC to include strong managerial leadership and innovative fund-raising. He tripled the number of DNC staffers, began a series of training seminars for state and local candidates, organized a State Party Works program that allowed state parties access to state-of-the-art campaign techniques and strategies, and devised a massive voter registration program. Most importantly, Manatt copied the Republicans and introduced the DNC's first direct mail program in 1981. Donors were given membership cards, "personal" notes from prominent Democrats, etchings of previous Democratic presidents, and other mementos designed to enhance the party connection.[14]

Assessing the success of Manatt's innovations is difficult. While Democratic coffers swelled from $15 million in 1980 to more than $46 million just four years later, and some state and local candidates benefitted from the seminars and expert services they received, Manatt was considerably less successful than Bill Brock.[15] Democrats were trounced in the 1984 Ronald Reagan–Walter Mondale presidential contest. Moreover, the huge staff increases at the DNC left little money to help individual candidates. One survey found that only a few Democrats received financial assistance or fund-raising help from the DNC.[16] Finally, the DNC-directed voter registration drive was an expensive flop.

New Technologies in the Information Age

One of the recurring themes in the history of American parties is that they have been willing to change their modes of operation as conditions dictate. It is no wonder then that both parties have moved full steam ahead into the technological age.

Just as the Republicans proved adept at harnessing the power of television advertising in the 1950s, and direct mail technology in the 1980s, they took an early lead over the Democrats in the use of cable television and the Internet in the 1990s. During the 1996 election season the RNC homepage received 75,000 hits a day. Republicans used the Internet to broadcast immediate responses to Bill Clinton's State of the Union address in 1997, and the RNC chair holds regular on-line chats. An e-mail list allows visitors to the RNC homepage to sign up to have the latest press releases sent directly to them on-line. The RNC homepage also offers updates on topical issues, television links, a "Café" for chats with other site visitors, listings of various campaign seminars and software, and "Tools," which allows visitors to download many RNC features. The homepage is so sophisticated and user-friendly, *USA Today* recently ranked it second only to the Disney site (see Figure 4.1). Republicans have landed feet first in the Information Age.

In addition to the World Wide Web, parties and satellite television technologies have become crucial Information Age partners. In 1997, the RNC produced and broadcast *Rising Tide*, which featured segments called "Insider Hotline," "GOP News," "Rising Stars," and "Under the Dome," a reference to Republican-led activities in Congress. With the aid of satellite technology, the program was broadcast live each week and took telephone calls from viewers. Scores of Republican organizations, including College Republicans, Young Republicans, and local Republican women's groups planned their meetings around broadcasts of *Rising Tide*. The cable show had a potential audience of 55 million households in 1997. Today, RNC broadcast facilities are used to disseminate daily fifteen-minute news feeds to local television stations. Often, Republican members of Congress line up for interviews with television reporters outside the Capitol, which are transmitted to their home districts via satellite. Each year nearly 1,500 such interviews were conducted.

Once again, Democrats are playing catch-up, although there are signs that they have narrowed the technology gap. In 1996, the DNC's Web site received 50,000 hits per day. One year later, the DNC updated its homepage to include a user survey, volunteer sign-up sheet, and a help page that downloads voter registration forms from the Federal Election Commission. Visitors can access daily news briefings and links to other state and local Democratic Party organizations (see Figure 4.2). Unlike Republicans, Democrats have relied more heavily on fax machines, using them to issue a morning briefing to over 2,500 individuals, including party leaders, elected officials, and grassroots activists. As for satellite press conferences and video teleconferences, they hold them only occasionally. As one former DNC press secretary said, "What is the value of reaching people you are already reaching?" Others have suggested that these technologies are essential, but remain out of the party's financial reach—at least for the time being.

Summary

The real story of this chapter is not which party has done a better job at fund-raising, restructuring, or developing new technologies, but what these changes suggest about the nature of contemporary politics. The reconfiguration of the national party committees is significant because it represents a shift of power away from

FIGURE 4.1 ▪ The Republican National Committee Web site contains topical press releases and encourages cyberspace volunteers to join the GOP.

states and localities toward Washington, D.C. Today, both national committees resemble large corporations with long-term staff members, clear lines of authority, and bureaucratic decision-making procedures—quite a departure from the way these organizations have historically operated. Once they were a string of semiautonomous, fragmented units comprising the national committee, fifty state

FIGURE 4.2 ▪ **The Democratic National Committee Web site gives the party's point of view on contemporary issues and contains links to the sites of its 2000 presidential candidates, Al Gore and Bill Bradley.**

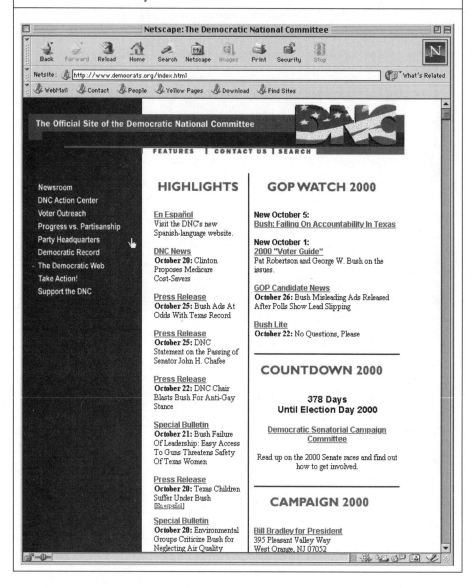

committees, and various local organizations and clubs. State parties were akin to mom-and-pop stores where the party faithful could gather and sample the local product. All that has changed, as state parties operate as franchise dealerships for the larger parent party corporation. The Democratic and Republican national committees operate in a Hamilton-like fashion—as strong, centralized leaders with greater control over the state parties than at any time in history. The Jeffersonian approach to party governance, with its deference to localism, seems anchored in the past.

THE EMERGENCE OF LEGISLATIVE CAMPAIGN COMMITTEES

But there is more to the story of party institutionalization than the growth of the national party committees. Another important development has been the creation of branch organizations designed to finance and manage legislative contests. At the national level, these organizations are called the **hill committees** because of their origins within the halls of Congress. There are four units, one for each party in each house of Congress: The **Democratic Congressional Campaign Committee (DCCC)**, the **Democratic Senatorial Campaign Committee (DSCC)**, the **National Republican Congressional Committee (NRCC)**, and the **National Republican Senatorial Committee (NRSC)**. Forty states now boast similar organizations, dubbed **legislative campaign committees (LCCs)**. In Illinois, for example, there is the Illinois House Republican Campaign Committee, the Illinois Republican State Senate Campaign Committee, the Illinois Democratic Majority Committee, and the Illinois Committee to Elect a Democratic Senate.

Each of these new organizations consists of elected members serving in the corresponding house of the legislature. They hire professional staffs to oversee campaign efforts—paying particular attention to those members seeking reelection, those contesting open seats, and competitive challengers. These legislative campaign committees are office and level-specific: House organizations help House candidates; Senate organizations aid only Senate candidates.

Few organizational developments have had a greater impact on parties than the ascendance of LCCs. They epitomize the merger of high technology, candidate-centered elections, and centralization into a single political unit. Because there are modest differences between state and national organizations, a brief review of each follows. In each case, however, important questions remain. To what extent have these committees transformed party politics? And at what cost?

The Hill Committees

The first congressional campaign committees emerged in the House of Representatives in 1866. During that year a struggle ensued between Andrew Johnson, who became president after Lincoln's assassination, and the Radical Republicans, most of whom were from the Northeast. Johnson, a Tennessean, was hesitant to support many of the policies espoused by the radicals, especially bills seeking reprisals against the South following the Civil War. Johnson opposed legislation that would have helped former slaves—including passage of the Fourteenth Amendment and the establishment of the Freedmen's Bureau. Because Johnson controlled the RNC by virtue of his holding the presidency, Radical Republicans feared political reprisals. They retaliated by establishing the NRCC. Not to be outdone, a group of pro-Johnson Democrats created the DCCC. Senators had little need for these legislative party organizations until the Seventeenth Amendment passed in 1913 instituting direct election of senators. Shortly thereafter, Senate campaign committees were established by both parties.

Until the 1970s, they were seemingly unimportant players, often serving merely as fund-raising apparatuses for incumbents to collect money in Washington and channel it back to local districts. No professional staff or permanent headquarters existed for these "poor sisters" in the party hierarchy. All that began to change in the 1960s, as the cost of campaigning began to escalate, television came to play an important role, and partisan loyalties weakened. Incumbents felt they could no longer take their victories on election day for granted. Their fears increased as progressive reformers stripped local parties of much of their patronage, with the result that fewer volunteers showed up at party headquarters. Accordingly, members of Congress turned to the congressional campaign committees for help. Once again, Republicans were the first innovators. Taking their lead from Bill Brock, the Senate and House Republican campaign committees devised extensive direct mail programs. Other "inside the Beltway" fund-raising schemes were pursued, including holding extravagant dinner parties in Washington, D.C. The result was an avalanche of cash. NRCC receipts quintupled from nearly $12 million in 1978 to $58 million in 1984. The NRSC posted an even greater gain, with receipts ballooning from $2 million in 1978 to $82 million in 1984. By the late 1990s, combined receipts for both GOP hill committees approached the $200 million mark.

Democrats followed a similar path. After losing the Senate in 1980 and seeing their majority wither away in the House, sweeping reforms were instituted. Under the aggressive leadership of California Representative Tony Coelho, the DCCC implemented scores of new fund-raising programs. Coelho made it a practice to visit hundreds of business and trade associations asking for contributions. According to Representative Barney Frank, "Tony Coelho was very good at explaining the fact of life to PACs: if you want to talk to us later, you had better help us now."[17] Thanks to these strong-arm tactics, DCCC receipts jumped from less than $3 million in 1980 to $10.4 million four years later. The DSCC also saw their war chest expand.

With both the Democratic and Republican hill committees awash in cash, they began spending on professional campaign managers and strategists, holding training seminars, and compiling computerized data to target voters. Today, the Republican congressional organizations conduct frequent in-house polling, while Democrats have forged agreements with private survey research firms that assist their candidates at bargain prices. Both parties have assembled vast files of opposition research on their opponents that is circulated to candidates and media outlets in targeted districts. The hill committees also issue briefings on local, state, and national issues to would-be candidates. Their national headquarters are outfitted with state-of-the-art radio and television facilities that can generate generic advertisements which are easily customized to specific localities. Candidates also receive help from professional event coordinators, who prepare them for large galas and rallies. Just about anything needed to run Information Age campaigns in the 1990s is provided for by the hill committees.

Services are one thing, but as California State Treasurer Jesse Unruh said many years ago, "Money is the mother's milk of politics." Here, too, the hill committees provide immeasurable assistance. Under existing law, House candidates can receive $5,000 per primary, runoff, and general election campaign from their respective party's hill committee, and Senate candidates can obtain $17,500. But such restrictions have proven meaningless as the various hill committees spend considerably larger sums on behalf of individual candidates. These **coordinated expenditures** are made in conjunction with a candidate's campaign. Typically, these expenditures are payments for services that candidates would have to otherwise purchase, such as polling or producing television advertisements. The amounts allowed currently total about $30,000 for House races and $60,000 for Senate contests in the smallest-populated state to $1.3 million for a Senate race in California, the largest state. Because hill committees have a vast array of in-house staff, facilities, and equipment (such as computers, print presses, and editing rooms), the itemized contribution per service rendered is small, but coordinated expenditures have allowed them to become modern-day political powerhouses.

Perhaps the biggest asset the hill committees bring to the fund-raising table is what has been termed their brokerage role—meaning that they serve as intermediaries between special interest groups and needy candidates. At meet-and-greet events, often organized in Washington, D.C., congresspersons and heads of PACs commingle. Like a blind date, the goal is to help candidates hit it off with the PAC representatives. To aid in this process, hill committees provide candidates with "PAC kits," which are tailored appeals to potential contributors. Afterwards, representatives from the congressional campaign committees spend hours on the telephone convincing would-be potential donors that their candidates stand a good chance of winning and will not forget their friends after election day. Finally, the hill committees send reams of data to the editors of the *Cook Political Report* and the *Rothenberg Political Report*—important newsletters that handicap individual congressional races and are closely read by political operatives. If it is reported that a particular challenger has a good or even fair, chance of winning, interest groups take notice and start sending checks. Poor notices in these newsletters are often the death knell for candidates, as contributions dry up and hapless challengers stand no chance of getting their messages out (see "The Parties Speak: Congressman David Price on the Role of Party in Campaigns").

Not every candidate benefits from the inner workings of the hill committees. While they are influential in close races, since even a marginal effort may make a difference, nonendangered incumbents often receive little or no help. Likewise, challengers with little or no chance of winning are left to their own devices. If the hill committee will not help, interest groups won't either. As one would-be congressional candidate described his first encounter with the DCCC: "All they did was show me a list of PACs and then tell me that the PACs wouldn't talk to me until I was the designated candidate. They promised me nothing. I could count on no help from them at all."[18]

The Parties Speak: *Congressman David Price on the Role of Party in Campaigns*

David Price first won his House seat in 1986 as a Democrat representing North Carolina's Research Triangle. He continued to represent the district until 1994 when he lost a close race to Republican Fred Heinemann. He recaptured the seat in 1996 and has maintained it ever since.

As a candidate for Congress, I had unusually strong party credentials. I had paid my dues through local party service and as a foot soldier in other Democrats' campaigns. My service as executive director and chairman of the North Carolina Democratic Party was the main factor giving me credibility as a congressional candidate. I chose the county Democratic conventions in my district—held simultaneously on April 13, 1985—to announce my candidacy. I did then and still do regard party activists as an essential core of my political base. After surviving the primary, I received substantial support from the Democratic Congressional Campaign Committee (DCCC) and integrated my grassroots campaign with that of county party organizations. My campaigns thus illustrate the role party can still play. But they also demonstrate the limits of that role, even when a candidate has an inclination (which many candidates do not) to run as part of the party team. . . .

I called on DCCC leaders during the primary season, knowing that a direct contribution was out of the question but hoping to convince them that I would be a strong, perhaps the best, general election candidate, so that they might informally pass the word to potential contributors that I was a good prospect. This happened only to a very limited degree. The fact is that the Democratic party nomination was not within the power of local, state, or national party organizations to deliver. I and my fledgling campaign team, including many active local Democrats, were largely on our own in pursuing it.

That changed some, but not entirely, after the primary. The DCCC was targeting four Democratic challengers in North Carolina in 1986—three of us attempting to regain seats that had been lost in 1984 and a fourth, D. G. Martin, trying again for the Charlotte seat he had failed to win by only 321 votes in 1984. Tony Coelho was an unusually active and aggressive DCCC chairman, greatly stepping up fund-raising activity and moving from the DCCC's natural tendency simply to shore up incumbents to a strategy of targeting those races where an infusion of funds could have the greatest impact. Martin's Charlotte race, where Coelho strongly disagreed with some of the tactics the candidate was adopting, showed how intrusive the chairman and his aides could be, using their financial support as leverage to try to move the campaign in certain directions. The DCCC leadership apparently had no such problems with my campaign, although we had many quibbles along the way. The committee contributed $39,848 to my campaign which, when added to the state tax checkoff monies funneled through the state Democratic Party, came close to the legal maximum. . . .

While my campaign evinced relatively strong participation by both the national campaign committee and local party organizations, it could not, when compared either to parliamentary elections in other western democracies or earlier American practice, be judged a party-centered campaign. We gained numerous foot soldiers and saved scarce campaign dollars by combining forces with other Democratic candidates in our canvassing and turnout operations. But even here we gave as much as we got; party precinct structures were spotty at best, and the cadres of volunteers often needed shoring up. So activists from the Price campaign helped make the party efforts work, as well as the reverse.

SOURCE: Excerpted from John Kenneth White and Jerome M. Mileur, eds., *Challenges to Party Government* (Carbondale: Southern Illinois University Press, 1992), 139, 140.

State Legislative Campaign Committees

State legislative campaign committees have been around since the 1970s—first sprouting up in large states like New York, Illinois, Wisconsin, California, Pennsylvania, and Minnesota, and later spreading to forty other states.[19] Like the congressional campaign committees, the heightened costs of state elections and a weakening of partisan ties have prompted the proliferation of state legislative party committees. They, too, dispense much-needed funds and provide state-of-the-art services, often concentrating their resources on close contests. Because most states do not limit campaign contributions, the result has been the transfer of considerable sums of cash from the state legislative campaign committees to a few candidates. In 1986, for example, the California Assembly Democratic Committee spent $589,000 on one Sacramento-area open seat, which accounted for 67 percent of that candidate's budget. That same year, the Indiana House Democratic Caucus gave a candidate $4,500, which totaled 43 percent of his entire account, and he won by five votes. The New York Republican Senate Committee targeted twelve races out of sixty-one in 1992, infusing each with massive resources.[20] In 1996, there were a handful of house races in Ohio where state legislative committee contributions approached the $500,000 mark.[21]

An interesting difference between state-level LCCs and the hill committees is how staff members are paid. Hill committees have large, year-round staffs consisting of full-time professionals. Most state committees do not have these resources, opting instead to call upon state employees who use vacations, sick time, or leaves of absence during election time to work for the legislative committee. By the late 1980s, such practices had become a serious legal problem. In 1987, Democratic operatives in New York were accused of conducting campaign activities on state time. The Democratic Minority Leader of the Senate was indicted on 564 counts of conspiracy, grand larceny, and related charges. One accusation claimed that an LCC employee was paid up to $10,000 per month by the state for conducting campaign activities. State courts dismissed the indictment, saying that while the hiring of legislative employees for campaign work might be unethical, no law prohibited it.[22]

The premier issue surrounding all of these new organizations is how they fit into the party rubric. In the past, most textbooks have placed the national committees at the top of a pyramid-like structure with the congressional and senatorial committees below them as subordinates. Similar characterizations were made for state legislative campaign committees. Today the picture is much more complex. As one former congressional campaign committee director said: "We take our instructions from the chairman and the other congressmen [sic] on the committee. They are selected by party members in the House and are responsible to them, if anyone. While members of the national committee may occasionally consult with the members of the committee, they certainly don't give them orders . . . and they don't tell us what to do either."[23]

Daniel M. Shea recently investigated many of these new organizations, interviewing more than three hundred state and county-level party leaders. He finds that these new entities more closely resemble campaign consulting firms than traditional party organizations. While some state legislative campaign committees work closely with the formal party structures, most do not. Indeed, a growing hostility has developed between local party officials and legislative campaign committees because these new organizations are stripping local parties of their historic functions in running election campaigns (see "The Parties Speak: Party Leaders Voice Concerns about Legislative Campaign Committees").

By 1988, political scientist Walter Dean Burnham maintained that the United States was undergoing a "radical recomposition of the American political system"

The Parties Speak: *Party Leaders Voice Concerns about Legislative Campaign Committees*

The following excerpts are from Transforming Democracy: Legislative Campaign Committees and Political Parties, *a study to discern the emerging relationship between traditional party organizations and state legislative campaign committees. In the spring of 1993, roughly three hundred state and county party leaders were surveyed regarding their interactions with state legislative campaign committees. The responses were varied, but a number noted mounting concerns. Below is a sampling of some of the more disparaging comments:*

- I'd get calls from people—and for that matter the media—and they would ask me about what the campaign was doing. To tell the truth, I really didn't know what was going on. . . . It made me look stupid.
- There were occasions when they will shun the head of the ticket if they believe it will hurt them. In the Dukakis campaign they walked away—in the Clinton campaign they embraced the candidate.
- I don't know of one county committee they have helped.
- [The LCCs] care only about a limited area, and preserving (or enhancing) the power of their leadership. The "party" is but a symbolic umbrella given lip service.
- It is my opinion that [the LCCs] use the county parties only for their best interest—to get to know the people and the lay of the land.
- We felt shut-out. They come here from [the state capital] and do things that might work there, but never listen to what we had to say. If you ask me, that's why we lost the race. . . .

In the face of a rapidly changing social and political order, local party committees have demonstrated surprising resilience. This study, nevertheless, should provide a warning sign. Party organizations, especially at the local level, are key components in our democratic system. Their displacement by myopic, level- and office-specific campaign organizations might bode poorly for popular governance. Among many other notable functions, local committees are one of the last direct, personal links between citizens and elected officials in a highly technical, complex world. Before we rush to congratulate the adaptability of parties, it should be considered what LCCs imply. This may not be the "party" we had in mind.

SOURCE: Excerpted from Daniel M. Shea, *Transforming Democracy: Legislative Campaign Committees and Political Parties* (Albany: State University of New York Press, 1995), 104, 160, 183.

due to the "accelerated decomposition of nominally partisan coalitions across office- and level-specific lines."[24] As voters lessened their party ties and party organizations splintered into scores of autonomous units—each concerned only with electing members to their branch of government— the unifying role once performed by parties was lost. Whereas local parties once controlled most congressional and state legislative races, today's organizations, centered in the state capitals and in Washington, fund and oversee these campaigns. Operatives from national or state headquarters are dispatched into targeted areas, creating a "party presence" of sorts. But this is a far cry from local party activists knocking on doors asking for support of the *entire* party ticket. And when the election is over, the campaign committee technicians leave—maybe to return for the next election, but perhaps not.

WITHER THE LOCAL PARTIES?

Given the growth of national and state campaign committees, have local parties disappeared? At first blush, the answer seems to be yes, but closer examination paints a more complex portrait. In some areas, local party organizations have survived, and even thrived; in other locales they are in serious decline. As the late House Speaker Thomas P. "Tip" O'Neill frequently remarked, "All politics is local." While the nationalization of the parties has made this political maxim less true than it was in O'Neill's time, party activity in local areas shows it still holds a ring of truth. (See Chapter 7 for more about the functions and character of state and local parties.)

Evidence of Local Party Renewal

In 1984, a team of political scientists conducted a comprehensive analysis of state and local party organizations. Their work, the Party Transformation Study (PTS), challenged traditional thinking about local parties and resulted in a small cottage industry to conduct local party studies.[25] The PTS interviewed 7,300 county-level party leaders and examined bushels of documentary evidence. Most local party organizations were found to be organizationally complex, complete with full-time staff and solid operating budgets. They also performed a myriad of tasks, including distributing literature; raising and donating money; publicizing party and candidate activities; and conducting voter registration drives. According to the PTS, the degree of party involvement in local campaigns was higher in the early 1980s than twenty years before. Furthermore, many local parties had ongoing activities during nonelection periods. As the authors of the study concluded, "It is clear that [party] organizations have not withered away and they do not appear to be in any danger of doing so."[26]

The PTS was replicated in 1992 and again in 1994 by political scientists John Frendries and Alan Gitelson. They reached a finding similar to the earlier PTS report: "It is clear that the local parties have not weakened over the last decade and, if anything, they have become slightly stronger."[27] A summary of their findings relating to the structural attributes of local parties is reported in Table 4.1, and data concerning their activity is found in Table 4.2.

TABLE 4.1 ▪ **Structural Attributes of Local Party Organizations, 1980, 1992, and 1994**

Attribute	Percent Republicans 1980	Percent Democrats 1980	Percent Republicans 1992	Percent Democrats 1992	Percent Republicans 1994	Percent Democrats 1994
Has complete set of officers	81	90	92	94	97	94
Chair works at least 6 hours per week (election period)	78	77	82	79	82	78
County committee meets at least bimonthly (election period)	57	59	57	75	72	72
Has constitution, rules, or bylaws	68	68	77	71	80	79
Has formal annual budget	31	20	34	23	39	22
Chair works at least 6 hours per week (non-election period)	26	24	40	34	35	34
County committee meets at least bimonthly (nonelection period)	49	53	58	56	63	60
Has some paid, full-time staff	4	3	4	2	6	3
Has some paid, part-time staff	6	5	8	4	8	4
Chair receives salary	1	2	1	1	2	2
Has year-round office	14	12	21	12	23	15
Has telephone listing	16	11	27	21	30	22
Has campaign headquarters	60	55	59	57	56	56
Maximum *N*	1,872	1,984	330	352	376	351

SOURCE: John Frendries, Alan R. Gitelson, Gregory Flemming, and Anne Ayzell, "Local Parties and Legislative Races in 1992 and 1994," in John C. Green and Daniel M. Shea, eds., *The State of the Parties: The Changing Role of Contemporary American Parties* (Lanham, Md.: Rowman and Littlefield, 1996), 154.

TABLE 4.2 ▪ Campaign Activity Levels of Local Party Organizations, 1980, 1992, and 1994

Direct Campaign Activity	Percent Republicans 1980	Percent Democrats 1980	Percent Republicans 1992	Percent Democrats 1992	Percent Republicans 1994	Percent Democrats 1994
Distributes campaign literature	79	79	88	90	88	88
Arranges fund-raising events	68	71	74	76	77	74
Organizes campaign events	65	68	77	81	81	78
Contributes money to candidates	70	62	75	67	79	68
Organizes telephone campaigns	65	61	58	62	64	57
Buys newspaper ads for party and candidates	62	62	60	65	68	62
Distributes posters or lawn signs	62	59	90	89	90	87
Prepares press releases for party and candidates	55	55	62	65	65	61
Sends mailings to voters	59	47	58	51	61	56
Conducts registration drives	45	56	39	50	39	39
Organizes door-to-door canvassing	48	49	52	55	59	56
Buys radio/TV time for party and candidates	33	33	24	31	25	26
Utilizes public opinion surveys	16	11	15	15	20	12
Purchases billboard space	13	10	9	7	10	5
Coordinates PAC activity	n/a	n/a	4	10	7	8
Conducts get-out-the-vote effort	n/a	n/a	60	70	71	66

continued

TABLE 4.2 ■ Campaign Activity Levels of Local Party Organizations, 1980, 1992, and 1994 *(continued)*

Direct Campaign Activity	*Percent Republicans 1980*	*Percent Democrats 1980*	*Percent Republicans 1992*	*Percent Democrats 1992*	*Percent Republicans 1994*	*Percent Democrats 1994*
"Very" or "somewhat" involved in candidate recruitment:						
a. for city and local offices	45	44	48	42	52	44
b. for county offices	71	69	94	87	92	97
c. for state legislative offices	71	69	94	87	87	78
d. for congressional offices	64	62	69	64	72	65
Makes formal or informal pre-primary endorsements	28	32	31	27	31	31
Maximum *N*	1,872	1,984	330	352	373	347

SOURCE: John Frendries, Alan R. Gitelson, Gregory Flemming, and Anne Ayzell, "Local Parties and Legislative Races in 1992 and 1994," in John C. Green and Daniel M. Shea, eds., *The State of the Parties: The Changing Role of Contemporary American Parties* (Lanham, Md.: Rowman and Littlefield, 1996), 156–57.

Evidence of Local Party Decline

Most claims of a local party resurgence have been overstated. Instead of promoting ideas, parties seem more candidate-centered. Instead of devising a platform, they take a poll. Instead of promoting themselves to skeptical voters, they hire consultants. These things happen because candidates want them to happen. Even in the one area of local party activity left, getting voters to the polls, parties seem to be failing. The decline in voter turnout that began in 1964 has continued virtually unabated in every election year since. Just 48.5 percent of the eligible voters cast a presidential ballot in 1996, the lowest total since 1924. In many state and local areas, the connections between local parties and citizens have all but disappeared. Consider the musings of a college graduate after his 1994 foray into local party politics:

> I'm young, I'm Ivy League educated, and I'm politically disenfranchised. When I graduated from college this past December, I thought I would assume certain social responsibilities. But the conventional American political institutions—namely the political

parties—can't use me. I don't know what gave me the idea that they could. Maybe it was the fact that I graduated in the top 2 percent of my class, or that I won the only award that the political science department gave out for the study of American politics. . . . But it seems that all of my academic achievements were self-indulgent tripe. When I went to the campaign headquarters of a mayoral race, something happened that I never expected: I was dissuaded from getting involved. . . . I was outright rebuffed.[28]

REVIVALISTS VERSUS DECLINISTS

Academic conferences are rarely tumultuous. This was not the case at "The State of the Parties: 1992 and Beyond" conference held at the University of Akron in 1993. The gathering brought together scholars, practitioners, and party activists for two days of haggling over the condition of the American party system. As the event proceeded, two camps quickly formed: revivalists and declinists. Armed with reams of survey data, revivalists argued that party organizations had adapted to life in the 1990s. As one revivalist stated: "Once cast as institutions of 'politics without power' in an increasingly candidate-centered political culture, the national party committees have responded to changes in their environment by expanding their institutional capacities and restructuring their operations to provide the services and resources candidates need in modern elections."[29] Revivalists believed that parties were more active, better funded, adequately staffed, and supplied more services than ever before.

Declinists were not convinced. In a harshly worded counteroffensive entitled "The Resurgence of Party Organizations? A Dissent for the New Orthodoxy," John J. Coleman railed against the revivalists' logic. He argued that recent party research had been shortsighted and misdirected. His arguments are summarized below:

- "Despite peculiarities in the data, the case that party organizations are performing more activities and raising more funds today is a strong one. But the party organization literature has leapt too quickly to words like *resurgence* and *revitalization*. Increased activity should only be the start of a conception of resurgent parties. That conception also needs to account for the party organization's relations with other actors and institutions in the political universe."
- "One striking anomaly in the contemporary party system is that scholars argue party organizations are reviving while the public has become increasingly skeptical about the relevance of political parties to governing. More citizens say that interest groups better represent them than do parties, particularly the young."
- "The new orthodoxy is generally very positive about party efforts to raise and distribute campaign funds. Other studies raise troubling questions about their reliance on large sums of money from special interests. The implicit stance of organization theories is that a party's *ability* to raise money is more significant than the *effects* of this reliance on massive fundraising."

- "Another normative issue concerns voter turnout. A party system correctly labeled resurgent or revitalized would not be one that witnesses sustained declining participation."
- "As party organizations claim increasing involvement in the strategy and conduct of campaigns, and acting as intermediaries between candidates and private market campaign services, they should be judged on the quality of these campaigns. In fact, campaigns have become shrill, uninformative, diverse, and unrelated to the real tasks of governance. Are the resurgent party organizations helping corrode the discourse of American campaigns?"[30]

Others joined Coleman's assault, comparing parties to a failing business. After all, they argued, if things are going so well, why are there so few customers? Although parties have new marketing schemes, these hardly matter if there are no new customers. The conference ended with little consensus about the "state of the parties." Since then, debates over the health of the party system have continued, and any conclusions reached are tentative at best. There are telltale signs of new party life—even as parties themselves are morphed into new and wholly different creatures than those we have been comfortable with in the past.

Two reasons explain why finding a consensus on the well-being of the American party system is difficult. First, the changes that have enveloped U.S. politics confound simple notions of party resurgence or decline. During most of the life of the parties, communications between politicians and citizens was either through word-of-mouth or in the local newspapers. With their legions of volunteers, parties were well-suited to carry out this vital communications function. In the Information Age, television remains the principal intermediary between the governed and the governors. If the parties have abandoned their labor-intensive activities for a thirty-second television advertisement, is that evidence of decline or simply smart thinking? Is it reasonable to expect voters to form personal allegiances to parties when they are inundated with appeals from hundreds of interest groups? During the heyday of party activity, social events sponsored by local organizations were well attended. But today most Americans are watching television or increasingly connecting to the Internet. What standard should be used to measure the extent and quality of civic involvement? As we enter a new century, family patterns, economic structures, and forms of entertainment, transportation, and communications are rapidly changing.

Second, there is considerable discord over the components that comprise a political party. Ever since the party-in-government (PIG), party-in-the-electorate (PIE), parties-as-organizations (PO) tripod was developed in the 1940s, students of parties have thought of these structures as interconnected. Failure of one leg of the tripod would, inevitably, hurt all others. If we adhere to this concept of parties, most would agree that they are in decline because one of the legs—the party-in-the-electorate—is withering. But seeing the model as interconnected is a mistake. Some parts do thrive, even as others suffer. Moreover, perhaps a fourth leg needs to be added: the "party-in-the-campaign." Although parties may be losing voters, they are making up for that loss by providing new and expanded services to candidates.

Whatever one's diagnosis about the state of the parties' health, there is little doubt that those who adhere to the Hamiltonian model generally would be pleased with their current condition. The new party elites, most of them centered in Washington, D.C., wield more authority than their predecessors. Their smooth, well-financed operations staffed with full-time professionals provide a glimpse of the future. Products of their time, the national party committees use all available Information Age resources to decide who gets help and in what form. State and local party organizations follow the leads of their national sisters for no other reason than those entities control the purse strings. To be sure, the local autonomy of these former mom-and-pop stores is lost. But the local leaders are well-supplied by the parent organizations, so few complain. And since the average voter no longer has a personal attachment to a party, parties are doing the only thing they can: providing technical expertise to their candidates.

From a Jeffersonian perspective, the picture is less commendable. Jeffersonians believe parties are essentially local institutions, paying due deference to local concerns. Historically, that has been the case—often a necessary by-product in a country as diverse as the United States. Absent strong national party organizations, partisanship mattered in local politics and lines of accountability were sharply drawn. If the ruling party was judged a failure, it was jettisoned from office and the opposition was given a chance. Candidates had less autonomy, but this created a sense that the official "belonged" to the folks in the district. Little of this remains. Local parties exist, but often they take their cues from state and national committees. They may have larger offices, better equipment, heftier budgets, and provide more services, but they arouse few passions. They may have adopted to the Information Age, but have lost their relevance as articulate spokespersons for traditional party values.

CONCLUSION

This chapter concludes our discussion of the history of American political parties. What role parties will play in the next century is open to debate. Drastic changes in what parties do and how they do it are inevitable in the Information Age. Some applaud the parties' newfound capacity for financing and orchestrating elections, and for their highly bureaucratic structures; others lament it saying that parties damage the quality of democratic institutions. Politics is best carried out at the community level where ordinary citizens often find it convenient to join a local interest group to articulate their concerns. Today's bureaucratic parties are not well-suited for this kind of town hall politics. Parties still show signs of life, but the challenge in the twenty-first century will be to integrate their technological skills with powerful ideas that enervate our democracy.

FURTHER READING

Aldrich, John H. *Why Parties: The Origin and Transformation of Political Parties in America.* Chicago: University of Chicago Press, 1995.

Herrnson, Paul S. *Party Campaigning in the 1980s.* Cambridge: Harvard University Press, 1988.

Kayden, Xandra and Eddie Mahe, Jr. *The Party Goes On: The Persistence of the Two-Party System in the United States.* New York: Basic Books, 1985.

Klinkner, Philip A. *The Losing Parties: Out-Party National Committees, 1956–1993.* New Haven: Yale University Press, 1994.

Schlesinger, Joseph A. *Political Parties and the Winning of Office.* Ann Arbor: University of Michigan Press, 1991.

Shea, Daniel M. *Transforming Democracy: Legislative Campaign Committees and Political Parties.* Albany: State University of New York Press, 1995.

Shea, Daniel M. and John C. Green, eds. *The State of the Parties: The Changing Role of Contemporary Party Organizations.* Lanham, Md.: Rowman and Littlefield, 1995.

NOTES

1. See Dick Morris, *Behind the Oval Office: Winning the Presidency in the Nineties* (New York: Random House, 1997), 139. Issue advocacy advertisements are sponsored by the national parties. They are not officially endorsed by the candidate and they do not ask voters to support a particular candidate, but the inference is clear.

2. Quoted in Warren P. Strobel, "President Improves on His 1992 Showing," *Washington Times,* November 6, 1996, A1.

3. David S. Broder, *The Party's Over* (New York: Harper & Row, 1972); Martin P. Wattenberg, *The Decline of American Political Parties* (Cambridge: Harvard University Press, 1996); John J. Coleman, *Party Decline in America* (Princeton, N.J.: Princeton University Press, 1996).

4. David S. Broder, "Politics Without Parties," *Washington Post,* January 5, 1993.

5. Xandra Kayden and Eddie Mahe, Jr. *The Party Goes On* (New York: Basic Books, 1985); Larry J. Sabato, *The Party's Just Begun* (Glenview, Ill.: Scott, Foresman/Little, Brown, 1988); Gerald M. Pomper, *Party Renewal in America* (New York: Praeger, 1980); L. Sandy Maisel, *The Parties Respond* (Boulder, Colo.: Westview Press, 1997).

6. There are scores of works along these lines, the most famous being Seymour Martin Lipset and Stein Rokkan, *Party Systems and Voter Alignments* (New York: Free Press, 1967).

7. Robert Merton, *Social Theory and Social Structure* (New York: Free Press, 1968) and John H. Aldrich, *Why Parties: The Origin and Transformation of Political Parties in America* (Chicago: University of Chicago Press, 1995).

8. Interview with Don Roch, October 22, 1979, Providence, Rhode Island. Cited in John Kenneth White, *The Fractured Electorate: Political Parties and Social Change in Southern New England* (Hanover, N.H.: University Press of New England, 1983), 79.

9. Philip A. Klinkner, *The Losing Parties: Out-Party National Committees, 1956–1993* (New Haven: Yale University Press, 1994), 39.

10. Ibid., 144.

11. A. James Reichley, *The Life of the Parties: A History of American Political Parties* (New York: Free Press, 1992), 356.

12. John F. Bibby, "Party Renewal in the National Republican Party," in Gerald M. Pomper, ed., *Party Renewal in America: Theory and Practice* (New York: Praeger, 1980), 113.

13. Anne Campbell quoted in Klinkner, *The Losing Parties,* 157.

14. See Paul S. Herrnson, *Party Campaigning in the 1980s* (Cambridge: Harvard University Press, 1988), 37.

15. Ibid., 32–34.

16. Klinkner, *Losing Parties,* 177.

17. Quoted in Reichley, *The Life of the Parties,* 365.

18. Linda L. Fowler and Robert D. McClure, *Political Ambition: Who Decides to Run for Congress* (New Haven: Yale University Press, 1989), 37.

19. Daniel M. Shea, *Transforming Democracy: Legislative Campaign Committees and Poltical Parties* (Albany: State University of New York Press, 1995), 18.

20. Anthony Gierzynski, *Legislative Party Campaign Committees in the American States* (Lexington: University Press of Kentucky, 1992), 73, 90.

21. Shea, *Transforming Democracy*, 27.

22. Ibid., 24–25.

23. Herrnson, *Party Campaigning in the 1980s*, 40.

24. Walter Dean Burnham, "The Reagan Heritage," in Gerald M. Pomper, ed., *The Election of 1988* (Chatham, N.J.: Chatham House, 1989).

25. This team included Cornelius P. Cotter, James L. Gibson, John F. Bibby, and Robert J. Huckshorn, and their first full-length publication from the analysis was *Party Organizations in American Politics* (New York: Praeger, 1984).

26. Ibid., 57–58.

27. John P. Frendries, Alan R. Gitelson, Gregory Flemming and Anne Ayzell, "Local Political Parties and Legislative Races in 1992 and 1994," in Green and Shea, *The State of the Parties*, 153.

28. Mark V. Ferraro, "Where's the Party," *Humanist* (March/April, 1996), 4.

29. Articles presented at the conference were compiled in Shea and Green, *The State of the Parties*. This particular quotation comes from Anthony Corrado's chapter entitled "The Politics of Cohesion: The Role of the National Party Committees in the 1992 Election," 61.

30. John J. Coleman, "The Resurgence of Party Organizations?," in Shea and Green, *The State of the Parties*, 313.

CHAPTER 5

Nominating Presidents in the Information Age

In 1962, President John F. Kennedy was asked by a reporter: "Somewhere in our land today there is a high school or college student who will one day be sitting in your chair. If you could speak to this future president, what advice and guidance would you give him or her?" Kennedy wisely replied, "It will help you to know the country you seek to lead," adding: "If you find the opportunity to know and work with Americans of diverse backgrounds, occupations and beliefs, then I would urge you to take eagerly that opportunity to enrich yourself." Kennedy also advised his successor to see the world since "the future of your own country is bound to your capacity to exercise leadership and judgment on a global scale."[1]

More than three decades later most Americans agree with Kennedy, but they have added even more qualifications to his list. These include some prior executive experience (such as serving as a governor or mayor), sound character, and effective advocacy of policies that are in the "public interest." But how to devise a presidential selection process that elevates such distinctive individuals to high office remains a mystery. For much of the past quarter century, many would-be presidents have bemoaned the fact that to be a successful candidate one must foreswear any other occupation, abandon one's family, and devote nearly every waking hour to seeking the office. In 1974, Walter Mondale appeared at a Johnstown, Pennsylvania, labor hall to test his potential 1976 presidential candidacy among a group of likely supporters. After a stem-winder, Mondale sank into a floral couch at a local motel and wondered aloud: "Hell of a way to make a living, isn't it?"[2] Indeed it is.

WHAT KIND OF PRESIDENT?

During the twentieth century, the presidency has survived two world wars, the Great Depression, and the Cold War. Americans have considerable pride in the institution of the presidency, but have an extremely low regard for how would-be presidents are chosen. According to a 1997 survey, 57 percent said they were "dissatisfied" with the way the political system is working. One reason for the profound public unhappiness is that it takes a vast amount of time, money, and energy to become president. Ever since Jimmy Carter won in 1976, those who have entered the White House have checked presidential aspirant as their primary occupation. Carter announced his candidacy on December 12, 1974, and for the next two years he and his family hit the road five days a week. Despite his limited credentials (at least according to the standards set by John F. Kennedy)—limited travel at home and abroad, no Washington experience, a relative unknown nationally, and a single term as Governor of Georgia—Carter promised: "I'll be good. You wait and see. I'll be damned good."[3] Yet shortly after his election victory, Carter admitted: "People say they don't know me. Well, I understand that. I really do, but I don't know how else to explain. I've tried, and I've tried hard. I've spent two years now trying to let people get to know me. I don't know what else I can do. I guess it's just one of those things. If they don't know me by now—well, I don't know, I just don't know."[4] Though he spent two years tenaciously running for president, "Iron Ass Jimmy" (Vice President Walter Mondale's nickname for Carter[5]) had few followers—even within his own party. That, coupled with rampant inflation and the Iran hostage crisis, ensured Carter's defeat in 1980.

Ronald Reagan emulated Carter by campaigning full-time for the presidency from 1976 to 1980. From southern California, Reagan took to the airwaves with a series of radio commentaries denouncing the Carter administration. Dressed in his neatly pressed suit, handkerchief just visible above the breast pocket, and polished shoes, Reagan was the perfect salesman. Having once hawked "twenty mule team Borax" (a soap powder) for the sponsor of television's *Death Valley Days,* in 1980 Reagan found himself pitching a much more personal commodity: himself. Reagan brought his unique sales abilities to politics with enormous success—first as a two-time governor of California and later as president.

Like Carter and Reagan, Bill Clinton's presidential ambitions long predated his 1992 campaign. Back in 1963, the young Arkansan shook hands with John F. Kennedy—an encounter that Clinton's mother believed lit the fires of ambition within her son. Nearly twenty years after that handshake, Clinton told Texas Democratic Party activist Billie Carr: "As soon as I get out of school, I'm movin' back to Arkansas. I love Arkansas. I'm going back there to live. I'm gonna run for office there. And someday I'm gonna be governor. And then one day I'll be callin' ya, Billie, and tellin' ya I'm running for president and I need your help."[6] Clinton biographer David Maraniss writes that the expectation and will to be president was always there "and it had built up year by year, decade by decade," climaxing in his 1992 victory.[7]

Besides those who list presidential candidate on a job application, vice presidents have been especially successful players in the nomination game. With the notable exceptions of Spiro Agnew, Nelson Rockefeller, and Dan Quayle, six of the last nine vice presidents have won their party's presidential nominations: Richard M. Nixon, 1960; Lyndon B. Johnson, 1964; Hubert H. Humphrey, 1968; Gerald R. Ford, 1976; Walter F. Mondale, 1984; and George Bush, 1988. Vice President Al Gore hopes to follow in their footsteps in 2000. One reason these men have captured their party's nod is that (with the exception of Gore) they were underutilized. A vice president's sole constitutional responsibility is to preside over the U.S. Senate and cast a vote in case of a tie. The Framers of the Constitution were reluctant to grant even this minimal duty, but relented when delegate Roger Sherman noted that without it, the vice president would be "without employment."[8]

To limit prospective presidents to otherwise unemployed men (and soon to be women) and standby vice presidents, excludes those who might be good chief executives but lack the time, money, or determination today's presidential selection system requires, including a willingness to cede all privacy to inquiring reporters. In 1988, after realizing the toll a presidential candidacy would take on their time and private lives, several prominent Democrats bowed out. Cynical journalists dubbed the remaining contenders, including nominee Michael Dukakis and his principal opponent Jesse Jackson, "the seven dwarfs." Four years later, more leading Democrats removed their names from contention—including New York Governor Mario Cuomo, New Jersey Senator Bill Bradley, West Virginia Senator Jay Rockefeller, and Jesse Jackson. Arkansas Governor Bill Clinton, who otherwise held a full-time job, entered the race partly because his state legislature has the distinction of meeting only once every two years (and the legislature was out of session in 1992).

A lack of qualified candidates is not just a Democratic problem. In 1996 and again in 2000, retired General Colin Powell shied away from a presidential candidacy because he lacked the dedication, organization, and money needed to make a serious bid. Likewise, Bob Dole had to make a hard choice in 1996. In 1988, Dole had tried to divide his time between his pressing Senate leadership duties and campaigning for the presidency. Dole lost to Vice President Bush in New Hampshire and soon exited the race. Eight years later Dole vowed not to repeat his mistake, concluding that he could not run for president and serve as Senate majority leader. Day after day during the Republican primaries, Senate Democrats tied Dole in one legislative knot after another. Dole, tired of the wrangling, told his staff, "If I'm going to run for president, I'm going to run for president."[9] With that, Dole ended his thirty-six year congressional career.

As Dole's dilemma indicates, time is a precious resource for would-be presidents. In the Information Age, most successful candidates require more than one attempt at a formal candidacy before succeeding. Bob Dole, for example, won the 1996 Republican nomination on his third try. Vice President Al Gore sought the Democratic nomination in 1988, an experience that has better prepared him to be a successful candidate in 2000. Second- and third-time candidates have a greater degree of public recognition than most unknown, first-time candidates. Thus, first-timers must invest vast quantities of time in order to introduce themselves to the party faithful. For example, in 1996, Lamar Alexander, a former Tennessee governor and secretary of education during the Bush administration, sought the Republican presidential nomination. Even though Alexander had long been active in GOP circles, most of the party's rank-and-file did not know him. To compensate for his lack of recognition, Alexander hit the campaign circuit—traveling around the country to introduce himself to the party faithful (see Table 5.1). Despite a back-breaking pace, Alexander finished third in the New Hampshire primary and was eliminated from contention.

Difficulties with the presidential selection process are nothing new. Since its inception, the United States has had no consistent method for choosing its presidents. This failure to devise a selection system that recognizes the national character of the presidency, yet provides some role for states and localities, has enormous

TABLE 5.1 ▪ Schedule of Lamar Alexander's Invisible Primary Campaign, February 6, 1993-June 24, 1994

Date	Event
February 6, 1993	Knox County, Tennessee, GOP dinner in Knoxville
February 8	Carter County, Tennessee, GOP dinner
February 19	Hudson Institute dinner in Indianapolis, Indiana
February 20	Shelby County, Tennessee, GOP dinner in Memphis
February 23	School visits in Akron, Ohio
March 6	Louisiana Women's GOP convention in New Orleans
March 8	GOP Lincoln Day dinner in Cleveland, Ohio
March 9	GOP Lincoln Day dinner in Albany, New York
March 12	President's dinner in Washington, D.C.
March 19	GOP National Congressional Campaign Committee breakfast in Palm Springs, California
March 30	Tarrant County GOP dinner in Fort Worth, Texas
April 16	Arkansas GOP dinner in Little Rock
April 26	Free Congress Foundation anniversary in Washington, D.C.
May 7	Southern GOP Exchange Conference in Louisville, Kentucky
May 9	William Penn commencement in Des Moines, Iowa
June 1	Republican neighborhood meeting in Milwaukee, Wisconsin
June 12	Pachyderm dinner in St. Louis, Missouri
June 18	Iowa Association of Business and Industry in Spencer, Iowa
June 19	Utah State GOP convention in Salt Lake City
June 24	CNN interview in Washington, D.C.
June 26	Young Republican convention in Charleston, West Virginia
June 26	*National Review* conference in Washington, D.C.
July 6	Republican neighborhood meeting in San Antonio, Texas
July 16	College Republican conference in Washington, D.C.
July 21	President's dinner, honoring Ronald Reagan, in Los Angeles
July 22	Republican National Committee dinner in Los Angeles
July 28	National Conference of State Legislators convention in San Diego
August 3	Republican neighborhood meeting in Orlando, Florida
August 10	Rochester-Buffalo tour with Congressman Bill Paxon of New York
August 18	Bull Moose Club of Des Moines, Iowa
August 21	Louisiana State GOP convention in New Orleans
August 28	Rhode Island GOP dinner in Newport
September 7	Republican neighborhood meeting in Springfield, Illinois
September 10	Campaigning for Republicans in Virginia
September 17	Ashbrook Center dinner in Ashland, Ohio
September 20	School Choice Initiative events in San Diego
September 25	National Federation of Republican Women conference in Las Vegas
October 1	Southern GOP Exchange in New Orleans
October 7	Alliance for Better Schools in Washington, D.C.
October 15	Western states leadership conference in Santa Fe, New Mexico
October 20	Board of Home Builders and Realtors in Akron, Ohio

continued

TABLE 5.1 ▪ Schedule of Lamar Alexander's Invisible Primary Campaign, February 6, 1993–June 24, 1994 *(continued)*

Date	Event
October 22	Alabama GOP Women's dinner in Birmingham
October 23	Tennessee GOP Women's lunch in Chattanooga
October 26	Sioux County GOP dinner in Sioux Center, Iowa
October 28	Public forum in Springfield, Massachusetts
November 2	Republican neighborhood meeting in Des Moines, Iowa
November 3	School Choice roundtable in Lansing, Michigan
November 5	New Hampshire State GOP dinner in Bedford
November 6	New Hampshire GOP town meetings in Derry, Rochester, and Dover; meetings with students and faculty at the University of New Hampshire
November 9	Dallas GOP forum in Dallas, Texas
November 20	Richmond forum in Richmond, Virginia
January 20, 1994	Nixon inaugural anniversary in Yorba Linda, California
February 3	Team 100 dinner in Washington, D.C.
February 8	Republican neighborhood meeting in San Francisco
February 11	Lincoln Day lunch in Springfield, Illinois
February 12	C-PAC meeting in Washington, D.C.
February 15	Lincoln Day dinner in Lake View, Iowa
February 16	*Larry King Live* interview in Washington, D.C.
March 5	Cobb County GOP breakfast in Atlanta, Georgia
March 8	Republican neighborhood meeting in Atlanta
March 16	New Hampshire Board of Education in Durham
March 21	New Castle Chamber dinner in Wilmington, Delaware
March 22	Don Sundquist campaign dinner in Memphis, Tennessee
March 29	Taft lunch in Cleveland, Ohio
March 29	Hudson dinner in Indianapolis, Indiana
March 30	Citizen's Insurance Symposium in Lansing, Michigan
April 6	Education forum in Augusta, Maine
April 7	WMUR-TV interview in Manchester, New Hampshire
April 11	Catholic Archdiocese in Louisville, Kentucky
April 12	Republican neighborhood meeting in Bedford, New Hampshire
April 16	Lincoln Day dinner in Portsmouth, New Hampshire
April 28	Lincoln Day dinner in Murfreesboro, Tennessee
April 30	Southern GOP leadership conference in Atlanta
May 4	Middlesex GOP Club dinner in Boston
May 10	Republican neighborhood meeting in Grand Rapids, Michigan
May 18	McKinley Day dinner in Akron, Ohio
May 21	Warren County GOP dinner in Carlisle, Iowa
June 24	Iowa State GOP convention and straw poll in Des Moines

SOURCE: Emmett H. Buell, Jr., "The Invisible Primary," in William G. Mayer, ed., *In Pursuit of the White House: How We Choose Our Presidential Nominees* (Chatham, N.J.: Chatham House, 1996), 5–6.

implications. Indeed, how a president wins will influence the direction of the government in Washington, D.C. Yet, most Americans seem quite content to leave the definition of the electoral process to the whims of fifty state legislatures and the ambitions of countless candidates. Thus, two questions that perplexed the Framers of the U.S. Constitution remain largely unanswered: (1) what kind of president do we want? and (2) how do we devise a nominating system that produces "good" presidents?

From John Adams to Bill Clinton: The Problem of Presidential Selection

The Framers understood the dilemma of picking a president, and their inability to solve it remains the single most conspicuous failure of the Constitutional Convention. Convening in Philadelphia, the delegates considered a myriad of schemes before finally settling upon the **Electoral College.** As devised by the Framers, each state would have a prescribed number of electors equalling its congressional delegation, based on the number of senators (two) plus the number of representatives (which varies from state to state). Under the Electoral College system, each elector would cast two votes for president. The Framers believed that state loyalties would determine the first vote (i.e., votes would go to "favorite sons"), but that the second vote would be for someone of national stature. Alexander Hamilton wrote in the *Federalist Papers* that the electors' "transient existence" and "detached situation" made the Electoral College a wise instrument for choosing the right kind of president.[10] In effect, the Electoral College would act as a presidential search committee (see "The Parties Speak: Alexander Hamilton on Choosing an American President").

However, only in the first two elections of George Washington in 1788 and 1792 did the Electoral College work as planned. Washington won unanimous victories—the only president to receive such a distinction. By 1796, however, the Federalist and Republican parties were competing for votes, thereby negating the Electoral College's role of finding the best person with the greatest national standing to serve as president. By 1804, the Electoral College that had been the object of Hamilton's effusive praise had been completely overhauled. Congress and the states approved the **Twelfth Amendment**—that part of the U.S. Constitution creating "tickets" of presidential and vice presidential candidates. The Electoral College remains one of the most flawed parts of the original Constitution (the other being how the Framers treated the issue of slavery), and two of that document's twenty-seven amendments mention it directly. Each time it appears that a presidential candidate could win the Electoral College and fail to capture a majority of the popular vote (something that happened in 1828, 1876, and 1888 and nearly happened in 1960, 1968, and 1976) calls for abolishing the Electoral College mount.

One riddle that confronted the constitutional Framers remains: how to choose a president in what is still a federal system of government? Clearly, the president must be a national leader, responding to what he/she sees as the public interest. As John Kennedy told reporters in 1962, the president has a "responsibility" to represent the public interest. But the United States consists of a myriad of interests, both special and regional. And as more money is needed to wage a successful presidential campaign, Americans increasingly resent the influence exercised by so-called

The Parties Speak: *Alexander Hamilton on Choosing an American President*

In this excerpt from The Federalist Papers, *Alexander Hamilton defends the newly-created Electoral College as the best means of choosing the president.*

[The Framers] have not made the appointment of the president to depend on any pre-existing bodies of men who might be tampered with beforehand to prostitute their votes; but they have referred it in the first instance to an immediate act of the people of America, to be exerted in the choice of persons for the temporary and sole purpose of making the appointment. And they have excluded from eligibility to this trust all those who from situation might be suspected of too great devotion to the President in office. No senator, representative, or other person holding a place of trust or profit under the United States can be of the number of the electors. Thus without corrupting the body of the people, the immediate agents in the election will at least enter upon the task free from any sinister bias. Their transient existence and their detached situation, already taken notice of, afford a satisfactory prospect of their continuing so, to the conclusion of it. The business of corruption, when it is to embrace so considerable a number of men, requires time as well as means. Nor would it be found easy suddenly to embark them, dispersed as they would be over thirteen States, in any combinations founded upon motives which, though they could not properly be denominated corrupt, might yet of a nature to mislead them from their duty.

Another and no less important desideratum was that the executive should be independent for his continuance in office on all but the people themselves. He might otherwise be tempted to sacrifice his duty to the complaisance for those whose favor was necessary to the duration of his official consequence. This advantage will also be secured by making his re-election to depend on a special body of representatives, deputed by the society for the single purpose of making the important choice.

All of these advantages will be happily combined in the plan devised by the convention [the Electoral College]; which is, that the people of each State shall choose a number of persons as electors equal to the number of senators and representatives of such State in the national government who shall assemble within the State, and vote for some fit person as President. . . . This process of election affords a moral certainty that the office of President will seldom fall to the lot of any man who is not in an eminent degree endowed with the requisite qualifications. Talents for low intrigue, and the little arts of popularity, may alone suffice to elevate a man to the first honors in a single State; but it will require other talents, and a different kind of merit, to establish him in the esteem and confidence of the whole Union, or of so considerable a portion of it as would be necessary to make him a successful candidate for the distinguished office of President of the United States. It will not be too strong to say that there will be a constant probability of seeing the station filled by characters pre-eminent for ability and virtue.

SOURCE: Excerpted from Alexander Hamilton, "Federalist 68," in Clinton Rossiter, ed., *The Federalist Papers* (New York: New American Library, 1961), 413–14.

special interests. In 1997, 66 percent said that excessive influence of political contributions on elections and government policy is a major problem; 63 percent maintained that elected officials in Washington spend too much time on political fund-raising; 55 percent claimed political contributions buy influence; and 48 percent thought these contributions had a significant influence on policymakers.[11]

Vast sums of money are required to run for president these days. In 1995, Democratic Party fund-raiser Terrence McAuliffe raised $42 million to thwart any Democrat from challenging Bill Clinton in the upcoming primaries—the largest war chest ever assembled for an incumbent president so far in advance of the balloting. When told how much money would be required to win, Clinton complained to his chief strategist, Dick Morris: "You don't know, you don't have any remote idea, how hard I have to work, how hard Hillary has to work, how hard Al [Gore] has to work to raise this much money."[12] Altogether, the major candidates spent $227.3 million just during the pre-nomination phase alone, including three contenders who emptied their wallets on their own behalf: Ross Perot contributed $8.5 million to his candidacy (which, if added to the $64 million he contributed to his 1992 campaign, makes him the largest contributor in American history); Republican Steve Forbes, $41.6 million; Morry Taylor (an industrialist who also sought the Republican presidential nomination), $6.5 million. According to two 1997 polls, 71 percent agree with the statement, "Good people are being discouraged from running for office by the high costs of campaigns," and 59 percent think that "elections are generally for sale to the candidate who can raise the most money."[13]

Complaints about how we choose our presidents are nothing new. At the close of the nineteenth century, author James Bryce wrote "Why Great Men Are Not Chosen Presidents," in which he maintained that "the ordinary American voter does not object to mediocrity." Bryce added, "Who now knows or cares to know anything about the personality of James K. Polk or Franklin Pierce? The only thing remarkable about them is that being so commonplace they should have climbed so high."[14] But the public's ongoing dissatisfaction with their presidential choices has attained new heights. A 1992 survey conducted by Louis Harris and Associates asked: "How satisfied are you with the candidates in this year's presidential election—very satisfied, somewhat satisfied, somewhat dissatisfied, or very dissatisfied?" Those who were dissatisfied totaled 63 percent.[15] These results sharply contrasted with answers given to pollster George Gallup in 1960. Back then, Gallup found 42 and 43 percent had a "highly favorable" opinion of John F. Kennedy and Richard M. Nixon respectively.[16]

Alexander Hamilton once observed that "the true test of a good government is its aptitude and tendency to produce a good administration."[17] Applying the same test to presidential nominations, the system seems to be malfunctioning. Not only are good candidates not forthcoming, information needed to make a sound judgment is sorely lacking. Instead of discussing the problems the next president must face, modern campaigns spotlight issues that have little relevance to governing. In 1960, for example, John F. Kennedy charged that the Republicans had allowed a missile gap to develop between the United States and the Soviet Union. But after assuming office the missile gap suddenly disappeared. Four years later Lyndon Johnson promised not to escalate the Vietnam War, saying that those who wanted to widen the conflict "call upon us to supply American boys to do the job that Asian boys should do."[18] But, once elected, Johnson sent 500,000 U.S. soldiers to Vietnam to fight a war that bitterly divided the country and cost more than 50,000 American lives. In 1988, George Bush decided to make Willie Horton, a convicted rapist and murderer who had been afforded a weekend pass by the administration of his Democratic opponent, Massachusetts Governor Michael S. Dukakis, a principal issue. Dukakis Campaign Manager Susan Estrich cried foul: "You can't find a stronger metaphor, intended or not, for racial hatred in this country than a black man raping a white woman. And that's what the Willie Horton story was."[19] The campaign left a bitter aftertaste: 64 percent polled by the Gallup Organization said the Bush-Dukakis race had been more negative than past campaigns; and 66 percent felt that "better qualified candidates should have been selected."[20] In 1992, controversy swirled around Bill Clinton and whether he had sex with Gennifer Flowers, evaded the draft during the Vietnam War, and inhaled marijuana.

Given the prevalent view that the presidential selection system is broken, ideas for fixing it have flourished. But the various instruction manuals differ. When it comes to selecting a chief executive, Americans want the process to be fair, yet provide for majority rule; deliberative as well as quick; representative, but with some having a greater voice than others. Political scientists have tried unsuccessfully to resolve these contradictions. Their discussions have centered around abstract details that have little to do with how to best pick a president, including: (1) which state or states should go first in selecting presidential candidates; (2) how many party officeholders should attend the convention; and (3) what proportions of men, women, blacks, Latinos, and American Indians should attend the conventions? Academicians have tracked, like bean counters, how both parties have addressed these issues. Delegates are polled about their race, sex, and issue positions, and determinations are made as to whether the system is performing better or worse than four years before. This immersion in minutiae is peculiar to the American party system. As Alexis de Tocqueville wrote: "Lacking great parties, the United States is creeping with small ones *and public opinion is broken up ad infinitum about questions of detail*" [emphasis added].[21]

Still, the quest for a better way of nominating and electing our presidents continues. This chapter focuses on the alternate roads taken in search of the best method for nominating a presidential candidate. Once again, the debates between Alexander Hamilton and Thomas Jefferson play a prominent role in the disagreements about which is the best path to take.

HAMILTON'S FAMILY VERSUS JEFFERSON'S COMMUNITY

Legendary party boss William Marcy Tweed once remarked, "I don't care who does the electin' as long as I do the nominatin'."[22] The issue of who should "do the nominatin'" of presidential candidates has vexed the American polity for nearly two hundred years. This argument, like so many of the debates in American politics, is rooted in the dispute between Alexander Hamilton and Thomas Jefferson as to how best to implement the American ideology of classical liberalism. As described in Chapter 1, Hamilton preferred to wed liberty to authority—preferring a strong central government that could act on behalf of a national family. Jefferson, meanwhile, wanted to marry liberty with local civic authority, believing that America was a series of diverse communities and deference should be paid to local customs.

The struggle between these two perspectives informs the controversy surrounding how presidents should be chosen. Throughout history, American political parties have at one time or another adopted a Hamiltonian or a Jeffersonian approach to the exercise of power. Initially, they thought they had a solution in the **Congressional Caucus.** The caucus consisted of House and Senate members who belonged to the same party. They would meet, discuss the pros and cons of various candidates, and emerge with a presidential nominee. As a national institution that represented state and local interests, it was thought that a gathering of congressional party leaders to choose a president made sense given the failure of the Electoral College. Moreover, it was generally assumed that presidents would come from the national legislature, so it seemed natural that Congress would choose from among the prospective candidates.

For a time, the Congressional Caucus seemed to work. But when the Federalist Party died in 1816, so did the caucus. The onset of one-party rule (described by historians as the "era of good feelings") meant that winning the Republican nomination was tantamount to winning the election. In 1820, James Madison won every electoral vote except one. With one-party rule, the idea of seeking a party nomination lost much of its meaning; why have a nominating system if there is no real opposition party? Moreover, King Caucus was depicted in the press as an elite institution where secret deals were cut. That perception became a reality in 1824 when fewer than half the congressmen attended the caucus and its nominee, William Crawford, was badly beaten in the election. By the late 1820s, the caucus system became a target of the Jacksonian forces, who argued the process epitomized aristocratic rule and thwarted the popular will.

The Rise of Nominating Conventions

When the Congressional Caucus collapsed, the search for another mode of making presidential nominations began. Initially, the youthful parties gravitated toward a **convention system** that took local sensibilities into account. Thomas Ritchie, editor of the *Richmond Enquirer,* urged a national convention, in a letter addressed to Martin Van Buren dated January 2, 1824:

> Vain is any expectation found upon the spontaneous movement of the great mass of the people in favor of any particular individual, the elements of this great community are multifarious and conflicting, and require to be skillfully combined to be made harmonious and powerful. Their action, to be salutary, must be the result of enlightened deliberation, and he who would distract the councils of the people, must design to breed confusion and disorder, and to profit by their dissensions.[23]

In Ritchie's view, party conventions allowed for a successful fusion of Hamiltonian Nationalism and Jeffersonian Localism. The convention spoke with an authoritative voice in selecting the nominee, but individual states maintained their sovereignty in choosing the delegates. In 1831, the Anti-Masonic Party held the first political convention in Baltimore. A year later the Democratic Party followed suit. The Democrats were driven toward the convention system not only because it seemed more "democratic," but President Andrew Jackson wanted to replace Vice President John C. Calhoun who had become an outspoken administration critic. One key Jackson operative pointed out: "the expediency, indeed absolute necessity, of advising our friends everywhere to get up a national convention to convene at some convenient point, for the purpose of selecting some suitable and proper person to be placed upon the electoral ticket with General Jackson, as a candidate for the vice presidency."[24] Eventually, the convention was held and the delegates chose a Jackson loyalist, Martin Van Buren, for the vice presidential slot.

Over the years, nominating conventions became a vital party instrument—providing a forum for making key decisions about who would head the presidential ticket, what issues might be stressed, and how to support those persons once elected. Conventions are held the summer before the general election, usually in one of the nation's largest cities. Until the 1970s, convention delegates were chosen by state and local party leaders. Party leaders ran the show, instructing delegates what platform planks to support and which candidates to back. Still, conventions were exciting affairs. Prior to the Progressive Era when party bosses wielded their greatest power, Democrats usually took ten ballots to select their nominees; Republicans, five. As boisterous and contentious as these gatherings could get, conventions were a way of merging the interests of local party leaders with the concerns of the national party to nominate a winner.

But the fusion of national party authority and states rights was not completely harmonious and differed for each party. Initially, it was the Republican Party of the late nineteenth century that was most hospitable to Hamilton's notion of a national family. When it came to governing, Republican presidents paid attention to state concerns. But when it came to nominating, they viewed their party as a national organization that was all-important in choosing their presidential ticket. During a credentials fight at the 1876 Republican Convention, one delegate asked "whether the state of Pennsylvania shall make laws for this convention; or whether this convention is supreme and shall make its own laws?" The delegate answered his own question, saying: "We are supreme. We are original. We stand here representing the great Republican party of the United States."[25]

Democrats adopted a wholly different approach, believing they should adhere to the traditions of their progenitor, Thomas Jefferson. At their first convention in 1832, the party adopted the **two-thirds rule** that no candidate could be nominated for president unless two-thirds of the delegates agreed. Whigs and Republicans eschewed calls for a super-majority, nominating their presidential candidates instead by a simple majority. Democrats also invented the **unit rule,** a device that allowed a state to cast all of its votes for one presidential candidate if a majority so desired. These changes presented considerable difficulties in getting the Southern and Northern wings of the party to agree on a nominee. Thus, it took forty-nine ballots to nominate Franklin Pierce in 1852, and seventeen to select James Buchanan four years later. Yet the two-thirds rule and the unit rule accentuated the federal character of the Democratic Party's nominating process—something the party desperately sought to protect. Rising to defend the unit rule, a delegate to the 1880 Democratic Convention excoriated the Republicans as "a party which believes . . . that the states have hardly any rights left which the Federal Government is bound to respect . . . [and] that the state does not control its own delegation in a national convention. Not so in the convention of the great Democratic party. We stand, Mr. President, for the rights of the states."[26]

At the beginning of the twentieth century, the debate over which approach to take in nominating presidents—one rooted in Hamilton's idea of nationalism or Jefferson's preference for localism—intensified. The struggle took place not only between the two parties, but within them. During the first years of the twentieth century, the Republican Party developed a growing progressive faction that wanted to nationalize party affairs. Local politics, as discussed in Chapter 3, was rife with corruption. Progressive leader Theodore Roosevelt advocated the creation of a **national presidential primary** in 1912. Failing that, Progressives wanted state parties to establish a direct presidential primary, believing that Teddy Roosevelt would dominate them. Fourteen states followed this route, and Roosevelt beat incumbent president William Howard Taft in all of the primaries. But Republican stalwarts, led by Taft, preferred having state GOP leaders retain their decisive voice in selecting presidential candidates. Taft's dismal third-place finish in 1912 resulted in a further nationalization of the nominating process. Progressive advocacy of the direct primary was extended to most elective offices, including the presidency. By 1916, twenty-three states with 65 percent of the delegates had adopted presidential primaries. Slowly, but surely, party regulars were being shown to the convention exits.

Democrats, meanwhile, continued to support a Jeffersonian-like approach in choosing their presidents. Although Woodrow Wilson backed Theodore Roosevelt's call for a national primary, the 1912 Democratic platform upheld the rights of the states and condemned as a "usurpation" Republican-inspired efforts "to enlarge and magnify by indirection the powers of the Federal Government."[27] Thus, any attempt to nationalize the party's rules would be turned aside. In fact, southern party leaders blocked the nomination of Speaker of the House Champ Clark who was unable to obtain the two-thirds support from the delegates needed to win the nomination. Seeking a compromise, the delegates turned to New Jersey Democratic Governor Woodrow Wilson whose birthplace was Staunton, Virginia.

But not all was harmonious within the Democratic ranks. The coming of the immigrant—beginning with the Irish in the 1840s and the eastern, central, and southern Europeans in the 1890s—wrought havoc in Democratic Party councils. These foreign-tongued Americans, mostly Roman Catholics, gravitated to the Democrats early and sought a voice in their state and national conventions. Most supported New York Governor Alfred E. Smith in his quest for the Democratic presidential nomination in 1924. But the two-thirds rule prevented Smith from capturing the nomination. After 103 ballots, the convention turned to John W. Davis, a well-known lawyer whose views on race were acceptable to the South.

These internal party squabbles—and the many attempts to quell them—did not solve the nominating dilemma. This is because the argument between the Hamiltonian and Jeffersonian perspectives became linked to the ongoing debate about what kind of president we should have. Those advocating a national-centered system suggested leaders make the best presidents, not party bosses. As Theodore Roosevelt espoused, the true test of leadership rests in an ability to reason with followers in an open, public fashion. Therefore, a national system of presidential selection is preferable because it provides an environment in which candidates can test their mettle in such a way that successful contenders will maximize their ability to govern. Those who subscribe to a Jeffersonian approach to presidential nominations hold that the selection of a nominee must be consensual, and to accomplish this the deliberations must necessarily be private. Candidates should be judged by their peers, even if that verdict is rendered in a smoke-filled room. From these deliberations, a candidate will emerge with sufficient institutional backing to make the party instrumental in mounting a winning campaign and crucial in forming successful administration.

THE RISE OF HAMILTONIAN NATIONALISM

During the nineteenth century, the youthful parties zigzagged between the Hamiltonian and Jeffersonian approach to presidential nominating—never quite sure how to balance the two. But during the twentieth century, Hamiltonian Nationalism gained the upper hand. Two individuals, both Democrats, were largely responsible: Franklin D. Roosevelt and George S. McGovern.

The movement towards a national-centered model was given its first push during the Progressive Era. A principal goal of this movement was to create a more open and democratic electoral process, as noted in Chapter 4. One means to accomplish this was to allow average voters a say in nominations. By 1912, a dozen states adopted presidential primaries and a few years later about one-half followed suit. Back then, however, the outcome of these primaries was only advisory, amounting to what some have called "beauty contests." The results provided information to the party leaders as to which candidates were popular, but the delegates chosen were not bound to a specific candidate. This gave local party leaders bargaining leverage at the conventions. Thus, while the growth of presidential primaries at the turn of the century appeared to shift the nomination process in a national direction, the change was mostly symbolic.

Beginning with Franklin D. Roosevelt, the Democratic Party adopted a Hamiltonian approach to picking its presidential candidates. In 1936, Roosevelt succeeded in having the Democratic Convention strike down the two-thirds rule despite vigorous resistence from southerners. Former Navy Secretary and Ambassador to Mexico Josephus Daniels spoke for the administration: "The Democratic party today is a national party, and Northern, Southern, and Western states would have greater representation in the party conventions under a majority rule."[28] Southerners argued that revoking the two-thirds rule would drastically reduce the role of individual states in the nomination process. On the surface, it was a call to a Jeffersonian-like system. Below the surface, southerners realized that as long as a two-thirds majority was needed for the nomination, they could veto any nominee by acting in unison. Even in the 1930s, racial issues divided the Democratic Party and the country, so the end of the two-thirds rule was a blow to southern party leaders.

Following Roosevelt's four terms in the White House, Democrats continued in the Hamiltonian tradition as their nominating process became increasingly nationalized. In 1952, a DNC member lost his seat because he supported Republican Dwight D. Eisenhower for president. Four years later, the Democratic Convention passed a resolution that required a state to list the party's presidential nominee on its ballot in order for its delegates to be seated in the convention hall. (Some southern states refused to list Democratic nominee Adlai Stevenson on the ballot in 1952.) A major step toward nationalizing the parties occurred in 1964, when the so-called Mississippi Freedom Democratic Party claimed to be more representative of that state's Democratic voters than the "regulars" who ran the state Democratic Party. Asked to settle the dispute between the two factions, the 1964 Democratic Convention passed a resolution forbidding discrimination in choosing delegates. Henceforth, delegates would be chosen without regard to their race, creed, or national origins. If a state delegation did not comply with the new rule, it could be ejected from the convention hall. A committee chaired by New Jersey Governor Richard Hughes would be responsible for implementing the rule. On July 26, 1967, Hughes wrote to the DNC and all state Democratic Party chairs outlining six requirements each state must meet in order to comply with the charge of the 1964 convention. Failure would mean that the seats would be vacated and filled by the convention—an unprecedented act at that time.

The McGovern-Fraser Commission

Not all states met Governor Hughes's criteria. In 1968, the Democratic Convention tossed out all of the Mississippi and half of the Georgia delegation from its convention for violating the Hughes resolution. In addition, the delegates abolished the 146–year-old unit rule that permitted a state to cast all of its votes for a presidential candidate even if other candidates had support within the delegation. The unit rule was a favorite among southerners who used it to maximize their power at Democratic conventions. But the pendulum toward a Hamiltonian-like nationalization of party affairs swung even further with the creation of the McGovern-Fraser Commission following the disastrous 1968 convention.

It was perhaps the worst year in the history of the Democratic Party. Early in 1968, it had appeared that the convention would be a dull affair since Lyndon B. Johnson, the sitting Democratic president, gave every indication of seeking renomination. Not since Chester Arthur in 1884 had an incumbent president been denied renomination by his own party. One lone Democrat had the temerity to challenge Johnson, a little-known U.S. senator from Minnesota, Eugene McCarthy. Propelled to oppose Johnson because of the Vietnam War, McCarthy had few resources and even less backing from party leaders. But with a battalion of antiwar activists drawn from several college campuses, McCarthy campaigned in New Hampshire, site of the first primary. Johnson defeated McCarthy, but the margin of victory was much smaller than expected—50 percent to 42 percent. In a dramatic turn of events, Johnson told a nationwide television audience: "I shall not seek, and I will not accept, the nomination of my party for another term as your president."[29]

Johnson's departure did not mean that most Democratic Party leaders were ready to back McCarthy—quite the contrary. If Johnson was out, their choice was Vice President Hubert H. Humphrey. Given the relative unanimity of party leaders supporting his candidacy, Humphrey did not campaign in any of the seventeen states holding primaries in 1968. This infuriated anti-Vietnam War demonstrators within the Democratic Party who charged that Humphrey was a member of the Johnson administration that had escalated U.S. involvement in Vietnam. Robert F. Kennedy, the brother of the late president and a U.S. senator from New York, entered the primaries and, along with McCarthy, fueled an anti-Humphrey movement. For a while, it looked as though Kennedy had a chance to win the nomination. He drew large crowds at every stop, received substantial media attention, and won most of the primaries he entered. Whether he would have been nominated is now left to historical debate—on the night Kennedy won the California primary, an assassin ended his life. Needless to say, the nation was in a state of shock and the party dumbfounded (see "The Parties Speak: The *New Republic*'s Reflections on the Assassination of Robert F. Kennedy and the Democratic Party of 1968").

The Parties Speak: *The* **New Republic's** *Reflections on the Assassination of Robert F. Kennedy and the Democratic Party of 1968*

The death of New York Senator Robert F. Kennedy in June 1968 left the Democratic Party reeling. Kennedy had just won the California primary, and his victory ensured a floor fight with Vice President Humphrey at the Chicago convention for the Democratic presidential nomination. This New Republic *article captures the strong emotions Kennedy's candidacy and death engendered among his supporters.*

On the eve of California's primary, Cesar Chavez, at 41 perhaps the most unassuming public figure in the land, sat in a restaurant in East Los Angeles at the end of a long day of campaigning for Robert Kennedy. Chavez and a hundred or so of his "campesinos" had played a key role in organizing the Mexican-Americans for the primary, and early the next day, would pour into the precincts to bring out that huge voting bloc. They slept on cots in the social hall of an Episcopal Church in the Mexican-American section. By day, they campaigned—first to register voters, then to organize them. To Chavez, some of whose closest "Anglo" friends were backing Eugene McCarthy, the choice was clear. He used, in a printed statement, the Spanish term *hechos son amor* (deeds of love) to describe Robert Kennedy's role in their troubled lives, explaining it in these words: "In the midst of our struggle in Delano against tremendous odds to gain dignity and social justice, Senator Kennedy came to us and helped us. He came without asking anything of us; he came without expectation of any benefit to him." To Chavez, a gentleman of unswerving purpose, the thing that was important was that he came when few others did. For the "campesinos," the answer to the taunt "Where was Kennedy in November" was a simple: "In Delano."

It will never be asked again where Robert Kennedy was in November. But it might be forgotten, even by some whose loyalty never wavered, why Kennedy became a presidential candidate. He had been reluctant to risk the fight. He was torn between anguish over Vietnam and the misery of life for so many Americans, and his keen sense of the odds against his succeeding. Having decided that he could not remain out of it, that he could not by his neutrality seem to consent to the policies of the Johnson-Humphrey Administration, he went at it hard. He was good-humored, decent to his rivals, but he fought. Now we weep for him and ourselves, as he could weep over one poor child. What that child and all our children will make of his passing is beyond comprehension. What does a generation that has watched the successive slaughter of good men become? What will children of the sixties make of their country?

The answers lie with the living, their will to overcome. For the campaign in which Robert Kennedy enlisted is not over, and not lost. It is a triumph Robert Kennedy shares with Eugene McCarthy that so many Americans rallied, refused to despair, took possession of themselves, and determined on change. Given a lead, the young proved what politics as "the art of the impossible" can do. Senator Kennedy, along with Senator McCarthy, felt in his bones the imperative of political renewal, the need for a politics radically different from the old, one of hopeful enterprise. "What all these primaries . . . and all of the party caucuses have indicated," Mr. Kennedy said, is that "the people in the United States want a change. . . . The country wants to move in a different direction. We want to deal with our problems within our own country, and we want peace in Vietnam." Minutes before he was shot, he congratulated McCarthy "and those who have been associated with him in their efforts that they have started in New Hampshire and carried through to the primary here in the state of California." They and Robert Kennedy were "involved in this great effort . . . on the part of the United States, on behalf of our own people, on behalf of mankind all around the globe and the next generation." His differences with Eugene McCarthy were nothing compared to this common effort they had undertaken.

The young cheered. So did their fathers and grandfathers. What brought them all to take practical politics seriously this year was not any superficial preference for one face, one name, one party over another. They were brought to politics by near-desperation, and by the sight of new leaders who dared to challenge the old ways. Theirs has been a quest for government of finer perception, more compassionate concern, more discriminating in its priorities. The popular movement which Robert Kennedy and Eugene McCarthy spotted and led was a movement of both revolt and resolve: revolt against physical and spiritual impoverishment, revolt against deepening enmities of race and class, revolt against needless massacre in Asia; and a resolve that something better than this is necessary and attainable. The Kennedy-McCarthy cause had no ideology; it springs from a fresher source, an earlier era of liberalism that was experimental, searching, that could confess failures and discern possibilities. . . .

The issues which brought Kennedy to California, and his death, remain. The campaign goes on. And those who have taken seriously the meaning of Kennedy's candidacy will not defect.

SOURCE: "The Kennedy Cause," *New Republic,* June 15, 1968, 3-4.

By the summer of 1968, the Democratic Party was in tatters. So deep were the divisions that two conventions were held: one in the hall, another in the streets of Chicago. Mayor Richard J. Daley, the Democratic boss of Chicago, refused to grant the crowds of young college students who descended upon the city a permit to demonstrate against the Vietnam War. Daley's police attacked the demonstrators with clubs and tear gas, creating what authorities subsequently described as a "police riot." Inside the hall, party leaders nominated Humphrey amid the usual hoopla and floor demonstrations. These jarring scenes led presidential chronicler Theodore H. White to describe Humphrey as "being nominated in a sea of blood."[30]

The protests in the streets, a widespread perception that Humphrey won his party's nod unfairly (since he did not compete in a single primary), and raucus dissent within the Democratic ranks led to the creation of the McGovern-Fraser Commission. As George McGovern, then a U.S. senator from South Dakota, recalled: "Many of the most active supporters of Gene McCarthy and Robert Kennedy and later of me, believed that the Democratic presidential nominating process was dominated by party wheel horses, entrenched officeholders, and local bosses. They believed that despite the strong popular showing of McCarthy and Kennedy in the primaries, a majority of the convention delegates were selected in a manner that favored the so-called 'establishment' candidates."[31] The McGovern-Fraser Commission arrived at a similar conclusion. In evocative language, it urged Democrats to change their ways: "If we are not an open party; if we do not represent the demands of change, then the danger is not that the people will go to the Republican Party; it is that there will no longer be a way for people committed to orderly change to fulfill their needs and desires within our traditional political system. It is that they will turn to third and fourth party politics or the anti-politics of the street."[32]

First chaired by McGovern and later by Minneapolis Mayor Don Fraser, the commission was officially called the "Committee on Party Structure and Delegate Selection." The McGovern-Fraser Commission adopted several recommendations that further nationalized presidential politics, including:

- A reaffirmation of the abolition of the unit rule, an action already approved by the 1968 Democratic Convention.
- Refusing to seat delegates chosen in back rooms.
- Prohibiting certain public or party officeholders from serving as delegates to county, state, and national conventions by virtue of their official position.
- Banning proxy voting, a practice used by party bosses to cast votes on behalf of absent delegates often without their knowledge.
- Ordering states to choose delegates during the calendar year in which the convention is held.
- Requiring states to post public notices announcing the selection of a delegate slate that would be committed to a particular candidate, and inviting the rank and file to participate in the selection process.
- Creating a Compliance Review Division within the DNC to ensure that states obeyed the McGovern-Fraser recommendations.

In effect, the commission told the party establishment to "reform or else." The nomination process needed to be more open, timely, and representative of the wishes of average Democrats. As McGovern recalled: "In public statements, speeches and interviews, I drove home the contention that the Democratic party had but two choices: reform or death. In the past, I noted, political parties, when confronted with the need for change chose death rather than change. I did not want the Democratic party to die. I wanted our party to choose the path of change and vitality. That was the function of the reforms."[33]

But behind the reforms lay another agenda: removing the so-called Old Democrats, mostly white, middle-aged, establishment types who supported the Vietnam War, and replacing them with New Politics Democrats, younger, professionals, female, and minorities who were antiwar, antiestablishment, and antiparty. The commission exceeded all expectations in achieving this objective. At the 1968 Democratic Convention, just 14 percent of the delegates were women, 2 percent were under age thirty, and only 5 percent were black. Four years later, women accounted for 36 percent of the delegates; those under age thirty, 23 percent; blacks, 14 percent. But these increased numbers for women, blacks, and young voters came with a high price tag. In an unprecedented act, the 1972 Democratic Convention voted to exclude the delegates from Cook County, Illinois (including Chicago), led by Chicago Mayor Richard J. Daley, and replaced them with pro-McGovern delegates led by a young, black civil rights activist named Jesse Jackson. In a subsequent legal action, the U.S. Supreme Court affirmed the convention's decision in *Cousins v. Wigoda* using decidedly Hamiltonian language: "The convention serves the pervasive national interest in the selection of candidates for national offices and this national interest is greater than any interest of any individual state."[34]

Establishment Democrats were astounded. Daley delegates had won the Illinois primary, while Jackson's slate had not even competed. Moreover, Daley was still viewed as key to winning this electoral vote-rich state in the fall. As it turned out, McGovern lost Illinois and forty-nine other states to Republican Richard M. Nixon. But in removing the Daley delegation on the grounds that it had less than the desired number of women, young voters, and blacks, the convention opened a Pandora's box of what became a virtual quota system for choosing delegates. As McGovern later acknowledged: "Whatever the commission originally intended, in administering the guidelines on minorities, women, and young people, it eventually moved very close to adopting a de facto quota system."[35]

Along with mandating specifics of the composition of each state's delegation, the commission also sought changes in how they were to be selected. The 1968 fiasco suggested that party regulars were excluded from the process in favor of party bosses who picked the president in smoked-filled rooms. The commission's proclamation that delegate selection must be "open, timely, and representative" was considered somewhat vague, but few states wished to jeopardize their role at the next convention. Most state Democratic Party leaders shrugged their shoulders and abandoned their state conventions in favor of primaries and caucuses where the rank and file would make their presidential preferences known. As compensation, however, Democratic leaders would retain a decisive voice in selecting their own candidates for state and local offices.

The shift from party leaders deciding who would be the next president to primary voters has been significant. In most of the states that hold primaries, voters choose how many delegates will go to the nomination convention for each of the various aspirants. A candidate who nets 50 percent of the primary votes, for instance, will receive 50 percent of the state's delegation. The actual delegates themselves are usually selected by state party meetings and conventions but, unlike the "advisory" primary system of the Progressive Era, they are bound to support the candidate they were sent to support, at least on the first ballot. Other states have a "pure" primary system where voters directly elect delegates to the national convention. Each would-be delegate's candidate preference is listed on the ballot. A delegate who has no preference is listed as "uncommitted." Delegates chosen under this system are duty bound to support the candidate listed on the ballot.

One unintended consequence of the McGovern-Fraser reforms has been a substantial increase in the number of presidential primaries. In 1960, John F. Kennedy ran in only three state primaries, West Virginia, Wisconsin, and New Hampshire. By 1996, more than three-quarters of the convention delegates were chosen in primaries and the number of states holding Democratic and Republican primaries had swelled to thirty-five, with many of them held between mid-February and late March (see Table 5.2). But the purpose of the primaries had changed dramatically. In 1960, Kennedy used the few contests available to convince a few party chieftains—notably, Chicago Mayor Richard J. Daley, Ohio Governor Mike DiSalle, Pennsylvania Governor David Lawrence, Connecticut Democratic State Chairman John M. Bailey, and New York City Mayor Carmine DeSapio—that he had requisite popular support to defeat Richard M. Nixon and that his Catholicism would not obstruct a victory.

The primary calendar is a long and complicated one. Candidates must know the dates of the scheduled state contests, and plan their calendars accordingly. But candidates must do more than be in three places at once. They and their staffs have to know the state laws that govern the primaries and caucuses. Most states hold **closed primaries** where voters are required to declare their party affiliation before voting. Often, this declaration is done when one registers to vote. In a few states, voters can register on the day of the primary. The idea behind a closed primary is to ensure that only loyal party members participate in selecting the nominee. About ten states have **independent primaries** where registered party voters and independents are allowed to participate in the primary election. Voters registered with another party cannot take part. Three states use **open primaries** where voters are permitted to cast a ballot for a nominee without disclosing a party affiliation. On entering the polling booth the voter is given a ballot for every party. The voter then selects one party ballot and casts a vote for a candidate of that party.

Caucuses are another popular means for selecting delegates. Instead of voting at one's leisure during the primary day, caucuses require the party's rank and file to appear at an organized meeting and publicly declare one's support for a candidate. The process is similar to a town hall meeting or a miniconvention. In 1996, fifteen states chose their national party convention delegates through caucuses. The most

TABLE 5.2 ▪ The 2000 Primary Calendar

Date	State	System
January 24	Iowa	Caucus (D and R)
January 24	Alaska	Straw poll (R)
February 1	New Hampshire	Primary (D and R)
February 1–7	Hawaii	Caucus (R)
February 8	Delaware	Caucus (R)
February 15	Delaware	Caucus (R)
February 19	South Carolina	Primary (R)
February 22	Arizona	Primary (R)
February 22	Michigan	Primary (R)
February 29	North Dakota	Caucus (R)
February 29	Virginia	Primary (R)
February 29	Washington	Primary (D and R)
March 7	California	Primary (D and R)
March 7	Connecticut	Primary (D and R)
March 7	Georgia	Primary (D and R)
March 7	Maine	Primary (D and R)
March 7	Maryland	Primary (D and R)
March 7	Massachusetts	Primary (D and R)
March 7	Missouri	Primary (D and R)
March 7	New York	Primary (D and R)
March 7	Ohio	Primary (D and R)
March 7	Rhode Island	Primary (D and R)
March 7	Vermont	Primary (D and R)
March 7	Hawaii	Caucus (D)
March 7	Idaho	Caucus (D)
March 7	Minnesota	Caucus (D)
March 7	North Dakota	Caucus (D)
March 7	South Carolina	Caucus (D)
March 7	Washington	Caucus (D)
March 7	Minnesota	Caucus (R)
March 7	Washington	Caucus (R)
March 10	Colorado	Primary (D and R)
March 10	Utah	Primary (D and R)
March 10	Wyoming	Primary (R)
March 11	Arizona	Caucus (D)*
March 11	Michigan	Caucus (D)*
March 12	Nevada	Caucus (D)
March 14	Florida	Primary (D and R)
March 14	Louisiana	Primary (D and R) **
March 14	Mississippi	Primary (D and R)
March 14	Oklahoma	Primary (D and R)
March 14	Tennessee	Primary (D and R)
March 14	Texas	Primary (D and R)
March 21	Illinois	Primary (D and R)
March 25	Alaska	Caucus (D)
April 4	Kansas	Primary (D and R)

continued

TABLE 5.2 ▪ The 2000 Primary Calendar *(continued)*

Date	State	System
April 4	Wisconsin	Primary (D and R)
April 15	Virginia	Caucus (D)***
April 17	Virginia	Caucus (D)***
April 25	Pennsylvania	Primary (D and R)
April 30	Alaska	Caucus (D)
May 2	Indiana	Primary (D and R)
May 2	North Carolina	Primary (D and R)
May 2	Washington, D.C.	Primary (D and R)
May 9	Nebraska	Primary (D and R)
May 9	West Virginia	Primary (D and R)
May 12–June 13	Virginia	Republicans hold congressional district conventions to choose a portion of their delegates
May 13–27	Virginia	Democrats hold congressional district conventions to choose a portion of their delegates
May 16	Oregon	Primary (D and R)
May 23	Arkansas	Primary (D and R)
May 23	Kentucky	Primary (D and R)
May 23	Idaho	Primary (R)
May 25	Nevada	Caucus (R)
June 6	Alabama	Primary (D and R)
June 6	Montana	Primary (D and R)
June 6	New Jersey	Primary (D and R)
June 6	New Mexico	Primary (D and R)
June 6	South Dakota	Primary (D and R)

* Tentative.

**GOP chooses seven of twenty-eight delegates; others picked at the January 22, 2000 caucuses.

***One hundred thirty-five cities and counties hold Democratic Party caucuses on either April 15 or April 17 to choose a portion of their delegates.

SOURCE: CNN/AllPolitics, Web site, <http://cnn.allpolitics.com>.

prominent of these is the Iowa caucuses, which provide the first test of a candidate's strength. On January 24, 2000, Republicans and Democrats gather at their individual caucus sites to announce their support for a particular individual. Once that task is completed, those attending a caucus may make platform recommendations which are forwarded to the state committee and the national convention. Each individual caucus can last as long as several hours before the proceedings are declared closed.

Are Primaries and Caucuses Representative?

One problem with both primaries and caucuses is that very few citizens bother to participate, and those who do are not exactly "average." It was assumed that when the nomination process was removed from the smoked-filled rooms that regular

Democrats would have a greater say in party affairs. Yet, only about 15 percent of eligible voters participate in primaries, and about one-third of the 15 percent attend caucuses. In a famous study of delegates attending the 1972 Democratic and Republican conventions, political scientist Jeane Kirkpatrick found them to be largely unrepresentative of the American electorate: 56 percent of the Democratic delegates had a college degree or more; 59 percent of GOP delegates also had college degrees.[36] Given this data, it was not surprising that George McGovern, the most liberal Democrat nominated for the presidency since William Jennings Bryan in 1896, received the Democratic nomination in 1972.

The more open system has allowed special interest groups to exercise greater influence. For example, in 1980, the National Education Association sent 464 delegates to the Democratic National Convention most of them supporting Jimmy Carter. The NEA was committed to Carter mainly for one reason: in 1976, he had promised to create a Department of Education and he kept that promise. Likewise, in 1984 the AFL-CIO broke with its past tradition not supporting a particular candidate prior to the Democratic Convention, and endorsed Walter Mondale for president prior to the Democratic Convention. So, too, did the National Organization for Women and the NEA. Each group exacted its price. For the AFL-CIO, it was a Mondale promise to impose a tariff on imported goods, particularly automobiles and steel; for the National Organization for Women, it was a Mondale pledge to consider a female candidate for vice president; for the NEA, it was a Mondale promise of more federal aid to education. In 1999, the AFL-CIO broke with precedent again, this time endorsing Vice President Al Gore for the Democratic presidential nomination. Several other labor organizations also formally endorsed Gore. Once more, the primary process has forced candidates from both parties to seek early endorsements from outside interest groups.

The Christian Right has greater numbers among Republican primary and caucus participants than within the total Republican electorate which includes more moderates. Given their passionate commitment to certain issues, especially their pro-life stance, the Christian Right has scored some surprising victories. The most significant of these was in 1988 when *700 Club* founder Pat Robertson upset Vice President George Bush in the Iowa caucuses.

The problem of representation persists for both parties as Tables 5.3 and 5.4 demonstrate. In 1996, Democratic and Republican delegates came from very different backgrounds and held opinions widely at variance from both the rank and file and the public at large. Democratic delegates tended to hold the liberal position; Republicans were staunch conservatives. On issues such as a constitutional amendment to balance the budget, the death penalty, gun control, immigration, defense spending, and school prayer, both the Democratic delegates and the Republican delegates hold opinions that are opposite of those of most voters. Thus, winning the nomination of either major party is often fraught with peril as the nominees then struggle to persuade the larger, detached segment of the electorate that they will refuse to bow to "extremists" within their party's ranks.

Even though participants in the current presidential nomination process are not "typical," most are hesitant to return to the smoked-filled rooms of days gone by. Precisely how to resolve the conflict between the types of candidates likely

TABLE 5.3 ▪ **Delegate Profiles to the 1996 Presidential Nominating Conventions versus Voter Profiles (in percentages)**

Characteristic	Democratic Delegates	Republican Delegates	All 1996 Voters
Ideology			
Liberal	36	1	21
Moderate	47	19	46
Conservative	3	74	31
Age			
18–29	4	2	16
30–39	12	14	21
40–59	60	52	38
60 and older	24	31	25
Race and Ethnicity			
White	67	92	81
Black	21	2	11
Latino	6	2	4
Other	6	3	3
Labor Union			
Member	34	2	11
Not a member	56	98	89
Sex			
Male	43	61	48
Female	57	39	52

SOURCE: *Washington Post* survey of 511 Republican delegates July–August 1996, and 496 Democratic delegates June–July, 1996. Public profiles obtained from Voter Research and Surveys, exit poll, November 5, 1996.

chosen by party leaders (those with mass appeal among the general electorate) and the types of candidates likely chosen by activists (ones more ideologically extreme) has remained an enigma. Compromise measures have been advanced, but the problem has left party leaders and activists who participate in primaries and caucuses alike scratching their heads.

Republicans Follow the McGovern-Fraser Lead

Although not subject to the recommendations of the McGovern-Fraser Commission, Republicans felt its effects when state legislatures passed laws mandating state presidential primaries. The gusts of change blowing through Democratic convention halls rattled Republican windows, too. Several state legislatures, largely controlled by

TABLE 5.4 ▪ Issue Comparison of Public to 1996 Democratic and Republican Delegates (percent agreeing)

Issue	All Voters	Democratic Delegates	Democratic Voters	Republican Delegates	Republican Voters
A constitutional amendment to require a balanced federal budget	82	32	77	88	87
The death penalty for people convicted of murder	76	48	67	38	81
Cut off public assistance payments a poor person can receive after a maximum of five years	73	38	67	88	81
Ban the sale of most assault weapons	73	93	78	47	67
Impose a five-year freeze on legal immigration	59	15	57	29	65
Reduce spending on social programs	55	20	44	84	71
Reduce spending on defense and the military	44	65	47	11	29
Amend the U.S. Constitution to allow organized prayer in public schools	66	19	66	50	73
Cancel affirmative action programs giving preference to women, blacks, and other minorities	45	82	63	11	31
Bar illegal immigrants from public schools, hospitals, and other state-run social services	48	16	36	65	61

SOURCE: *Washington Post* telephone poll of Republican delegates August 11, 1996 and Democratic delegates, August 25, 1996.

Democrats, passed laws mandating presidential primaries for both parties. Republicans also engaged in a modest effort to alter their rules in the name of fairness. The 1972 convention authorized the creation of a Delegate-Organization (DO) Committee. The purpose of the DO Committee (called the "Do-Nothing Committee" by critics) was to recommend measures for enhancing the numbers of women, youth, and minorities at future Republican conventions. The committee proposed that traditional party leaders be prohibited from serving as ex officio delegates; that party officials should better inform citizens how they could participate in the nomination process; and that participation should be increased by opening the primaries and state conventions to all qualified citizens. But the 1976 Republican Convention rejected several of the committee's more important recommendations, including: (1) allowing persons under twenty-five years of age to vote in "numerical equity to their voting strength in a state"; (2) encouraging equal strengths between male and female delegates; (3) and having one minority group on each of the convention's principal committees. Later, the RNC rejected a recommendation that it review state affirmative action plans, and the GOP has refused to abolish winner-take-all primaries such as the one in California. The winner-take-all system proved especially important to the 1988 campaign of George Bush, who finished first in each of the sixteen Republican primaries conducted on March 8, the day dubbed "Super Tuesday," thereby overwhelming his opposition who were unable to obtain any delegates. Republicans have generally preferred to leave delegate selection rules to the various state parties.[37]

Republicans have also been spared major changes in their delegate selection process because unlike the Democrats, Republicans avoided squabbles among presidential contenders involving party rules. This was possible because Republicans won most White House contests held between 1968 and 1988. Only once in this period did the rules figure in a GOP contest: in 1976, Ronald Reagan promulgated Rule 14C which would have required prospective candidates to name their vice presidential candidates in advance of their own selection by the convention. Reagan lost this battle and the nomination to Gerald Ford, and Rule 14C was relegated to the cobwebs of history.

The Unintended Consequences of the McGovern-Fraser Reforms

One result of the McGovern-Fraser Commission's actions has been a surge in ideological candidacies, beginning with McGovern's. Other ideologues include former Republican and current Reform Party candidate Patrick J. Buchanan, Republican Pat Robertson, and Democrat Jesse Jackson. McGovern admitted that the new rules spawned by the commission he led helped fuel such ideologically inspired candidacies: "My successful bid for the nomination in 1972 was based in part on the opportunity which the new rules offered to a candidate willing to take his case directly to rank-and-file voters rather than depending on big-name endorsements."[38] In fact, many who worked for the commission played key roles in McGovern's successful drive to win the Democratic nomination. But the exclusion of "big-name endorsements" has contributed mightily to a weakening of parties as institutions. By removing the most important function party leaders have—making its choice for president—what remained of the old establishment found itself with almost nothing to do.

The ongoing arguments about whether the rank and file or the party leadership should exercise a dominant role in selecting presidential candidates are virtually meaningless given the new presidential nomination system engendered by the McGovern-Fraser Commission—one that is dominated by primaries and where most voters learn about politics through television. Collectively, the media exercise a form of "peer review," where reporters act as political analysts and talent scouts. Political reporters are often fascinated with two things: who has raised the most money and from what sources and how the various candidates stand in the public opinion polls. From this information, the press determines what constitutes a "win" or a "loss" in any given contest. For example, Michael Dukakis's third-place showing in the 1988 Iowa caucuses was deemed good enough to continue. Likewise, Bill Clinton's second-place finish in the 1992 New Hampshire Democratic primary despite charges of draft evasion and womanizing was characterized as a "win." Bob Dole's first-place, but disappointing 23 percent showing in the 1996 Iowa caucuses, was deemed a "loss" by the pundits. Likewise, George Bush's first-place showing in the 1992 New Hampshire primary was a "loss," since Bush ceded 40 percent of the vote to conservative Patrick Buchanan. Ceaseless press coverage of the presidential "horse race" constitutes an exercise in reporting that Alexander Hamilton once derided as "the little arts of popularity."[39]

The Mikulski and Winograd Commissions

None of these unintended consequences of the McGovern-Fraser reforms stopped Democrats from tinkering with their presidential nominating system. The 1972 Democratic Convention authorized the creation of a Commission on Delegate Selection and Party Structure to be chaired by then-Baltimore City Council-woman Barbara Mikulski. The **Mikulski Commission** reaffirmed the idea of choosing convention delegates through direct primaries and state party caucuses and that a delegate's presidential preference should be clearly expressed on a state ballot. But even more radically, the commission recommended that winner-take-all primaries be ended. At the 1972 Democratic Convention, delegates loyal to Hubert Humphrey and George McGovern fought a bitter battle over the issue. McGovern had won the California primary, and under that state's rules he was entitled to all of its delegates. Humphrey argued for proportional representation, while McGovern said the rules should not be changed at the last minute. The issue was settled in McGovern's favor, but the zeal of the reformers could not stop the trend toward more openness and fairness in delegate selection. As the Mikulski Commission stated, "Delegations shall be allocated in a fashion that fairly reflects the expressed presidential preference . . . of the primary voters, or if there be no binding primary, the convention and caucus participants."[40] The commission recommended that anyone receiving ten percent of the primary or caucus votes receive a proportionate share of the delegates. The DNC agreed with the basic thrust of the recommendation, but raised the threshold to 15 percent. Together, the McGovern-Fraser and Mikulski Commissions represent a revolution in the nominating process. Old bosses became extinct—especially after Mayor Richard J. Daley died in 1976—and ideologues in both parties seized the reins of power.

Even though the old-style Democrats had been thoroughly defeated, reform commissions continued. In 1975, Democratic National Chairman Robert Strauss created the Commission on the Role and Future of Presidential Primaries, chaired by Morley Winograd, the Michigan State Democratic chairman. The **Winograd Commission** recommended that each state Democratic party "adopt specific goals and timetables" to carry out affirmative action programs, citing women, blacks, Hispanics, and Native Americans as groups for which remedial action was needed to overcome the effects of past discrimination. Upon receiving the commission report, the DNC immediately ordered that state delegations comprise equal numbers of men and women.

Taken together, these changes banished much of the Democratic Party establishment from the convention proceedings. Before the McGovern-Fraser Commission, 83 percent of Democratic governors, 68 percent of senators, and 39 percent of representatives attended the 1968 Democratic Convention as delegates or alternates; by 1976, only 76 percent of Democratic governors, 14 percent of senators, and 15 percent of representatives were delegates.[41] Proportional representation was introduced, and soon engendered disputes among prospective nominees. In 1984, Walter Mondale acceded to Jesse Jackson's demand to lower the delegate threshold, that proportion of votes in a primary or caucus needed in order to win a convention delegate. Jackson contended that the 20 percent threshold was unfair, since the percentage of the total vote he received did not correspond to actual delegates. Thus, the threshold was reduced to 15 percent. *New York Times* columnist Tom Wicker wrote that the Democratic Party's obsession with the purity of the process had overcome its desire to win presidential contests: "[Democrats have become] a *party of access* in which the voiceless find a voice while Republican control of the presidency has permitted them to "maintain enough coherence and unity to become a *party of government*."[42]

Enter the Superdelegates

Jimmy Carter's landslide loss to Ronald Reagan in 1980, coupled with the Democratic Party's loss of a majority in the U.S. Senate, prompted the creation of another commission to examine the delegate selection rules. This time there was a difference. The **Hunt Commission,** chaired by North Carolina Governor James Hunt, undertook to restore some modicum of federalism to the nominating process. It called for the creation of the **superdelegates**—that is, Democratic officials and party officeholders who would be automatic convention delegates. Totaling nearly 14 percent of the convention delegates in 1984, 16 percent in 1988, and 18 percent in 1992, these men and women would not be bound to a particular candidate, and could, if they wished, render a collective judgment on the prospective nominees. Despite attempts to reduce their numbers, superdelegates have remained a force and represent the Democratic Party's only attempt to graft an element of federalism back onto their presidential selection process. In fact, these superdelegates provided former Vice President Walter F. Mondale with his margin of victory over Gary Hart at the 1984 Democratic Convention.

Beyond the Hunt Commission, technological advances are a major factor in the nationalization of the presidential selection process. Television has helped to expand what the Framers hoped would be a federal contest. Yet even on that small screen, differences between the two party's nominating procedures are pronounced. Republicans tolerate winner-take-all primaries, while Democrats mandate proportional representation. Political scientist Martin P. Wattenberg claims the Democratic rules produce "Timex candidates" who "take a licking and keep on ticking."[43] Losers are expected to take their fight to the convention for ultimate adjudication. For example, although Republican Pat Robertson received almost as many votes in 1988 as Jesse Jackson did in 1984, there was one important difference. Robertson competed in a system where Jefferson's idea of community is not inconsistent with winner-take-all primaries, whereas Jackson fought in an arena where Hamilton's concept of family means that the national convention becomes the final arbiter. The result was to bench Robertson on the sidelines at the 1988 Republican Convention, while Jackson occupied center stage for much of the 1984 Democratic conclave.

LOOKING TO 2000

As noted previously, Americans are ambivalent about political parties. That ambivalence stems, in part, from the accent on individualism that permeates the American polity. When it comes to choosing a president, a focus on the individual, not the party, has prevailed. This emphasis on personalism has complicated the selection process. The Framers' attempt to devise a presidential selection system that would create a presidency free of partisan constraints resulted in the creation of the Electoral College, judged by nearly all historians to be a failure. By the mid-1800s, political parties became more firmly rooted in American soil, and the party convention, which emphasizes group activity rather than individual choice, supplanted the Congressional Caucus. The party convention has enjoyed a long life, in part because it fused federalism with nationalism and also because it became a source of social activity in an era when parties were an important socializing force. But the convention has fallen into disrepute—a victim of party decay and the ambitions of would-be presidents. Richard Reeves wrote that the most important feature of John F. Kennedy's political career was his own ambition:

> He did not wait his turn. He directly challenged the institution he wanted to control, the political system. After him, no one else wanted to wait either, and few institutions were rigid enough or flexible enough to survive impatient ambition-driven challenges. He believed (and proved) that the only qualification for the most powerful job in the world was wanting it. His power did not come from the top down nor from the bottom up. It was an ax driven by his own ambition into the middle of the system, biting to the center he wanted for himself. When he was asked early in 1960 why he thought he should be president, he answered: "I look around me at the others in the race, and I say to myself, well, if they think they can do it why not me? *'Why not me?'* That's the answer. And I think it's enough."[44]

Ever since John Kennedy uttered those words, nearly every other presidential candidate has said, "Why not me?" In presenting themselves to the public, these ambitious contenders have relied on their own persona rather than their party affiliations to help them get elected. Celebrity politics is not party politics. The evidence of the absence of parties in presidential campaigns is abundant. In 1968, for example, Richard Nixon rarely mentioned the word *Republican*. Instead, his theme was "Nixon's the one!"—a vague slogan to which voters could add whatever they wanted. The success of such empty sloganeering minus any reference to a political party was not lost on other presidential candidates. In 1980, third-party candidate John Anderson called for "a patriotism greater than party" and declared that "America needs an independent president."[45] Anderson eschewed a party convention, preferring to write his own platform and name a vice presidential running mate. In 1992, Ross Perot similarly presented himself to the American voter—minus any formal nominating process. Perot did much the same in 1996, cutting short a gathering of his Reform Party followers to appear on *Larry King Live*. Both Anderson and Perot waged their campaigns not just against the major parties, but against the idea of parties themselves.

While George Bush, Bill Clinton, and Bob Dole had the benefit of a nominating convention, it hardly resembled the days of yore. In the 1965 edition of *The World Book Encyclopedia*, major party conventions were described as allowing "all citizens an opportunity to observe one of the processes of representative government. And when two strong candidates seek nomination, a national convention is more exciting than a World Series."[46] But it has been years since a convention has been more exciting than any World Series. The last party gathering to take more than one ballot was in 1952 when the Democrats nominated Adlai E. Stevenson on the third ballot. Instead of cries of "Mr. Chairman, Mr. Chairman!" from the convention floor, party conventions have been relegated to C-SPAN where the most memorable phrase is likely to be that of the talk show host saying, "Virginia Beach, hello." In 1938, Franklin Roosevelt admitted that most voters saw the party convention as an event where the real decisions were made "by a little group in a smoke-filled room who made out the party slates."[47] By succumbing to such a caricature, and failing to overcome it despite the imposition of the direct primary, the party convention has itself become un-American. The major media no longer deem the nominating conventions worthy of much coverage. In a celebrated incident, ABC anchor Ted Koppel walked out of the 1996 Republican Convention saying that there was nothing for him to do. By allowing would-be presidents to present themselves to the electorate without the intermediary of a political party, we may be witnessing an end of a long era of two-party dominance (see Chapter 10) and a rebirth of emphasizing the personal qualities of presidential candidates.

The lack of connection exists not only between the public and the parties, but occurs within the parties themselves. In his highly acclaimed work *Consequences of Party Reform*, political scientist Nelson Polsby wrote:

> The sense of loss of autonomy among state party leaders in national affairs turned their concerns inward and reduced their incentives to contest with various interest groups and candidate enthusiasts for influence over the presidential nomination process. . . . The net effect on state and local party organizations of this discouragement of grassroots political activity during a presidential election year may be hard to access. At a minimum, it tends to diminish the value of state and local party leaders in their dealings with candidates, thus reinforcing trends that already have ample momentum.[48]

In a sense, we are back to square one, seeking to "fix" what many Americans see as a broken nominating system. Besides wondering about what kind of president we want, future tinkerers must also ask, "How do we get a president who can govern effectively?" The answers to both of these questions are harder to find as political parties become less important to most Americans. It is unlikely that voters in the next presidential election—nor the parties themselves—will be able to adequately solve these pressing questions in the near future.

FURTHER READING

David, Paul T., Ralph M. Goldman, and Richard C. Bain. *Presidential Nominating Politics in 1952.* 5 vols. Baltimore: Johns Hopkins University Press, 1955.

Jackson, John S. III and William Crotty. *The Politics of Presidential Selection.* New York: HarperCollins, 1996.

Kirkpatrick, Jeane J. *The New Presidential Elite: Men and Women in National Politics.* New York: Russell Sage, 1976.

Ladd, Everett Carll. *Where Have All the Voters Gone? The Fracturing of American Political Parties.* New York: Norton, 1978.

McGovern, George S. *Grassroots: The Autobiography of George McGovern.* New York: Random House, 1977.

Polsby, Nelson W. *Consequences of Party Reform.* New York: Oxford University Press, 1983.

Shafer, Byron. *Quiet Revolution: The Struggle for the Democratic Party and the Shaping of Post-Reform Politics.* New York: Russell Sage, 1983.

NOTES

1. Fred Blumenthal, "How to Prepare for the Presidency," *Parade Magazine,* 1962. Reprinted in *The World Book Encyclopedia* (Chicago: Field Enterprises Educational Corporation, 1965), 678–79.

2. Quoted in James Wooten, *Dasher: The Roots and the Rising of Jimmy Carter* (New York: Summit Books, 1978), 40.

3. Ibid., 22.

4. Ibid., 29.

5. Ibid., 40.

6. See David Maraniss, *First in His Class: A Biography of Bill Clinton* (New York: Simon & Schuster, 1995), 280–281. To which Carr replied, "Oh you are, are you?"

7. Ibid., 437.

8. Quoted in John Kenneth White, "YES—Vice-Presidential Candidates Should Be Selected from the Also-Ran Category," in Gary L. Rose, ed., *Controversial Issues in Presidential Selection* (Albany: State University of New York Press, 1994), 80.

9. Quoted in Evan Thomas, Karen Breslau, Debra Rosenberg, Leslie Kaufman, and Andrew Murr, *Back from the Dead* (New York: Atlantic Monthly Press, 1997), 74.

10. Alexander Hamilton, "Federalist 68," in Edward Meade Earle, ed., *The Federalist* (New York: Modern Library, 1937), 50.

11. See Larry Hugick, "Money and Politics," in *Polling Report* 13 (June 16, 1997): 6. The poll was conducted by the Princeton Survey Research Associates for the Center for Responsive Politics, April 1–24, 1997.

12. Quoted in Dick Morris, *Behind the Oval Office: Winning the Presidency in the Nineties* (New York: Random House, 1997), 150.

13. See Hugick, "Money and Politics," 6 and Gallup/CNN/*USA Today*, survey, October 3-5, 1997. Text of question: "I'm going to read you several pairs of statements. After I read each pair, please tell me which statement you agree with more. . . . Elections are generally for sale to the candidate who can raise

the most money. OR, Elections are generally won on the basis of who is the best candidate." Most money, 59 percent; best candidate, 37 percent; neither/other (volunteered), 2 percent; no opinion, 2 percent.

14. James Bryce, *The American Commonwealth* (New York: MacMillan, 1889), 72, 75.

15. Louis Harris and Associates, survey, April 22–27, 1992.

16. See Dr. George H. Gallup, *The Gallup Poll, Public Opinion 1935–1971, Volume Three 1959– 1971* (New York: Random House, 1972), 1681. Gallup poll, July 30–August 4, 1960. Text of question: "The ten boxes on this card go from the highest position of plus 5—for someone you like very much—all the way down to the lowest position of minus 5—for someone you dislike very much. Please tell me how far up the scale or how far down the scale you would rate each of the presidential and vice presidential candidates." Percentage responding "highly favorable": Richard M. Nixon, 43 percent; Henry Cabot Lodge, 42 percent; John F. Kennedy, 42 percent; Lyndon B. Johnson, 30 percent.

17. Hamilton, "Federalist 68," 444.

18. Lyndon B. Johnson, "Remarks Before the American Bar Association," New York City, August 12, 1964, in *Public Papers of the Presidents of the United States: Lyndon B. Johnson* (Washington, D.C.: U.S. Government Printing Office, 1964), 953.

19. Quoted in David R. Runkel, ed., *Campaign for President: The Managers Look at '88* (Dover, Mass.: Auburn House, 1989), 113.

20. Gallup Organization, survey, October 20–21, 1988. Text of question: "In your opinion, is this year's presidential campaign more negative or less negative than presidential campaigns in the past, just your own impression." More negative, 64 percent. Gallup Organization, survey, October 20–21, 1988. Text of question: "In your opinion, did this year's presidential primaries produce the best candidates or do you think there were better qualified candidates who should have been selected?" Better qualified, 66 percent.

21. Alexis de Tocqueville, *Democracy in America* (New York: New American Library, 1956), 177.

22. Quoted in James MacGregor Burns, *The Power to Lead* (New York: Simon & Schuster, 1984), 220.

23. Quoted in James W. Ceaser, *Presidential Selection: Theory and Development* (Princeton, N.J.: Princeton University Press, 1979), 147.

24. Quoted in A. James Reichley, *The Life of the Parties* (New York: Free Press, 1992), 92.

25. Ibid., 133–34.

26. Ibid., 134.

27. Quoted in E. E. Schattschneider, *The Semi-Sovereign People: A Realist's View of Democracy in America* (Hinsdale, Ill.: Dryden Press, 1975 reprint), 84.

28. Quoted in "Democrats End Two-Thirds Rule," *New York Times*, June 25, 1936, 1. It is interesting to note that Daniels equates the convention with the nation.

29. Lyndon B. Johnson, "Address to the Nation," March 31, 1968.

30. Theodore H. White, *The Making of the President, 1968* (New York: Atheneum, 1969), 376.

31. George McGovern, *Grassroots: The Autobiography of George McGovern* (New York: Random House, 1977), 130. Eugene McCarthy became a candidate in November 1967; Robert Kennedy entered in mid-March, 1968; Lyndon Johnson withdrew from the race on March 31st; Hubert Humphrey became an official candidate in late April (after most of the primary deadlines had passed). The charge that Humphrey was an unrepresentative candidate of the Democratic Party rank and file remains a contested issue. Humphrey easily led McCarthy in the Gallup polls as the party's choice for the presidential nomination, and was competitive in a three-way contest involving Eugene McCarthy, Robert Kennedy, and Humphrey. For more information see Richard Scammon and Ben J. Wattenberg, *The Real Majority* (New York: Coward-McCann, 1970).

32. *Mandate for Reform: A Report of the Commission on Party Structure and Delegate Selection to the Democratic National Committee* (Washington, D.C.: Democratic National Committee, April 1970).

33. McGovern, *Grassroots*, 137.

34. *Cousins v. Wigoda*, 419 U.S. 477 (1975).

35. McGovern, *Grassroots*, 148.

36. Jeane J. Kirkpatrick, *The New Presidential Elite: Men and Women in National Politics* (New York: Russell Sage, 1976), 68.

37. See Joseph A. Pika and Richard A. Watson, *The Presidential Contest* (Washington, D.C.: Congressional Quarterly, 1996), 15–16.

38. McGovern, *Grassroots*, 153.

39. Hamilton, "Federalist 68," 444.

40. Quoted in Everett Carll Ladd, *Where Have All the Voters Gone?: The Fracturing of American Political Parties* (New York: Norton, 1978), 55.

41. Cited in Nelson W. Polsby, *Consequences of Party Reform* (New York: Oxford University Press, 1983), 114.

42. Tom Wicker, "A Party of Access?" *New York Times*, November 25, 1984, E17.

43. Quoted in Thomas B. Edsall, "Bush Ascends Minus Solid Base," *Washington Post*, January 20, 1989, F10.

44. Richard Reeves, *President Kennedy: Profile of Power* (New York: Simon & Schuster, 1993), 14.

45. Quoted in Andrew E. Busch and James W. Ceaser, "Does Party Reform Have a Future?" in William G. Mayer, ed., *In Pursuit of the White House: How We Choose Our Presidential Nominees* (Chatham, N.J.: Chatham House Publishers, 1996), 350.

46. Walter F. Morse, "Political Convention," *World Book Encyclopedia*, vol. 15 (Chicago: Field Enterprises Educational Corporation, 1964), 553–54.

47. Quoted in Sidney M. Milkis, "Progressive Liberalism and Party Politics," in John Kenneth White and Jerome M. Mileur, eds., *Challenges to Party Government* (Cardondale: Southern Illinois University Press, 1992), 117.

48. Polsby, *Consequences of Party Reform*, 78–80.

CHAPTER 6

Party Brand Loyalty and the American Voter

Every four years Americans gather to follow a quadrennial series titled "Election Night" that answers an all-important question: who will be the next president? Some election nights have become legendary for their suspense and high drama. Running for an unprecedented third term in 1940, Franklin D. Roosevelt saw trouble in the early returns. Breaking into a cold heavy sweat, the president abruptly ordered everyone to leave the family dining room at his Hyde Park, New York, estate. Seated in his wheelchair, Roosevelt calculated whether he had enough votes to win as news tickers clattered away with the latest results. After a few suspense-filled hours, the numbers turned in Roosevelt's favor, whereupon family and friends rejoined him as he became his familiar, cheery self.[1]

Twenty years later, another election night was immortalized by journalist Theodore H. White. Spending the evening with John F. Kennedy at his Hyannisport, Massachusetts, compound, White described how the early figures were going Kennedy's way. At one point in the evening, Kennedy's wife, Jacqueline, exclaimed, "Oh, Bunny [her pet name for her husband], you're going to be president now!"[2] But as midnight approached, Kennedy's Republican opponent, Richard M. Nixon, had cut dramatically into Kennedy's lead, and the all-important Electoral College remained a few votes shy from a Kennedy majority. As night turned to day, no one knew who had won. Only when Chicago Mayor Richard J. Daley found enough votes to put Illinois in the Kennedy column was he declared the winner. Final figures showed Kennedy beat Nixon by just 112,881 votes out of nearly 70 million cast—a margin of just one-tenth of one percent.

Eight years later, Nixon was a central character in another election night melodrama—defeating Democrat Hubert H. Humphrey by half a percentage point out of nearly 73 million popular votes cast. As in 1960, the lead seesawed between the two candidates. At midnight, Humphrey was ahead. By 6:00 A.M. Nixon had taken a slim lead, but most television commentators were speculating that Mayor Daley was holding back Democratic votes in key Chicago precincts. When Mrs. Nixon heard that news, she became literally sick to her stomach.[3] Two hours later Daley recognized that he could not stop Nixon and released his votes. Illinois and the presidency went to Nixon.

In the Information Age, election night has lost much of its previous excitement. Exit polls conducted by the major television networks frequently provide strong indications of who has won or lost; before the polls even close. Relying on such information in 1980, Jimmy Carter telephoned Republican Ronald Reagan at 5:00 P.M. Pacific Standard Time, just as Reagan was stepping out of a hotel shower, to concede defeat. Eight years later Ronald Reagan and a group of intimates, including pollster Richard Wirthlin, gathered around a television set in the White House to watch the election results. At 8:00 P.M., CBS News informed Wirthlin that it would declare Vice President George Bush the winner some ninety minutes later. Wirthlin immediately took Reagan aside to tell him the news. With an actor's sense of timing the president responded, "Dick, don't tell anyone this. We've got to add a little excitement to the evening."[4] In 1996, any pretense of excitement was lost as both the major networks and principal presidential candidates knew the election outcome by midafternoon. That night, the roll call of states proceeded apace, and a little past 9:00 P.M. Eastern Standard Time Bill Clinton was declared the winner—even as people were still voting out West. Two hours later after the predictable victory and concession statements, ABC News television commentator David Brinkley, caught in an unguarded moment, acknowledged that this particular election night had been especially boring. Brinkley, no doubt, remembered Kennedy's remarkable win thirty-six years before which he had covered for NBC News.

The Information Age has created an interesting paradox. Exit polls and the computer-based projections that accompany them have taken away much of the drama that once surrounded election night. Yet, the behavior of individual voters is harder to predict as party brand loyalty is no longer what it used to be. In 1996, nearly one of every four voters who considered themselves to be either a Democrat or a Republican abandoned their party and voted for another presidential candidate.[5] According to a postelection poll by Wirthlin Worldwide, nearly 9 percent of voters indicated that information provided on the Internet had influenced their vote.[6]

This is quite a change from the nineteenth century. In 1884, the *Philadelphia Inquirer* observed that "party lines were as strictly drawn as were the lines of religious sects."[7] Southerners coined the nickname "yellow dog Democrat," meaning they would vote for a yellow dog instead of a dreaded Republican. Northerners, on the other hand, were often rock-ribbed Yankees and firmly committed Republicans. Then too, parental party identification had a strong influence on young, impressionable children as illustrated by two examples from the early twentieth century. Growing up in rural Texas, a young Lyndon B. Johnson followed politics through the eyes of his father, Sam, a powerful Democratic state legislator. Johnson remembered campaigning with his father when he was just ten years old: "We drove in the Model T Ford from farm to farm, up and down the valley, stopping at every door. . . . Families all the way opened up their homes to us. If it was hot outside, we were invited in for big servings of homemade ice cream. If it was cold, we were given hot tea. Christ, sometimes I wished it could go on forever."[8]

Richard M. Nixon remembered how his father's Midwestern Republicanism shaped his rise to power: "Lively discussions of political issues were always a feature of our family gatherings. My father started out as a hard-line Ohio Republican, [and his] interest in politics made him the most enthusiastic follower of my career from its beginnings. My success meant to him that everything he had worked for and believed in was true: that in America, with hard work and determination a man can achieve anything. . . . When I was running for Vice President, he wrote a typically straightforward letter to one of the newspapers he had read years before, suggesting that it support me: 'This boy is one of five that I raised and they are the finest, I think, in the United States. If you care to give him a lift, I would say the *Ohio State Journal* is still doing some good.'"[9]

Throughout much of American history, voting was not a soul-searching enterprise because most Americans were creatures of political habit. The excitement on election night came not because there was much doubt about what individual voters might do—they were loyal partisans—rather, it was because the parties were so evenly matched. Today, party brand loyalty is no longer habit-forming. Recalling the business analogy developed earlier in this text, voters are the political parties' consumers. In the Information Age, they tend to switch their purchasing habits from one election to the next, from one party to the other, and even from one candidate to another. Without much party brand loyalty, elections often are unpredictable and polls can change frequently. Perhaps the most famous instance of this occurred in 1988. That year Democrats salivated at the prospect of having Vice President George Bush serve as the GOP standard-bearer. The polls buoyed Democratic hopes. After their convention, a Gallup survey found Democratic nominee Michael Dukakis ahead of Bush by a whopping seventeen points. But on election night it was Bush who prevailed. Asked by a reporter the morning after the election why Dukakis lost, a frustrated Mario Cuomo curtly replied, "He got fewer votes."[10]

This chapter examines how political consumers—the voters—relate to the parties. First, we review how party brand loyalty develops and examine ways scholars have sought to measure it. Second, we discuss the decline of party brand loyalty in the Information Age. Third, we examine what political scientists call *realignment theory* and how its potential demise affects the way electoral politics is studied. Finally, we describe the electoral coalitions that have emerged in the 1990s and how the party-building demographics have changed in the last sixty years. In each case, one theme remains constant: When it comes to thinking about politics, voters are increasingly willing to select a generic brand instead of the old Democratic or Republican labels.

THE IMPORTANCE OF PARTY IDENTIFICATION

Few topics have received more scholarly attention over the last three decades than political behavior, an area of research that focuses on the attitudes, beliefs, and actions of individuals. Among the first to study how individual voters behave in the voting booths were Bernard R. Berelson and Paul F. Lazarsfeld who contributed to *The People's Choice* (1940)[11] and *Voting* (1948).[12] Berelson and Lazarsfeld developed a **sociological model** in which socioeconomic standing (education, income, and class); religion (Catholic, Protestant, or Jewish); and place of residence (rural or urban) formed an "index of political predisposition" that often determined party identification which strongly influenced choices made at the ballot box. Thus, for example, a well-educated, white, upper-class Protestant from upstate New York would most likely be a Republican, while a black, blue-collar worker from Detroit would most likely be a Democrat. Using this index of political predisposition, demography mattered most, and political campaigns counted little. Joining a political party was a declaration about who you were and where you were born. During the campaign season, Republicans shouted at other like-minded Republicans to vote for their candidates, and Democrats did much the same—with few minds being changed.

The sociological model was best-suited to explain the strong party era that existed from the post–Civil War period until the New Deal. The weakening of party loyalties, which began during the 1950s and accelerated in the 1960s, made the sociological model obsolete. In 1952, for example, millions of Democrats voted for Republican Dwight D. Eisenhower giving him a comfortable ten-point victory over Democrat Adlai Stevenson. What influenced many people, regardless of party affiliation, to support Eisenhower were issues—especially the Korean War. Gallup polls found 65 percent chose Eisenhower as best able to break stalemate in Korea; only 19 percent picked Stevenson.[13] In 1956, Eisenhower defied the existing Democratic majority to beat Stevenson again—this time with 57 percent of the vote to Stevenson's 43 percent. As in 1952, Eisenhower's advantage on the foreign policy issues that were vitally important in determining Cold War presidential elections proved decisive.

Eisenhower's landslide victories illustrated the deficiencies associated with the sociological model. Surely the attitudes held by voters about the candidates and issues were important factors in determining who won or lost on election night. Two questions remained: what individual political attitudes were important and how could they be measured?

Some answers were contained in *The American Voter* published in 1960.[14] Authors Angus Campbell, Philip Converse, Warren Miller, and Donald Stokes created the **sociological-psychological model.** They agreed with Lazarsfeld that demographics still counted for something, but that partisanship also had a strong psychological dimension. Accordingly, most Americans identified with their parent's party, while the children of parents without a clear partisan preference were ambivalent about politics. Once established, party identification often persisted throughout a person's adult life. Using data gathered in the 1950s, Campbell and his colleagues found that nearly 85 percent stuck with the same party throughout their adult lives, and a majority had *never* voted for a candidate of the other party.[15]

The American Voter is considered a seminal work because it introduced the **funnel of causality.** As shown in Figure 6.1, at the tip of the funnel is an individual's vote choice. The funnel's axis represents a time dimension, and events occur in sequence from the mouth to the stem. Numerous causes—each an outcome of prior events—converge into a single act of voting. At the mouth of the funnel are demographic characteristics (e.g., ethnicity, race, region, and religion); social status characteristics (e.g., education, occupation, and class); and parental characteristics (e.g., parental partisanship and social class). Together they create a person's party identification which is usually long-lasting. Once partisanship is formed, voters selectively screen information using the lenses of their preferred party. For example, when Independent Counsel Kenneth Starr accused Clinton of perjury and advocated his impeach-

FIGURE 6.1 ▪ The Funnel of Causality Predicting Vote Choice
("Michigan Model")

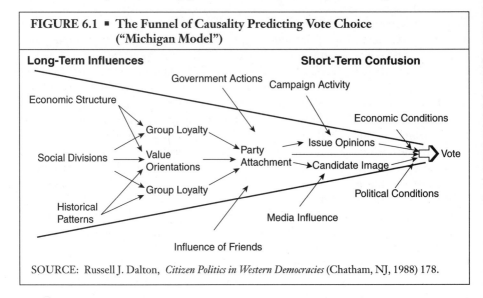

SOURCE: Russell J. Dalton, *Citizen Politics in Western Democracies* (Chatham, NJ, 1988) 178.

ment, voters reacted largely along party lines: 62 percent of Republicans believed that Starr's charges warranted Clinton's removal; 88 percent of Democrats disagreed.[16]

From its inception, *The American Voter* provided a baseline to measure how a person's party identification influenced individual voting choices. This is not to say that refinements were impossible and challenges were not forthcoming. In 1971, Gerald Pomper found a significant increase in the correlation between policy and party from the results reported in *The American Voter*. Using seven issues—federal aid to education; government provision of medical care; government guarantees of full employment; federal enforcement of fair employment, housing, and school integration; and foreign aid—Pomper found that in 1956 a linear relation between issue and party identification existed only for medical care. By 1968, there were correlations on all of the aforementioned issues except foreign aid. In addition, the proportion who viewed the Democrats as the more liberal party had risen on every question. Pomper concluded that between 1956 and 1968 "considerable political learning" had taken place.[17]

Building on Pomper's work, Norman Nie, Sidney Verba, and John Petrocik argued in *The Changing American Voter* that issues were important influences on voting behavior.[18] This approach, we call the **cognitive voter model,** assumed that citizens supported a particular candidate based on issue positions. For example, as the Vietnam War and civil rights debates of the 1960s and 1970s were given increased public prominence, and the two political parties nominated ideologues (Republican Barry Goldwater and Democrat George McGovern) who had strong positions on these issues, voters began to use candidate and party stances in a new manner as voting guides. Candidate-centered politics, with its focus on issues, had replaced party-centered politics. This did not mean that party identification no longer mattered; rather, voters paid attention to issues when candidates took clear, unequivocal stands on them. But if candidates adopted similar positions on the issues of the day, then party identification reemerged as the primary determinant of vote choice. It was a two-step process: issues first, party second.

Since the 1950s, several scholars have approached the study of parties and party identification using the **rational-choice** or **rational-actor model,** which postulates that voters establish goals and achieve them using cost-benefit calculations. For example, someone might aspire to become rich, but finds working eighteen-hour days to acquire wealth not worth the cost. Applying the same rationale to party identification, in his 1957 book titled *An Economic Theory of Democracy*, Anthony Downs argued that the benefits of arriving at a "correct" voting decision may not be worth the costs of compiling extensive information on the candidates.[19] Most voters want to cast an informed vote, but lack the time and energy to sift through the complex details of each candidate's policy stands and personal character. Party identification gives the busy voter a quick and easy solution. Voters can take an information shortcut by understanding the basic contours of what each party stands for, matching that information with their own values (thus developing a party identification), and then associate particular candidates with their party labels. Thus, an election day decision can be made in a few seconds, since the voter need only know each candidates' party to cast an "informed" vote.

If Downs and other rational-choice theorists are correct, we can better appreciate the importance of party brand loyalty—and what the loss of it has meant for the American polity. For instance, as the number of voters linking themselves to a particular party declines, under the rational-choice model it follows that electoral turnout will shrink. In fact, this has been the case since the 1960s. Without this information shortcut, voters are forced to either spend a great deal of time studying the candidates and issues or cast a random vote that does not square with their drive for rationality. Would-be voters find it easier to withdraw from the voting process than invest the time required to make an informed decision. The decline of party identification also has resulted in voters using other information shortcuts such as a candidate's gender, ethnic background, or incumbency. Use of the latter leads to high reelection rates, even though voters say they are frustrated with the overall direction of their government. Thus, from the perspective of rational-choice theorists, there is vastly more to party identification than meets the eye.

Measuring Party Identification

If the scholarly quarrel over how party identification influences vote choice has dominated the study of political behavior, a close second has been the controversy over how to *measure* party identification. The most commonly used technique employs a seven-point ordinal scale developed by public opinion pollsters. Voters are classified by their answers to two questions. First, voters are asked if they consider themselves Republicans, Democrats, independents, or something else. Respondents who answer that they are either Republican or Democrat, are then asked a follow-up question about how strongly they identify with their party. Those who classify themselves as "independent" are asked whether they are closer to the

Republican Party or the Democratic Party. Respondents are then grouped into one of seven categories: (1) strong Democrat, (2) weak Democrat, (3) independent-Democrat, (4) independent-independent, (5) independent-Republican, (6) weak Republican, (7) strong Republican. The advantage of this approach is that it suggests degrees of partisanship. It is reasonable to assume that some Democrats and Republicans are more closely connected to their party than others, and that many so-called independents lean more toward one of the parties. In fact, roughly two-thirds say they identify with the Democratic or Republican party to varying degrees, and 60 percent of self-identified independents exhibit political behaviors similar to those of overt partisans.[20]

But party identification is more complex and depends on a variety of other factors than merely asking whether a respondent is a Democrat, Republican, or independent. Herbert Weisberg offers three variables: (1) attitudes toward the Republican Party; (2) attitudes toward the Democratic Party; and (3) attitudes toward political independence.[21] Another approach to measure the strength of party identifiers is to have survey respondents rank each party on a thermometer with zero degrees representing very negative feelings and 100 degrees signifying very positive feelings. Scores for each party are compared and a partisan preference is determined. Others believe that the easiest way to gauge a citizen's disposition toward the parties is to ask how they vote on election day.

The debate surrounding the validity of and ways to measure party identification is likely to continue given the new technologies and modes of communication associated with the Information Age. Whereas voters once got most of their political information through interpersonal communications or daily newspapers, today's plugged-in electorate has vast options for election information through the media and on the World Wide Web. CNN, for example, has an "AllPolitics" Web site that the on-line browser can summon on a moment's notice. The other major networks—CBS, ABC, and MSNBC (the alliance formed by Microsoft and NBC)—also have sophisticated Web sites that contain vast amounts of political information. The *Washington Post*, *Congressional Quarterly*, and *National Journal* also provide Web sites for the interested voter. In addition, there are dozens of Web sites for individual newsletters and candidate organizations that Information Age voters can access. Project Vote Smart, for example, provided a Web site that outlined the major presidential candidates' issue positions in 1996. Other election-oriented Web sites include:

- Democracy Place, Pew Center for Civic Journalism: <http://www.democracy place.org>. This is a nonpartisan, issue-oriented Web site that encourages citizens to become involved in the democratic process.
- CNN/AllPolitics: <http://allpolitics.com>. This Web site examines the day-to-day stories of political campaigns with analyses by CNN correspondents and a look at public opinion polls.
- 4 Politics: <http://www.4politics.com>. A vast Web site that examines what others are saying about party campaigns that includes excellent linkages to other party-oriented Web sites.

- Conservative site, Right Side of the Web: <http://www.rtside.com>. The latest in conservative thinking.
- Liberal site, Turn Left, The Home of Liberalism on the Web: <http://www.turnleft.com>. The latest in liberal thought.
- *Congressional Quarterly:* <http://voter.cq.com>. Analyzes voting trends in Congress and the American electorate as a whole.
- The McLaughlin Group: <http://www.mclaughlin.com>. An on-line connection to the famous television program that provides weekly commentary on politics.

Is Party Identification Obsolete?

Advocates of strong political parties have had little to cheer about during the last few decades. Just when *The American Voter* was published in 1960, party identification began its decline. Back then, 74 percent said they were Democrats or Republicans; today, the figure is 66 percent.[22] Party identification is no longer the meaningful indicator it used to be. For example, in October 1990 when President Bush and the Democratic Congress were struggling with a budget compromise and government closings, 51 percent called themselves Democrats while 43 percent said they were Republicans. Five months later, after U.S. troops vanquished Saddam Hussein's forces in the Persian Gulf war, the figures were nearly reversed: 47 percent were Republicans; 45 percent were Democrats.[23] Democratic pollster Geoffrey Garin believes that emphasizing partisan identification is "silly," likening it to asking: "How do you feel about the way things are going in the country today?"[24] Like the weather, the answers often change from moment to moment. Such fleeting and tentative responses to such a basic question as which political party a person identifies with have important consequences when political scientists examine the structure of electoral politics.

THE MAKING OF AN IDEA: PARTY REALIGNMENT

So far, we have discussed how individuals form partisan attachments, but what of the electorate as a whole? Taken together, the party affiliations of the entire body politic form an underlying structure of voting behavior. Thus, for political scientists, election nights in the Information Age still retain an aura of their former excitement. Besides knowing who the next president is going to be, the next most important question to be answered is what the election means. Surely, there must be something more behind the collective *X*s placed next to a candidate's name. For example, after Franklin D. Roosevelt won a landslide victory in 1936, one analyst declared that he could "see no interpretation of the returns which does not suggest that the people of America want the president to proceed along progressive or liberal lines."[25] Similarly, after Ronald Reagan's stunning 1980 victory, many agreed with Reagan pollster Richard Wirthlin when he interpreted the result as "a mandate for change" that included "a rejection of the New Deal agenda that had dominated American politics since the 1930s."[26] In each case, many political scientists argued that the structure of the American party system had undergone a significant transformation. Thus, these elections provide important clues to a simple question: what does overall party change look like?

V. O. Key and Party Realignment

Behind the speculation about what the balloting in any given election means and which political party is favored, it is clear that some elections have far-reaching consequences. Political scientist V. O. Key, Jr. was the first to argue that some elections were more important than others. Who remembers, for example, whether Franklin Pierce won the presidency in 1852, or James Buchanan in 1856, or James Garfield in 1880? While the results of these contests might provide interesting material for a game of Trivial Pursuit, from Key's perspective, **realigning elections** are those in which catastrophe plays a significant role. The impending Civil War consumed everything in its wake in 1860. Lincoln's successful prosecution of that war along with his proclamation of a "new birth of freedom" in the Gettysburg Address convinced most voters that the Republican Party could be trusted to steer the ship of state. Likewise, the Great Depression and Franklin Roosevelt's collection of New Deal programs to combat it convinced most voters that the Democratic Party could best handle the nation's economy and look after the interests of the average American. When asked in 1951 what they would tell young people about whom the parties stood for, most said that the Democrats represented the "working man" while Republicans promoted the "privileged few."[27] These mental pictures of the "common man" Democrat and "country club" Republican still retain their bright colors among older Americans who remember Franklin Roosevelt. A 1996 Gallup poll found that among those aged seventy-five years and older, Democratic identifiers outnumbered Republicans, 46 percent to 32 percent.[28]

Building on this idea, in 1955 Key developed a category of elections he described as **critical elections.** Critical elections are contests characterized by sharp reorganizations of party loyalties over short periods of time. In these contests, voter turnout is quite high and new, long-lasting party coalitions are formed. Studying the election outcomes of several New England towns from 1916 to 1952, Key found that when the Democrats nominated Catholic New York Governor Alfred E. Smith in 1928, party support in urban areas increased significantly and remained high, while Democratic backing in rural, Protestant-dominated enclaves fell to record lows, where it remained in the years that followed (see "The Parties Speak: V. O. Key and the Theory of Party Realignment").[29]

Shortly after Key introduced the concept of critical elections, he published a major modification of his original idea. In 1959, he wrote that changes in partisanship are sometimes not as dramatic as those that occurred in 1928. Instead, party loyalties can erode among some groups and regions over many years. Key termed these changes **secular realignments,** defining them as "a movement of the members of a population category from party to party that extends over several presidential elections and appears to be independent of the peculiar factors influencing the vote at individual elections."[30] Key placed no time limit on the pace of this

---

The Parties Speak: *V. O. Key and the Theory of Party Realignment*

V. O. Key, a leading political scientist of the 1950s and early 1960s, was the first to broach the idea of party realignment. Key's notion of "critical elections," first outlined in this 1955 article, has prompted generations of political scientists in the decades since to amplify upon his basic idea.

Perhaps the basic differentiating characteristic of democratic orders consists in the expression of effective choice by the mass of the people in elections. The electorate occupies, at least in the mystique of such orders, the position of the principal organ of governance; it acts through elections. An election itself is a formal act of collective decision that occurs in a stream of connected antecedent and subsequent behavior. Among democratic orders elections, so broadly defined, differ enormously in their nature, their meaning, and their consequences. Even within a single nation, the reality of election differs greatly from time to time. A systematic comparative approach, with a focus on variations in the nature of elections, would doubtless be fruitful in advancing understanding of the democratic governing process. In behavior antecedent to voting, elections differ in the proportions of the electorate psychologically involved, in the intensity of attitudes associated with campaign cleavages, in the nature of expectations about the consequences of the voting, in the impact of objective events relevant to individual political choice, in individual sense of effective connection with community decision, and in other ways. These and other antecedent variations affect the act of voting itself as well as subsequent behavior. An understanding of elections and, in turn, of the democratic process as a whole must rest partially on broad differentiations of the complexes of behavior that we call elections.

While this is not the occasion to develop a comprehensive typology of elections, the foregoing remarks provide an orientation for an attempt to formulate a concept of one type of election—based on American experience—which might be built into a more general theory of elections. Even the most fleeting inspection of American elections suggests the existence of a category of elections in which voters are, at least from impressionistic evidence, unusually deeply concerned, in which the extent of electoral involvement is relatively quite high, and in which the decisive results of the voting reveal a sharp alteration of the pre-existing cleavage within the electorate. Moreover, and perhaps this is the truly differentiating characteristic of this sort of election, the realignment made manifest in the voting in such elections seems to persist for several succeeding elections. All these characteristics cumulate to the conception of an election type in which the depth and intensity of electoral involvement are high, in which more or less profound readjustments occur in the relations of power within the community, and in which new and durable electoral groupings are formed.

SOURCE: Excerpted from V. O. Key, Jr., "A Theory of Critical Elections," *Journal of Politics*, 17 (1955): 3-4.

change, noting that it could take as long as fifty years. But the premise was clear: gradual alterations in voting behavior, not a sharp reorganization of party loyalties, characterized secular realignments. Again, using election returns from some New England towns, Key found instances where the shift from Republican dominance to sustained Democratic victories during the New Deal era were slow, but steady. Key attributed the slow pace of change to the increased industrialization and urbanization of the region, and the last wave of European immigrants who eventually became acclimated to their new country and came to the polls in support of the Democrats.

Key's ideas about critical elections and secular realignment gained widespread popularity in the political science community. Enhancing its appeal was the pro-party argument that underpinned realignment theory. Instead of resorting to arms or radical ideas such as tearing up the Constitution when catastrophe struck, political scientists believed that voters used parties to engineer significant policy changes in the government. Political parties were often credited with being important agents in maintaining the stability of the American constitutional order. The Constitution works because political parties work—or so went the argument. Given this line of reasoning, the discipline had much at stake in the success of the realignment argument.

As analysis of electoral change moved away from actual election returns, as used by Key, to Information Age polling data that could pinpoint changes within narrowly defined population groups (e.g., white male Catholics between the ages of 18 and 24), party realignment took added significance. Walter Dean Burnham, a major proponent of the realignment concept, published the influential *Critical Elections and the Mainsprings of American Politics* (1970) in which he transformed Key's simple idea of critical elections into a generalized theory of party realignment. Burnham outlined five conditions that characterized the "ideal-typical" partisan realignment:

1. Short, sharp reorganizations of the major party voter coalitions which occur at periodic intervals nationwide.
2. Third-party revolts which often precede party realignments and reveal the incapacity of "politics-as-usual."
3. Abnormal stress in the socioeconomic system which is closely associated with fundamental partisan change.
4. Ideological polarizations and issue distances between the major parties which become exceptionally large by normal standards.
5. Realignments have durable consequences and determine the general outlines of important public policies in the decades that follow.[31]

Using this classification scheme, Burnham cited the elections of Andrew Jackson in 1828, Abraham Lincoln in 1860, William McKinley in 1896, and Franklin D. Roosevelt in 1932 as having met the conditions of party realignment. In each case, voter interest and turnout was high, there were significant third-party revolts either in the actual election or in the contests leading up to it, and the differences between the parties were exceptionally large by American standards. In making his calculations, Burnham discovered a rhythm to American politics—namely, that realigning elections occur once every twenty-eight to thirty-six years. Thus, if a realigning election happened in 1932 (as Burnham suggests) or in 1928 (as Key found in New England), one could expect another realignment to occur circa 1968.

Indeed, many believe that Richard Nixon's close victory over Hubert Humphrey in 1968 met the conditions of a classic party realignment. The issue differences between the Democratic and Republican parties on civil rights, the Vietnam War, and what became known as the "social issues" (crime, abortion, pornography, etc.) were significant. Moreover, there was a major third-party revolt in the person of Alabama Governor George Wallace, whose presidential candidacy garnered 14 percent of the popular vote—a feat not exceeded until Ross Perot captured 19 percent of the ballots cast in 1992. Kevin Phillips, an astute Republican political analyst, wrote in his 1969 book *The Emerging Republican Majority:* "Far from being the tenuous and unmeaningful victory suggested by critical observers, the election of Richard M. Nixon as president of the United States in November 1968, bespoke the end of the New Deal Democratic hegemony and the beginning of a new era in American politics."[32] The election nights that followed Nixon's 1968 win gave credence to Phillip's vision of a Republican realignment. From 1968 to 1988, Republicans won five of the six presidential contests (Nixon in 1968 and 1972, Reagan in 1980 and 1984, and Bush in 1988). Only Nixon's misadventures in the Watergate scandal permitted a Democratic victory—Jimmy Carter in 1976—and that for only one term. The Republican hold on the presidency was so great that some analysts thought the GOP had an impenetrable lock on the Electoral College that would prevent future Democratic victories.

But this Republican realignment had a very different feel from the ones that preceded it. Far from being vanquished, Democrats retained comfortable majorities in both houses of Congress for most of this period. Democrats controlled the Senate from 1968 to 1980—narrowly losing control in the 1980 Reagan landslide but reclaiming majority status in 1986. The House showed an even greater Democratic advantage. When Ronald Reagan won reelection in 1984, Democrats had a seventy-one–seat margin in the House—the largest edge given to a party that did not control the presidency since 1895. Thus, while the party system created by Franklin Roosevelt had died, the "ideal-type" party realignment forecast by Burnham had failed to take its place. Many wondered what happened. Some attributed the Republican failure to produce a classic realignment to the aftereffects of Watergate. In 1974, Democrats added forty-nine seats in the House—enough to ensure control until Newt Gingrich and his partisans took over twenty years later. Others attributed the failure of either party to achieve a classic realignment to presidents who were all too willing to eschew their party affiliations in order to win more votes.

This separation of president from party—coupled with television's capacity to frame questions candidates want voters to answer—means that voters can mark an X next to a name without regard to how they might fill in the rest of the spaces on the ballot. Television commercials allow politicians with enough cash to enter our living rooms and pose the questions they want answered. In this commercial-littered environment, candidate-centered contests—not party-centered ones—have become the norm. Realigning elections depend on partisan judgments rather than individual judgments. This calls into question the validity of the party realignment concept, since any change in power can be attributed to the artful strokes of skillful politicians rather than shifts in the collective judgments voters make about the political parties. During the 1980s, Democrats labeled Ronald Reagan the "Teflon president," an acknowledgment that his communication skills were the best since John F. Kennedy. Jimmy Carter and Walter Mondale were no match for Reagan, or so went the Democratic argument. Thus, Democrats explained away the 1980 and

1984 defeats as tributes to Reagan's acute sense of showmanship. Likewise, Republicans view Bill Clinton as an extraordinary political craftsman. GOP pollster Frank Luntz lauds Clinton as a better communicator than Reagan: "Reagan was likeable. People don't like Bill Clinton, and yet they follow him."[33] Thus, many Republicans explain their 1992 and 1996 presidential defeats as a testament to Clinton's political skills—and nothing more.

Party Realignment: The Death of a Concept?

Despite the attempts of V.O. Key and Walter Dean Burnham to develop a theory of party realignment and predict when it would occur, one problem persisted: voters refused to cooperate. During the 1970s and early 1980s, new terms to describe how the electorate was behaving came into vogue. The most common of these was **dealignment**—meaning that voters were moving away from both political parties. In 1980, political scientist Everett C. Ladd wrote: "All the anchors are being raised at the same moment in American politics, and the electoral ship is drifting as never before."[34] A new way of talking about politics suddenly was in style. Phrases like "Tweedledum and Tweedledee" or "There's not a dime's worth of difference between the two parties" were commonly heard. The widespread belief that parties did not count for much was reflected in public opinion polls. One 1983 survey found most respondents saying there was "no difference" between Democrats and Republicans on such major issues of the day as reducing crime, stopping the spread of communism, dealing effectively with the Soviet Union, providing quality education, reducing the risk of nuclear war, providing health care, reducing waste and inefficiency in government, and protecting the environment.[35] Instead of rooting for their "home team" Democrats or Republicans, voters adopted neutral attitudes toward them.

The failure of party realignment to live up to expectations caused many political scientists to question the concept. In a major critique of party realignment theory entitled "Like Waiting for Godot," Everett Ladd maintained that Key and Burnham's emphasis on a party realignment modeled after the New Deal had been "mostly unfortunate"[36] (see "The Parties Speak: Everett C. Ladd, Like Waiting for Godot: The Uselessness of Party Realignment"). In Ladd's view, the New Deal was a unique period when parties mattered and Franklin D. Roosevelt loomed over the political horizon. Key, Burnham, and other adherents to the party realignment idea grew up during the New Deal era and were shaped by it. Thus, said Ladd, by focusing on whether or not a party realignment happened in such interesting contests as 1968, 1980, 1992, or 1994, political scientists had been asking the wrong question. Rather than wonder whether each of these elections constituted a party realignment, Ladd suggested that it would be better to ask:

1. What are the major issues and policy differences between the two major parties and how do these separate political elites and the voting public?
2. What is the social and ideological makeup of each major party at both the mass and elite levels?

3. What are the principal features of party organization, nomination procedures, and campaign structure?
4. In each of the previous three areas, are major shifts currently taking place? What kind? What are their sources?
5. Overall, how well is the party system performing?[37]

Ladd's critique notwithstanding, political scientists have persisted in seeking a more traditional partisan realignment. They have done so despite Key's 1955 admonition that "the actual election rarely presents in pure form a case fitting completely any particular concept."[38] Instead of abandoning realignment, political scientists were busy refurbishing the idea to make it fit the new, candidate-centered Information Age. By the mid-1980s, party scholars were brandishing several new terms to explain what voters were doing. Phrases like **incomplete realignment, hollow realignment,** and **rolling realignment** were casually tossed about. During the Reagan era, John Kenneth White and Richard B. Wirthlin coined the phrase **rolling realignment** to describe the electoral changes that were taking place.[39] Building on Key's concept of secular realignment, they described party realignment as a process that involved four different stages:

1. A change in the political agenda. During the 1930s, Americans had a simple political agenda: big government works. By 1981, most Americans agreed with Ronald Reagan when he declared in his inaugural address: "In this present crisis, government is not the solution to our problem. Government is the problem."[40] The Reagan Revolution consisted of limiting the expansion of federal responsibilities and returning power to state and local governments and to the individual.
2. A change in partisan self-identification as expressed in the public opinion polls. How one answers the question, "In politics do you think of yourself as a Democrat, Republican, independent, or something else?" is a subjective query asked by most public opinion pollsters. When the political agenda changes, one's partisan identification will inevitably change as one party or another becomes identified with the new political thinking.
3. Changes in party registration. All states regulate party membership. In some places, people must visit a local town hall and formally declare which party they belong to. In other states, voting in a primary is a form of party registration. Either way, the commitment to a party involves an overt act. Frequently, alterations in party registration are lagging indicators of partisan change. For example, although Ronald Reagan had been campaigning for Republicans since 1952, it took him ten years to formally switch his California party registration from Democrat to Republican. As the Reagan illustration indicates, formal party registration is an imperfect barometer of how the electorate thinks about politics at any given moment.
4. Changes at the bottom of the ballot. Every state ballot lists offices that are usually invisible. New Yorkers, for example, elect their local county coroners; Texans vote for railroad commissioners and judges; in Illinois, state university trustees are elected. In such races, party identification means

---

The Parties Speak: *Everett C. Ladd, Like Waiting for Godot,*
the Uselessness of Party Realignment

In 1990, political scientist Everett C. Ladd launched what has become the most withering attack to date on the party realignment concept. An excerpt of his article, "Like Waiting for Godot," appears below.

Estragon: Charming spot. . . . Let's go.
Vladimir: We can't.
Estragon: Why not?
Vladimir: We're waiting for Godot.
Estragon: Ah! You're sure it was here?
Vladimir: What?
Estragon: That we were to wait.
Vladimir: He said by the tree. Do you see any others?
Estragon: What is it?
Vladimir: I don't know. A willow.
Estragon: Where are the leaves?
Vladimir: It must be dead.
Estragon: No more weeping.
Vladimir: Or perhaps it's not the season.
Estragon: Looks to me more like a bush.
Vladimir: A shrub.
Estragon: A bush.
Vladimir: A__. What are you insinuating? That we've come to the wrong place?
Estragon: He should be here.
Vladimir: He didn't say for sure he'd come.
Estragon: And if he doesn't come?
Vladimir: We'll come back tomorrow.
Estragon: And then the day after to-morrow?
Vladimir: Possibly.
Estragon: And so on.
Vladimir: The point is—
Estragon: Until he comes.
Vladimir: You're merciless.

For political scientists, "Waiting for Realignment" has been as bleak an experience as waiting for Godot was for Estragon and Vladimir. Indeed, the preoccupation of political science with realignment over the past thirty-five years has been mostly unfortunate, for the realignment focus is vastly too confining. It has served to deflect attention from the rich variety of changes that have transformed the contemporary party system. . . .

American political science proceeded to build on [V. O. Key's] modest foundation [of critical elections] an elaborate conceptualization of realignment as the centerpiece of a more general theory of partisan change. Many things besides Key's suggestions caused this to happen. The New Deal's burst of partisan change was alive in analysts' minds. It was the one such occurrence political scientists of the time had experienced personally. The vividness of the specific instance helped it masquerade convincingly as the general rule. With more perspective, we can now see that the massive shifts in the party system and voting alignments in the 1930s were in fact *sui generis*. In many essential structural regards, nothing like the New Deal transformation had ever occurred before, nor have they since.

For other reasons, a discipline seeking the neatness, precision, and predictability it naively attributed to "science" could not resist realignment's beguiling simplicity. We were highly susceptible. I remarked in a convention paper fifteen years ago that "it is truly a case of Key sneezing and political science catching a cold."

SOURCE: Excerpted from Everett C. Ladd, "Like Waiting for Godot: The Uselessness of Realignment for Understanding Change in Contemporary American Politics," *Polity* (Spring 1990): 511–12, 514–15.

---

everything, while the campaigns of individuals who seek these posts counts for little. Thus, when voters place an X next to these obscure candidates they are expressing a partisan preference. Alterations in outcomes of these races are suggestive that a party realignment has at last taken place.

The stages White and Wirthlin described were not linear—voters could move back and forth from step to step. But the final result was an inevitable realignment—however slowly and imperfectly that process rolled along. Yet, the rolling realignment they envisioned would help the Republicans failed to materialize. By the time Reagan left office in 1989, Republicans held fewer seats in the House and Senate than they did after Reagan won the presidency in 1980. Moreover, George Bush suffered a massive rejection at the polls in 1992 winning just 38 percent of the ballots cast. Even after Republicans seized Congress in 1994, GOP identifiers in the public opinion polls failed to increase measurably. Thus, while White and Wirthlin were right to suggest that successive realignments to the New Deal were not going to be the short, sharp reorganizations of party loyalties akin to the 1930s, something went awry in the inevitable steps toward a Republican realignment that, however slowly, would follow in Reagan's wake.

The 1994 midterm election gave party realignment theorists new ammunition with its apparent reorganization of voter loyalties—and right on schedule, twenty-six years after Richard Nixon's 1968 victory. For the first time in forty years—Republicans won majorities in both houses of Congress, gaining fifty-two seats in the House and eight seats in the Senate. Newt Gingrich and his fellow Republicans campaigned on a simple theme—the Contract with America, a document signed by all but four Republican House contenders in a flashy Capitol Hill ceremony. The contract promised that if Republicans won, party leaders would schedule votes during the first one hundred days of the new Congress on such issues as term limits, a line-item veto for the president, and a balanced budget amendment (see Chapter 9). Republicans were winning the war of ideas and the term *revolution*—commonly associated with ideal-type party realignments—was in vogue. Burnham claimed that the 1994 results closely resembled an old-fashioned party realignment and challenged his critics to disagree: "Those who have stressed partisan dealignment will now have to consider how this abrupt emergence of something remarkably like an old-fashioned partisan election fits their models. And those who have placed their bets on the argument that critical-realignment analysis is irrelevant to this modern candidate-driven electoral universe will have to reconsider their position."[41]

Certainly, voting behaviors in the South gave Burnham and other realignment advocates considerable ammunition. Fifty years ago the South was the most Democratic region in the nation. The Civil War, won by Republican Abraham Lincoln, created what seemed to be a permanent resentment among southern whites toward the GOP. Later, the New Deal proved especially popular south of the Mason-Dixon line as Franklin Roosevelt's "alphabet soup" agencies helped poor southern farmers recover from the agricultural disaster created by the Great Depression. In 1940, Roosevelt swept every state of the Old Confederacy (as he had in two previous elections), winning an astounding 96 percent of the vote in South Carolina—his highest percentage nationwide. Today, the South is reliably Republican. George Bush easily defeated Bill Clinton in South Carolina (48 percent to 40 percent) as did Bob Dole (50 percent to 44 percent). In the crucial 1994 midterm elections, 55 percent of southerners voted for Republican congressional candidates. Several examples from the 1994, 1996, and 1998 elections illustrate the depth of the party realignment that has taken place in the South:

- In 1990, Georgia Republicans fielded, for the first time this century, a complete congressional slate of candidates, with meager results—less than 40 percent of the statewide vote and just one winner (incumbent Newt Gingrich). Two years later they did somewhat better, winning 45 percent of the ballots and electing four members. But the payoff came in 1994, when Republicans captured 55 percent of the Georgia vote and took seven of eleven seats. In 1996 and again in 1998, Republicans won eight of the eleven congressional districts.
- Prior to the 1994 election, Democrats held fifty-one House seats in southern districts won by George Bush in 1988 and 1992. But in 1994 Democrats lost twenty-seven of these seats. For the first time since the Civil War, Republicans held most of the southern congressional districts. They maintained that edge in 1996, winning seventy-one southern House seats while the Democrats were held to fifty-four.
- Since the Republicans captured Congress in 1994, nearly all of the GOP leaders have called the South home: Newt Gingrich (Speaker, Georgia), Richard Armey (Majority Leader, Texas), and Tom DeLay (Majority Whip, Texas).
- Half of Bob Dole's ten best states in 1996 were south of the Mason-Dixon line: Alabama, South Carolina, Mississippi, North Carolina, and Texas. Bill Clinton and Al Gore, both southern whites, failed (as has every Democratic presidential contender since 1968) to win a majority of the southern white vote.

Still, the South has always been a political anomaly—hardly explaining where the country at large is headed. Given Clinton's 1996 win and the persistent Republican control of Congress, questions about where the American electorate is going persist. Is realignment as conceived by Burnham and Key still possible? Can Bill Clinton succeed in modifying the image of the Democratic Party such that his heir apparent, Vice President Al Gore, will win in 2000? Will Republicans consolidate their hold on the national political agenda to win control of the presidency and the Congress in 2000 for the first time since 1952, thus sparking anew questions about a GOP realignment?

WHERE ARE THE VOTERS GOING?

Speculating on the outcome of future elections is always dangerous. For instance, in 1980, Everett C. Ladd published an article in *Fortune* magazine titled, "Why Carter Will Probably Win."[42] Of course, Ronald Reagan easily defeated Carter that year. Nevertheless, one can make some determinations about the nature of the present party system and what its underlying structure looks like.

The End of the New Deal Coalition

The much-heralded New Deal coalition created by Franklin D. Roosevelt has long since passed away. Today, it is the Republicans who control both houses of Congress and have the largest number of appointments to the federal judiciary. But the GOP is far from the nation's majority. According to a Gallup poll conducted in February 1998, 38 percent of respondents called themselves Democrats, 28 percent said they were Republicans, and 34 percent called themselves independents.[43] These results are at sharp variance with the strongly pro-Democratic responses given in 1937 (see Table 6.1). Moreover, fewer Americans today identify strongly with either major party. According to a 1996 survey conducted by CBS News and the *New York Times*, just 17 percent were "hard-core Republicans," only 19 percent were "hard-core Democrats." The remaining 64 percent were "independents" or "soft partisans."[44] Thus, neither major party commands anything resembling a majority in the Information Age. Instead, they have been reduced to parity with each holding a minority share of the electorate as they compete for support from the ever-larger pool of independent voters.

Here Come the Ticket-Splitters

Absent a New Deal-like party system anchored in strong partisan loyalties, the present-day structure of electoral politics is characterized by large numbers of Americans willing to split their votes among candidates of all parties. According to data gathered by political scientists at the University of Michigan, those who voted for House candidates of one party and a president of another totaled 10 percent in the early 1950s, 15 percent in the 1960s, and 30 percent in the early 1970s—where it has remained stable for over two decades. As shown in Table 6.2, Americans from every age group and educational background told pollsters in 1996 that they often split their tickets between the two parties, with many expressing a willingness to vote for someone not affiliated with either major party. Even self-identified Republicans and

TABLE 6.1 ▪ Partisan Identification, Selected Gallup Polls, 1937–1998 (in percents)

Year	Democrats	Republicans	Independents
1937	53	32	16
1940	44	36	20
1944	43	39	18
1948	50	30	20
1952	51	29	20
1956	44	35	21
1960	47	29	24
1964	52	25	23
1968	42	28	30
1972	40	28	32
1976	48	24	28
1980	36	32	31
1984	39	35	27
1988	36	32	31
1993	36	30	32
1995	28	31	37
1997	31	29	33
1998	38	28	34

SOURCE: Gallup surveys, 1937–1998. Text of question: "In politics, as of today, do you consider yourself a Republican, a Democrat, or an independent?"

Democrats have regularly split their tickets (59 percent and 56 percent respectively). During the 1998 midterm elections, ticket-splitting was rampant. For example, in New York and Connecticut, voters returned Republican governors George Pataki and John Rowland to office, while choosing Democrats Charles Schumer and Christopher Dodd to represent them in the U.S. Senate. Of the twenty-two governor's races where the winning candidate won by ten percentage points or more, the winning governor's party did not net a single congressional seat. In fact, in two of these states—California and Kansas—the party whose gubernatorial candidate lost actually gained a House seat.

The rise of the ticket-splitters has resulted in a bewildering array of extremely close presidential elections followed by landslides, with the winning party often switching back and forth. Close elections, defined by percentage of popular vote as opposed to Electoral College votes, occurred in 1960, 1968, 1976, 1988, and 1992. Landslides happened in 1952, 1956, 1964, 1972, and 1984. The alternation between squeakers and blowouts is yet another illustration of the decline in party brand loyalty. Today, many Americans remain indifferent toward both parties. During the early 1950s, 10 percent were classified as neutral toward both parties; forty years later the figure has tripled. In responding to a 1997 poll about which party people thought was better for the country, 34 percent said the Democrats, 27 percent said the Republicans, while the remaining 39 percent weren't sure or had no opinion.[45]

TABLE 6.2 ▪ The Un-Anchored American Electorate, 1996 (in percents)

Social Group	Votes for Different Parties for President	Typically Votes Split Ticket	Typically Votes Straight Ticket	Very/Somewhat Likely to Vote for an Independent
Age				
18–29 years old	31	46	36	52
30–44 years old	59	65	27	41
45–59 years old	68	77	20	36
60+ years old	64	65	28	18
Education				
Less than high school	51	55	33	42
High school graduate	59	64	26	37
Some college	56	61	30	38
College graduate	59	68	25	32
Postgraduate	61	76	20	29
Party Identification				
Republican	50	59	32	27
Democrat	51	56	37	29
Independent	74	84	9	58

SOURCE: Survey by the Media Studies Center/Roper Center, February 1996. Text of question: "When voting in elections do you typically vote a straight ticket—that is for candidates of the same party, or do you typically split your ticket—that is vote for candidates from different parties? Have you always voted for the same party for president or have you voted for different parties for president? In 1996, how likely is it that you would vote for an independent candidate for president? Is it very likely, somewhat likely, not too likely, or not at all likely?" In Regina Dougherty, Everett C. Ladd, David Wilber, and Lynn Zayachkiwsky, eds., *America at the Polls, 1996* (Storrs, Conn.: Roper Center for Public Opinion Research, 1997), 190.

There has been much speculation as to why a growing number of voters have such disdain for political parties. A summary of the explanations include:

- The nature of issues changed during the 1960s and 1970s and the extent to which voters were guided by them increased.
- Interest groups are important competitors vying with parties for the voters' attention. In the early 1960s, there were roughly 5,000 issue-advocacy associations located in Washington, D.C.; today, there are more than 25,000. Thus, the parties' "market share" is down considerably.
- Candidate-centered politics causes voters to think of politicians as individuals rather than party advocates.
- Campaign consultants encourage candidates to take popular positions and soften their images rather than be depicted as uncompromising partisans.
- The news media often portrays partisanship in a negative light. The number of news stories linking a party to a candidate has declined dramatically

in the last three decades. During the 1960s, the press was much more focused on covering party activities, such as the national nominating conventions, and what the party platforms said.[46]

- During the heyday of party identification, voters worried about their physical sustenance, safety, and other material interests. After World War II, these concerns eased thanks to an extraordinary rapid economic expansion. An affluent society allows citizens to concentrate on postmaterialist concerns such as self-expression and quality of life issues that transcend traditional partisan politics.

- About the same time party identification began to wane, incumbent reelection rates soared. Incumbents, in effect, created their own "party" as they sought reelection. (A term-limits movement reflected voter backlash against this trend.)

- As people move more often, have fewer children, and spend more time in front of televisions and computers, civic life suffers. Because political parties are organizations that emphasize community involvement, it is not surprising that partisanship withers in such an individualistic, impersonal environment.

- In the Information Age, political communications spew forth from a dizzying array of impersonal and seemingly "neutral" sources—including television, radio, Internet, direct mail, and the telephone. This is a sharp contrast to the heyday of partisan politics when one's background and associations, including what newspapers one read, helped determine the degree and strength of partisanship.

Increasingly, party brand loyalty has been replaced by voter neutrality. The Information Age contributes to this new form of political neutralism by allowing candidates to present their personas to the public. John F. Kennedy cast himself as a dashing World War II hero who would add vigor to our politics following the desultory Eisenhower years. Ronald Reagan was seen as an amiable, grandfather-like figure. Bill Clinton likes to portray himself as a knowledgeable baby boomer who "feels our pain." We presently live in an age when the personality of a candidate, especially a potential president, becomes a central feature of the voting decision. Presidents and presidential candidates are regularly profiled in *People* magazine alongside movie stars or members of the British royalty.

PARTY COALITIONS IN THE CLINTON ERA

During the Clinton years, Democrats have seen their identifiers fluctuate from a low of 28 percent following the disastrous 1994 midterm elections to 38 percent in 1998. Clearly, the Democratic Party has not prospered by having one of its own occupy the White House. Following his pollster's advice after Republicans seized control of Congress in 1995, Bill Clinton adopted a strategy called "triangulation," whereby he positioned himself at the apex of a triangle separating himself from the congressional Democrats and Republicans. Public attention quickly shifted from the Republican-controlled Congress back to Clinton, as pollsters asked who could be trusted more to handle key issues—Clinton or the Republicans in Congress— the first time a president rather than a party had been presented so often as a choice to survey respondents. The results were startling: on nearly every issue, voters preferred Clinton. When asked in 1997 whether Clinton or the Republicans in Congress could handle a specific problem better, the results showed a fourteen–point Clinton lead on Medicare; the economy, ten points; Social Security, nine points; crime, eight points; taxes, three points; and the deficit, one point.[47]

But when voters were asked about which party they want to handle important national problems, the mental pictures voters conjure are much more abstract. Both parties have advantages on some issues, but not all. Republicans are generally preferred when it comes to maintaining a strong national defense, managing foreign affairs, balancing the federal budget, and handling crime. Democrats are preferred when voters are asked which party could better protect Social Security and Medicare, improve education and the schools, provide affordable health care, protect the environment, and help the middle class and the poor. Neither party has an advantage when respondents are asked which party could do the better job of encouraging high moral standards and values, handling the nation's economy, or holding taxes down (see Table 6.3). Because the mental pictures conjured by the two parties remain blurred, party realignment has yet to happen in the Clinton years—

TABLE 6.3 ▪ Voter Attitudes toward the Major Parties by Issue, 1998 (in percents)

Issue	Republicans	Democrats	No Opinion
Maintaining a strong national defense	**53**	37	10
Foreign affairs	**45**	41	14
Balancing the federal budget	**43**	41	16
Handling the crime problem	**42**	39	19
Reducing the problem of illegal drugs	**41**	33	26
Encouraging high moral standards and values	41	40	19
Handling the nation's economy	44	45	11
Holding taxes down	44	45	11
Coping with the nation's main problems	42	**45**	13
Protecting Social Security	38	**48**	14
Protecting Medicare	33	**52**	15
Improving education and the schools	34	**54**	12
Providing affordable health care	33	**54**	12
Protecting the environment	31	**54**	15
Helping the middle class	34	**57**	9
Helping the poor	27	**61**	12

NOTE: Partisan advantages are indicated in bold numbers.

SOURCE: ABC *News/Washington Post* survey, January 15–19, 1998. Text of question: "Which political party, the Democrats or the Republicans, do you trust to do a better job on [name of issue]?"

be it a traditional New Deal-style realignment, a secular realignment, or a rolling realignment.

Nonetheless, there have been dramatic shifts in the Democratic and Republican party coalitions since the New Deal era. As Table 6.4 shows, Democratic candidates in Franklin Roosevelt's time could count on support from low-income voters, those with a high school education or less, organized labor, urban dwellers, residents of the Northeast, white southerners, Catholics, ethnics (especially the Irish, Italians, and Poles), blacks, and Jews. Republicans won backing from farmers (including farm belt states from North Dakota to Kansas), Anglo-Saxon Protestants, rural dwellers, and high-income, well-educated voters.

Things have drastically changed as shown in Table 6.5. When Bill Clinton won reelection in 1996, the coalition he and his fellow Democrats assembled differed dramatically than Franklin Roosevelt's sixty years before. Democrats, including Clinton, have won backing from women, gays, singles, divorcees, Latinos, West Coast residents, Jews, those who live in the Northeast, those who infrequently attend church, and those with postgraduate degrees. Republicans count white men, members of the Christian Right, married voters, white southerners, Cubans, libertarians, and regular churchgoers in their ranks. White Catholics, those employed in the new Information Age technologies, middle-income voters, moderates, those who live in the Midwest, those with some college exposure, and true independents are swing voters, up-for-grabs by both major parties. Overall, the portraits of the two parties are fundamentally different than they were a mere three decades ago. Like sand on a beach, the grains have shifted with the blowing winds—some taken away from the Democratic portrait and added to the Republican one (and vice versa)—and new grains (e.g., gays, women, churched vs. un-churched) have been added. One is struck by the new contours and contrasts in the party mosaics.

TABLE 6.4 ▪ **Party Voting Blocks during the New Deal Era**

Democratic Voting Blocs	*Republican Voting Blocs*
Low-income voters (poor)	High-income voters (rich)
High school education or less	College education
Unskilled workers and semi-skilled workers	Professional white-collar workers
Urban residents (big cities)	Rural dwellers
Organized labor	Management/big business
Catholics	White Anglo-Saxon Protestants
Jews	Farmers
Northeast	Farm states
Blacks	Suburbs
White southerners	Western states
Liberals	Conservatives
Self-described Democrats	Self-described Republicans
Irish, Italians, Poles	Germans

TABLE 6.5 ▪ Party Voting Blocs in the 1990s

Democratic Voting Blocs	*Republican Voting Blocs*	*Swing Voters*
Union members	Management, small business	Employees in new Information Age technologies (e.g., computers, the World Wide Web)
Low-income voters (less than $15,000 per year)	High-income voters (more than $100,000 per year)	Middle-income voters (between $30,000 and $50,000 per year)
Liberals	Conservatives	Moderates
Self-described Democrats	Self-described Republicans	True independents
Postgraduates (graduate school education, e.g., Ph.D., lawyer)	Four-year college graduates (especially in the hard sciences and engineers)	Some college (two years or less)
Women	White men	
Blacks	Whites	
Jews	White Protestants	White Catholics
Northeast	South	Midwest
Upper Midwest	Farm states	
West Coast	Libertarians	
Hispanics	Cubans	
Unmarried singles or divorcees	Married	
Gays		
Attend church services infrequently	Attend church services at least once per week	

Given these electoral characteristics, two prominent features emerge that are likely to dominate twenty-first century electoral politics: the gender gap and divided government.

The Gender Gap

Until 1920, men dominated politics. After women were permitted to enter voting booths in 1920—thanks to the passage of the Nineteenth Amendment—politics changed, but only marginally. Women often followed their husbands' leads, and partisan differences between the two sexes were negligible. Things began to change in 1964 when, for the first time, women voted in slightly greater numbers for Democrat Lyndon B. Johnson who offered himself as the "peace candidate" by promising to let

Asian boys do the fighting in Vietnam. Republican Barry Goldwater was portrayed as a reckless, anticommunist zealot. Johnson exploited the public fears of a Goldwater presidency by running a television commercial showing a little girl plucking a daisy as the announcer began a countdown: "Ten, nine, eight . . ." When the fateful zero was reached, a nuclear bomb exploded and Johnson's voice was heard to exclaim: "These are the stakes. To make a world in which all of God's children can live—or go into the dark. We must love each other, or we must die." Many women were frightened of losing their sons in another war and 62 percent cast their votes for Johnson. But men were not far behind, with 60 percent supporting the Democratic president.

In the elections that followed, the status quo reigned with only marginal differences in the voting behaviors of men and women. All that changed in 1980. Divorced women with children were not enamored of Ronald Reagan and the revolution he promised by downsizing the federal government. Many depended on government help to make ends meet. In addition, most women, regardless of marital status, were frightened by Reagan's pledge to drastically increase military spending if he were elected. Because the economy was in poor shape with high inflation and unemployment, Reagan was able to beat Carter among women by the narrow margin of 47 percent to 45 percent. Among men, the race was no contest. Males liked Reagan's rugged individualism and his projection of U.S. military might, giving him 55 percent of their votes to just 36 percent for Carter.

Instead of being a flash in a pan, the **gender gap** persisted long after Reagan left the White House in 1989. Using combined 1997–1998 Gallup data, 31 percent of men call themselves Republicans and an equal number are Democrats. Among women the results are considerably different: 41 percent call themselves Democrats as opposed to 29 percent who say they are Republicans. The results are even more pronounced among the so-called Generation Xers. Among those aged eighteen to twenty-nine, women are 36 percent Democratic while just 26 percent are Republican. Young men are 28 percent Republican and 27 percent Democratic.[48]

These partisan differences are reflected in the voting booths. As Table 6.6 indicates, the gender gap has more closely resembled a gender canyon in nearly every presidential election held since 1980. In 1992, the gap narrowed slightly, only to widen once more four years later as men chose Bob Dole (44 percent to 43 percent) and women picked Bill Clinton (54 percent to 38 percent). Clinton won a second term propelled by the strong support he received from women.

The gender gap persists in other nonpresidential contests. In 1998, 51 percent of women sided with a Democratic congressional candidate as opposed to 45 percent of men. Even when a woman is nominated to head the Republican ticket, female support is not assured. For example, incumbent New Jersey Governor Christine Todd Whitman faced a tough 1997 reelection battle against male Democrat James McGreevey. Even though Whitman was the first woman to occupy the New Jersey governor's mansion and had done a credible job, women refused to support her. Whitman won just 46 percent of the female vote, while 48 percent of men supported her. McGreevey won backing from 49 percent of women, while 43 percent of men voted for the Democrat. Likewise, in the 1998 Maryland gubernatorial race, Republican Ellen Sauerbrey won 50 percent of the male vote while the incumbent, Parris

TABLE 6.6 ▪ **Gender Gap in Presidential Elections, 1980–1996 (in percents)**

Year/Candidates	Men	Women	Gender Gap
1980			
Carter	36	45	-9
Reagan	55	47	-8
			Total gap: -17
1984			
Mondale	37	44	-7
Reagan	62	56	-6
			Total gap: -13
1988			
Dukakis	41	49	-8
Bush	57	50	-7
			Total gap: -15
1992			
Clinton	41	45	-4
Bush	38	38	0
			Total gap: -4
1996			
Clinton	433	54	-11
Dole	44	38	-6
			Total gap: -17

Glendening, captured 60 percent of the female vote—enough for a comfortable Democratic victory in what many thought would be a hotly contested race.

Fueling the gender gap is a growing difference among the sexes on such questions as war and peace, entitlement programs, and social issues. When the United States contemplated a sustained bombing campaign against Saddam Hussein in 1998, seven years after his failure to comply with United Nations resolutions following the Persian Gulf war, men and women sharply differed as to the nature of the U.S. response. Fifty-five percent of men preferred a military strike against Iraq; 61 percent of women favored continued diplomacy and use of economic sanctions.[49] Closer to home, the sexes held substantially different opinions on domestic issues: 69 percent of women wanted more spending for Social Security compared to 57 percent of men; 83 percent of women favored improving the nation's health care compared to 76 percent of men; and 72 percent of women advocated spending more on programs for the homeless compared to 63 percent of men.[50] When asked in 1993 whether they favored ending the ban on homosexuals in the military, the sexes again split, with 51 percent of women compared to 34 percent of men in favor.[51] With the passage of time, partisan differences between males and females on military, social, and cultural issues have increased. One can easily imagine the arguments taking place between husbands and wives, boyfriends and girlfriends, over dinner tables across America every time a presidential election is upon us.

Divided Government

When Dwight Eisenhower was inaugurated for a second time in 1957, he was the first just-elected or reelected president to face an opposition-controlled Congress since Grover Cleveland in 1892. **Divided government** refers to the split in partisan control between the executive and legislative branches, with one party in charge of the presidency while the loyal opposition controls one or both houses of the legislature. From 1892 to 1954, divided government happened a mere eight years out of sixty-two. But in the forty-four years since 1954, divided government has reigned for thirty years—about 70 percent of the time.

Throughout the long Cold War years of 1947 to 1991, divided government became a fixture of national politics as Republicans won the confidence of voters on managing U.S. foreign policy (especially the superpower relationship with the Soviet Union), strengthening national defense, and running the increasingly defense-dependent economy. These three issues gave Dwight Eisenhower, Richard Nixon, Ronald Reagan, and George Bush victories on several election nights. But they counted for little in congressional contests, as illustrated by a 1984 exit poll that found just 1 percent naming foreign policy as an important factor in casting their congressional vote.[52]

During the Cold War years and continuing into the Information Age, congressional victories often were incumbent victories. Members of the House and Senate tended to business back home, often acting as ombudsmen and -women between the federal government in Washington and their local or state districts. The primary beneficiaries of pork barrel politics were House Democrats. From 1954 to 1994, Democrats ruled the House of Representatives as their personal fiefdom—an unprecedented streak of uninterrupted one-party control. The Democratic grasp was so strong that when the Republicans won their extraordinary victory in 1994, no Republican representative had previously served in the majority. Indeed, during the long Democratic reign, it was said that it was easier to change members in the old Soviet Politburo than it was to replace a sitting Democrat. Unless the member died, resigned, or got into a scandal, Democrats were usually assured of reelection. In fact, some members of Congress have even been reelected from jail.

An example of the once-powerful Democratic hold is Massachusetts' Eighth Congressional District. Encompassing parts of Boston and Cambridge (the area around Harvard University and MIT), the district has had a penchant for electing Democrats to Congress. When the district was created in 1942, the first winner was Democrat James Michael Curley who was famous for being the first Irishman to become governor of Massachusetts (1935–1937) and had been a long-time mayor of Boston (1914–1918, 1922–1926, 1930–1934, and 1946–1950). So confident was Curley of victory that he purchased a home in Washington, D.C., long before the ballots were counted. Curley was succeeded in 1946 by Democrat John F. Kennedy, who represented the district until 1952 when he won a hard-fought contest to enter the U.S. Senate. Kennedy, in turn, was replaced by Thomas P. "Tip" O'Neill who served in the Congress until 1986, rising in the ranks to become Speaker of the House in 1977. After O'Neill left, he was replaced by Joseph P. Kennedy II, John Kennedy's nephew and eldest son of Robert F. Kennedy. Joe Kennedy served in the

Congress without serious opposition—winning 84 percent of the vote in 1996 and outraising his hapless opponent $1,952,906 to *zero*. After tragedy struck the Kennedy clan once more in 1998 with the death of his brother Michael, Joe Kennedy decided not to seek reelection. His successor, Michael Capuano, won 82 percent of the votes cast in 1998—the highest percentage for his state's congressional delegation.

The story of the Eighth District is repeated in many others. Of course, it is not always the Democrat who emerges victorious. Upstate New York, for example, has several reliably Republican areas. In New York's Twenty-fourth Congressional District, Republican John McHugh has easily won four consecutive victories—the last with 79 percent of the vote. This is not surprising: no Democrat has represented the area since the late nineteenth century. As these congressional districts illustrate, only the cast of characters changes—not the outcome.

But instead of viewing congressional victories as either Republican or Democratic, in many cases these are incumbent victories. One of the distinguishing features of late-twentieth century politics has been the emergence of an incumbent party that is fairly secure in its reelection victories and allows legislators to build careers in the halls of Congress. These members serve for as long as they wish, sometimes even metaphorically checking "legislator" on their resumes under the box marked occupation. Over the years, resentment toward the incumbent party has grown—as is evident in the widespread support expressed for term limits. But voters often fail to exercise the ultimate term limit—that is, denying an incumbent reelection.

Aiding the incumbent party are perks that accompany the job of a modern-day member of Congress. During the long forty-year Democratic reign in the House of Representatives, Democrats refined these tools of incumbency and used them with increasing degrees of effectiveness. For example, all members of Congress are allowed to communicate with their constituents at no charge. Such communication often takes the form of a newsletter mailed out several times a year to constituents, which is paid for by the taxpayers instead of campaign funds. In addition, members can communicate directly with individual constituents "free" of charge. Whenever a member sends a letter to a constituent, the envelope does not have a stamp. Instead the member's stamped signature, called a "franking privilege," covers the cost of having the letter delivered by the post office. Democrats freely used (and often abused) the franking privilege, which in 1993 cost a total of $67.7 million.[53] (In 1995, members of the 104th Congress voted to cut the cost of the franking privilege by one-third.)

One key to continued Democratic control of the House was the explosion of personal and committee staff. In 1993, Congress had more than 26,000 employees—larger than the departments of State, Labor, or Housing and Urban Development—at an annual cost of more than $2 billion. This is a marked change from the turn of the century when representatives had no personal staff and senators had only 39 personal assistants. In 1993, 11,538 persons served on the personal staffs of representatives and senators, and more than 3,000 people were employed by congressional committees.[54] These staff persons were not partisans in the classic sense. While most had nominal ties to their local Democratic or Republican parties back home, what got them their jobs was a personal commitment to the winning candidate. Most who had worked on their candidates' campaigns followed them to Washington. Congressional staffs became an integral part of the incumbent party—keeping a watchful eye on the next election and dutifully looking after their member's interests. Not surprisingly, in 1996, 95 percent of House members from both parties who sought reelection won—including 83 percent of the Republican class of 1994. The incumbent party also prevailed in the Republican-controlled Senate, where 93-year-old Strom Thurmond won an eighth term and Jesse Helms was reelected to his fifth. Only South Dakota's Larry Pressler lost to a Democratic challenger.

Given the strength of the incumbent party, the victory House Republicans achieved in 1994 was a major, and rare, feat. Bill Clinton contributed mightily to the Democratic rout. Elected to fix the economy (a famous sign at the 1992 Clinton campaign headquarters proclaimed, "It's the economy, stupid!"), Clinton wandered far away from his mandate. First, he advocated a health-care reform bill that was depicted in a series of health insurance industry–sponsored television commercials as another intrusion of big government in the lives of ordinary Americans. The Harry and Louise characters in the advertisements deplored the massive bureaucracy and costs required to implement the Clinton plan. The ads had the desired effect, and the Democratic Congress was so divided on the issue, that Clinton's plan died without a formal vote being cast.

Clinton added to his difficulties by immersing himself in two issues sure to draw partisan fire: allowing homosexuals to serve in the military and endorsing the Brady Bill which required a ten-day registration period before any handgun could be purchased. Shortly after becoming president, Clinton advocated a "don't ask, don't tell" policy toward suspected gays in uniform. Clinton also made good on another campaign promise: signing into law the Brady Bill, named after former Reagan press secretary James Brady who was grievously wounded in the assassination attempt on President Reagan in 1981. Both issues reminded some voters why they disliked the Democratic Party stands on the so-called social issues. By becoming mired in the social and cultural quagmires that had previously given the Democratic Party fits, Clinton handed Republicans a splendid opportunity. Newt Gingrich devised a simplistic slogan that encapsulated voter grievances against Clinton and the Democrats: "God, Guns, and Gays." Using this political shorthand, Clinton was depicted as anti-religious, his support of the Brady Bill made him anti-gun, and his military policy made him pro-gay.

A crippled Bill Clinton, an ineffectual Democratic response to GOP attacks, and an energized Republican Party resulted in what many thought was unthinkable: Republican control of both houses of Congress. The "God, Guns, and Gays" slogan worked. Republicans won backing from 61 percent of evangelical Christians and 66 percent from members of the National Rifle Association, while 60 percent of those who were gay, lesbian, or bisexual (a minority of voters) backed the Democrats. Much more significantly, Republicans won support from married voters (54 percent), parents of a child under age 18 (53 percent), those employed full-time (52 percent), white southerners (55 percent), white Catholics (54) percent, and those who attended religious services once a week (53 percent). This coalition strongly resembled what Richard Nixon called the "silent majority," once described as consisting of the "un-young, un-poor, and un-black."[55]

The Republican congressional coalition held in 1996, making for the first back-to-back GOP Congresses in sixty-eight years. GOP control was assured by their consolidation of political power in the South, as Republicans added five House seats from states that comprised the Old Confederacy during the Civil War years. In addition, Republicans won Democratic-held seats in Texas, Oklahoma, Mississippi, Alabama, and even in Bill Clinton's native Arkansas, and control of the Alabama and Mississippi delegations switched from Democratic to Republican. Even the Senate was not immune to the new Republican-sounding southern accent. After Bob Dole left to do battle against Bill Clinton, Trent Lott of Mississippi became the new Majority Leader—the first time a southern Republican had been selected to lead the party in Congress since its formation in 1854. House Democrats scored gains in the Northeast, Midwest, and West—adding six, four, and two seats respectively from these regions—but these victories were not enough to deny the Republicans a majority in the House.

Divided government pleased the voters. After the 1996 ballots were counted, 65 percent said they were happy that the Republican Party had maintained control of the Congress (including 39 percent who voted to reelect Bill Clinton), and 53 percent were happy Clinton had won.[56] Claiming victory on an otherwise dull election night, Clinton saw a message in the returns: work together. The president later told cheering supporters that he would put country above party:

> The challenges we face, they're not Democratic or Republican challenges. They're American challenges. What we know from the budget battles of the last two years and from the remarkable success of the last few weeks of the Congress is the lesson we have learned for the last 220 years—what we have achieved as Americans of lasting good, we have achieved by working together. So let me say to the leaders of my Democratic Party and the leaders of the Republican Party, it is time to put country ahead of party.[57]

Newt Gingrich agreed: "Our goal is to find common ground [with Clinton] . . . We don't have to live in a world of confrontation. We ought to work with him and give him a chance to lead in the direction he campaigned on."[58]

The American electorate's desire for a grand coalition government has tremendous appeal. Divided government has not only become the norm in Washington, but in many statehouses as well. New York, Illinois, Rhode Island, Connecticut, Massachusetts, Michigan, and Wisconsin have one party controlling the governorship while another has a majority in one or both houses of the state legislature. Split-ticket voters are creating a new "check and balance" between the executive and legislative branches of government not accounted for in either the federal or state constitutions.

WHAT'S LEFT FOR PARTIES?

Electoral detachment from prior party ties, divided government, and the decline of institutional parties as important electing mechanisms have destroyed what linkages remain between the party-in-the-electorate, the party-in-government, and party organizations. Instead of pitching for broad-based support to alter the course of government, parties have become service-organizations—helping individual candidates raise money and marginally contributing to their victories (see Chapters 4 and 7). The release of the American electorate from their partisan moorings began in the 1950s, accelerated in the 1960s, and has continued apace, with few interruptions, ever since. This has wrought havoc with such heretofore sacred theories as party realignment, and political scientists have been grappling with the theoretical implications—often unsuccessfully. Concepts such as dealignment, rolling realignment, hollow realignment, and even a resuscitation of old-style party realignment theory are testaments to the discipline's dilemma. Clearly, in the Information Age candidates can personalize contests by demoting their opponents to the television equivalent of "brand X." Therefore, it is not surprising that voter images of the Democratic and Republican parties should be so blurred.

One consequence of fragmented, dealigned politics is the enhancement of a Hamiltonian-like party system where partisan activities are directed from the top down. Organizational competence—such as the ability to raise money and aid candidates with high technology services—become indicators of party accomplishment. Certainly, the Democratic and Republican national committees and their state party counterparts can boast of this type of prowess, in contrast to the Jeffersonian model which places a premium on civic involvement. Parties articulate the concerns of average folks and mobilize the faithful to the polls on election day. Jeffersonians do not see party brand loyalty as an impediment to civic involvement; instead, parties are necessary catalysts for mobilizing the grass roots. Emotional attachments to parties afford rational shortcuts and engage citizens in politics. Without any emotional connections to a party, voters are left adrift.

In this detached environment, the business analogy described earlier in this book has merit. If politics is about "who gets what, when, where, and how," to use political scientist Harold Lasswell's famous phrase, we know what candidates want: votes at election time.[59] Using new technologies—especially television and increasingly the World Wide Web—has allowed candidates to win even greater numbers of votes. But such vote-maximizing elections often say little about how the parties are faring. That does not mean that the parties are irrelevant after the victors have arrived in Washington or at their local statehouses—quite the contrary. But the partisan bickering that characterizes life in the nation's capital has assumed a personal character that counts for little beyond the Washington beltway.

This transformation of the electorate away from party brand loyalty increases the challenges parties face in the Information Age to redefine their place in electoral politics. How the parties are meeting these challenges is outlined in the next four chapters.

FURTHER READING

Campbell, Angus, Philip E. Converse, Warren E. Miller, and Donald E. Stokes. *The American Voter*. New York: Wiley, 1960.

Burnham, Walter Dean. *Critical Elections and the Mainsprings of American Politics*. New York: Norton, 1970.

Edsall, Thomas Byrne with Mary D. Edsall. *Chain Reaction: The Impact of Race, Rights, and Taxes on American Politics.* New York: Norton, 1992.

Fiorina, Morris P. *Divided Government.* New York: MacMillan, 1992.

Key, V. O., Jr. "A Theory of Critical Elections." *Journal of Politics,* 17 (February 1955): 3–18; and V. O. Key, Jr. "Secular Realignment and the Party System." *Journal of Politics* 21 (May 1959): 198–210.

Ladd, Everett Carll. "Like Waiting for Godot: The Uselessness of Realignment for Understanding Change in Contemporary American Politics." *Polity* XXII, no. 3 (Spring 1990).

Shafer, Byron E. *The End of Realignment? Interpreting American Electoral Eras.* Madison: University of Wisconsin Press, 1991.

Wattenberg, Martin P. *The Rise of Candidate-Centered Politics.* Cambridge: Harvard University Press, 1991.

White, John Kenneth. *Still Seeing Red: How the Cold War Shapes the New American Politics.* Boulder, Colo.: Westview Press, 1997.

NOTES

1. See James MacGregor Burns, *Roosevelt: The Lion and the Fox* (New York: Harcourt, Brace, 1956), 452–54.

2. Theodore H. White, *The Making of the President, 1960* (New York: Signet Books, 1961), 30.

3. See Julie Nixon Eisenhower, *Pat Nixon: The Untold Story* (New York: Simon & Schuster, 1986), 246–47.

4. John Kenneth White, interview with Richard B. Wirthlin, Washington, D.C., November 22, 1988.

5. William Crotty, "Political Parties in the 1996 Election: The Party as Team or the Candidates as Superstars," in L. Sandy Maisel, ed., *The Parties Respond: Changes in American Parties and Campaigns,* 3rd ed. (Boulder, Colo.: Westview Press, 1998), 217. Twenty-three percent of those who considered themselves either a Democrat or a Republican voted for a presidential candidate of another party.

6. Cited in Edward Sidlow and Beth Henschen, *America at Odds: An Introduction to American Government* (Belmont, Calif.: West/Wadsworth, 1998), p. 312.

7. Quoted in Michael E. McGerr, *The Decline of Popular Politics: The American North, 1865– 1928* (New York: Oxford University Press, 1986), 13.

8. Quoted in Robert A. Caro, *The Years of Lyndon Johnson: The Path to Power* (New York: Knopf, 1983), 74.

9. Richard M. Nixon, *RN: The Memoirs of Richard Nixon* (New York: Grosset & Dunlop, 1978), 7–8.

10. Quoted in Hedrick Hertzberg, "Hell, I Dunno," *New Republic,* December 5, 1988, 23.

11. Paul F. Lazarsfeld, Bernard R. Berelson, and Hazel Gaudet, *The People's Choice* (New York: Columbia University Press, 1940).

12. Bernard R. Berelson, Paul F. Lazarsfeld, and William N. McPhee, *Voting* (Chicago: University of Chicago Press, 1948).

13. Gallup Poll, October 9–14, 1952. Text of question: "Which presidential candidate—Stevenson or Eisenhower—do you think could handle the Korean situation best? Eisenhower, 65 percent; Stevenson, 19 percent; no difference (volunteered), 8 percent; no opinion, 8 percent.

14. Angus Campbell, Philip E. Converse, Warren E. Miller and Donald E. Stokes, *The American Voter* (New York: Wiley, 1960).

15. Ibid, 148.

16. CBS News/*New York Times* poll, October 26–28, 1998. Text of question: "Just from the way you feel right now, do you think President Clinton's actions are serious enough to warrant his being impeached and removed from office?" Yes, serious enough, 30 percent; no, 68 percent; don't know/no answer, 2 percent. Republicans: Yes, serious enough, 62 percent; no, 34 percent; don't know/no answer, 4 percent. Democrats: Yes, serious enough, 9 percent; no, 88 percent; don't know/no answer, 3 percent. Independents: Yes, serious enough, 28 percent; no, 70 percent; don't know/no answer, 2 percent.

17. Gerald M. Pomper, "Toward a More Responsible Two-Party System? What, Again?," *Journal of Politics,* 33 (1971): 936.

18. Norman H. Nie, Sidney Verba, and John R. Petrocik, *The Changing American Voter* (Cambridge: Harvard University Press, 1976).

19. Anthony Downs, *An Economic Theory of Democracy* (New York: Harper, 1957).

20. Cited in Bruce E. Keith, David B. Magleby, Candice J. Nelson, Elizabeth Orr, Mark C. Westlye, and Raymond E. Wolfinger, *The Myth of the Independent Voter* (Berkeley: University of California Press, 1992), table 1.1 and chapters 4–5.

21. Herbert F. Weisberg, "A Multidimensional Conceptulization of Party Identification," in Richard G. Niemi and Herbert F. Weisberg, *Controversies in Voting Behavior,* 2nd ed. (Washington, D.C.: Congressional Quarterly Press, 1984).

22. See Martin P. Wattenberg, *The Decline of American Political Parties, 1952–1988* (Cambridge: Harvard University Press, 1990), 140. The 1998 figures are contained in Gallup polls, February 20–22, 1998. Democrats, 38 percent; Republicans, 28 percent; independents, 34 percent.

23. ABC News/*Washington Post* surveys, October 10–14, 1990 and March 1–4, 1991. Party identification figures include those who said they "leaned" to the Democrats or the Republicans.

24. "Interview with Geoffrey Garin," *The Public Perspective* (May/June 1991): 9.

25. Quoted in Alan Brinkley, *The End of Reform: New Deal Liberalism and War* (New York: Knopf, 1995), 16.

26. "Moving Right Along? Campaign '84's Lessons for 1988: An Interview with Peter Hart and Richard Wirthlin," *Public Opinion* (December/January 1985): 8.

27. Gallup poll, August 3–8, 1951. Text of question: "Suppose a young person just turned 21, asked you what the Republican party (Democratic party) stands for today—what would you tell them?" The number one Republican response, 16 percent, was "for the privileged few, moneyed interests." The number one Democratic response, 19 percent, was "for the working man, for the public benefit, for the common man."

28. Combined Gallup/Cable News Network/*USA Today* surveys, January–June 1996. Independents were last with 22 percent.

29. V. O. Key, Jr., "A Theory of Critical Elections," *Journal of Politics* 17 (February 1955): 3–18.

30. V. O. Key, Jr., "Secular Realignment and the Party System," *Journal of Politics* 21 (May 1959): 199.

31. Walter Dean Burnham, *Critical Elections and the Mainsprings of American Politics* (New York: Norton, 1970), 10.

32. Kevin P. Phillips, *The Emerging Republican Majority* (New Rochelle, N.Y.: Arlington House, 1969), 25.

33. Evan Thomas, Karen Breslau, Debra Rosenberg, Leslie Kaufman, and Andrew Murr, *Back from the Dead: How Clinton Survived the Republican Revolution* (New York: Atlantic Monthly Press, 1997), 209.

34. Everett C. Ladd, "Realignment? No. Dealignment? Yes," *Public Opinion* (October/November 1980): 55.

35. Yankelovich, Skelly, and White, survey, September 20–22, 1983. Text of question: "Do you feel that the Democratic party or the Republican party can do a better job of handling . . . or don't you think there is any real difference between them?" The "no difference" results were as follows: Reducing crime, 58 percent; stopping the spread of communism 52 percent; dealing effectively with the U.S.S.R., 48 percent; providing quality education, 47 percent; reducing the risk of nuclear war, 46 percent; providing health care, 46 percent; reducing waste and inefficiency in government, 45 percent; protecting the environment, 45 percent.

36. Everett C. Ladd, "Like Waiting for Godot: The Uselessness of Realignment for Understanding Change in Contemporary American Politics," *Polity* XXII no. 3 (Spring 1990): 512.

37. Ibid., 518.

38. Key, "A Theory of Critical Elections," 16–17.

39. See John Kenneth White, "Partisanship in the 1984 Presidential Election: The Rolling Republican Realignment," paper prepared for the 1985 Annual Meeting of the Southwestern Political Science Association, March 20–23, 1985, Houston, Texas.

40. Ronald Reagan, "Inaugural Address," Washington, D.C., January 20, 1981.

41. Walter Dean Burnham, "Realignment Lives: The 1994 Earthquake and Its Implications," in Colin Campbell and Bert A. Rockman, eds., *The Clinton Presidency: First Appraisals* (Chatham, N.J.: Chatham House, 1996), 370.

42. Everett Carll Ladd, "Why Carter Will Probably Win," *Fortune*, July 28, 1980, 86–89.

43. Gallup poll, February 20–22, 1998.

44. CBS News/*New York Times* poll, September 2–4, 1996. A "hard-core Republican" was someone who was self-identified with their party, held a favorable opinion of it, and had an unfavorable opinion of the opposition. "Hard-core Democrats" met the same criteria. All others were lumped into a category labeled "independents" or "soft partisans."

45. *Time* magazine/Cable News Network, poll conducted by Yankelovich Partners, July 30–31, 1997.

46. Wattenberg, *The Decline of American Political Parties*, chap. 6.

47. Gallup Organization/Cable News Network/*USA Today* poll, August 22–25, 1997. Text of question: "Who can handle the following problems better, Clinton or the Republicans in Congress?" Medicare: Clinton, 49 percent; Republicans, 35 percent. Economy: Clinton, 48 percent; Republicans, 38 percent. Social Security: Clinton, 45 percent; Republicans, 36 percent. Crime: Clinton, 45 percent; Republicans, 37 percent. Taxes: Clinton, 43 percent; Republicans, 40 percent. Deficit: Clinton, 40 percent, Republicans, 39 percent.

48. Combined Gallup polls, January 1997–February 1998. Reported in *The Public Perspective* (April/May 1998): 8.

49. Gallup poll, January 30–February 1, 1998. Text of question: "As you may know, United Nation's inspectors are currently in Iraq to investigate that country's weapons producing capacity. Iraq recently announced that it would not allow these investigations to continue at certain sites. Which would you prefer the United States do right now to resolve the current situation—continue to use diplomacy and sanctions to pressure Iraq into compliance with the United Nation's inspections, or, take military action, even if other countries don't join in the effort, to force Iraq into complying?" Men: continue diplomacy, 42 percent; take military action, 55 percent. Women: continue diplomacy, 61 percent; take military action, 35 percent.

50. See Thomas B. Edsall, "Pollsters View Gender Gap as Political Fixture," *Washington Post*, August 15, 1995, A11.

51. Gallup poll, 1993. Cited in Benjamin Ginsberg, Theodore J. Lowi, and Margaret Weir, *We the People* (New York: Norton, 1997), 50, 197.

52. CBS News/*New York Times*, survey, November 4, 1984. Text of question: "What is the single most important reason you are for the (Republican/Democratic) candidate for the U.S. House of Representatives in your district? (open-ended)" Ideology, 35 percent; party affiliation, 25 percent; Reagan/Mondale, 4 percent; experience/done a good job, 19 percent; just like him/her, 6 percent; economy, 9 percent; domestic issues, 15 percent; foreign policy, 1 percent; other, 3 percent; don't know/no answer, 15 percent.

53. See Norman J. Ornstein, Thomas E. Mann, and Michael J. Malbin, *Vital Statistics on Congress, 1995–1996* (Washington, D.C.: Congressional Quarterly, Inc., 1996),129.

54. Ibid., 126.

55. See Richard M. Scammon and Ben J. Wattenberg, *The Real Majority* (New York: Coward-McCann, 1970).

56. *Los Angeles Times*, poll, November 5, 1995. Text of question: "Are you happy or unhappy that the Republican party maintained control of the U.S. Congress?" Happy, 65 percent; unhappy, 27 percent; don't know, 8 percent. See also Pew Research Center survey reported in Regina Dougherty, "Divided Government Defines the Era," in Regina Dougherty, Everett C. Ladd, David Wilber, and Lynn Zayachkiwsky, eds., *America at the Polls: 1996* (Storrs, Conn.: Roper Center for Public Opinion Research, 1997), 185.

57. Bill Clinton, "Victory Speech," Little Rock, Arkansas, November 5, 1996.

58. Quoted in Adam Clymer, "Top Republicans Say They Seek Common Ground with Clinton," *New York Times*, November 7, 1996, A1.

59. Harold D. Lasswell, *Politics: Who Gets What, When, How* (New York: Meridian Books, 1958).

CHAPTER 7

State and Local Parties: Mom-and-Pop Shops in the Information Age

Ohio license plates brag that their state is at "the heart of it all." This bit of sloganeering designed to attract tourists is also an apt descriptor of party politics in that state. While Ohio politics has its share of greed, corruption, and old-fashioned patronage, it also illustrates how partisan politics plays out in the Information Age. Nowhere is there a better example of the new Information Age politics than the Mahoning County Democratic Committee.[1]

Mahoning County is located on the eastern edge of Ohio, and includes the city of Youngstown. Until the early 1990s, the Mahoning Democratic Committee was headed by party boss Don Hanni. The Hanni machine was a one-stop supermarket for would-be candidates. Services included door-to-door canvassing, distributing party literature, and conducting voter registration drives. These tasks were performed by legions of Democratic Party members who worked for the city government in patronage jobs. In return for the machine's support, Hanni's candidates were expected to be "team players" who adhered to the party line. Although the late Chicago Mayor Richard J. Daley was better-known, it was the Don Hannis of the political world who gave the party machines described in Chapter 2 a life of their own.

For the Hanni machine, life ended in 1992, when after sixteen years as Mahoning County Democratic Chair, Hanni was beaten by a young, affluent upstart who promised to rein in the party machine. Michael Morley had felt the tight grip of the machine firsthand when Hanni refused to back his friend and law partner for county commissioner. Determined to exact revenge, Morley claimed that the "corrupt" Hanni machine was responsible for the region's economic downturn. But defeating the machine would not be accomplished with mere rhetorical thrusts. Thus, Morley launched a carefully planned campaign of sophisticated television commercials, "war-room" strategy sessions, phone banks, literature drops, and canvassing. Such an all-out battle for a party chairmanship was unheard of in Ohio politics. Hanni lost, and with his defeat two-thirds of the Mahoning County Committee was filled with Morley backers. The old machine had had its last hurrah.

Morley's victory prompted concerns that Youngstown would no longer enjoy the fruits of machine politics. Hanni loyalists emphasized that Youngstown prospered under Democratic presidents who depended on a sizable machine-generated vote to win in Ohio—or at least keep the Republicans at bay. Hanni's removal meant that if Morley could not deliver a strong Democratic showing in the upcoming 1992 presidential election, Youngstown could lose valuable federal aid.

In 1992, Ohio Democrats were determined to get their supporters to the polls. The Democratic National Committee (DNC) divided the state into eight regions, each with three DNC operatives. The state Democrats would be responsible for door-to-door canvassing, voter registration drives, literature drops, distributing absentee ballots, using volunteers as media watchers to respond to Republican charges, and having local party workers offer rides to the polls. But a large part of this "coordinated campaign" relied on high-technology Information Age techniques, such as providing computerized targeting data from the DNC to Youngstown Democrats, sponsoring survey research, producing slick media ads in conjunction with the DNC, and spending large sums to buy air-time on local radio and television stations. In short, the "locals" hit the streets, while the "nationals" hit the airwaves. On election day, Clinton narrowly defeated Bush statewide, but in Mahoning County he won by a two-to-one margin. Once more—but now in an entirely new way—the Mahoning Democratic County Committee delivered.

After the election, Chairman Morley told President-elect Clinton that he expected federal economic development grants as a "thank you" for help given during the campaign. Shortly after assuming office, scores of projects found their way to northeast Ohio, including an $11.5 million Federal Aviation Administration grant to expand the Youngstown-Warren Regional Airport. Less than a year after his election, Morley, who had won on a platform opposed to pork, had taken home a sizable slice of bacon.

Of course, not all local party organizations are like the Mahoning County Democratic Committee. Most are not nearly as sophisticated, and in some communities local parties are virtually nonexistent. The point of this anecdote—a theme repeated throughout this chapter—is that for the Mahoning Democratic organization to survive in the Information Age, it had to adapt. Besides getting rid of Hanni, survival meant using new voter contact technologies and a willingness to take direction from the national party. Survival, however, was not without a price, as will be seen in the pages that follow.

STATE AND LOCAL PARTIES IN THE INFORMATION AGE

We have already described several forces that contributed to the nationalization of the party system. That process, begun at the turn of the century, was given a further boost by Franklin D. Roosevelt's New Deal, and later by new sophisticated campaign technologies and the ever-growing need for large sums of money. The result has been a highly centralized and professional party operation located in Washington, D.C., but this does not mean that state and local party organizations have disappeared. Their stories vary from place to place. In some areas they are virtually nonexistent, while in others state and local parties have thrived, such as in Mahoning County. But wherever they are, state and local parties face several challenges in the Information Age.

This chapter examines state and local party organizations—the "mom-and-pop" shops of the American party system. It is divided into five interrelated sections. First, we discuss the numerous regulations that define what state and local parties do, the changing party structure, and the growing role of allied groups. Second, we examine who belongs to the parties. Third, we describe what state and local parties actually do by presenting four case studies of county party organizations. Fourth, we describe how the local political culture influences local party operations. And finally, we examine the growing use of computers and the Internet by state and local party organizations.

Regulating State Parties

Throughout much of American history, state and local party organizations were considered private associations beyond the reach of the law. In 1932, Texas Democrats adopted a resolution stating that "all white citizens of the State of Texas who are qualified to vote under the Constitution and laws of the State shall be eligible to [sic] membership in the Democratic party and, as such, entitled to participate in its deliberations."[2] This rule excluded blacks from voting in Texas Democratic primaries which, given the solid Democratic majority in the state at the time, were tantamount to the general election. Texas Democrats defended their rule stating that they were a voluntary organization that was free to determine its own membership and limit primary participation to whites only. In 1944, the Supreme Court rejected this argument in *Smith v. Allwright*, stating: "It may now be taken as a postulate that the right to vote in a primary for the nomination of candidates without discrimination by the State, like the right to vote in a general election, is a right secured by the Constitution. . . . Under our Constitution the great privilege of the ballot may not be denied a man by the State because of his color."[3]

As noted in Chapter 3, progressive reformers believed that the only way to end corrupt machine-dominated politics was to strip the party bosses of their powers. One way to do this was to have the government regulate party activities. Parties would continue to exist, but as quasi-public agencies subject to legislative control. Although the range of government regulation varies considerably from state to state, the trend has been toward more regulation. A 1986 study by the Advisory Commission on Intergovernmental Affairs found that five states were relatively unregulated, nine were lightly regulated, seventeen were modestly regulated, and nineteen were heavily regulated.[4] Most of these restrictions concern how parties nominate candidates for statewide office and whether this should be accomplished through state-managed direct primaries. Other regulations govern the composition, selection methods, meeting dates, and duties of both state and county party committees.

Some of these regulations are highly intrusive. For example, during the 1970s the California state legislature passed a series of laws designed to curtail party activity, enacting statutes to determine the terms and qualifications for party officers; force parties to organize on a countywide basis (instead of a regional basis as preferred by third parties); limit the party chairs to a single, nonrenewable term of office; and even mandate that party chairs alternate between northern and southern California. When former California Governor Jerry Brown became state Democratic Party chair in 1988, he changed his voting address from Los Angeles to San Francisco in order to comply with the state law.[5] Indeed, Californians so zealously disliked parties that they prohibited them from formally endorsing candidates for office, and made it a misdemeanor for any candidate to claim such party backing. In 1989, the Supreme Court unanimously struck down these laws claiming that they violated the free speech clause of the First Amendment and its "right of association" guarantees for all interest groups.[6]

The cumulative effect of all state laws has been to reduce the powers exercised by state and local party chairs. Gone are the days when the bosses could anoint someone as the party's nominee or handpick a central committee. At the same time, these regulations have woven the parties into the legal fabric. This means that the Democratic and Republican parties cannot die as the Whig Party did in the 1850s because state and federal laws help ensure their continued existence. Thus, no matter how frail a party organization might be, it remains a player because the law proscribes it.

Party Structure

Another part of our inquiry is to define the place of state and local party organizations in the overall party structure. How are the various party pieces arranged? Are they akin to giant corporations like IBM, ITT, or the Ford Motor Company? Or are they a matrix of numerous autonomous entities comprising one national, fifty state, and thousands of county and municipal committees? The answer has varied over the years and from one region of the county to another. In 1964, political scientist V. O. Key, Jr. thought he had solved the riddle:

> Viewed over the entire nation, the party organization consists of no disciplined army. It consists rather of many state and local points of power, each with its own local following and each comparatively independent of external control. . . . Each has a base for existence independent of national politics. Each in fact enjoys such independence that more than a tinge of truth colors the observation that there are no national parties, only state and local parties.[7]

That same year political scientist Samuel Eldersveld arrived at a very different conclusion, likening the party organizations to a *stratarchy*.[8] Eldersveld wrote that American parties were unique because each unit operates within a well-defined sphere and is largely unresponsive to outsiders. Instead of a centralized party structure issuing directives, there exists a strata of commands. Formal and informal linkage mechanisms provide some coherence, but each unit knows its place within the overall structure. Interaction among national, state, and local parties is generally reciprocal and assistance flows in all directions—especially at election time. For example, a city committee may work with a county committee on a congressional race, or a county organization may help the state committee get out the vote for a gubernatorial candidate.

Debates about the precise structures and relationships among various party layers are important because they provide clues as to how parties are faring in the Information Age. Political scientists have theorized that the party structure is pyramid-shaped—akin to a large company in which there are various levels of bosses and workers. At the top of this centralized structure are the national party committees followed by the state committees, and numerous county party committees and municipal organizations. This structure mirrors the Hamiltonian conception of political parties, which presumes that national leaders issue directives to state and local subordinates with the expectation that they will be carried out. It also assumes that party organizations located at the bottom can express their concerns to the national leadership (see Figure 7.1).

A competing vision is the Jeffersonian approach to party structure (see Figure 7.2). It assumes that each party unit is autonomous of the other. Rather than a hierarchy, political parties have decentralized power structures that share the same label. Thus, a Republican Party organization in Boise, Idaho, is independent from other local GOP organizations in the state. The Republican National Committee (RNC), located in faraway Washington, D.C., has little impact on the day-to-day activities of the Boise Republicans.

The Jeffersonian model recognizes the diversity of the American political landscape. It has often been said that we have fifty Democratic and fifty Republican state parties. To cite just one example, in Minnesota the Democratic-Farmer-Labor Party formed by Hubert H. Humphrey dominated state politics from 1948 until Humphrey's death thirty years later. Successive defeats, followed by the Watergate disaster, led Minnesota Republicans in 1975 to rename their party the Independent Republicans in a desperate attempt to appeal to independent voters. Twenty years later, after Ronald Reagan changed the Republican Party's image and Republicans won the governorship and a U.S. Senate seat, Minnesota Republicans changed the name of their party once more to the simple "Republicans," saying: "We are unabashedly and unambiguously part of the Republican revolution in the United States of America."[9]

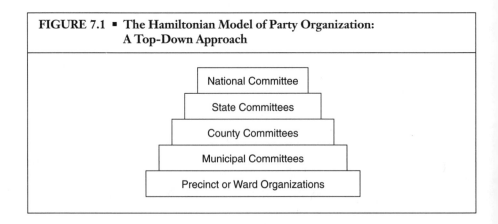

FIGURE 7.1 ▪ The Hamiltonian Model of Party Organization: A Top-Down Approach

FIGURE 7.2 ▪ The Jeffersonian Model of Party Organization: The Stratified Approach

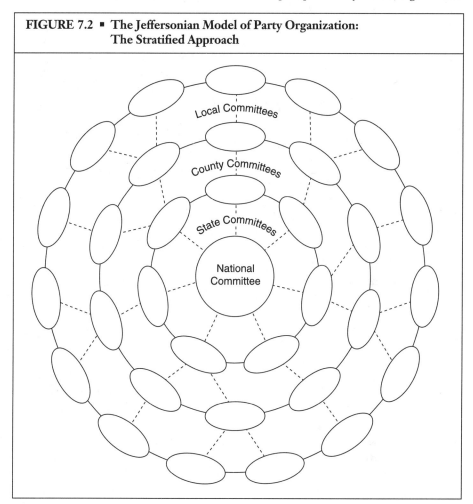

Even visits to party headquarters illustrate the widespread disparities that exist from state to state. In the early 1980s, John Kenneth White paid contemporaneous visits to Democratic Party headquarters in Massachusetts, Rhode Island, and Connecticut. In Massachusetts, the Democratic headquarters was so devoid of any furniture that voices echoed from the walls. Bay State Democrats won on their own and paid little attention to the party apparatus. Things were quite different in Rhode Island. There, the Democratic headquarters was filled with activists waiting for an interview with the party chair for state government patronage jobs. In Connecticut, an interview with the Democratic state chairman was interrupted by a phone call from the governor who wanted help persuading Democratic state legislators to support his agenda.

At first glance, the Jeffersonian style bottoms-up approach to party organization seems better-suited to fit the U.S. system of long ballots with multiple candidates for different offices. National party organizations help elect presidents; state parties concentrate on gubernatorial races; and county committees focus on state legislative and local campaigns. In such a system, it would appear that centralized parties are an impossibility. But, in fact, present trends favor the Hamiltonian model with its top-down, centralized approach. The catalyst for this change has been two-fold: (1) the infusion of large sums of money into campaigns and (2) the importance of information technologies. Over the course of the past two decades, the parties have come to resemble the federal government's grant-in-aid system—namely, before state and local organizations can receive aid they must accept the conditions imposed by the national party. The result has been to give the national party committees a voice in local politics heretofore thought impossible.

An old saying has it that money is "the mother's milk of politics." Today, **soft money** has become the principal tool used to strengthen all party organizations. Soft money refers to the unlimited sums of cash party committees can solicit from individuals and corporations. In 1995–1996, the RNC raised $161 million in soft money, while the DNC raised $128 million. Most of it was used for issue advocacy spending, transfers from national to state and local party coffers, and so-called party-building activities such as get-out-the-vote drives. At first glance, it would seem that state parties would be flush with cash, allowing them to purchase high-technology gadgetry and hire campaign professionals. Yet, upon closer inspection, state party committees are often "silent partners" who take orders from the national party committees. As one Republican state party chair observed: "I figure I should go along with the Republican National Committee as much as possible, because I want as much of their money as I can get for my state."[10] Put another way, "He who pays the piper calls the tune." Any activities that fall outside the purview of the national parties can expect to receive little soft money from the national committees.

New campaign technologies have transformed the Democratic and Republican national committees into one-stop high-technology centers. Increased staff, state-of-the-art equipment, and glistening new headquarters have meant that the DNC and RNC can send campaign managers to the various states, conduct public opinion polls, provide issue and opposition research, undertake media development and production, and help raise money for local candidates. If local party leaders want up-to-date polling information, they can ask the national party committees; or they can surf the Internet. Just as individuals have been empowered, and sometimes overwhelmed, by the wealth of information available on the World Wide Web, party organizations have experienced the same sense of empowerment. On the eve of the twenty-first century, the national parties have achieved a degree of autonomy and power that they could not ever have imagined at the turn of the twentieth.

A Network of Allied Party Groups

In the Information Age, many conceive of party structures as stretching beyond local, state, and national organizations to include affiliated groups. For years, parties have relied on outside interests for help with their campaigns. During the 1940s, for example, labor unions gave Democrats much-needed money and manpower. In 1943, the Congress of Industrial Organizations (CIO) established the Political Action Committee (PAC). Sidney Hillman, president of the Amalgamated Clothing Workers of America which was then affiliated with the CIO, put $1.5 million of his local union's money into the PAC. This helped the CIO distribute campaign literature to 1,500 labor publications and 255 black newspapers on behalf of Democratic candidates. Thus, when it came to choosing a vice president in 1944—a task that eventually assumed unusual importance since Franklin Roosevelt would be dead within a year—Roosevelt reputedly told the Democratic party bosses to "Clear it with Sidney."[11]

In addition to labor unions, those groups with strong ties to today's Democratic Party include the National Organization for Women, National Abortion Rights League, National Education Association, Sierra Club, and other assorted environmental groups. Republican-oriented groups include Americans for Tax Reform, U.S. Chamber of Commerce, Christian Coalition, National Rifle Association, National Beer Wholesalers Association, and the National Federation of Independent Businesses.

The nexus between the Republican Party and the National Beer Wholesalers Association provides an interesting case study. Back in the 1930s, the beer industry restricted its lobbying efforts to state governments because the repeal of Prohibition left the regulation of alcohol to the states. But after a series of federal setbacks, the beer industry targeted Congress. During the Reagan administration, Transportation Secretary Elizabeth Dole pushed for an increase in the drinking age from eighteen to twenty-one in order to reduce traffic fatalities. Then in 1990, George Bush and the Democratic Congress raised beer taxes by 100 percent. Three years later, the beer wholesalers were vehemently opposed to the Clinton health care plan because it would have mandated coverage for workers in small businesses and, most importantly, threatened to raise the federal excise tax on beer as a revenue source. The Beer Wholesalers became players in Republican politics in order to secure their policy objective of less federal regulation. Allying themselves with conservative Republicans such as House Whip Tom DeLay, the Beer Wholesalers became an influential group within GOP circles. Determined to keep the Republican Party committed to its antitax, anti–big government policies, the Beer Wholesalers contributed much-needed cash in 1994 to nearly four-hundred candidates who were pro-beer and pro-small business. In 1996, the Beer Wholesalers gave nearly 80 percent of their contributions to Republicans, many of them House candidates (see "The Parties Speak: David Rehr on the National Beer Wholesalers Association and the GOP").[12]

A recent example of how influential Democratic-affiliated groups can be occurred in the January 1996 special election held in Oregon to replace Republican Senator Bob Packwood. The AFL-CIO dispatched twelve full-time staff members to the state while state and local unions provided another twenty-five more to help Democrat Ron Wyden get elected. In addition, the League of Conservation Voters and the Sierra Club spent more than $200,000 on Wyden's behalf. The Sierra Club ran a television commercial charging that Wyden's Republican opponent, frozen vegetable tycoon Gordon Smith, allowed spills from his plant to pollute a nearby

---

The Parties Speak: *David Rehr on the National Beer Wholesalers Association and the GOP*

David Rehr is an influential lobbyist and vice president of the National Beer Whole-salers Association. He formerly worked for Republican Congressman Vin Weber and the National Federation of Independent Business.

The National Beer Wholesalers Association (NBWA) is a non-partisan organization representing the interests of family-owned and operated malt beverage distributorships before the federal government. With more than 1,800 members located in virtually every congressional district, these prominent local citizens are involved in various civic and charitable community activities, and are politically active at all levels of government.

The political goal of the NBWA is to elect and sustain a "Pro-Beer Wholesaler, Pro-Business" Congress. It works to achieve this objective through legitimate and legal support for congressional incumbents seeking reelection to the Senate and House, aiding candidates in so-called "open-seats" where the incumbent is not seeking reelection, and by helping challengers run against an incumbent Member of Congress when the incumbent has a philosophy which is against the interests of beer wholesalers or has a hostile voting record on key legislative initiatives.

The legislative goal of NBWA is to ensure that Congress enacts legislation which does not inhibit small business growth and provides an environment where beer can be moderately and responsibly consumed by 80 million Americans.

The NBWA works to advance its political goal in three primary ways. First, and foremost, the NBWA Political Action Committee financially supports candidates. In the 1993–94 election cycle, the NBWA PAC spent almost $1.5 million in more than four-hundred campaigns. NBWA PAC support is based upon successful completion of an issues questionnaire, contact with local wholesaler(s) and a discussion of legislative issues with their constituents, and a review of campaign data which helps determine the seriousness of the effort being undertaken by the candidate. During the 1993–94 cycle, the Federal Election Commission (FEC) ranked the NBWA PAC forty-ninth largest out of more than 4,000 PACs.

Second, local wholesalers and industry contacts provide political intelligence which can enhance or detract from a candidate's effort. The NBWA staff, in routine legislative issue discussions with other representatives of interest groups, share information on polling, campaign fundraising reports, candidate contact, and perceptions about the ability of various candidates to win their elections. This intelligence is invaluable to the Washington, D.C., political community which is inundated with thousands of requests from incumbents and candidates for campaign support. Information is exchanged with the House and Senate campaign committees. Both the collection and dissemination of this information falls under the Free Speech Clause of the First Amendment.

Third, the NBWA regularly hosts events where a candidate can meet with influential Washington, D.C., "movers and shakers" so each party can have a dialogue on issues of concern. These "Meet n' Greet" functions are not fundraisers and are not under the purview of FEC regulations. The meetings provide incumbents and candidates with a better understanding of issues they will face as Members of Congress and provide the Washington community with an opportunity to become better acquainted with the featured guest.

The political marketplace is extremely competitive. At NBWA, we look for every legitimate opportunity to help our philosophical allies enhance their power and signal our adversaries that opposing the interests of family businesses will not be taken lightly by their wholesaler constituents.

SOURCE: David K. Rehr, vice president, National Beer Wholesalers of America, December 1998.

---

creek. Finally, the Human Rights Campaign—the largest gay and lesbian political organization in the country—raised a large sum of money and sent its organizers to the state. These groups, together with the state and national Democratic committees, produced television commercials, canvassed voters, sent direct mail, and attended neighborhood rallies. Thanks to these efforts, Wyden eked out a 48 percent to 47 percent victory.[13]

Special interest groups like the Beer Wholesalers and the Sierra Club are not the only players in party politics. Others include **unofficial party organizations** whose members are party loyalists who wish to change the direction of the national party. For Democrats, a prime example is the Democratic Leadership Council (DLC). Founded in 1985 by a group of moderate-to-conservative Democrats, the DLC rejects the "Old Left" and the "New Right" in favor of a "Third Way" that makes government a catalyst between individuals and private associations that can solve problems. For example, the DLC hailed the efforts of the Oakland, California, public schools to encourage businesses to donate computers by creating a public-private partnership called the Oakland Technology Exchange. The exchange receives used computers from area businesses and employs students after school to refurbish them and install new software. By 1998, 3,000 computers were sent to 90 public schools. DLC leaders tout the program as helping local schools achieve universal computer access and giving those employed by the exchange a chance to develop the necessary job skills to succeed in the Information Age.[14]

On the Republican side, a number of unofficial party organizations vie for influence. These include the Christian Coalition, Republican Mainstream Committee, Ripon Society, National Republican Coalition for Choice, Empower America, and the Heritage Foundation. Empower America is one place where many thoughtful Republicans have looked for new ideas. Founded in 1993, Empower America cast itself as a "pro-growth, free market political advocacy organization whose mission is to steer public policy in favor of individual freedom and opportunity, responsibility and excellence." This empowerment agenda includes (1) fostering economic growth, entrepreneurship, job creation, and expanded opportunity for all people through low taxes, reduced government spending, sound money, and less government regulation; (2) facilitating cultural renewal by removing bureaucratic impediments and empowering families and individuals to improve education, combat poverty, and restore peace and security to their local communities; and

(3) advancing freedom and democracy around the world through strong international leadership and open trade policies.[15]

In recent years, much attention has been paid to the powerful voice that the Christian Coalition exercises in Republican affairs. The Christian Coalition believes that religion and politics are necessarily intertwined, and that social issues stances, such as abortion and school prayer, should be decisive in choosing prospective presidents. This led to a showdown in 1997 when the Christian Coalition supported a measure that would refuse party funding for any Republican who supported partial-birth abortion. After an acrimonious debate, Republicans defeated the ban. As this example illustrates, the influence of affiliated party groups remains controversial, and how both parties will resolve the conflicts is unclear. But their overall effect has been to make the party structure far more fluid, as new allied groups enter and depart with each passing election.

WHO BELONGS?

A unique aspect of the American party system relates to membership. Who belongs to state and local parties? In Chapter 6, we discussed the concept of party identification as it pertains to personal allegiances, but party loyalty is different than party membership. One can be a loyal Democrat or Republican, and never attend a party meeting. This is a far cry from most European party systems where party membership is determined by payment of dues. In the United States, however, party membership is open to whoever wishes to support a particular party's candidates for office. There are three ways to define party membership: (1) those who vote in primaries, (2) those who hold official positions in the party structure, and (3) those who take part in party-sponsored activities.

Primary Voters

Prior to the Progressive reforms, party bosses argued that voters should participate in party activities through periodic caucuses, conventions, and party-sponsored primaries. But these gatherings were controlled by the machines, thereby making the activities of the members mostly symbolic. Progressive reforms legitimized the role of average citizens in party functions. Progressives believed, quite rightly, that who the parties nominated was as important as who got elected. Thus, the Progressives were strong supporters of state-sponsored primary elections.

By regulating how nominations were made and who was allowed to participate, state laws determined who belonged to which party. Today, thirty-five states use primaries as the sole means to nominate state and local candidates.[16] Two states, Indiana and Michigan, require that primaries be used to nominate candidates for important statewide office such as governor and U.S. Senate, but that conventions should select candidates for lesser offices such as the state legislature. (State conventions are where delegates from local areas, usually county party committees, gather to vote for their favorites.) In four southern states, state party committees choose between primaries or conventions. For instance, in 1994 Virginia Republicans opted to use a convention to choose their U.S. Senate candidate. Oliver North, who gained fame during the Iran-Contra affair, was quite popular with GOP activists while his rival, James Miller, was far more favorably viewed by the rank and file. North won his party's nomination with 55 percent of the vote, but lost to incumbent Democrat, Chuck Robb, 46 percent to 43 percent. Two years later, Virginia Republicans used the primary method to renominate incumbent Senator John Warner who won his bid for reelection.

In sixteen states, some combination of primary and convention is used. For example, Colorado restricts access to the primary ballot to candidates who win 20 percent of the convention votes. Connecticut and Massachusetts have a lower threshold of 15 percent. In Iowa, if there are more than two candidates for any nomination and each receives less than 35 percent of the primary vote, the primary is deemed inconclusive and the nomination is made at a party convention. In New York, the person who wins a majority of votes at the convention becomes the party's designated candidate. But anyone who receives at least 25 percent of the convention votes can appear on the primary ballot.

Rules matter. But of equal importance is the prevailing political culture under which parties operate. In Connecticut, for example, there is a bias toward the state party convention as the ultimate authority. From 1955 until 1982, Connecticut Democrats held just one gubernatorial primary, because no one was able to win 20 percent support at a state party convention. Quite the opposite is true in New York. There, convention delegates are prone to give 25 percent of their votes to candidates just to ensure that their names appear on the primary ballot. And New Yorkers are likely to overrule choices made at the party conventions. For example, in 1982, Democrats had a classic gubernatorial primary battle between New York City Mayor Edward I. Koch and Lieutenant Governor Mario M. Cuomo. Koch received 69 percent of the ballots at the Democratic State Convention, but with 31 percent Cuomo won enough support to enter the Democratic primary. More than 1.2 million Democrats trekked to the polls on primary day, and Cuomo defeated Koch, 52 percent to 48 percent. Cuomo subsequently edged out his Republican rival and went on to serve three terms as governor.

Added to this complexity, the form of a primary election varies widely (see Table 7.1). Most states use a **closed primary system** that requires voters to formally declare a party affiliation in order to vote. Thus, once voters declare themselves Republicans or Democrats, they become, in a legal sense, members of that party and are allowed to help pick the party's candidates for the general election.

Because state primaries are regulated by individual state legislatures, there are several varieties of closed primaries. Two types stand out: **completely closed** and **partially closed.** Completely closed primary systems mandate that party enrollment must be entered into the official state records and made public. There are opportunities to alter one's enrollment, but that must occur by a prescribed date long before election day. South Dakota, for example, sets its deadline at fifteen days; Oregon, twenty days, and in New York, nearly a year. The average time requirement is about sixty days. In **partially closed systems,** used in nine states, voters are

---

TABLE 7.1 ▪ Open, Closed, and Blanket Primaries: An Overview of the Fifty
State Systems

Completely Closed: Voters must register with a party in advance of the primary election. Switching to a different party must be done well in advance of the primary.

Arizona	Nebraska	Oklahoma
Connecticut	Nevada	Oregon
Delaware	New Mexico	Pennsylvania
Florida	New York	South Dakota
Kentucky	North Carolina	West Virginia
Maryland		

Partially Closed: Voters must preregister with a political party, but are allowed to change party registration on election day.

Colorado	Maine	New Jersey
Iowa	Massachusetts	Ohio
Kansas	New Hampshire	Rhode Island

Partially Open: Voters are required to choose a political party or a party ballot at the polls. There is no long-term party registration, but their choice on primary day is public information. Crossover voting is not possible.

Alabama	Indiana	Texas
Arkansas	Mississippi	Virginia
Georgia	Missouri	Wyoming
Illinois	Tennessee	

Completely Open: Voters are not required to state any party preference. Usually, the voter is given two ballots and is required to pick one of them once they are in the privacy of the polling booth. Crossover voting is not possible.

Hawaii	Montana	Utah
Idaho	North Dakota	Vermont
Michigan	South Carolina	Wisconsin
Minnesota		

Blanket: Voters may choose candidates of different parties for different offices.

Alaska	California	Washington

Nonpartisan: All voters participate in a single primary.

Louisiana

SOURCE: The National Conference of State Legislatures, Denver, Colorado, November 1998.

allowed to change their registration on primary day itself. Ohioans, for example, can sign a declaration altering their party membership on primary day. Of course, voters can only pick candidates from one party's ballot. The idea behind a closed system is to ensure that only party members vote in primaries. Although somewhat of a simplification, closed primary states tend to be those that historically were dominated by party machines.

Open primaries allow voters to participate without declaring their political affiliation. Open primaries can be of two types: **completely open** and **partially open.** Ten states hold completely open primaries. Voters in these states can request whatever party ballot they desire. Although poll-watchers know which party ballot is requested (they watch the voter walk into a party voting booth), no official record is kept. This is not the case in partially open states. There, voters declare their party preference in the privacy of the polling booth. No record is kept because no one is aware of which ballot was chosen. As with closed systems, voters must choose candidates from only one party. States using this partially open system, or open-private model, tend to have had a strong progressive heritage, such as Minnesota and Wisconsin, which was the first state to adopt the direct primary nomination system in 1903.

A third model, termed **blanket primaries,** is used in California, Washington, and Alaska. In these states, voters are allowed to participate in primaries for both parties at the same time. For example, an Alaskan might support a Republican candidate for governor *and* a Democratic state representative in the same primary election. California's recent switch to a blanket system is especially noteworthy. The move away from a closed system was spearheaded by U.S. Representative Tom Campbell. Campbell entered the Republican U.S. Senate primary in 1992 and was widely believed to be the strongest candidate to challenge his Democratic opponent. He was conservative on economic issues, but moderate on social questions such as abortion and gay rights. Campbell was defeated in the primary by ultraconservative television commentator, Bruce Herschensohn, 38 percent to 36 percent. Herschensohn subsequently lost to liberal Democrat Barbara Boxer, 48 percent to 43 percent.

Campbell contended that the closed primary process was dominated by "extremists" within the Republican Party. After securing financial backing from several civic-minded organizations and Silicon Valley billionaire David Packard (founder of Hewlett-Packard), Campbell mounted a campaign to open the primary system. In 1996, voters overwhelmingly approved Proposition 198 which created a blanket primary system, marking the most radical overhaul of California election laws in forty years.

The first test of California's blanket primary occurred in 1998. Campbell's theory that more moderate candidates would be chosen proved correct. In the Republican primary for U.S. Senate, two candidates sought the GOP endorsement: moderate Matt Fong, son of the former Democratic secretary of state, and conservative Darrell Issa, a steadfast abortion foe. Exit polls found that 25 percent of self-described Democrats and independents cast a ballot in the GOP contest, and thanks to those crossover votes Fong beat Issa.[17]

This in not to say a shift from a closed primary to a blanket primary is not without problems. First, the nomination process is taken completely away from the party organization. Second, blanket primaries accentuate the trend away from partisan labels—a development discussed in the previous chapter. Finally, some crossover voters in blanket primaries are motivated by a desire to sabotage the opposition by supporting an inferior candidate certain to be a sure-loser in a general election. In 1972, Republicans were nearly unanimous in choosing Richard M. Nixon to be their party's nominee. But the Democratic race was far more interesting. Former Vice President Hubert H. Humphrey who had been the party's 1968 nominee, Maine Senator Edmund S. Muskie, who was Humphrey's 1968 vice presidential candidate, South Dakota Senator George S. McGovern, an ardent foe of the Vietnam War, and Alabama Governor George C. Wallace, a segregationist who appealed to blue-collar Democrats upset with the Vietnam War and the sexual revolution, vied for the nomination. Some Republicans, knowing that Nixon did not need their primary votes, supported Wallace as a protest to the social and cultural unrest knowing that he would be an easy target for Nixon to beat in November.

One state, Louisiana, holds **nonpartisan primaries.** There all candidates, regardless of their affiliation, appear on a single ballot listed alphabetically. Anyone receiving more than 50 percent of the vote is elected. If no candidate receives more than 50 percent, a runoff election is held between the top two contenders regardless of their party affiliation. This peculiar election process drew national attention in 1991. The incumbent Republican governor, Buddy Roemer, was unpopular because he had raised taxes after promising he would not. Roemer was challenged by former Democratic governor Edwin Edwards, who was tried in 1985 for bribery and was charged in 1986 with making $2 million on a kickback scheme involving state hospitals. One jury voted eleven-to-one for acquittal; another found Edwards not guilty. A third candidate was Ku Klux Klan leader and State Senator David Duke. Duke received 32 percent of the primary vote, compared to 34 percent for Edwards and 27 percent for Roemer. Faced with a two-way contest between Edwards and Duke, many Republicans bolted to Edwards, including President George Bush. In a contest that saw a record turnout helped by intense national media coverage, Edwards walloped Duke, 61 percent to 39 percent.

Whether states have open or closed primaries usually depends on the state legislature. But this, too, may be changing. In 1986, the Supreme Court issued an important decision in *Tashjian v. Republican Party of Connecticut,* a case that arose from a decision by the Connecticut Republican Party to allow the large number of unaffiliated independent voters to participate in its statewide primaries. The state's Democratic-controlled legislature refused to amend the state laws to conform with the Republican Party's rules. In a narrow five-to-four decision, the Court sided with the Republicans, saying: "Any interference with the freedom of a party is simultaneously an interference with the freedom of its adherents."[18] But in a strongly worded dissent, Justice Antonin Scalia wrote:

> The Connecticut voter who, while steadfastly refusing to register as a Republican, casts a vote in the Republican primary, forms no more meaningful an "association"

with the Party than does the independent of the registered Democrat who responds to questions by a Republican Party pollster. If the concept of freedom of association is extended to such casual contacts, it ceases to be of any analytic use.[19]

Scalia's dissent notwithstanding, less than a year after the Court's ruling in *Tashjian* seven state parties changed their primary rules to allow unaffiliated voters to participate.

Officials in the Party Organization

Defining party membership according to those who vote in primaries is easy. But it is also far too inclusive because in some states it includes unaffiliated voters who can vote in party primaries. An alternative way to define party membership is to look at those holding formal positions in the party organization. Party organizations are numerous. Each state, for example, has a Republican and Democratic central committee. So, too, do nearly all of the three thousand counties scattered throughout the nation. No one has ever done a census of municipal party organizations since there are tens of thousands of local governments, but it is safe to assume most have party organizations as well.

Perhaps the best way to conceptualize state party organizations is to review Figure 7.1 (see p. 178). At the bottom are local committeepersons, sometimes referred to as "precinct captains." They are elected on primary day, except in those places where county party leaders appoint them. Generally speaking, precinct captains represent the smallest electoral unit, usually about six hundred people. There is usually one party official per precinct, though some states have two. The bylaws of the New York State Democratic Committee, for instance, stipulate that each precinct elect a man and woman as committeepersons. Since there are nearly 16,000 election districts in the Empire State, the Democratic and Republican state parties would have 32,000 members at the base of their organizations if they were all filled—a highly unlikely eventuality. Committeepersons represent the party in their neighborhood, bring voters into the party fold, and get out the vote on election day.

As to why one might choose to serve as a party committeeperson, the incentives are mixed. In the heyday of party machines these were highly coveted posts, because those who occupied them got the best patronage jobs. One 1970 study found that three-fourths of Pittsburgh's Democratic committee members held public jobs.[20] Today, just 10 percent of county/municipal committeepersons are also local public employees.[21] Party committeepersons get involved because of their concerns about issues, as well as their desire to enter politics, socialize with like-minded people, or fulfill their civic duty. There is really no way to describe a "typical" committeeperson. Some are from middle- and upper-class backgrounds; others are working class. Their level of political skill also varies. Some are well-versed in local politics, while others are amateurs. Although they tend to be more ideological than the general public, many are middle-of-the-road types. Historically, most committeepersons have been men, but this is no longer true. But whatever their background, political orientation, or sex, the numbers of those willing to serve in local party organizations are dwindling. In vast areas of the country, precinct-level party operatives are nonexistent—especially in places dominated by one party.

Moving upward from the base of the pyramid is a series of progressively larger organizations. As one observer noted, "The precinct caucus is the seed from which the mighty party organization grows."[22] The committeepersons from a municipality comprise a city or town committee. For instance, all the Republican committeepersons from the city of Meadville, Pennsylvania, are part of the Meadville Republican City Committee. The next layer is the county organization which is composed of all the committeepersons from each election district in the county. Thus, all of the GOP committeepersons in Crawford County, Pennsylvania, including those from the city of Meadville, make up the Crawford County Republican Committee. This is a critically important layer in the overall structure, because county committees are the key cogs of the party system. Also, the county is the geographical electoral area from which members of Congress, state legislative personnel, and county government employees are selected. Consequently, county committees are subject to numerous statutory regulations.

Most municipal and county party organizations elect chairs, vice chairs, treasurers, secretaries, and executive committee members. Often, their vitality is directly linked to the chairperson and his/her officers. Aggressive party leaders can create dynamic organizations; ineffectual leaders often have inept ones.

State party committees usually comprise county committee members. The size of state party committees varies from as few as twenty in Iowa to more than a thousand in California. State party leaders (chairs, executive officers, etc.) are generally selected by the central committee at annual party conventions or through some form of ballot procedure. Usually, the governor chooses the state party chair. When a party does not control the governorship, the contest for state party chair can be a spirited one with several contestants.

If membership in a political party is defined as the number of those holding official party posts, the tally would shrink considerably from those who vote in primaries. There are approximately 100,000 election districts in the United States. If each of them had a committeeperson from each party, there would be 200,000 party members. They, in turn, would serve on their county party committee; a smaller portion of those individuals would serve on the state central committee, and an even smaller portion would serve on the national party committee. However, as previously noted, many election districts do not have a precinct captain. Even where parties are active, the county committees often remain only two-thirds filled. One of the toughest tasks for a county party leader is getting and keeping a full list of committeepersons. Optimistically, we might assume each party boasts three-fourths of their committeeperson potential, suggesting each has about 75,000 members. About 150,000 party members across the nation might seem impressive, but given the number of voting age Americans this amounts to roughly one per 1,300 citizens. By contrast, 18,139,881 Democrats cast votes in their contested 1992 presidential primaries between Bill Clinton, Paul Tsongas, and Jerry Brown. Republicans cast 12,424,284 primary votes, dividing them between President George Bush and his erstwhile challenger Pat Buchanan.[23]

Activists

A final way to define party membership involves looking at the activities held by the party organization. State and local party organizations conduct numerous activities from barbecues to black-tie galas. Conceivably, the best way to define a party member is by counting the number of those attending party-sponsored events, which might include most party officials, elected officials from the community, concerned citizens, and the true believers. Unfortunately, there is no accurate measure of how large this group is. The University of Michigan's American National Election Study is the best available resource. Every two years respondents are asked whether they have "worked for a party or candidate." As noted in Table 7.2, those answering "yes" during the 1960s totaled 6 percent. But in the decades since, the percentage has steadily declined, falling to just 2 percent in 1996. Likewise, those who have contributed to a political campaign fell from 12 percent during the 1960s to 7 percent in the 1990s.

TABLE 7.2 ▪ **Activism in Local Party Organizations, 1960–1996 (in percents)**

Year	Those Who Worked for a Party or Candidate during the Last Election	Those Who Gave Money, Bought Tickets, or Did Anything to Help a Party or Candidate
1960	6	12
1962	4	9
1964	5	11
1966	*	8
1968	6	9
1970	7	*
1972	5	10
1974	5	8
1976	4	16
1978	6	13
1980	4	8
1982	6	9
1984	4	8
1986	3	10
1988	3	9
1990	3	7
1992	3	7
1994	3	6
1996	2	7

*Not available.

SOURCE: National Election Study, 1960–1996. Text of questions: "Did you do any work for one of the parties or candidates during the last election?" "Did you give any money, or buy any tickets, or do anything to help the campaign for one of the parties or candidates?"

Summary

There are several ways to define members of state and local party organizations. Those subscribing to the Jeffersonian view of parties may wish to count primary voters, since they are fairly inclusive. Hamiltonians may wish to count only those elites who hold official party positions. But no matter what method is used, parties in the Information Age are likely to rely on resources other than volunteers. Given the increased professionalization of the parties, grassroots party activism may become an arcane piece of Americana.

LOCAL POLITICAL CULTURE

At the heart of the Jeffersonian model lies a belief in the diversity of local politics. Toward the end of his life, Jefferson worried about the decline of local politics. The "salvation of the republic," he argued, rested on the regeneration of community-based politics.[24] If Jefferson had lived into the 1840s (he died in 1826), he would have been pleased to find a diversity of local communities, each with a distinct modus operandi. With the Progressive reforms some of that diversity was lost, as each state followed a similar path in regulating party activities. Nonetheless, a dominant characteristic of the American party system has been differing local political cultures. But this, too, is changing in the Information Age.

Local political culture refers to those values and beliefs that form a rough consensus within which political behavior and government policies are bound. The foremost student of political culture has been Daniel Elazar, who has identified three political cultures throughout the United States:

1. **Individualistic** states have a business-like mentality where politicians and politics are viewed as "necessary evils." Typically, an individualistic political culture is built on principles of commerce and is generally accepting of diverse ethnic, religious, and social structures. Examples include Pennsylvania, Indiana, New Jersey, Nevada, and Alaska.
2. **Moralistic** states are those where politics is a means for creating a better society, and government acts on behalf of the public interest. Vermont, Maine, Michigan, Wisconsin, Minnesota, North Dakota, Colorado, Utah, and Oregon are illustrations of this type of culture.
3. **Traditionalistic** states tend to adhere to established traditions of leadership under a hierarchical social structure. Like the moralistic culture, politics is undertaken for the common good, but those involved are elites who have a vested interest in maintaining the status quo. Examples include Virginia, Tennessee, Mississippi, and North Carolina.

Not all states perfectly adhere to the three cultural models. For example, Elazar suggests that Iowa, Kansas, Montana, New Hampshire, and California are mostly moralistic, but each has an individualistic strain. Nebraska, Idaho, Massachusetts, and New York are considered individualistic, but they also have a moralistic strain. Table 7.3 summarizes Elazar's typologies.

TABLE 7.3 ▪ Elazar's Typologies of Political Subcultures

Individualistic

Pure Individualistic	*Individualistic with Traditionalistic Strain*	*Individualistic with Moralistic Strain*
Pennsylvania	Delaware	Nebraska, New York,
Indiana	Maryland	Wyoming, Ohio,
New Jersey	Missouri	Idaho, Illinois,
Nevada	Hawaii	Connecticut, Rhode Island,
Alaska		Massachusetts

Traditionalistic

Pure Traditionalistic	*Traditionalistic with Individualistic Strain*	*Traditionalistic with Moralistic Strain*
Virginia	Florida, Texas,	Arizona
Tennessee	Alabama, Kentucky,	North Carolina
South Carolina	Georgia, Louisiana,	
Mississippi	Arkansas	
	West Virginia	

Moralistic

Pure Moralistic	*Moralistic with Individualistic Strain*	*Moralistic with Traditionalistic Strain*
Vermont	Iowa	None
Maine	Kansas	
Michigan	Montana	
Wisconsin	South Dakota	
Minnesota	New Hampshire	
North Dakota	California	
Colorado	Washington	
Utah		
Oregon		

SOURCE: Daniel J. Elazar, *The American Mosaic: The Impact of Space, Time and Culture on American Politics* (Boulder, Colo.: Westview Press, 1994).

　　While Elazar's work has been groundbreaking, it does not account for different political cultures within a given state. In his 1962 work, *The Amateur Democrat: Club Politics in Three Cities*, James Q. Wilson found great diversity in local party politics. Wilson noted that in some political subcultures, especially several California cities, "amateurs" were engaged in party activity in order to achieve ideological goals (see "The Parties Speak: The 'Amateur Democrats'"). In other places such as Chicago and New York, winning elections mattered most. Wilson dubbed these the "professionals." Since Wilson first published his book in 1962, several scholars have also found differences in the core objectives of party organizations.[25]

The Parties Speak: *The "Amateur Democrats"*

James Q. Wilson was among the first to discern differences between political party activists. Surveying those participating in local party committees, Wilson discovered a new type of participant—the amateur, whose primary motivation for political involvement was not personal loyalty to an individual or a job, but agreement with their fellow partisans on issues.

Since the Second World War a new kind of politician has appeared in large numbers in several of the biggest American cities. Although they are nowhere in complete control of their parties, these new politicians have played a crucial part in the defeat of the boss of Tammany Hall and have contributed to the election of several important officials. . . . Their ambitions extend far beyond these offices, however, for they intend to alter fundamentally the character of the American party system, and accordingly of all governing institutions. . . .

It is not his liberalism or his age, education, or class that sets the new politician apart and makes him worth studying. Rather, it is his outlook on politics, and the style of politics he practices. This is sensed by the politicians themselves; the conventional and the new politicians, in almost every case, find it hard to "understand" one another or to "get along," even in those cases in which their interests or policies happen to coincide. . . . Although in New York the new politicians are called "reformers," their counterparts in Wisconsin or California are not reformers at all, for in these states they are not preoccupied with matters of reform. Nor, as we shall see, are they all "intellectuals" or "eggheads," although some of the new politicians are fond of describing themselves and their colleagues in these terms. Although no single word is completely satisfactory, the word which I will use in this study is "amateur." . . .

An amateur is one who finds politics *intrinsically* interesting because it expresses a conception of the public interest. The amateur politician sees the political world more in terms of ideas and principles than in terms of persons. Politics is the determination of public policy, and public policy ought to be set deliberately rather than as the accidental by-product of a struggle for personal and party advantage. Issues ought to be settled on their merits; compromises by which one issue is settled other than on its merits are sometimes necessary, but they are never desirable. . . . The amateur takes the outcome of politics—the determination of policies and the choice of officials—seriously, in the sense that he feels a direct concern for what he thinks are the ends these policies serve and the qualities these officials possess. He is not oblivious to considerations of partisan or personal advantage in assessing the outcome but (in the pure case) he dwells on the relation of outcome to his conception, be it vague or specific, of the public weal. Although politics may have attractions as a game of skill, it is never simply that.

SOURCE: Excerpted from James Q. Wilson, *The Amateur Democrat: Club Politics in Three Cities* (Chicago: University of Chicago Press, 1962), 1–4.

Today, local political cultures still matter although nationalizing trends have lessened their impact. An apt analogy might be the glut of hamburger stands along busy roadways. Just a few decades ago, these were individually owned and operated. Now many have been taken over by national chains such as McDonald's or Burger King, and everywhere the same burger is made, tasting more or less the same, from Maine to California.

Thankfully, we have not reached the point where the American party system has become completely "franchised." In 1997, Joel Paddock examined survey data from thousands of party leaders and overlaid this information with Elazar's typologies.[26] The results were fascinating. In moralistic states, party competition revolved around competing conceptions of the common good. Amateurs dominated and their goals were highly ideological. Party leaders in moralistic states were likely to agree with the statement, "I'd rather lose an election than compromise my basic philosophy." The same was true when asked whether "a candidate should express his conviction even if it means losing the election" or "the party platforms should address controversial issues, even if they are unpopular."

In individualistic states, professional party leaders are inclined to distribute favors (patronage) rather than change public policy. Party leaders there were less likely than the moralists to agree with the idea that candidates should hold to their beliefs, even if it meant losing. Traditionalistic states have a minimum of activity because, says Paddock, "they encourage a degree of openness that goes against the fundamental grain of an elite-oriented order."[27]

WHAT STATE AND LOCAL PARTIES DO

In the Introduction, we listed what might be called latent party functions—namely, those by-products of party activity that often are not immediately recognizable but are very important. Quite often, party leaders and their followers do not fully understand how important their handiwork is to the democratic process. Here we address the manifest activities of state and local party organizations.

Manifest Party Functions

When it comes to the overt activities conducted by state and local party organizations, most are centered on winning elections and controlling government. Manifest party activities include, but are not limited to, the following:

- **Nominating Candidates.** A core activity performed by parties is choosing which candidates to run under their banner. Put another way, party organizations choose their sales force (i.e., candidates).
- **Recruiting Public Servants.** Party activists often ask prominent local citizens to run for public office. Sometimes they are willing to toss their hats into the ring; on other occasions it takes a bit more coaxing.

- **Slating.** An important party activity is to secure a full slate of candidates. Sometimes in one-party areas this is not possible, but local parties try hard anyway to fill all positions listed on the ballot.
- **Aiding Candidates.** Once nominations are complete, party organizations help candidates with their general election campaign. Although there has been a shift toward candidate-centered elections, this does not mean parties are irrelevant.
- **Raising and Distributing Money.** In the Information Age, high-technology campaigns are fueled by money. State and local party organizations spend a considerable amount of time collecting funds from activities as diverse as black-tie dinners to potluck suppers.
- **Registering New Voters.** Party organizations seek out those who are not registered to vote and ask them to register. Sometimes they are motivated by a belief that "everyone should participate in the process." More often they want a potential voter's support in the next election. Either way, parties bring people into the political process.
- **Getting Out the Vote.** Parties do everything they can to get the "faithful" to the polls on election day. Several studies have shown that turnout is highest in communities that have viable party organizations.[28]
- **Educating Voters.** Party organizations articulate policy positions and debate issues. The outcome is a more informed electorate.
- **Overseeing the Election Process.** Most local party organizations watch what is happening at the polls using poll-watchers and inspectors. In New York, for example, state law mandates that paid poll-watchers be appointed from the two parties that received the highest vote totals in the last gubernatorial election. Thus, Democrats and Republicans can keep an eye on each other.
- **Uniting Diverse Interests.** Political parties often bring together scores of interest groups behind a candidate. For example, it is not unusual to find individuals from women's groups, environmentalists, and labor unions all making telephone calls from the local Democratic party headquarters. Likewise, members of anti-abortion groups, conservative activists, and small business men and women often populate local Republican party headquarters.
- **Allocating Patronage.** Even with civil service reform, there are many government jobs that must be filled at the municipal, county, and state levels. Elected officials frequently turn to party leaders to find qualified men and women to occupy these posts.
- **Providing Information to the Media.** Party officials are often called upon by the media to provide comments and to interpret events.
- **Providing a Social Outlet.** Local party organizations provide civic-minded citizens an opportunity to gather at party events and discuss politics.
- **Promoting Patriotism.** Political parties sponsor patriotic events (especially Fourth of July speeches) that promote a love of country.

One way to gauge the extent to which these activities are undertaken by party committees is to spend time watching them. We present some brief narratives that describe the activities of four contemporary county party committees: the Nassau County Republican Committee (New York), the Kings County Republican Committee (Washington), the Loudoun County Democrats (Virginia), and the Dare County Democratic Committee (North Carolina). Although this is not a scientific approach (any generalizations would be tenuous), these groups say much about how local parties are coping (or not) with the Information Age.

Nassau County Republicans: A Machine That Keeps on Ticking

Lurking among the pristine lawns and expensive shopping plazas in the affluent suburbs surrounding New York City one finds an endangered species: the political machine. The Nassau County Republican Party has been virtually unchallenged since 1916, save one brief lapse in the early 1960s. The party organization's strength rests in its ability to disburse government jobs, amass legions of campaign volunteers, and retain a high degree of party loyalty among local voters. The *New York Times* once described the Nassau County Republicans as having "the best political organization in the country."[29]

With an average median income approaching $50,000 and a large number of residents commuting to Manhattan, Nassau County has been fertile Republican territory. The county's favorite son, former U.S. Senator Alfonse D'Amato, began his career as a loyal machine politician—first as supervisor of the town of Hempstead (1971–1977), and later as vice chairman of the Nassau County Board of Supervisors (1977–1980). In a 1995 book titled *Power, Pasta, and Politics*, D'Amato wrote, "The deal-making and politicking I witnessed in my own backyard equaled anything I have done in the U.S. Senate."[30] Nassau County Republicans are traditionalists in their desire to win elections rather than adhere to a strict ideology. And win they do. In 1998, the GOP controlled five of seven state senate seats, seven of eleven assembly seats, and thirteen of nineteen slots in the county legislature. They also won every countywide post including county executive, district attorney, comptroller, and county clerk.

The corporate ethos, which pervades the Nassau County commuter's life in Manhattan, is reflected in how Nassau County Republicans run their party. Cigar-toting boss Joseph Mondello sits at the top and all party workers follow his directives. As one local mayor observed: "The party has treated politics like a business for the last fifty years. That's not a compliment."[31] Like a corporate hierarchy, the county's 298 square miles are divided into military-like zones with 71 "executive leader areas," 1,000 election districts, and 2,077 committee members. The machine annually evaluates the fund-raising and vote-delivering performance of its executive committee. Performance is based on sponsorship of local party events, manning telephone banks, conducting door-to-door canvassing, and distributing party literature. Committee members record the name, address, and phone number of every registered Republican in their district, and these folks are contacted before election day. These efforts are essential if an aspiring Republican hopes to win his party's nomination. As one member stated, "Everyone ultimately answers to Mr. Mondello."[32]

If one expects to get a government job, you must be active in local Republican politics. Several Nassau County employees have testified that they are required to contribute 1 percent of their salary to the party.[33] In addition, they are expected to purchase tickets, attend picnics, and work for the party on election day. Mondello brags, "Our people are out in the street working hard, going to every little podunk party."[34] A previous party chair revealed his philosophy on government workers' obligations by reminding them, "You have eaten of my food and drunk of my drink and now you must pay of my bill."[35] But by paying one's dues, party workers have their pick from a variety of high-paying patronage jobs. Mondello himself holds a $141,000–a-year government post.

The Nassau County Republican Committee is an active, omnipotent organization, and one of the last party machines in the United States. It depends on the traditional capital of party machines—local volunteers. Ironically, it is one of the few local party organizations that does not have a homepage on the World Wide Web. The Information Age has arrived in many other locales, but in Nassau County old-fashioned machine-style politics still rules.

The Kings County Republican Committee: Fighting the Nonpartisan Tide

The 1.5 million voters who reside in Kings County, Washington, live in one of the trendiest places in the country. Home to Starbucks Coffee and Microsoft computers, Washington State has been a national trendsetter during the 1990s. Not surprisingly, it is the state's affinity for the latest political fad—nonpartisanship—that concerns us here. Washington State is one of only three states that holds a blanket primary. Moreover, the state discourages voters from adopting a partisan affiliation by placing severe restrictions on campaign contributions and designating many elected offices as nonpartisan. This makes Reed Davis's job as chairman of the Kings County Republican Committee, which encompasses the city of Seattle, extremely difficult.

Reed Davis is a party man, who believes that parties should be the "exclusive organizational source of funding and recruiting for [sic] candidates." But nonpartisanship has resulted in lower voter turnout and elected officials who are unaccountable to the public. As Davis states: "If candidate endorsements were the province of the party, they would work with us to raise money. They [would] buy tables for my Lincoln Day Dinner and introduce me to the people with money. When they don't need our endorsement, why should they help us raise money?"[36] Still, the Kings County Republican Party fights hard for media recognition, volunteers, and for the attention of candidates. But without money, success is limited.

Kings County is divided into 2,689 precincts, each with its own Republican leader. Half are truly interested in local issues—the rest are aspiring candidates. Davis employs an unofficial system of networking designed to cultivate candidates who have displayed an interest in party politics. But in a nonpartisan state like Washington, the battle has been uphill. The party sponsors few events—just a Lincoln

Day dinner and a booth at the county fair. Official meetings are sparsely attended. To make matters worse, the committee is not on good terms with state and national Republican organizations. A particular sticking point is the disagreements between Davis and operatives of the RNC: "There's a horrible misconception that people from the national [party] organizations know what they're doing. They should recognize that folks at the grass roots know more about a given area than a group of fly-by-night national operatives. The RNC is fine, but to bring in out-of-town talent is a waste of time. They're all kids under thirty."

Can the Kings County Republican Committee recoup? Any chance lies in mobilizing affluent citizens to take part in party politics. Prospects are, however, that voters will opt for a second cup of coffee and new computer software rather than for revamping of local party organizations.

The Loudoun County Democrats: An Information Age Revival Story

Loudoun County, Virginia, is located just outside Washington, D.C. One would surmise that proximity to the nation's capital keeps voters attuned to politics. But in this instance, the opposite is true. According to David Whitmer, chairman of the Loudoun County's Democratic Committee, fewer people are paying attention to state and local politics. Dwindling ranks of volunteers has meant that the party organization has suffered. Whitmer believes the solution is to build a candidate-centered party using the tools of the Information Age.

The transformation of the Loudoun County Democratic Committee is a recent development. Buoyed by an influx of newcomers, Whitmer won the local party chairmanship in 1994. He advocated a shift from an ideological to a candidate-centered approach. In a 1998 interview, Whitmer stated: "Candidates should take policy stands, not the party. Our first objective is to get Democrats in office. I don't want to handcuff them."[37]

The Loudoun Democratic Committee sponsors a "fire-house primary" held before the regularly scheduled primary to identify strong candidates. The county committee informally gathers to debate candidate strengths and weaknesses and makes a quasi-endorsement. (The official endorsement is made by the primary voters.) Then the party applies Information Age technologies to identify potential supporters. For example, the committee compiles lists of union households and sends them targeted mailings throughout the campaign season. It also identifies residents of publicly subsidized housing—a group thought "ripe" for Democratic candidates—and mails them voter registration cards and absentee voting information.

Even so, Whitmer worries that candidates are less dependent on the party. He blames voter nonpartisanship, a development that pushes candidates to pitch themselves as "independent," and television, saying, "The parties just can't compete with media advertising." Moreover, Whitmer contends that because Virginia law does not limit the size of campaign contributions, candidates are free to court private donors that leave the often bankrupt party organization even further behind. Still, the Loudoun County Democratic Committee has found creative ways to adapt, including a sophisticated homepage on the World Wide Web that claims 17,000 hits since 1995. Thus, the Information Age has provided an opportunity for Loudoun County Democrats to find their niche in the political process.

Dare County Democratic Committee: Hoping for a Policy Makeover

Dare County, North Carolina, is perched along the Atlantic coast's easternmost point. The string of islands is home to Sir Walter Raleigh's lost colony on Roanoke Island in 1587 and the Wright Brothers first airplane flight on Kitty Hawk Island in 1903. Today, Dare County is a popular vacation site with a multimillion dollar tourist industry. The county's beautiful surroundings have induced many northerners to relocate there. Prior to this influx, Dare County was solidly Democratic and Democrats often ran unopposed. With the invasion of wealthy new residents and a Republican realignment in the South (see Chapter 6), the county has become increasingly Republican. The first Republican was recently elected to county government since the Civil War.

Given the GOP resurgence, Dare County's Democratic Committee now asks party workers in each precinct to identify sympathetic voters and get them to the polls. The party also relies on social activities such as picnics and fish fries to energize the faithful. These events often feature popular Democratic leaders including State Senator Mark Basnight and Governor Jim Guy Hunt. But in the day-to-day governing of the county, tradition rules. Two-thirds of county jobs are classified as patronage. According to Chris Hardy, chair of the Dare County Democrats, "Patronage is the greatest thing created."

But Hardy laments that voters turn away from partisan politics. Hardy recalls that on Sunday afternoons everyone would visit the Basnight Lone Cedar Restaurant, owned by a local Democratic state senator, where they would talk politics and socialize. But with the influx of northern strangers, such old-fashioned southern back-slapping has become passé. Dare County Democrats need to adjust their tactics to fit the new socioeconomic situation in which the county finds itself. Unlike other local party organizations that are in transition, such as the Loudoun County Democratic Committee, Hardy says that issues are the key to revitalization. Mirroring the moderate-to-conservative viewpoints of the Democratic Leadership Council, Hardy believes a more conservative focus will help attract the area's new residents to the party cause and keep the remaining loyalists in the Democratic fold.

Summary

One should not presume that these four county party committees exclusively reflect the state of local politics in America, but their experiences are indicative of profound party change. First, local parties are incorporating Information Age technologies into their day-to-day operations. While there are some exceptions, such as the Nassau County Republican machine, many local parties use direct mail, the mass media, and the Internet to reach out to the electorate. Second, the trend toward nonpartisanship is taking a toll on local party organizations, as evidenced in Kings County. Third, both parties are having trouble attracting volunteers due to a voter preference for nonpartisanship and competition from television, movies, and the Internet. Finally, there is a trend toward providing candidate-centered services (other than in Dare County) and a centralization of party structures. While each of these developments are not found everywhere, there is no escaping that what local parties do and their place in the overall scheme of party structures is changing. How each locality will cope with the changing lifestyles generated by the new postindustrial economy and the communications revolution created by the Information Age will undoubtedly differ.

STATE AND LOCAL PARTIES, COMPUTERS, AND THE INTERNET

Few should be surprised to learn that many state and local parties are joining the information revolution by taking advantage of computers and the Internet. Computer usage has spread in two directions: desktop tools and reaching voters via the Internet. Each has profound consequences for political parties in the Information Age.

Desktop Tools

Clearly, the most important advances in computer technology are those that help parties win elections. Leading the way is the creation and manipulation of databases. According to one 1997 survey of state party leaders, all Republican state parties and almost all Democratic ones (93 percent) have databases of voter information.[38] Both parties use their databases to compile fund-raising lists, gather voter information, and recruit potential volunteers. Twenty-nine percent of state Democratic parties have sought outside computer consultants to operate their system, only 4 percent of Republican parties did so. Moreover, 82 percent of state Republican parties report receiving computer assistance from the RNC; only 24 percent of Democratic organizations got help from the DNC. This has helped the GOP maintain a financial advantage, since better use of databases can yield more direct mail fund-raising responses. Seventy-one percent of Republican state parties report raising more than $100,000 in small contributions from 10,000 donors compared to less than 50 percent of Democratic organizations.

State Parties on the Net

Table 7.4 contains a range of information pertaining to state party development and use of Web sites. State party committees use Web sites to attract volunteers, raise money, mobilize activists, and register voters. For example, the Indiana Republican State Committee homepage tells visitors that they believe that "economic growth and prosperity are fueled by individual initiative, freed from the burdens of government regulation and taxation." State party Web sites often promote particular candidates, and most have direct links to their homepages. For instance, the Idaho Republican Web page allows visitors to click on the Helen Chenoweth for Congress

TABLE 7.4 ■ State Parties and the Internet*

Internet Technology in State Parties	Republicans	Democrats
Have a party e-mail address	79%	100%
Utilizing an electronic mailing list	39%	67%
Have a party Web site	68%	67%
Have integrated voter e-mail addresses into their databases	18%	32%

State Parties and Internet Activity	Republicans	Democrats
Volunteering/Member solicitation	57%	57%
Voter registration	26%	25%
Election day reminders	32%	50%
Persuasion mailings	32%	45%
Fund-raising	47%	20%
Mobilization for rallies	26%	55%

Internet Volunteers and Donations	Republicans	Democrats
Have attracted volunteers with their Web site	74%	85%
Have received donations	37%	35%

State Party Spending on Web Site Development	Republicans	Democrats
Less than $1,000	68%	55%
$1,001–$5,000	11%	25%
$5,001–$10,000	5%	0%
$10,001–$25,000	5%	5%
More than $25,000	0%	5%

* Information based on a survey of 59 state party organizations conducted in February of 1997.

SOURCE: Noah J. Goodhart, "The New Party Machine: Information Technology in State Political Parties," in John C. Green and Daniel M. Shea, *The State of the Parties* (Lanham, Md.: Rowman and Littlefield, 1999).

placard and review her campaign literature. It also contains links to Republican Governor Phil Batt's Web site. The Massachusetts Democratic Party Web site connects visitors directly to the homepages of Democratic Senators John F. Kerry and Edward M. Kennedy. Many local party sites make it possible to volunteer for a campaign, submit an internship application, or, in the case of the Republicans, become a "cyber-volunteer."

Due to the relative newness of the Internet, many Web sites are rather generic. One estimate is that, as of 1998, a majority of state and local parties have spent less than $1,000 on Web site development. On the Republican side, many states have two homepages: one accessible from the RNC's Web site; another that is self-created (see Appendix A). Those linked to the RNC homepage are most common. Although a disclaimer at the bottom of the page reads, "Not an official page of the RNC," one suspects that the "Washington folks" provided some help. The

DNC, on the other hand, has not established homepages for every state committee (see Appendix B). Instead, it provides links only to state parties that have instituted their own Web sites. Not surprisingly, there is only modest similarity in content and quality between Democratic state committee homepages. The New Jersey Democratic State Committee, for example, allows visitors to view photos of political fund-raisers, read a message from the state chair, volunteer for an upcoming campaign, make monetary contributions, or download pro-Democratic articles like "What Is Wrong with the GOP?" Other Democratic state party sites are far less ambitious and contain only cursory information on upcoming events—most of them fund-raisers.

Most state and local parties tailor their Web sites to draw in Internet surfers by highlighting a national issue and coaxing the user to support their candidates. For example, the October 1998 homepage of the Oregon Republican State Committee has a mystery quote from a political leader calling for the president's resignation: "Yes, the president should resign. He has lied to the American people, time and time again, and betrayed their trust. He is no longer an effective leader. Since he has admitted guilt, there is no reason to put the American people through an impeachment. He will serve absolutely no purpose in finishing out his term; the only possible solution is for the president to save some dignity and resign."[39] The mystery speaker is Bill Clinton, who called upon President Nixon to resign back in 1974. Having drawn in the Clinton-haters, Oregon Republicans make volunteering to campaign for state and local candidates just a mouse click away. Other state party Web sites post "talking points" for visitors to include in their day-to-day conversations with others.

While Web site development is in its infancy, and many sites are rather bland, there are differences based on local political culture. Some sites focus almost exclusively on policy alternatives; others simply promote candidates. There is also a close connection to allied groups. For example, the Idaho Republican homepage proudly displays a "Right-to-Life of Idaho, Inc." insignia with a direct link to the Christian Coalition Score Card. More moderate Republican states, like Massachusetts, provide no such links on their homepages. In fact, the Massachusetts Republican platform "leaves it to individuals, and individual candidates, to form and clearly articulate their own position on the issue of abortion"—a far cry from the pro-life banner of the Idaho Republicans.

COMPUTERS TO THE RESCUE?

Clearly, the parties have entered cyberspace. This is to be expected, because parties are adaptive creatures. Indeed, Democratic and Republican parties at all levels are reaching more voters than ever before. According to Xandra Kayden and Eddie Mahe, the dwindling ranks of party activists "may not be so catastrophic for democracy as it seems because it does not affect the flow of information to the voters."[40] Today, few campaigns are conducted without computerized targeting, mail lists, and survey research. If parties are to be players, they must use the new tools of the trade.

But reaching voters via direct mail or through the Internet is qualitatively different than meeting them at their doorstep. Computerized communications are often one-directional, since voters receive information but are rarely given the opportunity to express their concerns. E-mail and chat rooms provide some opportunity for feedback, but this is far less satisfying than a face-to-face encounter with a party member. It is possible that such a lack of personal contact will lead to increased voter cynicism as frustration levels rise over not being heard. Moreover, not everyone is connected to the information superhighway. Those without access to the Internet are often the poor and the elderly. Thus, the newcomers who are drawn into politics by computers are generally young, college-educated, and affluent. Finally, computerized politics adds to the nationalizing trends discussed at the beginning of this chapter. Presently, the national party committees are within reach of developing large databases that can be made available to their state and local party organizations. While this improves efficiency (instead of fifty databases there would only be one), state and local parties would be subordinates to the national parties. Hamiltonian party advocates, who prefer a national party with directions given from the top, welcome this trend. But those who believe in Jeffersonian-style local parties that are relatively autonomous have much to fear.

APPENDIX A: REPUBLICAN STATE COMMITTEE WEB SITES AS OF 1998

State	RNC-Sponsored Web Site Address	State Committee Site
Alabama	http://www.fastlane.net/homepages/weide/algop.shtml	http://www.algop.org
Alaska	http://www.fastlane.net/homepages/weide/akgop.shtml	
Arizona	http://www.fastlane.net/homepages/weide/azgop.shtml	http://www.azgop.org/
Arkansas	http://www.fastlane.net/homepages/weide/argop.shtml	
California	http://www.fastlane.net/homepages/weide/cagop.shtml	http://www.cagop.org/
Colorado	http://www.fastlane.net/homepages/weide/cogop.shtml	http://www.cologop.org/
Connecticut	http://www.fastlane.net/homepages/weide/ctgop.shtml	http://www.ctrepublicans.org/
Delaware	http://www.fastlane.net/homepages/weide/degop.shtml	www.delawaregop.org.com/
Florida	http://www.fastlane.net/homepages/weide/flgop.shtml	http://www.rpof.org/
Georgia	http://www.fastlane.net/homepages/weide/gagop.shtml	http://www.gagop.org
Hawaii	http://www.fastlane.net/homepages/weide/higop.shtml	http://www.hawaiigop.org/
Idaho	http://www.fastlane.net/homepages/weide/idgop.shtml	
Illonois	http://www.fastlane.net/homepages/weide/ilgop.shtml	http://www.ilgop.org/
Indiana	http://www.fastlane.net/homepages/weide/ingop.shtml	http://www.indgop.org/
Iowa	http://www.fastlane.net/homepages/weide/iagop.shtml	http://www.iowagop.org/
Kansas	http://www.fastlane.net/homepages/weide/ksgop.shtml	
Kentucky	http://www.fastlane.net/homepages/weide/kygop.shtml	http://www.rpk.org/
Louisiana	http://www.fastlane.net/homepages/weide/lagop.shtml	http://lagop.org/
Maine	http://www.fastlane.net/homepages/weide/megop.shtml	www.midcoast.com/~naubegop/
Maryland	http://www.fastlane.net/homepages/weide/mdgop.shtml	http://www.mdgop.org/
Massachusetts	NO DIRECT LINK	http://www.massgop.com
Michigan	http://www.fastlane.net/homepages/weide/migop.shtml	http://www.migop.org/
Minnesota	http://www.fastlane.net/homepages/weide/mngop.shtml	http://www-mn.org/

State	RNC-Sponsored Web Site Address	State Committee Site
Mississsippi	http://www.fastlane.net/homepages/weide/msgop.shtml	
Missouri	http://www.fastlane.net/homepages/weide/mogop.shtml	http://www.mogop.org/
Montana	http://www.fastlane.net/homepages/weide/mtgop.shtml	
Nebraska	http://www.fastlane.net/homepages/weide/negop.shtml	http://link-up.com/gop-nc/
Nevada	http://www.fastlane.net/homepages/weide/nvgop.shtml	http://www.nevadagop.org/
New Hampshire	http://www.fastlane.net/homepages/weide/nhgop.shtml	http://www.nhgop.org
New Jersey	http://www.fastlane.net/homepages/weide/njgop.shtml	http://www.njgop.org/
New Mexico	http://www.fastlane.net/homepages/weide/nmgop.shtml	http://www.swcp.com/gopnm/
New York	http://www.fastlane.net/homepages/weide/nygop.shtml	http://www.nygop.org/
North Carolina	http://www.fastlane.net/homepages/weide/ncgop.shtml	http://www.ncgop.org/
North Dakota	http://www.fastlane.net/homepages/weide/ndgop.shtml	http://www.tradecorridor.com/ndrepublicans
Ohio	http://www.fastlane.net/homepages/weide/ohgop.shtml	http://www.ohiogop.org/
Oklahoma	http://www.fastlane.net/homepages/weide/okgop.shtml	http://members.aol.wm/gopOK/
Oregon	http://www.fastlane.net/homepages/weide/orgop.shtml	http://wwwteleport.com/~orgop/
Pennsylvania	http://www.fastlane.net/homepages/weide/pagop.shtml	htt://www.pagop.org/
Rhode Island	http://www.fastlane.net/homepages/weide/rigop.shtml	
South Carolina	http://www.fastlane.net/homepages/weide/scgop.shtml	http://www.netside.com/~scgop/
South Dakota	http://www.fastlane.net/homepages/weide/sdgop.shtml	
Tennesee	http://www.fastlane.net/homepages/weide/tngop.shtml	http://www.tngop.org
Texas	http://www.fastlane.net/homepages/weide/txgop.shtml	http://www.texasgop.org/
Utah	http://www.fastlane.net/homepages/weide/utgop.shtml	
Vermont	http://www.fastlane.net/homepages/weide/vtgop.shtml	http://www.rpv.org/
Virginia	http://www.fastlane.net/homepages/weide/vagop.shtml	
Washington	http://www.fastlane.net/homepages/weide/wagop.shtml	http://www.wsrp.org/
West Virgina	http://www.fastlane.net/homepages/weide/wvgop.shtml	
Wisconsin	http://www.fastlane.net/homepages/weide/wigop.shtml	http://www.wisgop.org/
Wyoming	http://www.fastlane.net/homepages/weide/wygop.shtml	

APPENDIX B: DEMOCRATIC STATE COMMITTEE WEB SITES AS OF 1998

State	DNC-Sponsored Web Site Address
Alaska	http://www.alaska.net/~adp/
Arizona	http://www.asdem.org/
Arkansas	http://www.arkdems.org/
California	http://www.ca-dem.org/dems/cadems.nsf/index
Georgia	http://www.mindspring.com/~gaparty/
Idaho	http://www.webpak.net/~iddems/
Indiana	http://www.indems.org/
Iowa	http://www.netins.net/showcase/democrat
Kansas	http://democratic-party.org/cgi-shl/dbml.exe?template=statepage/statepage.dbm&state=Ks&month=6

State	DNC-Sponsored Web Site Address
Maine	http://www.maine.com/dems/
Maryland	http://www.clark.net/pub/mddem/
Massachusetts	http://www.massdems.org/
Michigan	http://www.nvcn.org/info/mdp/
Mississippi	http://www.missouridems.org/
Montana	http://incolor.inetnebr.com/nebrdems/
New Hampshire	http://www.njdems.org/
North Dakota	http://www.ohiodems.org/
Oklahoma	http://dpo.org/
Rhode Island	http://www.scdp.org/home.html
South Dakota	http://www.isdn.net/tdp/
Tennessee	http://www.txdemocrats.org/
Vermont	http://www-vademocrats.org
Virginia	http://www.wa-democrats.org/
West Virginia	http://www.execpc.com/democrat/

NOTE: Missing states have not yet established Web site homepages.

FURTHER READING

Appleton, Andrew M. and Daniel S. Ward, eds. *State Party Organizations: A Resource Guide.* Washington, D.C.: Congressional Quarterly, 1996.

Davis, Richard. *The Web of Politics: The Internet's Impact on the American Political System.* New York: Oxford University Press, 1999.

Drew, Elizabeth. *Whatever It Takes: The Real Struggle for Political Power in America.* New York: Viking, 1997.

Eldersveld, Samuel J. *Political Parties: A Behavioral Analysis.* Chicago: Rand McNally, 1964.

Lorch, Robert S. *State and Local Politics: The Great Entanglement.* Englewood Cliffs, N.J.: Prentice-Hall, 1986.

Wilson, James Q. *The Amateur Democrat: Club Politics in Three American Cities.* Chicago: University of Chicago Press, 1962.

NOTES

1. The following information rests heavily on Melanie J. Blumberg, William C. Binning, and John C. Green, "The Grassroots Matter: The Coordinated Campaign in a Battleground State," in John C. Green and Daniel M. Shea, *The State of the Parties: The Changing Role of Contemporary Party Organizations,* 3rd ed. (Lanham, Md.: Rowman and Littlefield, 1999).

2. Cited in *Smith v. Allwright* (1944). Reported in *United States Reports, Volume 321, Cases Adjudged in the Supreme Court at October Term, 1943* (Washington, D.C.: U.S. Government Printing Office, 1944), 656.

3. Ibid., 661–62.

4. See Timothy Conlan, Ann Martino, and Robert Dilger, *The Transformation in American Politics* (Washington, D.C.: Advisory Commission on Intergovernmental Affairs, 1986), 141–42. Modified by Paul Allen Beck, *Party Politics in America,* 8th ed. (New York: Longman, 1997), 67–68.

5. Dan Freedman, "Justices Hear Case on State Primary Law," *San Francisco Examiner,* December 6, 1988, A8.

6. See *Eu, Secretary of State of California, et al. v. San Francisco County Democratic Central Committee, et al.* (1989). Reported in *United States Reports, Volume 489, Cases Adjudged in the Supreme Court at October*

Term, 1988 (Washington, D.C.: U.S. Government Printing Office, 1992). The vote was eight to zero. Chief Justice William Rehnquist did not participate in this case.

7. V. O. Key, Jr. *Parties, Politics, and Pressure Groups,* 5th ed. (New York: Crowell, 1964), 329.

8. Samuel J. Eldersveld, *Political Parties: A Behavioral Analysis.* (Chicago: Rand McNally, 1964) 9.

9. Quoted in Michael Barone and Grant Ujifusa with Richard E. Cohen, *The Almanac of American Politics, 1998* (Washington, D.C.: National Journal, 1997), 773.

10. Philip A. Klinkner, *The Losing Parties: Out-Party National Committees, 1956–1993* (New Haven: Yale University Press, 1994), 153.

11. See John Kenneth White, *Still Seeing Red: How the Cold War Shapes the New American Politics* (Boulder, Colo.: Westview Press, 1997), 37.

12. See Elizabeth Drew, *Whatever It Takes: The Real Struggle for Political Power in America* (New York: Viking, 1997), 15, 17.

13. Smith eventually succeeded Oregon's other Republican senator, Mark Hatfield, who retired in 1996.

14. See "The DLC Update," Friday, September 18, 1998. On the Democratic Leadership Conference homepage, <http://www.dlcppi.org>.

15. Empower America brochure.

16. *The Book of the States, 1996–1997.* (Lexington, Ky.: Council of State Governments), 157–58.

17. Mark Paul, "Primary Gave Political Theorists a Reason to Smile," *Sacramento Bee,* June 8, 1998, B5.

18. *Tashjian v. Republican Party of Connecticut (1986).* Reported in *United States Reports, Volume 479, Cases Adjudged in the Supreme Court at October Term, 1986* (Washington, D.C.: U.S. Government Printing Office, 1989), 215.

19. Ibid., 235.

20. M. Margaret Conway and Frank B. Feigert, "Motivation, Incentives Systems, and the Political Party Organization," *American Political Science Review* 62 (1968).

21. Samuel J. Eldersveld, *Political Parties in American Society* (New York: Basic Books, 1982), 144.

22. Robert S. Lorch, *State and Local Politics: The Great Entanglement* (Englewood Cliffs, N.J.: Prentice-Hall, 1986), 86.

23. Delegate count is from the Associated Press. Cited in Charles D. Hadley and Harold W. Stanley, "Surviving the 1992 Presidential Nomination Process," in William Crotty, ed., *America's Choice: The Election of 1992* (Guilford, Conn.: Dushkin Publishing, 1993), 36.

24. Quoted in Robert F. Kennedy, *To Seek a Newer World* (New York: Doubleday, 1967), 56.

25. John W. Soule and James W. Clarke, "Amateurs and Professionals: A Case Study of Delegates to the 1968 Democratic National Convention," *American Political Science Review* 64 (September 1970): 888–98. See also Anne N. Costain, "Changes in the Role of Ideology in American National Conventions and Among Party Identifiers," *Western Political Quarterly* 33 (March 1980): 73–86.

26. Joel Paddock, "Political Culture and the Partisan Style of Party Activists," *Publius: The Journal of Federalism,* 27 (Summer 1997): 127–32.

27. Ibid., 128.

28. See for example, John P. Frendries, James L. Gibson, and Laura L. Vertz, "The Electoral Relevance of Local Party Organizations," *American Political Science Review* 84 (1990): 225–35.

29. Dan Barry, "Science of Politics: L. I. Style Prevails," *New York Times,* March 8, 1996, B9.

30. Quoted in Barone, Ujifusa, and Cohen, *Almanac of American Politics, 1998,* 965.

31. Barry, "Science of Politics: L. I. Style Prevails."

32. Ibid.

33. Anne Freedman, *Patronage: An American Tradition* (Chicago: Nelson-Hall, 1994).

34. Barry, "Science of Politics, L. I. Style, Prevails."

35. Freedman, *Patronage,* 135.

36. Reed Davis, telephone interview by Wendy Erdly, on July 24, 1998. Ms. Erdly was working as a research assistant to Daniel Shea.

37. David Whitmer, telephone interview conducted by Wendy Erdly, July 21, 1998.

38. Noah J. Goodhart, "The New Party Machine: Information Technology in State Political Parties," in John C. Green and Daniel M. Shea, *The State of the Parties* (Lanham, Md.: Rowman and Littlefield, 1999).

39. Quoted in ORP: The Official Website of the Oregon Republican Party, <http://www.teleport.com/~orpgop>.

40. Xandra Kayden and Eddie Mahe, Jr., *The Party Goes On: The Persistence of the Two-Party System in America* (New York: Basic Books, 1991), 121.

CHAPTER 8

Campaign Finance and Information Age Political Parties

On November 21, 1864, Abraham Lincoln warned the nation of a "crisis approaching:"

> As a result of the war, corporations have become enthroned, and an era of corruption in high places will follow. The money power of the country will endeavor to prolong its rule by preying upon the prejudices of the people until all wealth is concentrated in a few hands and the Republic is destroyed.[1]

Today, many Americans would agree that Lincoln's prophecy has become reality. It is often said that we now have "the best Congress money can buy," and few would be surprised that in a recent survey 75 percent agreed (39 percent agreeing "strongly") that "our present system of government is democratic in name only. In fact, special interests run things."[2] In another poll, conducted in 1997, the same percentage agreed that "many public officials make or change public decisions as a direct result of money received from contributors."[3] The American public has become more cynical, and much of their distrust centers on the way elections are financed.

Many Americans would also contend that the "high places" where corruption is to be found is the party system. The most frequent reference made to political parties in the media during the last decade has been around campaign finance scandals. In the spring and summer of 1997, a media frenzy ensued over the Democratic National Committee's (DNC) fund-raising activities in the previous presidential election. The Republicans tried to make hay with the uproar, claiming that the Democrats had broken laws, but the media soon turned their attention on them. The public was left bewildered by a series of charges and countercharges. Two years later, the media again turned its spotlights on money and party politics, this time looking into the phenomenal sums raised by several of the GOP candidates. George W. Bush alone had raised nearly $60 million by the end of 1999. This amount surpassed Bob Dole's entire budget for the 1996 election. Speaking of the perception of corruption of money and party activities, one scholar noted that "an illness that had plagued previous elections [has] developed into an epidemic."[4]

The intimate relationship between money and party politics is a long one, however. Like nearly every aspect of party politics, the rate of change in the last few decades is staggering—it is difficult for even the most informed observer to keep abreast. Early-1970s federal regulations, aimed at limiting the flow of big contributions into congressional and presidential campaigns, and a landmark campaign finance court decision, had the unintended consequence of creating a series of loopholes that thrust parties into the center of the elections-finance matrix. By the 1990s, a host of techniques were being used to circumvent state and federal regulations, further pushing parties into the center of things. Although there are limits on the amount a group or individual can give to federal-level candidates, there are no restrictions on how much can be donated to the parties. Trunkloads of money are simply given to the parties, which then use it to help candidates. This loophole, generically called "**soft money,**" was somewhat a secret in the recent past—or at least something the parties did not openly flaunt. By the late 1990s, however, that had changed. A full year before the 2000 presidential nominating conventions, both parties were actively and openly soliciting soft money contributions. The Republicans mailed thousands of letters to potential contributors, noting that a contribution to a candidate need not be the end of their help; they could go a step further by sending a soft money check to the RNC as well. Not surprisingly, each election seems to usher-in new soft money records.

The Democrats started the "issue advocacy" stampede in 1996, when Bill Clinton and his advisers made a decision to use the DNC to circumvent expenditure restrictions. During the spring of 1996, they ran a series of television advertisements in swing states that highlighted Clinton's commitment to a number of policy initiatives. These early expenditures seemed to be in violation of federal laws, given that Clinton had accepted public financing of his election and that there are limits on how much can be spent in each state during the primary season. But the Democrats purported that these spots were not designed to build support for Clinton per se, but rather for certain policies. "Issue advocacy," they argued, is protected by the First Amendment. Though this argument seemed consistent with recent federal court rulings, because Clinton was the actor used in the ads and numerous shots were fired at Bob Dole and the Republicans, the controversy surrounding the commercials grew. The Republicans voiced loud objections, but soon joined the act. Within two years they would vastly outdo the Democrats with their own issue advocacy spots. Most political pundits agree that this latest loophole has the potential to shatter expenditure restrictions—the floodgates are wide open.

But why would citizens and pundits voice strong objections to big money in elections? Perhaps contributing money during elections is a basic civil liberty—akin to free speech. And if there is to be lots of money in elections, why would voters reject parties as the proper vehicle to deliver it? Are not parties better instruments for allocating funds than wealthy individuals, labor unions, or business groups? This chapter charts the role of money in the contemporary electoral system and where parties fit into the mix. We begin with a brief history of money in elections and then turn to several reform efforts designed to stem the flow of big money into campaigns. Special attention is paid to the Federal Election Campaign Act of 1971 and subsequent amendments. This is followed with a discussion of recent "innovations" by the parties to get around FECA limits. The chapter concludes with some thoughts about what these changes mean for party politics in the next century. It is not surprising that the growing role of money in party politics is conceivably the most powerful force pushing the system toward the Hamiltonian pole. It is, we argue, the fulcrum of the new professionalized, centralized party system.

A BRIEF LOOK AT MONEY IN ELECTIONS

Money has always played a role in American elections. It was not until the turn of the twentieth century, however, that money became the pillar of electioneering. This section outlines the transformation of elections from a labor-intensive, interpersonal process, to the money-driven, technical state we are now in. This history is broken into three phases: money as a supplement to party activities; the rise of corporate politics; and the rise of media-centered elections.

Phase 1: Money as a Supplement to Party Activities (1790s to 1880s)

The dominant means of reaching voters during the early days of campaigning in America was the print media. As discussed in Chapter 1, the battle between Jefferson and Hamilton was waged mostly in the newspapers. The surest way to win favorable media attention for policies or candidates was simply to own the newspaper, or at the very least sponsor the editor. Jefferson gave Philip Freneau a part-time clerkship in the State Department in 1791, so that he would move to Philadelphia to become editor of the *National Gazette*. This paper proved instrumental in helping the Jeffersonian Republicans clobber the Federalists in the election of 1800. Hamilton, for his part, was a major financial backer of the competing *Gazette of the United States*. As late as the middle of the nineteenth century, newspapers were a major source of campaign expenditures. When a wealthy backer wanted to aid the political ambitions of James Buchanan, he simply contributed $10,000 to start a sympathetic newspaper. Even Abraham Lincoln secretly purchased a small newspaper in Illinois in 1860.[5]

"Treating" was another common form of electioneering during the early days of the republic. Candidates would sponsor events or parties where voters would be treated to lavish feasts. "Rum punch, wine, and beer were served in ever-larger quantities, together with all sorts of other fare."[6] Even George Washington was charged with this form of campaign spending when, in a race for the Virginia House of Burgesses in 1751, he reportedly purchased a quart of rum, wine, beer and hard cider for every voter in the district (there were only 391 voters).[7] In 1795, one would-be Delaware officeholder "roasted a steer and half a dozen sheep . . . as a kind of snack for his friends." Another candidate gave a "fish feast" and also a "turtle feast."[8] Four decades later, Ferdinand Bayard, a Frenchman traveling the United States, commented that "candidates offer drunkenness openly to anyone who is willing to give them his vote."[9] In addition to newspapers and treating, candidates also sent mailings to voters, printed pamphlets for distribution, and organized rallies and parades. By the 1840s, pictures, buttons, banners, and novelty items were being distributed to voters.

Although the control of newspapers, treating, and the distribution of campaign paraphernalia were costly endeavors, massive war chests were not necessary for several reasons. Prior to Jacksonian democracy in the late 1820s, the size of the electorate was rather small. Only white males could vote, there were property qualifications in some states, and voting was even restricted in some states to those belonging to the proper religious denomination.[10] Fewer voters meant lower expenditures. Modes of communication were limited to interpersonal connections—word of mouth—and the print media. Simply put, there were not many "big ticket" campaign items. A vast majority of campaigning was conducted by volunteer party activists, especially after the formation of the spoils system in the 1830s. Parades and canvasses, for example, were conducted at very little cost. Most importantly, party loyalty among voters was extremely pronounced in the latter half of the century, as discussed in Chapter 2. There was simply little movement within the electorate from one election to the next and straight-ticket voting was the norm. As noted by Frank Sorauf, a leading scholar in the field of campaign finance, "To a considerable extent, campaigning in those decades was an exercise in activating both party loyalties and responses to party positions on the great issues of the day."[11]

Phase 2: The Rise of Corporate Politics (1880s to 1950s)

Mark Hanna might be credited with being the first campaign consultant in American history. Among other notable achievements, Hanna was instrumental in orchestrating William McKinley's victory in 1896. He also helped transform the role of money in party politics. In 1895 he is quoted as saying, "There are two things that are important in politics—the first is money and I can't remember what the second one is."[12] This would seem an astonishing statement, given the secondary role of money in elections during the first century of our nation's history. How did things change so quickly?

Following the Civil War the Industrial Revolution was in full swing. The nation's industrial infrastructure was booming and the nation was headed westward. As noted by historian Richard Hofstadter, "capitalists seeking land grants, tariffs, bounties, favorable currency policies, freedom from regulatory legislation and economic reform, supplied campaign funds, fees and bribes, and plied politicians with investment opportunities."[13] A relationship existed between party machines and the captains of industry, in which the latter pumped money into party coffers in exchange for preventing elected officials from interfering with the "free market" (see Chapter 2).

The election of 1896 marked a turning point in the tale of money and politics in America. The stakes of the election were high: McKinley had pledged to continue the GOP's laissez-faire economic policies, meaning that he would afford the business community a free hand, while William Jennings Bryan, McKinley's Democratic opponent, offered a much more "intrusive" outlook on the link between government and business. According to Bryan, the election marked a struggle of the masses against the classes (see Chapter 10).

Fearing a Democratic groundswell and the ruin of the economic system if Bryan were to enter the White House, Republicans mounted the most efficient and best bankrolled campaign the country had ever seen. For the first time in American history, corporations made political contributions directly from their company treasuries. The Republicans' massive war chest, estimated at $5 million (some estimates have been as high as $7 million), allowed RNC chair Hanna to conduct a vigorous campaign and to use cutting-edge tactics. Republicans sponsored hundreds of speakers for small gatherings and debates, produced over 200 million pamphlets (their headquarters employed over 100 full-time mail clerks), hundreds of thousands of posters, buttons, and billboards, invested heavily in newspaper advertising, and hired legions of workers to register new Republicans and to get them to the polls on election day. McKinley was simply instructed to say at home in Canton, Ohio, where trainloads of supporters, many carrying envelopes of cash, were brought to his front porch. The Democrats relied on the great oratory skills of their nominee, sending him via train to cities and towns across the nation. Their entire treasury that election amounted to just $650,000. McKinley won the election with 51.7 percent of the vote.[14]

Hanna's efforts were significant in two ways. First, this was the first election in which party operatives employed systematic fund-raising techniques. No longer would the parties wait patiently for money to come in; they would go out and get it. Second, Hanna demonstrated that hard-core political advertising could rule the day. Campaigning through word of mouth, volunteer party activists, and newspaper ads was fading into the history books. Press releases, direct mail, billboards, and soon radio (and later television) would transform electioneering. Obviously, this change put a premium on raising money—lots of it.

In addition to the shift in campaign tactics, the nation was also experiencing a rapid expansion of the electorate through immigration and later women's suffrage. With more voters to reach, the parties needed more resources, and so the age of aggressive fund-raising began. It was reported that when a union leader came to a U.S. senator to urge him to support anti-child-labor legislation at the turn of the century, the senator replied, "But, Sam, you know damn well as I do that I can't stand for a bill like that. Why those fellows this bill is aimed at—those mill owners—are good for $200,000 a year to the party. You can't afford to monkey with a business that friendly."[15]

Political parties continued to be the focal point of the campaign finance system during this period. Elections were still conducted by party activists, especially below the presidential level, and the remnants of party machines exerted control over public policy. Party bosses expected elected officials to ante up during elections and anyone interested in shaping public policy were expected to woo them. Party coffers were filled through a small number of huge contributions from those dubbed "fat cats" (aggressive fund-raising is often called "frying the fat"). One study of party finances found that during the late 1920s a vast majority of state party funds came from less than one hundred contributors. During the presidential race of 1928, for example, over half of both Democratic and Republican funds were from contributions of $5,000 or more; a sum that could buy ten family cars at that time.[16]

Phase 3: Media-Centered Elections (1960s to the Present)

If the cost of elections rose during the Industrial Revolution, it skyrocketed during the technological revolution of the 1960s. Total spending during presidential election years went from $175 million in 1960, to over $1.2 billion two decades later, a jump that vastly outpaced inflation. That amount trippled to $3.2 billion by the early part of the 1990s, and by the end of the decade approached the $4 billion mark. The cost of running for any office has grown at a staggering rate. Whereas in the early 1970s few competitive campaigns for the House of Representatives topped the $100,000 mark, by 1992 over fifty races spent at least $1 million. Today, it is generally accepted that in order to run a strong race for the House, especially if the candidate is a challenger, one's war chest must come near to or exceed the million-dollar mark.

What forces compelled this staggering change? The single greatest development has been the way candidates communicate with voters. Again, during most of the nation's history a candidate's message was spread via party activists, and to some degree in print material. Today, most voters hear from candidates through the electronic media—televison, radio, and the Internet. The first television advertisements for candidates at the presidential level appeared during the early 1950s. By the 1980s, candidates at nearly all government levels had come to rely on television. Nine out of ten U.S. senatorial campaigns used televison advertisements in the 1990s, and over 70 percent of House candidates did the same. These figures are even higher for competitive House and Senate races. Candidates have simply found it more efficient to broadcast their message through radio and television advertisements than through volunteer party activists. This form of voter communication is, of course, expensive. Abraham Lincoln's entire campaign in 1860 cost just over $100,000. A century later, that amount bought just 30 minutes of televison airtime.[17]

Another reason for the growing cost of elections—closely connected to the rise of electronic communications—has been declining party brand loyalty within the electorate. A number of forces pushed voters away from the party system in the late 1960s and 1970s, including social unrest, Vietnam, Watergate, and the interest group explosion (see Chapter 6). This movement has led to unpredictable elections with pools of voters up for grabs in each election. Candidates and their handlers believe that such uncertainty compels them to reach out more often, and consequently raise even more money. It is entirely possible that electronic-based, candidate-centered campaigns push voters away from party labels, leading to erratic outcomes and more costly elections.

A third reason for the rapid rise in the cost of elections has been the emergence of professional campaign consultants. Prior to the 1950s, most campaigns were headed by candidates, their spouses, or party activists—usually the most seasoned "hack" in the organizations. These handlers were trained in the school of hard knocks and served on a volunteer basis. With the advent of television advertising, product marketing experts became useful during campaigns and by the 1960s a new profession blossomed—campaign consulting. There was also a specialization within the profession, leading to a broad range of consultants: media gurus, pollsters, strategists, fund-raising professionals, direct mail experts, and so on. Today, there are numerous graduate school programs designed to train campaign professionals. In their book *Gold-Plated Politics*, scholars Dwight Morris and Murielle Gamache note that in modern politics "candidates turn themselves over to a cadre of highly skilled advisers who develop candidate strategy, mold and project the candidate's image, make certain people show up to vote on election day, and find the money to pay for it all."[18] Obviously, as professionals have taken over campaigning, the cost of elections has grown, and it might be said that campaign consultants are the real winners in contemporary politics. In 1990, the consulting firm of Squier and Associates alone billed fourteen congressional campaigns for a total of $11,273,185.[19] It is little wonder that the cost of getting elected has skyrocketed.

What role have parties played in the age of high-cost, media-centered electioneering? On the one hand, parties have inadvertently contributed to the rising cost of elections. As previously noted, dealignment has led to uncertainty, which, in turn, leads to greater spending by candidates. If party brand loyalty had remained at 1950s levels, it is likely that less money would be needed even with the growth of electronic advertising. It is also true that when the media age arrived, party organizations—based on the localized, Jeffersonian model—were not equipped to play a lead role. Most of the early campaign consultants were not directly affiliated with a party. Many of the scholarly works of the 1970s that highlighted the decline of party politics drew our attention to the parties' inability to compete with new-style campaign consultants. One scholar noted, "Children of electronic politics, the new specialists vaulted past the parties as the masters of the new campaigning in less than a generation." Yet, by the 1980s the parties had adapted to the realities of new-style elections and became full participants in high technology, media campaigning. Not only have they adjusted to high-cost elections, they have become the mechanism for raising and spending the necessary sums of money.

It is worth mentioning that, during the beginning of the media age, most of the money fueling the shift came from big contributors. Some candidates, such as Barry Goldwater in 1964, George Wallace in 1968, and George McGovern in 1972, tried to raise money from a broader group of "average" Americans, the idea being to bring the election process "back to the people." But broad-based fund-raising was inefficient, "for losers running ideological campaigns of the left or right," suggested one observer.[20] Most candidates continued to garner massive donations from a small group of individuals, the most notorious during this period was insurance executive Clement Stone, who gave nearly $3 million to Richard Nixon in 1968.

EFFORTS TO REGULATE THE FLOW OF MONEY IN ELECTIONS

What difference does it make that some groups and individuals give money during elections, often large sums, while others do not? One could argue that contributing money is simply one way Americans participate in the democratic process; whereas in the past people gave their time and energy to a candidate, today they simply send a check. Indeed, Republican Senator Mitch McConnell of Tennessee has led the battle against greater campaign contribution restrictions in the late 1990s. His argument is that by opening up the finance system, more Americans will become involved in politics. He is unabashed in his advocacy of more money in electoral politics, proclaiming that "money is free speech." After spearheading opposition to a proposal endorsed by Bill Clinton designed to slow down the growing cost of elections, McConnell stated, "I make no apologies for killing this turkey of a bill."[21] A few years later, in 1997, McConnell once again led the opposition to a campaign finance reform measure sponsored by Senators John McCain (R-Ariz.) and Russell Feingold (D-Wis.). Not coincidently, McConnell is chair of the National Republican Senatorial Committee (NRSC), where his first duty is to help raise money.

It is fair to say that most Americans do not share McConnell's optimism about the positive aspects of money in elections. There is a long-standing belief that money plays a corrupting role during elections and later in the development of public policy. Most Americans never send a check to a candidate or a political party. In the 1990s, just over 4 percent of Americans contributed money to candidates or a political party. And when it comes to sending large contributions, the percentage is even smaller. In 1990, for example, one-tenth of a percent of the voting-age population accounted for 46 percent of the money raised by congressional candidates. In 1994, residents of one zip-code area (10021) on New York City's upper East Side contributed more money to congressional races than did all the residents of each of twenty-one states.[22] This sort of disparity leads average Americans to wonder about the true incentives behind contributions. There is deep-seated belief that campaign contributions are intimately linked to government outputs—that money can "buy" favorable public policy decisions.

There were, however, few efforts to curb the flow of money in elections prior to the Progressive movement. In the early 1800s, some states sought to limit treating, but there was little enforcement of these laws. Campaign finance reform was simply not a major consideration during the nineteenth century. All this changed with the Industrial Revolution and the growing accounts of corruption in government exposing politicians who were being bought by industrial fat cats. The first wave of reforms came in the 1880s.

The **Civil Service Reform Act** was passed by Congress in 1883. It included a prohibition against assessing government employees for contributions. Under the spoils system model, it was common for public employees to "kick back" a portion of their pay to the party machine. The practice continued at the state and local level, but was outlawed at the federal level through this act.

As noted earlier, the election of 1896 marked a potent effort by industrial giants to keep Bryan from the White House. The contribution floodgates were opened and within a decade there was a growing outcry for reform. Following the lead of Teddy Roosevelt, Congress passed the **Tillman Act of 1907.** This measure made it a crime for any corporation or national bank to contribute to candidates for Congress or for the presidency. Three years later, Congress again acted by establishing requirements that compelled candidates to disclose the source of contributions. In 1925, the **Corrupt Practices Act** was passed, a measure that went beyond the mere disclosure of receipts and expenditures to limiting expenditures for House and Senate campaigns. A similar reform tide swept through the states; only fourteen states had disclosure laws in 1905, but by 1920 some forty-four states had joined the act.

Another flurry of reform measures occurred in the late 1930s and early 1940s, most notably the **Hatch Act of 1939**, officially called the Clean Politics Act. This measure made it a crime for any employee of the federal government to become an active participant in politics, and for anyone to solicit funds from people receiving federal relief. Within a year, several amendments were added, including the first federal limit on contributions from individuals (they could give no more than $5,000 to a candidate for federal office) and a prohibition against contributions to federal-level candidates from any business doing work for the United States. By 1943, Congress extended the prohibition on contributions from banks and corporations to include labor unions. A similar pattern of regulations again followed at the state level.

The surprising thing about all of these reform efforts is how utterly meaningless they proved to be. The flow of big money into elections did not slow at all; it was simply channeled along different paths. Reform efforts failed for several reasons.[23] First, while these statutes placed impressive laws on the books, most failed to create public authorities responsible for collecting disclosure reports and prosecuting illegal activity. Disclosure failed to curb contributions because this information was rarely brought to the public's attention. Second, there were large loopholes. Reporting requirements, for example, often pertained to "campaign periods," so contributors simply gave prior to the start of these periods. Expenditure limits applied only to the candidate, not to the separate committees that sprung up on the candidate's behalf (i.e., Friends to Elect John Doe to Congress). Corporations evaded contribution prohibitions by reimbursing corporate executives who sent money to candidates. "Under the table" gifts also were common. Finally, and perhaps most importantly, there was simply a lack of will among elected officials to enforce regulations; they were elected under the existing system and rocking the boat created risks. Sorauf writes, "the prohibition against contributions by businesses contracting with the U.S. government was very widely ignored."[24] It is no wonder that from the Corrupt Practices Act of 1925 until the 1970s, there is no record of a single prosecution for campaign contributions violations.

Meaningful Reform: Watergate and Federal Reforms

By the late 1960s, reform was back on Congress's agenda. Unlike prior movements, where a public backlash drove the reform efforts, the roots of this phase lay in the fears of the members of Congress. The cost of elections was rising, owing to the growing use of television. In 1956, for example, just over $6 million had been spent on televison during the general election. By 1968 this figure had jumped to over $27 million.[25] Members of both parties, but especially Democrats—given that they were in the majority and had the most to lose—were increasingly worried that well-financed challengers would connect with voters through the mass media and thus toss them out. There were also disclosures of continued fat cat contributions, including businessman Clement Stone's gift to Nixon in 1968.

Two significant measures were passed in 1971: The **Revenue Act** created a fund for presidential campaigns and allowed voters to check off a dollar donation on their tax forms to help support the fund. (To get around a veto threat by Richard Nixon, the act did not go into effect until the 1976 election.) The **Federal Election Campaign Act (FECA)** was an ambitious attempt to tighten reporting requirements and limit expenditures on media advertisements. Unlike prior disclosure laws, FECA mandated that all expenditures and contributions of over $100 would be disclosed, regardless of when they were given. Moreover, reports would be filed with the General Accounting Office and be made public with forty-eight hours of being received. Media expenditures, including televison, radio, billboards, and newsprint, would be limited to $50,000 or ten cents per voting-age resident, whichever amount was larger. The largest allotment was for the California senatorial contests at $1.4 million. Only 60 percent of the maximum could be spent on radio and television combined.[26]

FECA did improve disclosure levels, but had little impact on overall spending in the 1972 election. Candidates once again found different channels through which to spend their funds. In fact, that election proved to be the most expensive to date in American history. But the story of finance reform was about to take a dramatic turn. The focusing event for meaningful reform came with disclosures surrounding the **Watergate** scandal. In the course of investigating Richard Nixon's involvement in the break-in of the Watergate Hotel, it was found that the Committee to Reelect the President (CREEP) had established a secret fund-raising program. A great number of the donations to Nixon's war chest were illegal, ranging from $200,000 delivered in an attache case, to nearly $1 million in illegal corporate donations. Of the overall $63 million collected by Nixon, $20 million was from 153 donors who gave $50,000 or more. In July of 1974, the Senate Watergate Committee further reported that foreign subsidiaries were used to channel corporate money to CREEP. Commenting on the breadth of the Watergate finance scandal, John Gardner, head of Common Cause, said in April 1973:

> Watergate is not primarily a story of political espionage, nor even of White House intrigue. It is a particularly malodorous chapter in the annals of campaign financing. The money paid to the Watergate conspirators before the break-in—and the money passed to them later—was money from campaign gifts.[27]

Two forces came together for meaningful reform: a shocked public and a Congress dominated by those less able to tap into fat cat contributions—the Democrats. Technically, the new measure came as a series of amendments to the 1971 FECA, but these measures amounted to the most sweeping campaign finance laws ever passed by Congress. The **FECA Amendments of 1974** did a number of things:

- Established a Federal Election Commission, consisting of six members, with the overall charge of enforcing federal election statutes.

- Instituted numerous contribution limits, including $1,000 for individuals per primary, run-off, and general election, not to exceed $25,000 to all federal candidates annually; $5,000 for PACs per election with no aggregate limit; $1,000 for independent expenditures on behalf of a candidate; and a complete ban on contributions from foreign sources.
- Set limits on spending by all federal candidates and national parties, including a total of $10 million per candidate for all presidential primaries; $20 million per candidate in presidential general elections; $2 million for each party's nominating convention; $100,000 or eight cents per voter, whichever is greater, for Senate primary candidates and $150,000 or twelve cents per voter for general election races; $70,000 for House primary and $70,000 for House general elections.
- Limited party spending to $10,000 per candidate in House elections and $20,000 or two cents per voter, whichever is greater, for each candidate in Senate general elections; and two cents per voter in presidential general elections.
- Expanded public funding of presidential elections not only to general elections but to primary elections as well, with a matching formula used for the latter.
- Created an extensive list of disclosure and reporting requirements, including the establishment by each candidate of one central campaign committee through which all contributions and expenditures on behalf of that candidate would be reported.[28]

In all, the 1974 amendments represented sweeping change in the way federal elections were financed—one that continues to shape American politics. Several states have followed a similar path, but most have not gone nearly as far. While raising his own objections to the bill, President Gerald Ford signed the amendments into law noting that "the times demand this legislation."[29]

A Challenge in the Courts: Buckley v. Valeo

The jubilation over reform did not last long. As soon as the FECA amendments took effect they were challenged in the courts. The case comprised a diverse set of plaintiffs, including U.S. Senator James Buckley, a Conservative from New York; Senator Eugene McCarthy, a Democrat from Minnesota; the New York Civil Liberties Union; and *Human Events*, a conservative publication. In *Buckely v. Valeo* (Francis R. Valeo was then the secretary of the Senate),[30] the core arguments on each side were rather simple. Buckley and his colleagues argued that spending during elections is a form of speech protected by the First Amendment. Political speech, they argued, must be especially sensitive to regulatory limits. They further contended that the law discriminated against minor parties and lesser-known candidates. The government, on the other hand, argued that money had a corrupting influence on elections and that in order to promote fair contests—the cornerstone of the democratic process—some restrictions were necessary. In other words, the democratic process compels a level playing field and in an age of media-centered elections this implies limits on campaign contributions and expenditures.

On January 30, 1976, the Supreme Court handed down its decision in *Buckley*, arguably the most important election case in American history. In an unsigned 137-page decision, the Court found that some, but not all, of the FECA restrictions were constitutional. They let stand the provisions that set limits on how much individuals and political committees could contribute to candidates, both to individual candidates and in the aggregate; allowed for the public financing of presidential elections, so long as it was voluntary, meaning that candidates could refuse public monies and spend their own; and required disclosure of campaign contributions and expenditures of more than $100. Perhaps more significantly, the Court struck down several features of the law. They found unconstitutional: the overall spending caps; the limits on what candidates and their spouses could contribute to their own campaigns; and limits on independent expenditures. Concerning their rejection of overall spending limits, the Court noted:

> A restriction on the amount of money a person or group can spend on political communication during a campaign necessarily reduces the quantity of expression by restricting the number of issues discussed, the depth of their exploration and the size of the audience reached. This is because virtually every means of communicating ideas in today's mass society requires the expenditure of money.

Regarding the rejection of limits on independent expenditures, the Court stated:

> While the . . . ceiling thus fails to serve any substantial interest in stemming the reality of corruption in the electoral process, it heavily burdens core First Amendment expression. . . . Advocacy of the election or defeat of candidates for federal office is not less entitled to protection under the First Amendment than the discussion of political policy generally or advocacy of the passage or defeat of legislation.

The decision was a strong defense of free expression, but also quite contradictory. How could campaign spending be akin to free speech, while at the same time open to limits by Congress? The Court reasoned that some restrictions are more burdensome than are others:

> By contrast with a limitation upon expenditures for political expression, a limitation upon the amount that any one person or group may contribute to a candidate or political committee entails only a marginal restriction upon the contributor's ability to engage in free expression. . . . The quantity of communication by the contributor does not increase perceptibly with the size of his contribution, since the expression rests solely on the undifferentiated, symbolic art of contributing. Expenditure ceilings impose significantly more severe restrictions on protected freedoms of political expression and association than do its limitations on financial contributions.

Finally, an important qualification was made regarding the role of parties in election finance. The Court agreed that limits on party contributions to candidates were reasonable. Under FECA provisions, money spent by a party "for the purpose of influencing" the candidate's campaign or made on behalf of a candidate to benefit his or her campaign, is considered a qualified campaign expense. Assistance of this sort is subject to spending limits. But in the now-infamous footnote 52 seized upon by party operatives in the late 1990s, the Court noted that these limits apply *only* to communications that contain express words of advocacy, such as "vote for or against," "elect," "Jones for Congress," or "defeat." That is, if the party's communication does not expressly advocate the election or defeat of a candidate, they fall beyond the realm of regulations. This loophole has become a powerful mechanism to circumvent contribution limits and has thrust parties into the center of the election-finance matrix.[31]

The Rise of PACs

Interest groups have played an important role in funding elections for over a century. During the Industrial Revolution, businesses, trade associations, and labor unions channeled immense donations to parties and candidates. Even though reform measures limited direct contributions from corporations, banks, and later labor unions, many loopholes were available. In 1943, the Congress of Industrial Organizations decided to circumvent contribution restrictions by creating a separate fund to receive and spend voluntary contributions, a new organizational unit they called the **political action committee** (PAC). It was legal, they argued, because none of the monies used to support the group or given to candidates came directly from the labor union.

By the late 1950s, scores of business and professional associations began to develop similar organizations, picking up the name PAC. The Business-Industry PAC and American Medical PAC were created during this period. The true growth period for PACs, however, occurred after the finance reform measures of the early 1970s. Because FECA imposed limits on how much an individual could give to a campaign ($1,000 per primary, runoff, and general election), and also set aggregate individual limits at $25,000, candidates were, and still are, compelled to solicit donations from a broad range of sources. PACs fit the bill nicely. Even though FECA never specifically mentions PACs, it does stipulate that "multi-candidate committees", which raise funds from at least fifty donors and spends it on at least five candidates, can contribute up to $5,000 per election. Even though individuals can give just $1,000 to a candidate, they can give up to $5,000 to a PAC. In 1975, the Federal Elections Commission provided Sun Oil Company (SunPAC) with an "advisory opinion"—a statement on what they believe the court would say if the issue came up—that the company could pay the overhead and solicitation costs of its PAC. This allowed all PACs to use their funds to help candidates and made these organizations an even more attractive means for channeling special interest money to candidates. Finally, the court's ruling in *Buckley* allows PACs to spend unlimited sums on a campaign, so long as it is in the form of an independent expenditure (expenditures made without the knowledge of candidates or their staffs).[32]

The number of PACs exploded, and so too did their role in election finance. In 1974, there were roughly 600 PACs; by 1998 there were nearly 4,500. Their expenditures in federal campaigns went from approximately $35 million in the late 1970s to $220 million in 1998. The average competitive congressional candidate (both House and Senate) nets about 40 percent of his/her contributions from PACs.

It was common for House candidates in the late 1990s to raise upwards of $.5 million from PACs each election cycle. For Senate candidates, aggregate PAC totals of $2 million are now common. In 1996, labor PACs gave congressional candidates a total of $47 million, corporate PACs gave $70 million, and trade association PACs another $57 million.[33] There has been a similar explosion at the state level. Simply put, contributors have found PACs to be an efficient means for getting money to their preferred candidates, and candidates have raised few objections.

Many had assumed that the proliferation of PACs would hinder the party system. It was speculated, especially during the early days of PAC growth, that these units would quickly replace parties. Even the chair of the RNC, Bill Brock, commented in 1976 that "the emergence of PACs poses a serious threat to the role of parties." Robert Strauss, head of the DNC during that same time, stated that "the availability of PAC money has contributed to the undermining of party discipline."[34] By the 1990s, a new picture had emerged—one of cohabitation and mutual assistance.

Overall, labor union PACs support Democrats and business-related organizations help Republicans. This is not a perfect fit, but the relationship is quite strong. For instance, during the 1996 election, corporate PACs gave a full 72 percent of their contributions to Republicans and labor PACs gave 91 percent of their funds to Democrats.[35] Eighty-four percent of all money given to federal-level candidates by gun rights PACs during the 1996 election was given to Republicans. Just over 80 percent of insurance industry PAC money was also given to the GOP, as was 83 percent of oil industry money. The Democrats consistently benefit from donations by lawyers and lobbyists (75 percent of their contributions); and from environmental groups (upwards of 80 percent of contributions). There are several industries, such as finance, real estate, agriculture, and defense contractors that spread the wealth more or less evenly. The most uniform relationship concerns incumbency—a vast majority of contributions from all sectors goes to those already in office. In 1998, 78 percent of PAC contributions went to incumbents, 57 percent of which was given to Republicans. Whichever party holds the majority of seats in a legislature can expect to get more PAC funds than their opposition.

Both parties maintain a close working relationship with PACs, especially when it comes to targeting resources to competitive races. As the campaign season progresses, party operatives share information with PAC managers on their "hot prospects." Once party and PAC operatives team up on a race, a great deal of information is shared, including polling data, opposition research, and strategic approaches. The parties also help candidates solicit funds from these PACs in a number of innovative ways. And a good deal of evidence suggests the relationship between parties and PACs is becoming even more coordinated, as both groups realize the importance of a concerted effort. Scholar Paul Herrnson has been watching this growing relationship for some time. He writes:

> By helping candidates understand how the PAC community works and by furnishing PACs with information about candidates, the congressional and senatorial [party] committees have become important intermediaries in the fund-raising process. [The parties] have entered into symbiotic relationships with some PACs, enabling them to become brokers between candidates and PACs.

Each party has benefitted from a growing bundle of direct PAC contributions. In 1998, for example, the Republicans received $21.4 million and the Democrats $18.9 million in PAC contributions. These figures are roughly double what they were during the previous off-year election cycle in 1994.

Once again, political parties have adapted to new conditions. At first it seemed that modest contribution limits would push candidates to gather funds from a wide range of sources, including PACs, relagating parties to the sidelines. The parties realized that in order to remain players in elections, they needed to make adjustments. This meant coming to grips with new-style voter communication technologies, centralizing party resources, providing candidates with new services, and raising the money to pay for it all (see also Chapter 4). Overall, it meant turning away from the amateur-based, Jeffersonian model to the Hamiltonian approach. The coupling of Washington-based PACs and the national party organizations is another piece of evidence that dramatic changes are underway and will continue, even if it means exploiting loopholes in the law.

CREATIVE PARTY FINANCES IN THE INFORMATION AGE

The cornerstone of Hamiltonian parties is money. The organizational response to the movement away from party brand loyalty has been greater services to candidates. Without money, party organizations could not help their clients, especially with the new tools of the Information Age, like survey research and television advertisements. It is not a coincidence that the drive to amass larger war chests began at precisely the time the national party committees adopted their professional, service-oriented outlook. By the end of the 1980s, both national parties had honed sophisticated fund-raising techniques, and they were working.

Party coffers swelled. In the mid-1970s, the Republicans collected roughly $40 million per election cycle. The Democrats lagged behind, bringing in approximately $18 million in receipts. By the late 1980s, these figures had jumped to well over $300 million and nearly $100 million, respectively. Within a decade these numbers had doubled again, and by 1996 the GOP raised over $416 million, with the Democrats compiling $221 million. Table 8.1 charts the receipts of Republicans during the last two decades.

Two things make this growth particularly impressive. First, party fund-raising has been successful in spite of FECA regulations designed to reduce the flow of big money in elections. Second, and much related, these figures do not include an entire category of receipts, comprising hundreds of millions per election, dubbed "soft money." Soft money refers to funds raised outside the restraints of federal laws, but spent on activities to influence federal elections. An important distinction was made in a 1979 FECA ruling that permitted a portion of money raised for party building to be set aside in a special account. For example, money raised by the DNC to register voters in a given state or to run commercials designed to get out the vote can be stored in a special "non-federal" or soft money account. Hard money, on the other hand, refers to party money raised specifically for federal election

> **TABLE 8.1** ▪ National Party Hard Money Receipts 1980 through 1998 (in millions of dollars)*
>
> | Party | 1980 | 1982 | 1984 | 1986 | 1988 | 1990 | 1992 | 1994 | 1996 | 1998 |
> |---|---|---|---|---|---|---|---|---|---|---|
> | Democrats | $32 | $39 | $98 | $65 | $127 | $87 | $178 | $140 | $222 | $160 |
> | Republicans | $168 | $215 | $297 | $255 | $263 | $205 | $267 | $246 | $416 | $285 |
>
> * Federal (hard dollars) only.
> SOURCE: Federal Election Commission New Release, April 9, 1999.

campaigns. It is given to candidates either as a direct contribution or as a coordinated expenditure.

Several forces have contributed to the unprecedented fund-raising bonanza. Competition for control of the House of Representatives became a reality in the early 1990s. During the prior three decades, the Democratic lock on the House seemed impenetrable. But as GOP gains continued to mount, especially in the South, both parties realized a change was possible. The "earthquake of 1994" was actually quite predictable. As the uncertainty of the Democrats' hold on the House grew, so too did party spending on these races (see "The Parties Speak: Ten Myths about Money in Politics"). From 1986 to 1994, the amount of money spent by Democrats on congressional races more than tripled—from $6.4 million to nearly $22 million. The rate of growth for the GOP was a bit slower, perhaps because they were already spending heavily on these races, but even so went from just under $17 million in 1986 to $21.4 million a decade later. Of course, greater spending means a greater emphasis on raising funds.

Once the Republicans took control of the House in 1994, the ability for the parties to raise money from access-seeking groups and individuals was much simpler. The GOP found themselves in the unique position of being able to recast the direction of government, a prospect that excited many groups in their coalition and struck fear among those aligned with the Democrats. It is likely that this uncertainty compelled influence-seekers to hedge their bets, as best they could, and give lavishly to both parties (or anyone else who would/could take it, for that matter). This uncertainty factor was played out in other ways, at both the congressional and presidential election levels.

Finally, both parties demonstrated a bold willingness to test the limits of campaign finance regulations. The real story of party finances in the 1990s is one of clever ways of subverting and stretching FECA limits, including issue advocacy, independent expenditures, soft money, state transfers, and bundling.

Issue Advocacy

At Bill Clinton's urging, the DNC implemented an aggressive fund-raising plan and engineered a novel way of spending money. From July 1995 until election day 1996, the DNC bombarded the television airwaves with thousands of commercials.

The Parties Speak: *Ten Myths about Money in Politics*

The Center for Responsive Politics is a nonprofit, nonpartisan research organization based in Washington, D.C. Its mission is the study of Congress, with a particular focus on the role that money plays in its election and actions. The Center has become one of the major "good government" groups dedicated to ridding big money from the political process. They regularly publish material on the corrupting influence of money. These are excerpts from their pamphlet "Ten Myths About Money in Politics," published just after the 1994 elections.

MYTH #1—PACS ARE THE PROBLEM

- In presidential races, where tens of millions of dollars in private contributions are raised during the primaries, most all of it comes from individuals, not PACs.
- PACs accounted for only 40 percent of the campaign dollars collected by House candidates in 1994, and less than 25 percent of the money collected by U.S. Senate winners.
- Large individual contributions often come from the same sources and represent the same interests as PAC contributions.

MYTH #2—THE SPECIAL INTERESTS BALANCE EACH OTHER OUT

- Between January 1991 and December 1994, business PACs gave three times as much money to members of Congress as did labor PACs—$257 million vs. $85 million.
- During the 1992 election cycle, all environmental groups combined gave members of Congress less than $2 million, whereas the energy and natural resources industry, which often opposes strict environmental safeguards, gave ten times as much—more than $21 million.
- The National Rifle Association supported gun rights with PAC contributions totaling just under $2 million in 1994. On the opposing side, Handgun Control, Inc., the largest gun control PAC, gave just over $200,000.

MYTH #3—MAKING CAMPAIGN CONTRIBUTIONS IS ONE OF THE WAYS THAT AMERICANS PARTICIPATE IN DEMOCRACY

- Of the 250 million people who live in the U.S., fewer than 900,000, or one-third of one percent, gave over $200 to congressional candidates in 1992.
- In 1990, one-tenth of one percent of the voting-age population accounted for 46 percent of all the money raised by congressional candidates.

MYTH #4—MONEY DIDN'T MATTER IN THE 1994 ELECTIONS THAT GAVE CONTROL OF CONGRESS TO THE REPUBLICANS

- More money than ever before was spent by congressional candidates in 1994—$724 million. This was an increase of 15 percent over 1992, and that was a presidential election year.
- In October, just prior to the election when fund-raising is most intensive, Republican candidates enjoyed an almost unprecedented $4.2 million edge over Democrats in individual contributions of over $200.
- In contributions of less than $200, Republicans outpaced Democrats by a margin of $73.6 million to $46.6 million.

MYTH #5—THE MONEY ONLY BUYS ACCESS— NOT VOTES

- On the tax side, the appropriations side, the subsidy side, and the expenditure side, decisions are clearly weighted and influenced . . . by who has contributed to candidates." (Former Congressman Mel Levine, D-Calif.)
- [Legislators] can scarcely avoid weighing every decision against the question, 'How will this affect my fund-raising prospects." (Former Senator Barry Goldwater, R-Ariz.)
- "The pay-off may be as obvious and overt as a floor vote in favor of the contributor's desired tax loophole, or it may be subtle as a floor speech not delivered, a pigeonholed in subcommittee, or an amendment not offered." (Former Senator William Proxmire, D-Wis.)

MYTH #6—PRIVATELY FINANCED ELECTIONS DON'T COST TAXPAYERS MONEY

- Corporate tax breaks are high on the agenda of corporate campaign contributors. During the 1980s, U.S. corporations paid $67.5 billion in federal taxes, while receiving tax breaks (loopholes) of $92.2 billion.
- The Cato Institute identified $425 billion in pork-barrel funding programs, subsidies, or tax breaks for corporations and industry groups.

MYTH #7—MONEY IN POLITICS IS ONLY A SERIOUS PROBLEM AT THE FEDERAL LEVEL

- Between 1976 and 1988, spending by statewide and legislative candidates across the country increased by 450 percent—from $120 million to $540 million.

continued

The Parties Speak: *Ten Myths about Money in Politics* (*continued*)

MYTH #8—THE PUBLIC FINANCING SYSTEM FOR PRESIDENTIAL ELECTIONS IS A MODEL FOR REFORMING OTHER ELECTIONS

- Presidential Candidates raise most of their money prior to the beginning of the election year.
- During the 1992 election, the two parties combined raised over $80 million in "soft money"—that is, money that is not regulated by the Federal Election Commission.
- Since 1980, the candidate who raised the most money by the January before the primary season has won his party's nomination.

MYTH #9—TAXPAYERS OPPOSE THE PUBLIC FINANCING OF ELECTIONS

- When the idea of full public financing of elections (i.e., no private contributions at all) is put to people in a straightforward manner, most polls show majority support.
- In a 1990 survey in the *Los Angeles Times*, 75 percent of respondents wanted to ban private contributions and adopt public financing of state legislative races.

MYTH #10—IT'S ALWAYS BEEN THIS WAY AND ALWAYS WILL BE

- The history of democracy in the U.S. is the history of periodic waves of protest followed by evolutionary change. The right to vote, once reserved to white, male property owners, has been won by successive groups of Americans.
- As the cost of federal, state, and municipal campaigns has greatly increased in recent years, so has the public's awareness of the problem. Three-quarters of Americans believe our system is democratic only in name, and that in fact special interests run things. Our "long habit" of thinking that privately financed elections are compatible with democracy has already begun to change.

SOURCE: Center for Responsive Politics, *Ten Myths About Money in Politics* (Washington, D.C.: Center for Responsive Politics, 1995)

These spots cost $34 million, none of which was drawn from Clinton's campaign committee accounts.

How was this possible? As already noted, provisions of the Federal Election Commission stipulate that any money spent by a party "for the purpose of influencing" a candidate's chance in an election are considered a qualified expense, and therefore subject to limits. Such restrictions were upheld in *Buckley* v. *Valeo*. The

Court noted, however, that limits can be applied only to expenditures that expressly advocate the election or defeat of a candidate. Put differently, if an advertisement does not contain the magic words, like "vote for candidate X" or "vote against candidate Y," it cannot be considered a campaign advertisement and therefore is not subject to limitations.

The DNC picked up on this loophole and ran with it. They crafted a series of issue advocacy spots that steered clear of expressly advocating Bill Clinton's reelection. This did not mean that the actor in the commercials could not be the president himself. Quite the contrary, the advertisements showed a hard-working Clinton in the serenity of the Oval Office acting as a barrier against "radical Republicanism." Voters in a dozen key states saw these DNC advertisements about once every three days for a year-and-a-half. To them, the ads were simply pro-Clinton commercials, but to the operatives at the DNC they were issue ads, protected by the First Amendment. The scheme worked. The Republicans eventually caught on to the issue advocacy scam and spent approximately $20 million. As noted by one party finance scholar, "this innovative form of party spending essentially rendered the contributions and spending limits of the FEC meaningless."[36] Table 8.3 notes two televison commercials that were dubbed "issue ads." To most observers, they implied a good deal more than a discussion about public policy.

A study conducted by Paul Herrnson and Diana Dwyre examined the differences between television advertisements directly sponsored by candidates and those sponsored by the parties considered issue advocacy. Pundits have argued that the difference between the two is artificial, based on a poor understanding of campaign communications. The courts have found some sort of difference, they argue, where none exists. By examining a 1996 U.S. Senate race in careful detail, Herrnson and Dwyre conclude that the critics are essentially correct: There are more similarities than differences between candidate ads and party ads. The only real difference they find is that party-sponsored commercials tend to be more negative. They conclude by suggesting that the shift to party-based independent expenditures and issue ads has the potential to change the nature of congressional elections.[37]

By 1998, both parties had stepped-up their issue advocacy spending. The tack was still rather new, but national party operatives from both sides of the aisle seemed willing to learn. The Republicans orchestrated an aggressive fund-raising scheme called "operation breakout." The goal was to raise upwards of $20 million, divided equally between soft money expenditures and issue advocacy.

Independent Expenditures

But there is more to the story of innovative finance in the 1990s than issue advocacy. A second line of assault has been independent expenditures. In June of 1996, the Supreme Court issued a ruling in *Colorado Republican Federal Campaign Committee v. Federal Elections Commission*, a case that involved a decade-old complaint. In 1984, Democratic Representative Tim Wirth had thrown his hat in the ring for the U.S. Senate, but before any Republican candidate had done the same, the Colorado Republican Party launched a series of television ads attacking Wirth. The Federal

TABLE 8.3 ▪ When a Campaign Ad Is Not a Campaign Ad: Issue Advocacy
Spots from the 1996 Election

#1. Clinton Spot: "Finish" (released May 6, 1996)

Announcer:

Head Start. Student Loans. Toxic Cleanup. Extra Police. Anti-Drug Programs.
Dole-Gingrich want them cut. Now they're safe.
Protected in the '96 budget because the President stood firm.
Done-Gingrich? Deadlock. Gridlock. Shutdowns.

The President's plan? Finish the job. Balance the budget. Reform welfare. Cut Taxes.
Protect Medicare.

President Clinton says, get it done.
Meet our challenges. Protect out values.

#2. Dole Spot: "More" (released June 20, 1996)

Announcer:

Did you know there are over five million illegal immigrants in the United States?
And that you spend five and one-half billion dollars a year to support them with
welfare, food stamps, and other services?
Under President Clinton, spending on illegals has gone up. While wages for the
typical worker have gone down.
And when efforts are made to stop giving benefits to illegal immigrants, Bill
Clinton opposed them.
Tell President Clinton to stop giving benefits to illegals, and end wasteful
Washington spending.

---

*Both of these television advertisements were declared issue advocacy, and therefore not subject to
federal spending restrictions.

SOURCE: Brooks Jackson, "Financing the 1996 Campaign: The Law of the Jungle," In Larry J.
Sabato, ed., *Toward the Millennium: The Elections of 1996* (Needham Heights, Mass.: Allyn & Bacon,
1997), 237.

Election Commission ruled that this expenditure, totaling a mere $15,000, should
be counted against the party's spending limits that are applied to all senatorial campaigns. The Colorado Republicans disagreed, arguing their ad campaign was an
independent expenditure—a form of speech protected under *Buckley.*

The Court sided with the Colorado Republicans, but the decision was far from
unanimous. Four fragmented opinions were handed down, with three justices writing the plurality opinion. It was agreed that restrictions on "independent" advertisements are constitutionally protected, especially for political parties. Building upon
this decision, and the fact that four of the other justices (in two separate opinions)
were willing to strike down restrictions on party spending coordinated with the candidates, both parties pushed the envelope and began independent expenditure campaigns. In 1996, it was limited mostly to U.S. Senate races, with the amount totaling
just over $11 million. (The Republicans were the most aggressive in this regard.) At

first glance this amount might appear insignificant; yet considering that no party funds were spent in this way prior to 1996, this tactic marked yet another clever innovation—and provided a blueprint for future party spending. Moreover, the *Colorado* decision assured operatives in both parties that their issue advocacy programs would receive a friendly hearing in the courts if push came to shove.

Hard and Soft Money

Hard money refers to contributions to particular candidates that are subject to federal and state limits. Once these contributions are made, the party relinquishes control of the funds to the candidate. In 1998, congressional candidates could receive a $10,000 hard money contribution from their national party committees for a total contribution limit of $30,000 per election cycle. There is an additional $17,000 limit for Senate candidates shared by the national committee and the senate campaign committee. State parties can give up to $5,000 per Senate candidate each election.

Related to hard money contributions, parties can use **coordinated expenditures** to help candidates. Here, both the party and the candidate share control of the funds. Several common coordinated expenses including polling, direct mail, get-out-the-vote drives, and the production of radio and television commercials. In 1998, national parties were allowed to spend a maximum of $32,550 in coordinated expenditures per race. State party committees were limited to the same amount, and were allowed to transfer their spending limits to the national party through what is dubbed **agency agreements.** In effect, these agreements allow the national parties to double their spending limits. Coordinated expenditure limits for Senate races vary by population, ranging from just under $62,000 to a high of $1.5 million.

Both hard money and coordinated expenditures are fully disclosed. Table 8.4 highlights both of these more traditional forms of party giving, spanning from 1980 to 1998. The table suggests party giving is significant. There are fluctuations, based on whether it is a presidential election year, but on the whole both parties afford congressional candidates a great deal of help. There has been a shift away from direct contributions. Given that the national party committees have become more centralized and professional (i.e., more Hamiltonian), it makes sense that they would be anxious to play a role in how their money is spent. The table underscores the import role that "hill committees" (see Chapter 4) now play in congressional elections. A few decades ago these units were minor players, but today they provide massive sums. The role of the National Republican Senatorial Committee (NRSC) and the NRCC in the early 1990s is most impressive. Between 1990 and 1994, the NRSC spent well over $40 million in direct contributions and coordinated expenditures. Finally, by comparing this table to Table 8.5, we find that the most significant growth in party involvement in congressional campaigning is not direct contributions or coordinated expenditures, but rather in soft money expenditures. Although reported contributions have remained somewhat level over the last two decades, soft money disbursements have shot up.

TABLE 8.4 ▪ National Party Committee Hard Money and Coordinated Expenditures, 1980–1998 (in millions of dollars)

Party	1980	1882	1984	1986	1988	1990	1992	1994	1996	1998
Democrats										
DNC										
Direct contributions	.78	.21	1.5	.03	.19	.06	<.01	.09	.03	<.01
Coordinated expenditures	7.8	.24	4.2	.51	11.2	.15	13.1	.38	7.0	6.0
DSCC										
Direct contributions	.95	.90	.66	.86	.60	.53	.69	.59	.56	.30
Coordinated expenditures	1.2	3.2	6.2	9.1	8.5	5.6	13.1	13.5	8.7	<.01
DCCC										
Direct contributions	1.2	.95	1.2	.91	.92	.56	.97	1.1	1.1	.43
Coordinated expenditures	.68	.34	1.8	2.3	3.3	3.6	4.8	8.1	5.9	2.9
Totals	11.3	5.8	15.5	13.6	24.8	10.5	32.6	23.7	23.2	9.7
Republicans										
RNC										
Direct contributions	1.6	2.8	1.3	.52	.45	.32	.91	.60	.50	.44
Coordinated expenditures	10.6	.39	10.7	<.01	11.4	.06	13.1	5.18	23.7	3.9
NRSC										
Direct contributions	.82	.94	.88	.94	1.0	.87	.80	.69	.72	.28
Coordinated expenditures	9.9	14.7	10.6	14.8	14.1	9.6	19.1	12.0	.32	.04
NRCC										
Direct contributions	3.9	4.3	4.1	2.5	2.1	1.2	.85	.87	1.3	.78
Coordinated expenditures	2.4	8.3	9.8	6.1	5.6	3.5	6.0	4.3	7.6	5.1
Total	29.4	31.6	37.4	62.2	34.9	15.5	40.8	23.6	34.1	10.5

SOURCE: Federal Election Commission data.

Collecting and disbursing soft money has become a full-time occupation for both national party committees and the hill committees. The soft money strategy is where the national party committees raise massive sums of money, but instead of spending it on behalf of a particular candidate, which would be subject to federal limits, they give it to state party committees or spend it on general party-building activities. There are a number of common soft money activities, including joint

TABLE 8.5 ▪ National Party Soft-Money Activity in the 1990s
(receipts in millions of dollars)*

Party	1992	1994	1996	1998
DNC	36.4	48.3	103.3	56.9
DCCC	.51	5.6	11.3	16.8
DSCC	.66	.41	14.6	25.9
Total	42.1	54.1	127.1	92.8
RNC	41.8	49.3	114.6	74.8
NRCC	7.1	8.1	18.9	26.9
NRSC	10.5	6.1	27.7	37.9
Total	57.8	57.7	146.6	131.6

*Disbursements were nearly identical.

SOURCE: Federal Elections Commission press release, April 9, 1999.

fund-raising costs, voter mobilization programs, administrative costs shared with state party organizations, and voter registration drives. In 1992, about 20 percent of soft money was transferred directly to state party organizations. By 1996, this increased to about 50 percent, probably due to the large number of joint television campaigns in target states. As noted in Table 8.5, the national parties collected and disbursed nearly $300 million in soft money in 1996—a whopping 200 percent increase over 1992, the previous presidential election year. There is also a near doubling of off-year soft money collection between 1994 and 1998.

Soft money has also become the means by which fat cat contributors can channel money into the process. There are limits on the amount of money an individual, corporation, labor union, or interest group can give to candidates, but no restrictions on how much they can give to a national party committee. It has become the loophole of choice. In 1998, George Bush and the GOP organized what they dubbed "Team 100," a group where membership was limited to those who had donated at least $100,000 to the party. The Democrats actually out-raised the Republicans that year in soft money. Just after the 1994 election, the GOP announced that it had received a $2.5 million donation from Amway Corporation. In 1996, the tobacco manufacturer Philip Morris contributed over $2 million to the Republicans and Seagrams liquor gave over $1 million to the Democrats. That year, some 303 contributors gave at least $100,000. Table 8.6 notes the top ten soft money contributors to both parties in the 1996 election.

Transfers to State Party Committees

Federal laws require disclosure of soft money contributions, so we know who is giving these large sums to the parties at the national level. Several states, however, have limited reporting requirements and many have none at all. It is increasingly common to have large contributors send their checks to state party committees; the money is then used to support a specific candidate or transferred to the national

TABLE 8.6 ▪ Top Ten Soft Money Donors to the National Party Committees
for the 1996 Election Cycle

Republican Donors	Amount	Democratic Donors	Amount
Philip Morris	$2,185,118	Jos. E. Seagram & Sons	$1,155,000
RJR Nabisco	$995,175	Walt Disney Co.	$866,800
Atlantic Richfield	$702,921	Communications Workers of America	$770,750
Jos. E. Seagram & Sons	$646,600	Food and Commercial Workers Union	$573,050
American Financial Corp.	$562,000	MCI	$536,136
AT&T	$549,590	Dream Works SKG	$525,000
Brown and Williamson	$515,000	Integrated Health Services	$524,000
U.S. Tobacco	$502,403	Assn. of Trial Lawyers	$515,000
Mariam Cannon Hayes	$500,000	Goldman, Sachs & Co.	$510,000

SOURCE: Brooks Jackson, "Financing the 1996 Campaign: The Law of the Jungle," In Larry J. Sabato, ed., *Toward the Millennium: The Elections of 1996* (Needham Heights, Mass.: Allyn & Bacon, 1997), 245.

party committees. A similar trick is for the national party committees to send money to the state committees, where it is then channeled back to the national party as a hard money contribution. Generally, the state committee is allowed to skim some of the funds for their trouble. In 1997, the DNC approached several state committees with a scheme for trading soft for hard dollars; they were offering a 10 percent commission, and there were many takers. Between January 1997 and April 1998, the DNC sent soft money contributions ranging from $11,000 to $172,000 to several states, and within days received back from these state hard dollar contributions—minus the commissions, of course.[38]

The outcome of this activity has allowed the state party committees to play an increasing role in congressional elections. Their coffers are swelling and candidates are now expecting help from these organizations—a drastic change from the 1970s. On the other hand, money transferring is just another example of how the party system has become top-down, or Hamiltonian. State and local committees have more resources than in the past, but have also lost autonomy to the national parties. State party leaders are increasingly frustrated by the strings attached to these deals, but go along with them because of the money involved.

Bundling

The parties, along with scores of favor-seeking interest groups, have devised a tool recently dubbed "bundling." This practice entails collecting checks made payable to a specific candidate by an intermediate agent, such as a party operative. These checks are individually within the legal limit (under $1,000 for an individual contribution and $5,000 for a PAC contribution), but combined to allow the party to contribute an immense "bundle of joy" to needy candidates. Of course, it also allows the party to receive credit for its efforts from the candidate.

Funding Nominating Conventions

Finally, the parties have discovered yet another finance regulation loophole, this one related to the funding of their presidential nominating conventions. In 1996, both parties received $12.4 million in public funds to pay for their conventions. According to FECA rules, the only other money that the parties can receive would be gifts from companies with a local business connection in the city where the convention is being held—"host committees." Not a single *Fortune 500* company is located in San Diego, the site of the GOP convention in 1996, but the party took the position that any business selling its products in the city had a "local connection." Philip Morris, Time Warner, Microsoft and AT&T gave the party millions for the event. Amway Corporation, the same company that gave the Republicans $2.5 million in 1994, gave another $1.3 million for the convention in 1996. As for the Democrats, the Chicago Committee raised just under $21 million from private donors. Many corporations gave to both conventions. As noted by Brooks Jackson, a CNN correspondent, "The post-Watergate limits broke down in spectacular fashion. . . . Both parties consumed record amounts of money even though the conventions had long since lost their original function: choosing a candidate."[39]

THE FUTURE OF PARTY FINANCE IN AMERICA

We noted at the start of this chapter that the tale of party money in American elections is long, convoluted, and ever-changing. Certainly the variations during the 1990s are enough to make one's head spin. Each election, it seems that new court decisions, FECA rulings, and strategic approaches push parties and candidates down new fund-raising paths. Not long ago coordinated expenditures were voguish; today it seems that issue advocacy and soft money are on top.

Since the 1960s, the means by which parties and candidates could reach out to voters has been revolutionized. Not long ago legions of party activists hit the streets to rally support for their ticket, but today televison commercials do the same in a fraction of the time. Computerized mailing lists have replaced literature drops, sophisticated telemarketing operations have taken over for the local phone bank, and satellite teleconferencing has replaced smoke-filled rooms. The Internet is also bursting onto the campaign scene. Immense sums are used by candidates to develop sophisticated Web sites. One year prior to the 2000 presidential primary season, George W. Bush, Al Gore, and Bill Bradley had already invested a fortune in their sites.

An interesting mix of Internet campaign technology and old-style politics came to light in the summer of 1999. It seems that Texas businessman, Karl Rove, a close advisor to George W. Bush, bought more than sixty Internet Web site names or domains—such as <www.bushsucks.com>—to keep them out of the hands of opponents. He also registered names for Web sites for possible Bush running mates, such as <bushwhitman.com> (Christine Whitman, governor of New Jersey); <bushpataki.net> (George Pataki, governor of New York); and <bushridge.com> (Tom Ridge, governor of Pennsylvania).[40] Apparently, the cost of Internet campaigning is on the move as well.

The potential power of the Internet as a fundraising tool was realized in February 2000. Arizona Senator John McCain stunned the GOP establishment with a 19-point victory over the frontrunner, Texas Governor George W. Bush, in the first-in-the-nation presidential primary held in New Hampshire. Within 72 hours after his big win, McCain's Website had collected $1.45 million. While it is common for upset winners to have a surge in fundraising, the Internet adds a new twist: Most on-line contributors use a major credit card to make their donations. Thus, the turnaround time between sender and recipient is virtually immediate—in McCain's case, 55 seconds. Thus, McCain was quickly able to receive and spend money in time for the next round of primaries. Momentum is a powerful force in presidential campaigns, and the Internet has now demonstrated its might for collecting quick cash and keeping a candidate's bandwagon rolling.

This chapter has also underscored that America's parties have demonstrated an ability to adapt and refine their role to changing environmental constraints—this time to new technologies, federal regulations, and the spiraling cost of elections. Both parties have devised new ways of squeezing the fat from the frying pan. With immense war chests, the parties are today key players in the election process. This is true at all levels of government, but especially so at the national level.

What is perhaps most surprising about this turn is that it has occurred even though average voters seem increasingly frustrated with partisan politics. Candidates need money and the parties are now in a position to help. But this does not mean that the voters have been lured back into the system. Although issue advocacy, independent expenditures, transfers, bundling, and soft money have given party organizations renewed energy, these activities have worsened the public's skepticism about the party system. Most see the proliferation of borderline fund-raising as a pestilence. Calls for reform, this time directed at party-based loopholes like soft money, are growing. It is likely that the parties will continue to fall back on the Court's interpretation of money and free speech in *Buckley*, but this does not mean that the public will be onboard. From their perspective, it is all a scam.

The best way to characterize the turn parties have taken with regard to raising and disbursing funds, then, is to return to our models of party politics. Without question, the focus that the national party committees place on raising ever-larger sums has led to a professionalization and centralization of the party system. Neighborhood-based electioneering, where activists visit their neighbors and rally support for a ticket, is gone—or at the very least fading fast. The Jeffersonian model has been replaced nearly overnight with electronic communications, campaign consultants, and aggressive national party committees. The party system has also maintained its tight connection to wealthy individuals and affluent groups. One might even suggest that the fat cat-party connection is as strong in the Information Age as at any point in our nation's history. How one interprets this development depends greatly on their outlook about the proper course of party politics and the role of the average citizen in democracy. We can only imagine that while Thomas Jefferson is rolling in his grave, Alexander Hamilton is resting peacefully.

FURTHER READING

Corrado, Anthony. *Campaign Finance Reform: A Sourcebook*. Washington, D.C.: Brookings Institution, 1997.
Corrado, Anthony. "Financing the 1996 Elections," in Gerald M. Pomper, ed., *The Election of 1996*. (Chatham, N.J.: Chatham House, 1997.
Dinkin, Robert J. *Campaigning in America: A History of Election Practices*. Westport, Conn.: Greenwood Press, 1989.
Jackson, Brooks. "Financing the 1996 Campaign: The Law of the Jungle," in Larry J. Sabato, ed., *Toward the Millennium: The Elections of 1996*. Needham Heights, Mass.: Allyn & Bacon, 1997.
Morris, Dwight, and Murielle E. Gamache, *Gold-Plated Politics: The 1992 Congressional Races*. Washington, D.C.: Congressional Quarterly Books, 1994.
Sorauf, Frank J. *Money in American Elections*. Boston: Scott, Foresman/Little Brown, 1988.

NOTES

1. As cited in the Center for Responsive Politics, *A Brief History of Money in Politics* (Washington, D.C.: Center for Responsive Politics, 1995), 4.
2. Roper Center for Public Opinion Research, 1994, as cited in the Center for Responsive Politics, *The Myths about Money in Politics* (Washington, D.C.: Center for Responsive Politics, 1995), 19.
3. Christopher Lehmann, "In the End: Cynical and Proud." *New York Times*, May 12, 1997, 40.
4. Anthony Corrado, "Financing the 1996 Elections," in Gerald M. Pomper, ed., *The Election of 1996* (Chatham, NJ: Chatham House, 1997), 152.
5. Herbert E. Alexander, *Financing Politics: Money, Elections, and Political Reform*, 3rd ed. (Washington, D.C.: Congressional Quarterly Press, 1984), 5–6.
6. Robert J. Dinkin, *Campaigning in America: A History of Election Practices* (Westport, Conn.: Greenwood Press, 1989), 8.
7. Center for Responsive Politics, *A Brief History of Money in Politics* (Washington, D.C.: Center for Responsive Politics, 1995), 3.
8. Ibid.
9. As cited in Dinkin, *Campaigning in America*, 13.
10. Center for Responsive Politics, *A Brief History of Money in Politics*, 3.
11. Frank J. Sorauf, *Money in American Elections* (Boston: Scott, Foresman/Little Brown, 1988), 16.
12. As cited in the Center for Responsive Politics, 3.
13. Richard Hofstadter, *The American Political Tradition* (New York: Knopf, 1948), as cited in Center for Responsive Politics, *A Brief History of Money in Politics*, 5.
14. For an interesting discussion of the role of money in the election of 1896, see Keith Ian Polakoff, *Political Parties in American History* (New York: Wiley, 1981), 259–66.
15. The union leader here is Samuel Gompers, founder and first president of the American Federation of Labor; the senator was Boies Penrose. This quotation is cited in the Center for Responsive Politics, *A Brief History of Money in Politic*, 5. See also George Thayer, *Who Shakes the Money Tree? American Campaign Practices from 1789 to Present* (New York: Simon & Schuster, 1974).
16. The study was conducted by Louise Overtaker, in *Money in Elections* (New York: Macmillan, 1932). See also Frank J. Sorauf, *Money in American Elections*, 16–25.
17. Alexander, *Financing Politics*, 12.
18. Dwight Morris and Murielle E. Gamache, *Gold-Plated Politics: The 1992 Congressional Races* (Washington, D.C.: Congressional Quarterly Books, 1994), 198.
19. Ibid., 199.
20. Ibid.
21. As cited in Philip D. Duncan and Christine C. Lawrence, *Politics in America, 1998* (Washington, D.C.: Congressional Quarterly Press, 1999), 580.
22. Center for Responsive Politics, *The Myths about Money in Politics*, 5.
23. Sorauf, *Money in American Elections*, 32–33.
24. Ibid., 33.

25. Ibid., 35.

26. Ibid., 36.

27. As cited in Mary W. Cohn, editor, *Congressional Campaign Finances: History, Facts, and Controversy* (Washington, D.C.: Congressional Quarterly, 1992), 42.

28. Ibid., 44–46.

29. As cited in Alexander, *Financing Politics*, 38.

30. *Buckley* v. *Valeo*, 424 U.S. I, 44.

31. For an excellent discussion of issue advocacy and its ramifications, see Corrado, "Financing the 1996 Elections," 145–50.

32. Paul S. Herrnson, *Congressional Elections: Campaigning at Home and in Washington* (Washington, D.C.: Congressional Quarterly Press, 1995), 104–9.

33. Norman J. Ornstein, Thomas E. Mann, and Michael J. Malbin, *Vital Statistics on Congress: 1997–1998* (Washington, D.C.: Congressional Quarterly Press, 1999), 108–9.

34. As cited in A. James Reichley, *The Life of the Party: A History of American Political Parties* (New York: Free Press, 1992), 369–70.

35. Norman J. Ornstein, Thomas E. Mann, and Michael J. Malbin, *Vital Statistics on Congress: 1997–1998*, 112.

36. Corrado, "Financing the 1996 Elections," 148.

37. Paul S. Herrnson and Diana Dwyre, "Party Issue Advocacy in Congressional Election Campaigns," in John C. Green and Daniel M. Shea, eds., *The State of the Parties*, 3rd ed. (Lanham, Md.: Rowman and Littlefield, 1999), 86–104.

38. Wilson Scott, "DNC Swaps Funds with State Affiliates: Exchange Increases Latitude in Spending by Avoiding Limits." *Washington Post*, April 24, 1999, A1.

39. Brooks Jackson, "Financing the 1996 Campaign: The Law of the Jungle," in Larry J. Sabato, ed., *Toward the Millennium: The Elections of 1996* (Needham Heights, Mass.: Allyn & Bacon, 1997), 240–41.

40. *The Economist*, May 29, 1999, 26.

CHAPTER 9

Elected Officials: The Reluctant Sales Force of the Party System

On Thanksgiving eve 1994, a buoyant Newt Gingrich drove along the country roads of Georgia with his wife, Marianne. Only two weeks before, House Republicans received 9 million new votes and added fifty-two representatives to their ranks—enough to form a majority for the first time in forty-two years. Not since 1946, the year John F. Kennedy and Richard M. Nixon entered Congress, had there been this many new Republicans. As the car raced along the roadside, an excited Gingrich exclaimed, "This is really a big change!" At this, Marianne turned to her husband and gently reproved him: "You don't have any clue how big this change really is."[1] Six months later the change seemed quite real indeed as House Republicans strutted down the west front steps of the U.S. Capitol while a band played, reporters milled about, and a partisan crowd held small American flags and signs that read, "Contract with America—Promises Made—Promises Kept—Restoring the American Dream." The occasion was to mark the one-hundredth day since Gingrich put the House under new management. At precisely 10:00 A.M., Arizona Congressman J. D. Hayworth stepped to the microphone to serve as master of ceremonies. A former television sportscaster, Hayworth's booming voice reverberated over the sunny Capitol grounds. Seated next to him was a beaming Sonny Bono, the former half of the Sonny and Cher pop music duo and now the duly elected congressman representing Palm Springs, California. Spirits ran high as each speaker took center stage to extol the Contract with America.

The rally's highpoint came when Speaker Gingrich took center stage. Rising to chants of "Newt, Newt!," Gingrich strode to the podium, stared into the bank of television cameras arrayed before him, and declared: "Editorial writers and pundits scoffed. But we did mean it. We made promises and we kept promises."[2] This was not the first time Republicans made promises to act if voters would only give them the authority. In 1980, GOP congressional candidates, together with Ronald Reagan, gathered on the Capitol steps and pledged to cut government spending and promote private investment. One of the organizers of that event dubbed Governing Team Day was a little-known House member from Georgia named Newt Gingrich.

Fourteen years later Gingrich was creating a new sense of team spirit. This time the vehicle he used was the Contract with America signed by 367 Republican House candidates on September 27, 1994, on the very same Capitol steps that once served as a backdrop for Governing Team Day. The contract was a list of ten promises that included among others balancing the budget, overhauling the welfare system, and placing term limits on members of Congress (see "The Parties Speak: The 1994 House Republicans' Contract with America"). If voters would put the Republicans in charge of the House, Gingrich pledged that each item would receive an up or down vote at the conclusion of the first hundred days of the 104th Congress.

The Parties Speak: *The 1994 House Republicans' Contract with America*

Prior to the 1994 midterm elections, Republicans outlined their Contract with America. The GOP promised to introduce and vote on each of the ten bills listed below during the first one hundred days of a Republican-led 104th Congress.

1. **Fiscal Responsibility Act** would propose a constitutional amendment requiring the president to submit, and the Congress to pass, a balanced federal budget for each fiscal year; and would give the president a line-item veto over specific budgetary provisions in a bill passed by Congress.
2. **Taking Back Our Streets Act** would limit federal and state *habeas corpus* appeals; mandate minimum sentences for and victim restitution from those convicted of gun-related crimes; replace recently passed crime-prevention programs with block grants for local law-enforcement programs; relax rules for admission of evidence at criminal trials; and speed deportation procedures for aliens convicted of serious crimes.
3. **Personal Responsibility Act** would limit eligibility for the federal Aid to Families with Dependent Children (AFDC) program; deny AFDC benefits to teenage mothers; impose work requirements for those receiving AFDC benefits; and transfer much of the responsibility for social welfare programs to the states.
4. **Family Reinforcement Act** would grant tax credits for adoption and for care of elderly dependents and increase penalties for sexual offences against children.
5. **American Dream Restoration Act** would grant tax credits for families with children; reduce taxes on some married couples; and expand uses for Individual Retirement Accounts (IRAs).
6. **National Security Restoration Act** would restrict participation of U.S. forces in UN peace-keeping activities; subject all funding for and participation in UN peace-keeping activities to congressional approval; and reinstate development of the "Star Wars" antiballistic missile defense system and other such systems.
7. **Senior Citizens Equity Act** would double the income level beyond which Social Security benefits are reduced; reduce taxes on upper-income recipients of Social Security; and create tax benefits for the purchase of private long-term health care insurance.
8. **Job Creation and Wage Enhancement Act** would cut the capital gains tax; increase the estate tax exemption; and impose additional requirements for and restrictions on federal regulation.
9. **Common Sense Legal Reforms Act** would require the loser to pay the legal expenses of the winner in lawsuits filed in federal courts; reform product liability laws; and limit lawsuits by shareholders against companies whose stock they hold.
10. **Citizen Legislature Act** would propose a constitutional amendment to limit tenure of senators and representatives to a maximum of twelve years.

SOURCE: House Republican Conference, *Legislative Digest*, September 27, 1994.

With seven days to spare, Speaker Gingrich kept his promise. At the pep rally, Republican National Committee (RNC) Chairman Haley Barbour heaped praise on his party's lawmakers for having voted on the ten contract items in an astounding ninety-three days. Such speed, said Barbour, was the by-product of "the most issue-oriented campaign of my lifetime."[3] Indeed, not since Franklin D. Roosevelt's famous first hundred days in 1933 when many of his New Deal measures won congressional approval, had there been this much legislative activity. But while the first ninety-three days of the new Congress had been unusually active, only two contract items—those applying federal labor laws to Congress and a curb on unfunded mandates to the states—had won Senate passage and been signed into law by President Clinton. By the time the 104th Congress adjourned, the remainder of the contract's provisions had been stymied by GOP Senate moderates, vetoed by President Clinton, or declared unconstitutional by the Supreme Court—and the "big change" Gingrich and his wife expected seemed rather small indeed.

There is an adage that says, "Winning is not everything—it's the only thing." Chapters 4 and 7 of this book describe how national, state, and local party organizations use Information Age technologies to win votes. But what happens after the ballots are counted is often even more important. In the United States, the victor in any given election wins an office, but elections alone do not confer power. That often must come from the wily efforts of leaders able to grasp the levers of power and move the creaky machinery of government into action. This is in sharp contrast to **parliamentary systems** where elections confer both office and power. British Prime Minister Tony Blair, for example, won an astounding victory in 1997 when his Labour Party captured 419 seats to just 164 seats for the opposition Conservatives. Blair's landslide did more than make him prime minister, it gave him a strong party platform and the ability to enforce party discipline in the British House of Commons in order to reshape the institutions of British government.

In the **presidential system** devised by the Framers of the U.S. Constitution, presidents and members of Congress cannot rely on their party connections to make things happen. The Framers believed that parties would corrupt leaders and prevent them from doing the right thing. Like most of his compatriots, Alexander Hamilton maintained that if noble citizens gained office, their outstanding characters and concern for the nation's well-being would be enough to allow them to act in the public interest. Defending the Electoral College as a means for choosing a president, Hamilton wrote in the *Federalist Papers* that "there would be a constant probability of seeing the station filled by characters pre-eminent for ability and virtue," adding that "the true test of a government is its aptitude and tendency to produce a good administration."[4] Hamilton's equation of character with the effective administration of the government still appeals to many Americans. Seeking office in 1998, Minnesota Reform Party candidate and ex-wrestler Jesse Ventura cast himself as honest and un-corruptible. When asked how he would fare as governor—especially since the state legislature has one house controlled by the Democrats and another held by the Republicans—Ventura responded: "Well, I think it's an advantage because now you're truly getting a three-prong approach, aren't you? You're getting the head executive to be neutral from the other two parties, and the two parties—one controls the House, one controls the Senate, and I will act as a mediator to bring them together and do what's best for Minnesota and cut out the partisan politicking. And like I said in my campaign, let's put Minnesotans first. There's more of us than there are Democrats and Republicans. And, obviously, I was right, wasn't I?"[5]

While Ventura's answer resonated with Minnesotans, the pages of American history are replete with examples demonstrating that character alone is an insufficient basis for prompting government, with all of its checks and balances, into taking decisive action. During his single term as president, Jimmy Carter was extolled for his honesty and trustworthiness—qualities deemed especially desirable following the Watergate scandal. But Carter's outstanding character did not often translate into effective leadership. When the public was asked in 1985 to rank the nine presidents from Franklin D. Roosevelt to Ronald Reagan, 49 percent gave Carter the dubious honor of being the president "least able to get things done."[6] The separation of powers between the executive, legislative, and judicial branches; the "special interests" that populate Washington, D.C.; and getting 535 members of Congress to agree on anything are huge obstacles to making things happen—as Carter learned to his regret.

THE PRESIDENT AS PARTY LEADER

Historically, political parties have been viewed as necessary mechanisms to make governments of all types work. Local machine mayors, like former Chicago Mayor Richard J. Daley, used parties as instruments to wield power. Likewise, presidents who have understood the value of effective party leadership have, on occasion, been able to overcome the constitutional obstacles placed by the Framers and get government to act. Franklin D. Roosevelt, for example, corralled a wily bunch of congressional Democrats into passing his liberal-oriented New Deal program in a breathtaking one hundred days back in 1933. The legislative pace was so swift that bills were hardly given more than passing consideration as cries of "vote, vote" echoed from the chambers. Nearly five decades later, Ronald Reagan used the Republican Party to effect a conservative change. The "Reagan revolution" cut taxes, raised the federal deficit, and substantially increased defense spending.

Franklin Roosevelt and Ronald Reagan form opposite ends of the ideological spectrum, but most presidents who want to accomplish great things (especially in domestic affairs) have, like them, paid attention to their party. Running for president in 1912, Democrat Woodrow Wilson promised to create a Federal Reserve Board to control the flow of the nation's money supply, a Federal Trade Commission that would rein in corporate interests, workmen's compensation for those injured on the job, and an easing of child labor laws. Wilson won with just 42 percent of the vote but, more significantly, Democrats added seventy-three seats in the House and six in the Senate. Wilson made much of the election results in his inaugural address: "No one can mistake the purpose for which the Nation now seeks to use the Democratic party. It seeks to use it to interpret a change in its own plans and point of view."[7] Likewise, a conservative Republican president, Herbert Hoover, saw his party as an indispensable partner: "We maintain party government not to promote intolerant partisanship but because opportunity must be given for the expression of the popular will, and organization provided for the execution of its mandates. It follows that Government both in the executive and legislative branches must carry out in good faith the platform upon which the party was entrusted with power."[8]

Since the rise of television, Americans have chosen their presidents without paying much attention to their partisan affiliations. Consequently, presidents often feel free to ignore their party-in-government. Bill Clinton, for example, raised large sums of cash for his Democratic Party. Yet, as president, Clinton favored a strategy of triangulation—setting himself above the partisan wrangling when Republicans assumed control of Congress in 1994. In this sense, Clinton emulated Jesse Ventura in his willingness to be a referee in the struggles between himself and an increasingly partisan Congress. While Clinton's strategy of triangulation helped him win reelection in 1996, it produced little of consequential legislation.

THE PARTY IN CONGRESS

While presidents have sometimes attempted to use their party as a way of bringing the executive and legislative branches together, Congress has been incapable of achieving a similar result. Regional diversity and the special interests have often overwhelmed appeals for party loyalty. This has not stopped key legislators from trying to use parties as action-centered instruments of government. Helping them is the fact that parties remain important organizing mechanisms. For example, which side of the aisle one sits in Congress is determined on the basis of party affiliation. Likewise, committee chairmanships are often reserved for the senior party member of a particular committee. Ideological appeals also help bind Democrats and Republicans together. And, as noted in Chapter 4, both parties have established congressional campaign committees that have assumed a growing role in the recruitment and election of members of Congress.

From the outset, congressional parties were an important "extra-constitutional" device that were inserted into the Framers' handiwork. As noted in Chapter 2, the Federalists, led by Alexander Hamilton, were strong supporters of the Jay Treaty while their Democratic-Republican rivals, headed by Thomas Jefferson, were unified in their opposition. As their policy disagreements escalated, party voting became the norm. From the third Congress (1793–1795) to the seventh Congress (1801–1803), Federalist Party unity scores increased from 83.3 percent to 89.9 percent. Likewise, the Democratic-Republicans saw their bloc voting rise from 73.5 percent to 79.6 percent. Looking at this period, political scientist John F. Hoadley writes that party development passed through four distinct stages: (1) factionalism, (2) polarization, (3) expansion, and (4) institutionalization. In the first stage, factions developed and were centered on a variety of disparate issues and charismatic personalities. But these divisions were rarely organized and lasted only a short while. In the second stage, the factions stabilized into permanent groups who opposed each other on a broad range of issues. During the expansion phase, the public was drawn into the partisan arguments. Finally, in the institutionalization phase, a permanent linkage was made between the party organizations, party-in-the-electorate, and the party-in-government.[9] (See Chapters 2 and 3.)

Formalized party structures have developed over the centuries in Congress, as well as in the forty-nine state legislatures. (Nebraska has a nonpartisan unicameral legislature.) Both parties in both houses of Congress meet every two years at the beginning of each congressional session to select its leadership. There are two institutionalized leadership positions, one for each branch of the legislature. Article I of the Constitution states that the House "shall choose their **Speaker**." Interestingly, it does not require that this person be an actual member of the House although all of them have been. The Speaker presides over that chamber, rules on points of order, announces results of votes, refers legislation to committees, names lawmakers to serve on conference committees, and maintains order and decorum. In addition, the Speaker sets the House's agenda, controls the Rules committee, chairs his/her party's committee assignment panel, and can bestow or withhold various tangible and intangible rewards to members of both parties. In sum, the Speaker controls both the political and administrative activities of the House. Both parties nominate candidates for the Speakership, but the majority party's candidate always prevails. It is extremely rare that a member will cross over and support the nominee of the other party.

The next step is for each party to complete their internal party organization. These spots are filled by the entire party membership, or what the Democrats call their "caucus" and the Republicans call their "conference." The **majority leader** is the second-in-command of the majority party, and works closely with the Speaker. The **minority leader,** on the other hand, serves as the head of his or her party in the House. Minority leaders are the "speakers in waiting" should their party become a majority. Congressman Gerald Ford of Michigan, for example, was elected House minority leader in 1965. Ford's ambition was to become Speaker, but instead he was tapped by Richard Nixon in 1973 to serve as vice president following Spiro Agnew's resignation. Nixon's involvement in the Watergate scandal subsequently led to Ford's assuming the presidency a year later. Next are the majority and minority **whips.** Each party uses a variety of whips—ranging from head whip to deputy, at-large, regional, and assistant whips. The whips gather intelligence, encourage attendance at important votes and party events, count votes, persuade colleagues to support party measures, and forge lines of communication between the rank and file and party leaders. The foremost job of a whip is, of course, to encourage party discipline. Two other party positions are the **chair of the policy committees** and the **heads of the campaign committees.** The former is responsible for developing a policy plan for the coming session and the latter for fundraising and distributing party funds during elections.

In the Senate, the Constitution stipulates that the **vice president** serve as the presiding officer and, in the case of a tie, cast the deciding vote. Other than ceremonial occasions and when votes are expected to be very close, the vice president hardly ever sits in session. In the vice president's absence, the Constitution stipulates that a "president pro tempore" preside. Recently, a custom has developed where this officer is the majority party senator with the longest continuous service. Today, that person is ninety-seven-year-old Strom Thurmond, a South Carolina Republican who was first elected to the Senate in 1954, and currently holds the record for the longest period of continuous Senate service. When it comes to the head of the party, the **majority leader** is the head of the majority party in the Senate. For the minority party, the highest post is the **minority leader**. Both are elected biennially by secret ballot. The remaining leadership posts in the Senate is much the same as in the House. There are whip organizations and chairs of policy committees and campaign committees. Table 9.1 notes the leadership of both parties and in both chambers, as of the spring of 1999.

Despite the institutionalization of political parties in the Congress, **party government**—where a political party is the primary instrument for engineering change—has been a rarity during the latter half of the twentieth century. The multitude of viewpoints within both the Democratic and Republican ranks often prohibits both parties from enunciating clear policies. Senate Democrats have a range of views from liberals such as Edward M. Kennedy (Mass.) and Paul Wellstone (Minn.), to the more conservative Ernest Hollings (S.C.). Likewise House Democrats have established liberals such as Barney Frank (Mass.) and Maxine Waters (Calif.) and conservatives such as Gene Taylor (Miss.) and Ralph Hall (Tex.). Republicans have a disparate group in the Senate: moderates such as Lincoln Chafee (R.I.) and Jim Jeffords (Vt.) find it hard to coexist with hardline conservatives such as Jesse Helms (N.C.) and Phil Gramm (Tex.). In the House, there are moderate Republicans such as Constance Morella (Md.) and Christopher Shays (Conn.) who often vote with the Democrats, but their ranks were reduced when the Republican class of 1994 saw the entry of zealous conservatives like Bob Barr (Ga.) and Lindsay Graham (S.C.).

This intraparty diversity has often meant that congressional coalitions have transcended party lines. For example, from 1937 until 1994, Congress was controlled by the **Dixiecrat coalition**—an alliance of conservative Southern Democrats (the Dixiecrats) and old guard Republicans who opposed extending the New Deal. Virginia Democrat Howard Smith was a potent symbol of the Dixiecrat coalition. As chairman of the powerful House Rules Committee, Smith vetoed proposed legislation presented by Democratic presidents and congressional leaders, and actually opposed the elections of John F. Kennedy in 1960 and Lyndon B. Johnson in 1964.

TABLE 9.1 ▪ Party Leadership Position in the U.S. House and Senate, 106th Congress, 1999–2000

House	*Senate*
Speaker: J. Dennis Hastert	**Vice President:** Al Gore
Majority Leader: Dick Armey	**President Pro Tempore:** Strom Thurmond
Majority Whip: Tom DeLay	**Majority Leader:** Trent Lott
Minority Leader: Richard A. Gephardt	**Assistant Majority Leader:** Don Nickles
Democratic Whip: David E. Bonior	**Minority Leader:** Tom Daschle
	Democratic Whip: Harry Reid

When Smith once proclaimed, "I will cooperate with the Democratic leadership of the House of Representatives, just as long and just as far as my conscience will let me," a loud chorus of laughter erupted on the House floor.[10] With Smith and the Dixiecrat-Republicans opposing his legislative agenda, John F. Kennedy (who had served in both the House and Senate) lamented: "The fact is that the Congress looks more powerful sitting here than it did when I was there in Congress. But that is because when you are in Congress you are one of one hundred in the Senate or one of four-hundred-thirty-five in the House. So the power is divided. But from here I look at Congress, particularly the bloc action, and it is a substantial power."[11]

As John Kennedy's frustrations with an intractable Congress demonstrate, only when there are grave national crises, such as the world wars or the Great Depression, or when foreign policies require congressional approval, as was the case during the Cold War, or when there are periods of political abnormality, such as Lyndon Johnson's 1964 landslide following John Kennedy's assassination and Ronald Reagan's 1980 Republican sweep, are party-oriented presidents momentarily able to overcome congressional opposition. The inability of both Democratic and Republican presidents to produce a truly party-oriented government has frustrated political scientists and led them to search for ways of achieving greater party accountability. Those who believed that parties should have a decisive role in making public policy advocate a doctrine commonly referred to as **responsible party government.** Simply put, responsible party government is when the party-in-power manages the government and enacts the program spelled out in its platform. For its part, the opposition party develops alternative policies and makes its case to the voters. The public is asked to judge whether the party in power has done a good job, and which party has the better program for the future.

The doctrine of responsible party government was best expressed in a 1950 report commissioned by the American Political Science Association (APSA) entitled *Toward a More Responsible Two-Party System* (see "The Parties Speak"). This little book was the capstone of a multiyear effort by an APSA-sanctioned Committee on Political Parties consisting of the leading party scholars of that time. After four years of deliberations, *Toward a More Responsible Two-Party System* operated from the following premise: "Throughout this report political parties are treated as indispensable instruments of government."[12] Thus, it followed that if the parties were in trouble, so was our system of government. This is exactly the conclusion the committee reached—noting the doubts that surrounded Democratic President Harry S Truman's ability to lead following the death of Franklin D. Roosevelt, the division of power created by the 1946 elections when Republicans assumed control of both houses of Congress, and the inability of either branch to agree on much-needed civil rights legislation. By the time the report was published, the APSA committee concluded that both parties had disintegrated to the point where they could no longer effectively propose solutions to the problems facing the country. The report warned that unless the party system was overhauled, three disastrous consequences would follow: (1) the assumption of "excessive responsibility to the president," who would have to generate support for new public initiatives through personal efforts without the benefit of party; (2) continued disintegration of both

The Parties Speak: *Toward a More Responsible Two-Party System*

In 1950, the APSA's Committee on Political Parties published Toward a More Responsible Two-Party System. *The report outlined the responsible party argument made by political scientists in the decades following its publication. This excerpt captures the sense of urgency that characterized the thinking of that time.*

For the great majority of Americans, the most valuable opportunity to influence the course of public affairs is the choice they are able to make between the parties in the principal elections. While in an election the party alternative necessarily takes the form of a choice between candidates, putting a particular candidate into office is not an end in itself. The concern of the parties with candidates, elections, and appointments is misunderstood if it is assumed that parties can afford to bring forth aspirants for office without regard to the views of those so selected. Actually, the party struggle is concerned with the direction of public affairs. Party nominations are no more than a means to this end. In short, party politics inevitably involves public policy in one way or another. *In order to keep the parties apart, one must consider the relations between each and public policy. . . . The crux of public affairs lies in the necessity for more effective formulation of general policies and programs and for better integration of all of the far-flung activities of modern government.*

Only large-scale and representative political organizations possess the qualifications needed for these tasks. The ascendancy of national issues in an industrial society, the impact of the widening concern of government with problems of the general welfare, the entrance into the realm of politics of millions of new voters—all of these factors have tended to broaden the base of the parties as the largest political organizations in the country. *It is in terms of party programs that political leaders can attempt to consolidate public attitudes toward the work plans of government. . . .*

Responsibility of the party in power centers on the conduct of the government, usually in terms of policies. The party in power has a responsibility, broadly defined, for the general management of the government, for its manner of getting results, for the results achieved, for the consequences of inaction as well as action, for the intended and unintended outcome of its conduct of public affairs, for all that it plans to do, for all that it might have foreseen, for the leadership it provides, for the acts of all of its agents, and for what it says as well as for what it does.

Party responsibility includes the responsibility of the opposition party, also broadly defined, for the conduct of its opposition, for the management of public discussion, for the development of alternative policies and programs, for the bipartisan policies which it supports, for its failures and successes in developing the issues of public policy, and for its leadership of public opinion. The opposition is as responsible for its record in Congress as is the party in power. It is important that the opposition party be effective but it is equally important that it be responsible, for an irresponsible opposition is dangerous to the whole political system.

SOURCE: Committee on Political Parties, *Toward a More Responsible Two-Party System* (New York: Rinehart, 1950), 15, 16, 22.

major parties caused by their relative ineffectiveness; and (3) a presidential-congressional logjam that "might set in motion more extreme tendencies to the political left and the political right."[13]

In the decades following its publication, *Toward a More Responsible Two-Party System* became required reading for party scholars. Most extolled the report for its analysis of the problems parties faced, and saw the report's warning of a weaker party system fulfilled in a more powerful, but partyless presidency. To commemorate its fiftieth anniversary, the APSA plans a major symposium at its 2000 meeting. But celebrations aside, the APSA committee's work actually stifled a lively debate about the role parties should play in government begun at the turn of the twentieth century. Back then, scholars viewed the responsible party doctrine with considerable skepticism. As one wrote: "This theory [of responsible party government] appeared alluring enough to be adopted by some writers of prominence, and expanded in certain cases, with brilliancy of literary style. It has, however, one defect: it is not borne out by the facts."[14]

Perhaps no better party scholar demonstrated the inexorable movement of political scientists toward accepting the doctrine of responsible party government during the twentieth century than Woodrow Wilson. A prominent political scientist who once served as APSA president, Wilson told the Virginia Bar Association in 1897: "I, for my part, when I vote at a critical election, should like to be able to vote for a definite line of policy with regard to the great questions of the day—not for platforms, which Heaven knows, mean little enough—but for *men* known and tried in public service; with records open to be scrutinized with reference to these very matters; and pledged to do this or that particular thing; to take a definite course of action. As it is, I vote for nobody I can depend upon to do anything—no, not even if I were to vote for myself."[15] A decade later, Wilson saw party-centered government more favorably: "There is a sense in which our parties may be said to have been our real body politic. Not the authority of Congress, not the leadership of the President, but the discipline and zest of parties has held us together, has made it possible for us to form and to carry out national programs."[16]

The doctrine of responsible party government got a powerful grip on the academic community, even as events made the idea of a strong party-in-government less of a possibility. During the forty-year Democratic reign in the House of Representatives (1954–1994), responsible party government had little meaning. Instead of relying on their party to win, Democrats used the tools of incumbency to preserve their offices. Congressional staffs, for example, became a new-style permanent campaign staff—answering mail, acting as ombudsmen, and serving as the "eyes and ears" of the legislator in the district. Between 1967 and 1980, for example, the personal staff allocated to each House member grew by 114 percent.[17] Money also helped Democrats win as PAC directors steered their dollars to incumbents, with a demonstrated ability to win.

Once in Congress, however, Democrats generally were free to ignore their party. Southerners had long abandoned appeals to party loyalty—as exemplified by the emergence of the Dixiecrat coalition. By the 1970s, Democrats began stripping their congressional leaders of the few remaining powers they had left. Following the Watergate-dominated elections of 1974, a crop of newly elected freshman Democrats were determined to substitute party leadership for a more openness. In a surprising move, these Watergate babies deposed three incumbent committee chairs—a repudiation of the once ironclad seniority rule. Moreover, they adopted a **Subcommittee Bill of Rights** that reduced the power of both the Speaker and the committee chairs. These changes allowed committee Democrats to pick their chairs; fix the jurisdictions of subcommittees so that their ability to control certain subjects would not be given to another committee; gave each subcommittee an adequate budget that it controlled; created more staff positions; and guaranteed that members of the full committee would have a right to at least one "choice" subcommittee assignment. These reforms stripped the recalcitrant conservative Southern Dixiecrats, many of whom had accumulated enough seniority to become committee chairs, of their jealously guarded powers to frustrate the Democratic majority. But in so doing, they fragmented power among members who served on an ever-larger number of committees and spent their days literally running from one meeting to another.

By 1994, party leadership in Congress was at a low ebb. A series of relatively weak Democratic speakers were held hostage by recalcitrant committee chairs who were quite willing to resist demands for party loyalty. Bill Clinton, who had high hopes that unified Democratic Party control of the presidency and Congress would result in significant legislative accomplishments, found his hopes dashed when his health care initiative went down in flames. Even Clinton's much-touted economic recovery program—the basis for his 1992 election and his promise to focus on the economy "like a laser beam"—barely won House approval and was passed by the Senate only after Vice President Al Gore cast the decisive tie-breaking vote. Democrats limped into the 1994 midterm contests, hoping that history would prevail yet again and incumbents—meaning Democrats—would be reelected. It was not to be.

THE CONTRACT WITH AMERICA

The Republican takeover of the 104th Congress following the 1994 midterm election was more than a mere shift from one party to another. The incoming seventy-three Republican freshmen differed significantly from their predecessors in both style and ideological persuasion. Stylistically, many saw themselves as "citizen politicians"—dispatched by their constituents to Washington, D.C., for a brief period before coming home. In this respect, they were throwbacks to the nineteenth century when most House members served just a single term. Abraham Lincoln, for example, spent two years in Congress (1847–1849) before returning to Springfield, Illinois, to resume his law practice. Thus, when many of the Republican freshmen endorsed a six-year term limit, it was to ensure that they would never become "beltway insiders." To further fortify themselves from becoming too comfortable, many of the Republican newcomers chose to live in their congressional offices—sleeping on their couches by night and showering in the House gymnasium by day. This practice differentiated them from their predecessors whose families lived year-round in the nation's capital. During the 1960s, for example, House Minority Leader Gerald Ford had a home in Alexandria, Virginia, where he resided with his wife, Betty, and their children. Once, President Lyndon Johnson called from the White House during a Thanksgiving recess and thought he had reached Ford in Michigan only to discover that he was just a few miles away.[18]

But it was in their politics that these freshmen were truly different. Motivated by conservative principles, the 1994 class of House Republicans was especially responsive to pleas to keep the faith when it came to implementing their Contract with America. As noted, the contract consisted of ten poll-tested items that included balancing the federal budget, tough anti-crime measures, a line-item veto for the president, welfare reform, and tax cuts targeted at families (see "The Parties Speak on p. 238). Of thirty-three House roll calls taken in 1995 on contract-related items, House GOP members were unanimous on sixteen. For the entire series of roll calls, the median number of Republican dissents was one.[19] On average, 97 percent of the Republican freshmen voted in lockstep with their party, and no one fell below 90 percent.[20] Such uniform party voting is more common in parliamentary democracies such as Great Britain or in the old communist regimes that once controlled the Soviet Union.

The contract gave Speaker Newt Gingrich an opportunity to assume powers that none of his Democratic predecessors dared imagine. He twice passed over Carlos Morehead, the ranking Republican on the Judiciary and Commerce committees, in favor of Gingrich loyalists Henry Hyde and Thomas Bliley. As Judiciary Chairman Hyde candidly admitted, "I'm really a sub-chairman. . . . I am a transmission belt for the leadership."[21] But Gingrich's most famous promotion was that of Robert Livingston, who was fifth in seniority to head the Appropriations Committee. Just to make sure that everyone knew who controlled this all-important committee, Gingrich required each Republican member to sign a "letter of fidelity" that gave the speaker the final say over how much the federal budget would be cut. In addition, Gingrich abolished three committees that had been liberal Democratic bastions: District of Columbia, Merchant Marine and Fisheries, and Post Office and Civil Service. Others were renamed to fit the new GOP-led conservative agenda. The Education and Labor Committee became Economic and Educational Opportunities, Government Operations became Government Reform and Oversight, and Public Works and Transportation became Transportation and Infrastructure. As one Republican put it: "The old names implied a desire to perpetuate and expand the size and scope of government. The new names were needed to put our *imprimatur* on Congress and indicate the direction in which we're taking the institution."[22]

Gingrich also gave his freshmen firebrands unusual access to the inner circles of power. In a highly irregular move, the so-called exclusive committees of the House—Rules, Ways and Means, and Appropriations—got new freshmen members over the objections of their Republican chairs. Usually, members have to wait several terms before securing these plum assignments. Three newcomers were assigned to the Ways and Means Committee, which deals with taxation, seven were placed on the Appropriations Committee, which controls the federal budget, and one was put on the Rules Committee, which has jurisdiction over the business of the House. As one grateful recipient observed: "Newt really enjoys seeing some of us work because he sees the same rabble-rouser that he was a few years ago. Without Newt, the class wouldn't be such a dynamic class. Newt Gingrich asks: 'What do the freshmen think?' And he's giving us more than anyone else would have."[23] Such largesse paid off handsomely. In less than one hundred days, eight of the contract's ten items had been approved by the House thanks to near-unanimous support from the GOP freshmen. Only two measures failed: term limits, thanks to the opposition of Judiciary Committee Chairman Henry Hyde, and a provision prohibiting the Pentagon from using funds for UN peace-keeping operations.

Thus, for a brief moment it appeared that House Republicans had constructed a party-in-government akin to the responsible party that political scientists had long desired. But there was a difference: this parliamentary-like system did not include the voters. Prior to the 1994 elections, 71 percent said they had never heard of the Contract with America. Of those who knew something about it, only 15 percent said it made a difference in how they voted.[24] As one Republican ruefully admitted: "Most of the voters in my district didn't have a clue about it. But I did like the idea of writing down what I stood for and the voters later holding me accountable."[25]

Indeed, the Republican takeover of Congress culminated a rise in party-centered voting that began during the 1980s. Many Republicans were captivated by Ronald Reagan who led a large, activist, conservative following. During the 1990s, the Reaganites were succeeded by religious-minded conservatives who had strong antiabortion, antigay, and antigun control beliefs.

Democrats, too, became more ideologically liberal, given their bitter opposition to Ronald Reagan's assault on Lyndon Johnson's Great Society and other Democratic-sponsored government programs. The exit of southern conservatives from the party's congressional ranks, and the introduction of social and cultural issues (such as abortion and gay rights), transformed congressional Democrats into a far more homogeneous group. House Minority Leader Dick Gephardt exemplified the transition. First elected in 1976, Gephardt styled himself as a different kind of Democrat who did not represent the old New Deal liberalism. He supported Ronald Reagan's 1981 tax cut and voted for Reagan's tax reform plan in 1986. Gephardt differed with many of his fellow House Democrats on such hot-button issues as abortion, busing, and raising the minimum wage. But when Gephardt climbed the party leadership ladder in the House, his positions began to change. He altered his stance on abortion from pro-life to pro-choice and supported minimum wage increases. In 1993, Gephardt was a strong supporter of the big government–oriented Clinton health care plan. But Gephardt later joined with his fellow Democrats in opposing Clinton on the North American Free Trade Agreement (NAFTA), fast-track trade legislation, welfare reform, and the balanced-budget agreement Clinton reached with House Republicans. In each case, Clinton had to settle for an accommodation with the majority House Republicans at the expense of his own party.

Negative campaigns have added to the growing ideological polarization in Congress, as well as in state legislatures. In their book *Going Negative: How Political Advertisements Shrink and Polarize the Electorate*, Stephen Ansolabehere and Shanto

Iyengar maintain that contemporary electioneering has alienated less partisan voters, leading to a highly party-oriented group of elected officials: "The hostile tenor of political campaigns contributes in no small part to the disaffection of the independent voter. . . . As their base of support becomes more partisan (or at the least less independent and centrist) members of Congress will work harder to represent those partisan interests."[26]

Clearly, ideological purists from both parties have altered the way Congress conducts its business. Those who once subscribed to the late Democratic House Speaker Sam Rayburn's wisdom that the best way to "get along" in Congress is to "go along" suddenly found themselves in the minority. House Minority Leader Bob Michel, an old-school Republican who was often chummy with his Democratic colleagues, first spotted the change. Of the forty-seven GOP newcomers elected in 1992, Michel concluded that "seven are thoughtful moderates, and the other forty are pretty darn hardliners, some of them really hardline."[27] The Republican class of 1994 was even more zealous. Arizona freshman John Shadegg said his colleagues were not "interested in coming here to be reasonable and to settle for what they can get. They don't want to go along to get along." Matt Salmon, another Arizona newcomer, agreed: "This is an ideological class . . . that really believes we were sent here to make a difference."[28]

Liberal Democrats were also more apt to place their ideology on display. During the 105th Congress (1997–1998), the House Judiciary Committee was a microcosm of the increased presence of Democratic liberals eager to battle conservative Republican ideologues. Of the sixteen Judiciary Committee Democrats, there were eleven northerners, six Jews, five blacks, three women, and one declared homosexual. Rich Boucher, a Virginia Democrat, was the lone white, male, southern Protestant. Together, they sided with the liberal interest group Americans for Democratic Action 90 percent of the time.[29] For their part, Republicans stacked the Judiciary Committee with conservative white Christian men, the single exception being Mary Bono who replaced her late husband, Sonny, on the committee. Eleven of the twenty-one committee Republicans hailed from the South.

Because the Judiciary Committee deals with such hot-button issues as abortion, school busing, civil rights, and the death penalty, ideological polarization has increased since members find the committee a convenient forum to advance their social agendas. Democrat Maxine Waters is a case in point. Representing Watts and South Central Los Angeles, Waters used her rhetorical wrath against GOP-backed legislation to crack down on criminals. As she once stated, "I don't have time to be polite."[30] Opposing her were two conservative committee Republicans: Bob Barr of Georgia and Lindsey Graham of South Carolina. Barr believed that conservatives must declare war on big government: "It's really come to the point of no return with government taking so much power. I really have a tremendous fear of government taking away our freedoms."[31] But when it came to social issues, Barr favored more government supervision—sponsoring the Defense of Marriage Act, which banned homosexual marriages. Graham is a long-time advocate of conservative causes ranging from term limits to opposing gays in the military. During his 1994 campaign, Graham made his opposition to Clinton clear: "I'm one less vote for an agenda that makes you want to throw up."[32]

Perhaps no issue has divided the Judiciary Committee more than the impeachment proceedings launched against President Clinton following his admission of an "inappropriate" relationship with former White House intern Monica Lewinsky. When Chairman Henry Hyde stepped before television cameras to announce that a bipartisan decision on the impeachment ground rules had been reached, Democrat Barney Frank interjected, "If this is bipartisanship, the Taliban wins a medal for religious tolerance."[33] Ranking Democrat John Conyers agreed, stating that the public was not threatened by Clinton's extramarital affair; instead it was endangered by the "tactics of a win-at-all-costs prosecutor [Kenneth Starr] determined to sink a president of the opposition party." Conservative Republican Bill McCollum countered: "When people believe that the president of the United States can lie, commit perjury, and get away with it, what are they going to say the next time they have to go to court?"[34]

In December 1998, the Judiciary Committee debated four articles of impeachment. Article One stated that President Clinton provided "perjurious, false and misleading testimony" before Independent Counsel Kenneth Starr's grand jury. Article Two charged Clinton with lying in a deposition he gave to Paula Jones's lawyers. Article Three accused Clinton of obstructing justice so as to "delay, impede, cover up, and conceal the existence of evidence" related to the Jones case. Finally, Article Four claimed Clinton lied to Congress in his answers to eighty-one questions posed by the Judiciary Committee. The Judiciary Committee approved three of the four impeachment articles on a straight party-line vote, twenty-one to sixteen. Only Republican Lindsey Graham dissented from supporting Article Two (see "The Parties Speak: The House Judiciary Committee and the Question of Impeachment").

The impeachment debate is the latest manifestation of the growing partisanship that afflicts all members of Congress covering a wide variety of issues. For four decades, *Congressional Quarterly* has traced the number of roll calls where a majority of Democrats has opposed a majority of Republicans. In 1970, for example, Republicans held together 59 percent of the time; Democrats, 57 percent. The Reagan years saw an increase in party unity, with Republicans holding together 75 percent of the time; Democrats, 79 percent in 1985. This rise in party unity scores was not surprising given Reagan's strong conservative beliefs. But after the Republicans took control of the Congress, party harmony reached record levels. In 1995, 91 percent of Republicans in both chambers of Congress voted alike, as did 80 percent of Democrats. In 1998, party unity scores remained high with 86 percent of Republicans and 83 percent of Democrats toeing the party line (see Table 9.2). Regional party unity scores also were unusually high. In the Senate, northern and southern Republicans supported their party 84 percent and 91 percent, respectively. Among Senate Democrats, northerners had an 88 percent record of support and southerners were not far behind with 83 percent. The relative lack of regional differentiation was also evident in the House. In 1998, northern and southern Republicans backed their party 84 and 88 percent of the time, while northern and southern Democrats had party unity scores of 85 percent and 74 percent, respectively.[35] Such percentages are more evocative of parliamentary democracies where party discipline remains high than in presidential systems such as the United States.

The Parties Speak: *The House Judiciary Committee*
and the Question of Impeachment

In December 1998, the House Judiciary Committee voted along partisan lines to refer four articles of impeachment following publication of Independent Counsel Kenneth Starr's report. The following are excerpts from the Judiciary Committee's debate on impeachment.

F. James Sensenbrenner (R-Wis.): To me, making a false statement under oath to a criminal grand jury is an impeachable offense, period. . . . The truth is the truth, and a lie is a lie, no matter who says it. And no amount of legal hair-splitting can obscure that fact.

John Conyers, Jr. (D-Mich.): Most Americans believe that their personal sex life is personal and should not serve as a basis for a wide-ranging criminal investigation of themselves or any citizen and yes, not even the president. It should not serve as the foundation for overturning the will of the American people to a twice-elected, popular and successful president.

Bill McCollum (R-Fla.): If he has committed these crimes and is not impeached, a terrible message will go out across the country that will undermine the integrity of our court system. We will not only send the message that there is a double standard and that the president of the United States is above the law in these matters, but also a message that these crimes are not as serious as some people once thought they were. More people in the future will likely commit perjury in the courts than would be the case if the president were impeached.

Barney Frank (D-Mass.): After many years of investigations by every possible investigative tool of the federal government, congressional committees, the FBI under the command of the independent counsel, we have the following charge against Bill Clinton. He had a private, consensual sexual affair and lied about it. Let's be very clear that that is what we are talking about.

Charles T. Canady (R-Fla.): Unfortunately, the president's sins led him to commit crimes. His sins led him to engage in a calculated and sustained pattern of lying under oath and obstructing the due administration of justice. And that, indeed, is the proper subject of our inquiry.

Jerrold Nadler (D-N.Y.): The effect of impeachment is to overturn the popular will of the voters as expressed in a national election. We must not overturn an election and remove a president from office except to defend our very system of government or our constitutional liberties against a dire threat.

SOURCE: "We Stand Poised on the Edge of a Constitutional Cliff," *Washington Post*, December 11, 1998, A28.

THE RISE OF THE PUBLIC SPEAKERSHIP

One obvious consequence of the Republican takeover of the House has been a more visible Speakership. Newt Gingrich's public recognition was at a level unequaled by his immediate predecessors and his successor, J. Dennis Hastert. Indeed, during the long reign of Democratic rule, Speakers often ceded much of their power to committee chairs—many of them conservative Southern Democrats—who were the

TABLE 9.2 ▪ **Party Unity Average Scores in Both Chambers of Congress, 1963–1998 (in percents)**

Year	Republicans	Democrats
1963	72	71
1964	69	67
1965	70	69
1966	67	61
1967	71	66
1968	63	57
1969	62	62
1970	59	57
1971	66	62
1972	64	57
1973	68	68
1974	62	63
1975	70	69
1976	66	65
1977	70	67
1978	67	64
1979	72	69
1980	70	68
1981	76	69
1982	71	72
1983	74	76
1984	72	74
1985	75	79
1986	71	78
1987	74	81
1988	73	79
1989	73	81
1990	74	81
1991	78	81
1992	78	81
1993	84	85
1994	83	83
1995	91	80
1996	87	80
1997	88	82
1998	86	83

SOURCE: "Party Unity Background," *Congressional Quarterly Weekly Report*, January 9, 1999, 92.

undisputed "kings of the hill." This suited most Speakers, as many of them were old-style operatives who worked behind closed doors. Sam Rayburn, one of the most powerful of the Democratic Speakers, had his famous "Board of Education" where favored members would gather to discuss pending business and make deals over bourbon and branch water. Once when asked to appear on a Sunday talk show,

Rayburn responded: "I do appreciate your wanting me to be on *Meet the Press*, but I never go on programs such as yours. . . . The trouble about my going on one program is then I would have no excuse to say to the others that I could not go on their program. It is a chore that I have never relished and one that I doubt would be any good. . . . I would have to tell you what I tell all the others, and that is that I do not go on these programs."[36]

John McCormack and Carl Albert were far less powerful Speakers, yet like Rayburn they were ineffectual party spokesmen. In 1969, McCormack was mentioned on the three network evening television newscasts (CBS, NBC, and ABC) a mere seventeen times.[37] Media inquiries were so few that McCormack did not even bother hiring a press secretary. Carl Albert got a press secretary, but still refrained from assuming a public role. Thomas P. "Tip" O'Neill was much more visible, but his heightened recognition was due to a unique political situation: Republican control of the presidency and U.S. Senate in 1980—leaving O'Neill as the only viable Democratic party spokesman. Thus, in 1984 O'Neill was cited 168 times on the big three network evening news programs.[38] His successor, Jim Wright, sought O'Neill's visibility, but became much better known thanks to Newt Gingrich's charge that Wright had violated congressional ethics rules. Wright resigned and was succeeded by Democrat Tom Foley. Although Foley appeared on the various Sunday talk shows, he was eclipsed by other Democratic party spokespersons—most notably President Clinton.

All that changed with Newt Gingrich. In 1995, for the first time in history, the House Speaker delivered a nationally televised address to the American people. The following June, Gingrich shared a stage with President Clinton in a small New Hampshire town to debate the issues. Television, which had transformed the presidency, was now working its magic on Congress. Gingrich became the first public Speaker in memory, as he freely acknowledged: "Each generation produces its own style of being effective. The most accurate statement of how I see the Speakership [is] somebody who could somehow combine grassroots organizations, mass media, and legislative detail into one synergistic pattern."[39] Gingrich redesigned the Speaker's office to accommodate his desire to "go public" by creating four media-oriented staff positions: press secretary, deputy press secretary, press assistant, and communications coordinator. Unlike his predecessors, Gingrich had little appetite for the machinations of the House floor—preferring to leave those duties to his number two man, Majority Leader Dick Armey.

The effects of the new public Speakership were immediate. During the first three months of the 104th Congress, Gingrich was mentioned in 114 stories that ran on the three network nightly news programs, and was six times more likely than his Democratic predecessor, Tom Foley, to appear on these news shows. NBC congressional correspondent Lisa Myers gave Gingrich a thumbs-up review: "Newt is the star. Newt's setting the agenda." Kenan Block, a producer for public television's *MacNeil/Lehrer's NewsHour*, agreed: "Speaker Gingrich is surrounded by people who are incredibly sophisticated about how to use the media and how to use television." Refusing to seek the presidency in 1996, Gingrich declared, "I hardly need to run for president to get my message out."[40]

An old saying has it that "imitation is the sincerest form of flattery." Democrats paid attention to Gingrich's skilled use of the media during the early months of his Speakership and emulated his tactics, if not his style. House Minority Whip David Bonior (D-Mich.)—a Gingrich nemesis—described his job this way: "My new role will not only be counting the votes by which we are going to lose. My role will be to emphasize the message which we are trying to convey to the American people."[41] Toward that end, Democrats established a communications team that coordinated appearances on the House floor by party members and ensured that each Democrat "stayed on message." Today, both congressional parties have message groups and communication strategy teams. Former House Republican Conference Chair John Boehner justified the need for having large communications staffs, "It's not what you're doing but the perceptions that are so important."[42]

The Internet has become an important tool for all party leaders in Congress to get their message out. Gingrich's successor as Speaker, Dennis Hastert, has his own homepage, as does Minority Leader Dick Gephardt. Each seeks to tell his side of the party story to a Web-connected audience (see Figures 9.1 and 9.2). Increasingly, the World Wide Web has also become a forum for important Congress-related stories. For example, the sexual indiscretions of Louisiana Republican Bob Livingston were conveyed over the Internet before *Hustler* publisher Larry Flynt made them public. These revelations caused Livingston to forego the Speakership in 1998 after being designated to lead by the Republican team.

HAMILTON'S CONGRESS?

The fall of Newt Gingrich following the 1998 elections marked the last chapter of the Republican revolution. The gain of five Democratic House seats marked the first time since 1934 that the president's party added to its members in an off-year election. Gingrich tried to put the best face on the results: "For the first time in seventy years, the Republicans are going to retain control of the House for a third term. Every chairmanship will be a Republican, the agenda will be Republican. . . . I think in that sense, it's a big victory."[43] But the returns told a far different story. Several of the Republican revolutionaries from the class of 1994 had been defeated for reelection or in campaigns for other offices, while only one Democratic incumbent was beaten at the polls. Moreover, in assessing Gingrich, voters took a dismal view: 58 percent had a negative impression of him; only 36 percent were positive.[44] Representative Lindsey Graham (R-S.C.) gave Gingrich his final epitaph: "His shining moment may forever remain the day that the polls closed in November 1994."[45]

The fall of Newt Gingrich also meant the end of any semblance of responsible party government. In 1998, virtually no Republican seeking reelection mentioned the Contract with America. In fact, Republicans had long ago consigned the contract to the dustbin of history after discovering that governing meant making compromises with a Democratic president. This left many Republican conservatives profoundly disenchanted. As one of them stated: "My point of view is one of disgust. I don't think our leadership has the courage to make us take tough votes."[46]

> **FIGURE 9.1** ■ House Speaker Dennis Hastert's Web site contains daily press releases on topics under congressional consideration and invites respondents to e-mail the Speaker.

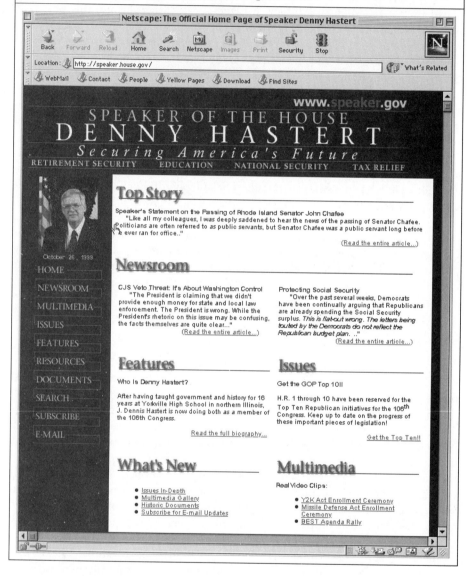

Even some political scientists were rethinking the responsible party doctrine. Nelson Polsby thought that the Contract with America had created a destructive partisanship: "The trouble began when we political scientists finally got our wish—'responsible' political parties instead of broad, nonideological coalitions. The idea was, of course, completely nuts from the start."[47]

FIGURE 9.2 ▪ House Minority Leader Richard Gephardt's Web site includes statements issued by the Democratic Caucus and speeches by Congressman Gephardt, and also solicits views from cyberspace surfers.

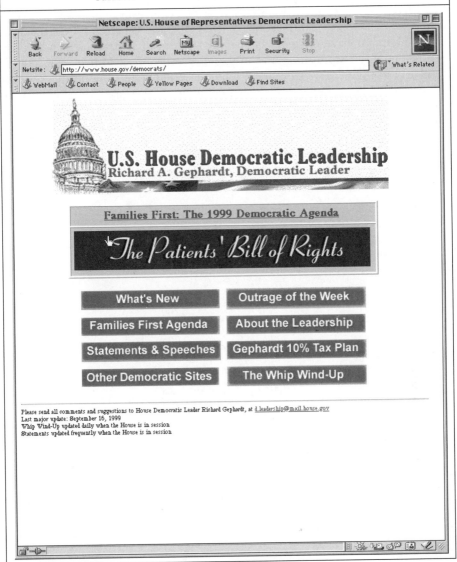

Increased partisanship hit a high-water mark in 1998 when the House of Representatives approved two of four articles of impeachment against President Clinton. Ninety-eight percent of House Republicans supported Article One, accusing Clinton of lying before a federal grand jury; 88 percent passed Article Two, which claimed that Clinton gave false testimony in his deposition in the Paula Jones case;

95 percent approved Article Three, which charged Clinton with obstruction of justice; and 64 percent backed Article Four, which stated that Clinton had abused his office. Democrats were just as united: 98 percent voted nay on the first three articles and 99 percent rejected the fourth (see Table 9.3).

In the U.S. Senate, partisanship was also much in evidence. Sitting as a court of impeachment, party identification overtook whatever penchant for dispassionate judgment might have existed. On the two articles of impeachment before the Senate—perjury before the grand jury and obstruction of justice—not a single Democrat voted to convict President Clinton. Republicans were nearly as united: 45 of the 55 Senate Republicans voted guilty on the perjury charge and 50 said Clinton was guilty of obstructing justice. In each instance, Republican defectors included northeast moderates whose electorates were strongly supportive of Clinton, who had twice carried their states (Arlen Specter, Pennsylvania; John Chafee, Rhode Island; James Jeffords, Vermont; Olympia Snowe and Susan Collins, Maine). Although the Senate conducted the impeachment trial with considerable

---

TABLE 9.3 ▪ House Vote on Articles to Impeach President Clinton

Article/Party	Yes	No	Not Voting
Article One			
Republicans	223	5	
Democrats	5	200	1
Independent*		1	
Total	228	206	
Article Two			
Republicans	200	28	
Democrats	5	200	1
Independent*		1	
Total	205	229	
Article Three			
Republicans	216	12	
Democrats	5	199	2
Independent*		1	
Total	221	212	
Article Four			
Republicans	147	81	
Democrats	1	203	2
Independent*		1	
Total	148	285	

*Refers to Representative Bernard Sanders, a Vermont Socialist, who often votes with the Democrats.

dignity, partisanship remained the key factor in the Senate's decision to allow Clinton to finish his term.

The demise of the Dixiecrat-Republican coalition in Congress and its replacement with highly charged partisanship has met with a general public revulsion. During the impeachment debate, House Minority Leader Richard Gephardt called for an end to "the politics of personal destruction": "We are now rapidly descending into a politics where life imitates farce. Fratricide dominates our public debate and America is held hostage with tactics of smear and fear. We need to start healing. We need to start binding up our wounds. We need to end this downward spiral which will culminate in the death of representative democracy."[48] Republican representative Bob Livingston also pleaded for harmony: "I very much regret the enmity and hostility that has been bred in the halls of Congress for the last months and year. I want so very much to pacify and cool our raging tempers and return to an era when differences were confined to the debate; not to a personal attack or assassination of character."[49]

But the Republican-led votes to impeach and convict Bill Clinton are signs that partisanship remains strong—even though the GOP may have endangered its House majority in 2000. It is clear that the public strongly disapproves of how Republicans have handled the impeachment issue. On the eve of the House vote, 61 percent were opposed to impeaching Clinton, and 74 percent said that "political events in Washington are out of control."[50] The public was equally unhappy with the Republican-controlled U.S. Senate. Fifty-six percent disapproved of its handling of the trial; just 37 percent approved. These figures translate into significant advantages for Democrats on issues ranging from Social Security, education, and health care. By a margin of 50 percent to 33 percent, respondents said Democrats have better ideas for solving the nation's problems. Even on issues long-considered the province of Republicans, like reducing taxes and curbing crime, Democrats run even with the Republicans. Only when asked which party could better uphold traditional moral values did the GOP have a decisive advantage.[51]

Given such poor showings in the public opinion polls, Republicans have tried to cast themselves as heroes by their willingness to impeach Clinton. During the Senate trial, the House managers repeatedly described themselves as lonely defenders of the "rule of law." Henry Hyde, chairman of the Judiciary Committee and chief manager, captured the feelings of House Republicans when he told the Senate: "Equal justice under the law is what moves me and animates me and consumes me. And I'm willing to lose my seat any day in the week rather than sell out on those issues. Despite all the polls and the hostile editorials, America is hungry for people who believe in something. You may disagree with us, but we believe in something."[52]

Hyde's statement is representative of a long-held belief that members of Congress should act as **trustees** who vote their consciences, and ignore the pleas of either their party or the voters to do otherwise. Such a view is juxtaposed to the **delegates** who see themselves as duty-bound to vote the way folks back home want them to. Alexander Hamilton believed that the best representatives were trustees who acted in the national interest. Writing in the *Federalist Papers*, Hamilton derided "the little arts of popularity"[53]—a dig at those who paid too much attention to the public opinion polls of their day. Thomas Jefferson was much more sensitive to the need of lawmakers to pay attention to the folks back home—no doubt one reason why he was elected president and Hamilton was not. Given his predilection for viewing the country as a diverse collection of communities, Jefferson believed that legislators should act as delegates. In 1825, he wrote that the "salvation of the republic" rested on the regeneration and spread of devices like the New England town meeting.[54]

Ironically, though the Republican takeover of the Congress has been accompanied by a call to transfer power from the federal government to the states, a throughly Jeffersonian view; when it comes to the method of representation, it is Hamilton's concept of trustees that has prevailed among Republicans. But Hamilton's trusteeship has come at a price. In addition to their poor showings in the public opinion polls, the trustee-like congressional Republicans are less willing to defer to their leaders. The post-Gingrich Speakership is stripped of the powers he once amassed. The downsizing of the Speakership was foretold in an impertinent letter sent to Gingrich by his initial successor, Bob Livingston. After the 1998 midterm disaster, Livingston made the following demands upon Gingrich:

- I, as Chairman of the Appropriations Committee, shall run the Committee as I see fit and in the best interest of the Republican majority, with full consultation with the Leadership, but without being subject to the dictates of any other Member of Congress.
- That I be the final authority to determine content of legislation within the Appropriations Committee and the schedule under which legislation is produced, without interference.
- I, as Appropriations Chairman, shall be present in all Leadership discussions of the budget affecting Appropriations matters. No decisions on Appropriations issues will be made within the context of budget negotiations without consultation (and not necessarily approval) with me.
- No Member or Subcommittee Chairman will be removed from my committee or from their post on my committee without my approval.
- No Republican will be assigned to the Appropriations Committee without my approval.
- I, as Chairman of the Appropriations Committee, during last-minute negotiations with Democrats or with representatives of the White House on all appropriations bills, will make all final decisions, but with full consultation with the leadership.[55]

J. Dennis Hastert, Gingrich's successor, is not the prominent figure that Gingrich was. One reason is the slender five-vote majority Hastert has to work with—the smallest since 1952. This means that Hastert must be a conciliatory figure in order to accomplish anything—often working together with opposing Democrats behind closed doors. In addition, like his Democratic predecessors, Hastert is a backroom pol who never had much media exposure or aspired to the spotlight. This is quite different from Newt Gingrich as Hastert readily admits:

"Newt was a visionary. He was articulate. He had his own ideas, and I mean he was on TV a lot. My job is to make sure that we can put the right people in the spotlight to get the job done. I guess that's part of going back to my old coaching career, where we made stars out of a lot of people, but I was never in the spotlight much myself. That's how I see this job."[56]

Thus, for the second time in a decade, the stage has been set for a redefinition of power within the House. This restructuring is likely to affirm a primary theme of this chapter: elected officials have, once again, become the reluctant sales force of the American party system.

FURTHER READING

Committee on Political Parties. *Toward a More Responsible Two-Party System.* New York: Rinehart, 1950.

Gingrich, Newt. *Lessons Learned the Hard Way.* New York: HarperCollins, 1998.

Hoadley, John F. "The Emergence of Political Parties in Congress, 1789–1803." *American Political Science Review* 74 (1980).

Killian, Linda. *The Freshmen: What Happened to the Republican Revolution?* Boulder, Colo.: Westview Press, 1998.

Rae, Nicol C. *Conservative Reformers: The Republican Freshmen and the Lessons of the 104th Congress.* Armonk, N.Y.: Sharpe, 1998.

NOTES

1. Newt Gingrich, *Lessons Learned the Hard Way* (New York: HarperCollins, 1998), 1, 2.
2. Quoted in Linda Killian, *The Freshmen: What Happened to the Republican Revolution?* (Boulder, Colo.: Westview Press, 1998), 7.
3. Ibid., 4.
4. Alexander Hamilton, "Federalist 68," in Alexander Hamilton, James Madison, and John Jay, *The Federalist Papers* (New York: Mentor Books, 1961), 414.
5. Jesse Ventura, *Meet the Press,* November 8, 1998.
6. Louis Harris and Associates, poll, April 1–3, 1985.
7. Woodrow Wilson, "Inaugural Address," Washington, D.C., March 4, 1913.
8. Quoted in Stanley Kelley, Jr., *Interpreting Elections* (Princeton, N.J.: Princeton University Press, 1983), 127.
9. See John F. Hoadley, "The Emergence of Political Parties in Congress, 1789–1803," *American Political Science Review* 74, (1980): 761, 768–69.
10. Quoted in Tom Wicker, *JFK and LBJ: The Influence of Personality on Politics* (Baltimore: Penguin Books, 1968), 58.
11. Quoted in Dale Vinyard, *The Presidency* (New York: Scribner's, 1971), 107.
12. Committee on Political Parties, *Toward a More Responsible Two-Party System* (New York: Rinehart, 1950), 15.
13. Ibid., 92, 94, 95.
14. M. I. Ostrogorski, *Democracy and the Party System* (New York: Macmillan, 1910), 380.
15. Woodrow Wilson, "Leaderless Government," an address before the Virginia Bar Association, August 4, 1897, in *Public Papers,* vol. 1, 336–59. Quoted in Austin Ranney, *The Doctrine of Responsible Party Government: Its Origins and Present State* (Urbana: University of Illinois Press, 1954), 33. The emphasis is Wilson's.
16. Quoted in David E. Price, *Bringing Back the Parties* (Washington, D.C.: Congressional Quarterly Press, 1984), 103.

17. See Randall B. Ripley and Grace A. Franklin, *Congress, the Bureaucracy, and Public Policy* (Homewood, Ill.: Dorsey Press, 1984), 45.

18. See Michael R. Beschloss, *Taking Charge: The Johnson White House Tapes, 1963–1964* (New York: Simon & Schuster, 1997), 64.

19. Gerald M. Pomper, "Parliamentary Government in the United States?," in John C. Green and Daniel M. Shea, eds., *The State of the Parties: The Changing Role of Contemporary American Parties* (Lanham, Md.: Rowman and Littlefield, 1999), 260.

20. See John H. Aldrich and David W. Rohde, "The Transition to Republican Rule in the House: Implications for Theories of Congressional Politics," *Political Science Quarterly*, 112, (Winter 1997–1998): 563.

21. Quoted in John E. Owens, "The Return of Party Government in the U.S. House of Representatives," *American Political Science Review*, 27, (April 1997): 245.

22. Nicol C. Rae, *Conservative Reformers: The Republican Freshmen and the Lessons of the 104th Congress* (Armonk, N.Y.: Sharpe, 1998), 69.

23. Ibid., 70–71.

24. See Killian, *The Freshmen*, 6.

25. Quoted in Rae, *Conservative Reformers*, 44.

26. Stephen Ansolabehere and Shanto Iyengar, *Going Negative: How Political Advertisements Shrink and Polarize the Electorate* (New York: Free Press, 1995), 113.

27. Quoted in Aldrich and Rohde, "The Transition to Republican Rule in the House," 561.

28. Ibid., 562.

29. Adam Cohen, "We Fight Like Cats and Dogs," *Time*, September 28, 1998.

30. Quoted in Michael Barone and Grant Ujifusa, *The Almanac of American Politics, 1998* (Washington, D.C.: National Journal, 1997), 230.

31. Ibid., 425.

32. Ibid., 1281.

33. Quoted in Cohen, "We Fight Like Cats and Dogs."

34. "We Are Not Here to Pass Judgment," *Washington Post*, October 6, 1998, A8.

35. "Party Unity Background," *Congressional Quarterly Weekly Report*, January 9, 1999, 92.

36. Quoted in Douglas B. Harris, "The Rise of the Public Speakership," *Political Science Quarterly* (Summer 1998): 198.

37. Ibid., 195.

38. Ibid.

39. Ibid., 195.

40. Ibid., 193, 196, 202, 210.

41. Ibid., 203.

42. Ibid., 210.

43. Quoted in Charles Pope, "'Hollow Victory': A Chronology of Rebellion," *Congressional Quarterly*, November 3, 1998.

44. Voter Research and Surveys, exit poll, November 3, 1998.

45. Quoted in Killian, *The Freshmen*, 433.

46. Quoted in Alan Greenblatt, "Despite Drop in Partisan Votes, Bickering Continued in 1997, *Congressional Quarterly*, January 5, 1998, 18.

47. Quoted in Joe Klein, "The Town That Ate Itself," *New Yorker*, November 23, 1998, 80.

48. Richard Gephardt, "Remarks on the House Floor," December 19, 1998.

49. Bob Livingston, "Remarks on the House Floor," December 19, 1998.

50. CNN/*Time*, poll, December 17–18, 1998. Text of questions: "As you probably know, the House of Representatives is considering a resolution to impeach President Clinton. If the majority of the House votes for impeachment, the Senate would have to decide whether Clinton is guilty and should be removed from office. Based on what you know, do you think the House should vote for or against the impeachment of Bill Clinton?" Yes, 37 percent; no, 61 percent. "Please tell me whether you agree or disagree with this statement: 'Political events in Washington are out of control.'" Yes, 74 percent; no, 24 percent. "Please tell me whether you have generally favorable or generally unfavorable impressions of the Democrats/Republicans in Congress, or whether you are not familiar enough to say one way or the other?" Democrats: Favorable, 53 percent; unfavorable, 27 percent. Republicans: Favorable, 36 percent; unfavorable, 47 percent.

51. Richard L. Berke with Janet Elder, "Damaged by Clinton Trial, Senate Sinks in Public's Eye; GOP Is Hurt More," *New York Times*, February 3, 1999, A1.

52. Peter Baker, "Judge Orders Lewinsky to Cooperate," *Washington Post*, January 24, 1999, A18.

53. Hamilton, "Federalist 68," 414.

54. Quoted in Robert F. Kennedy, *To Seek a Newer World* (New York: Doubleday, 1967), 56.

55. "Bob Livingston's Fifteen Demands of Newt Gingrich," *Wall Street Journal*, November 9, 1998.

56. Quoted in David E. Rosenbaum, "Road to Reconciliation Appears Long and Hard After Acquittal," *New York Times*, February 14, 1999, A1.

CHAPTER 10

Third Parties and the Information Age: The Orphans of American Politics

Washington, D.C., must have seemed a lonely place for freshman Congressman Bernie Sanders in the spring of 1991. Some of his isolation had to do with being in that vast, sprawling metropolis of the nation's capital. As the sole member of the House of Representatives from Vermont, Sanders undoubtedly found the traffic congestion, high crime, rank pollution, sultry heat, and rapid pace of life a drastic change from his cool, bucolic "Green Mountain State." Other representatives from different parts of the United States also experience a degree of culture shock upon arriving in the nation's capital. Moreover, first-timers often feel lost as they struggle to learn the rules that govern the world's most important lawmaking body. But Sanders's isolation was due to more than mere geography or the complex procedures of Congress. Ideologically, Sanders was out-of-step with the times. An unabashed liberal, Sanders's 1990 win ran contrary to the conservative tide that still dominated American politics. But the real cause of Sanders's isolation was due to the fact that of 535 members of Congress, Sanders was, and still is, the only one who is neither a Democrat nor a Republican. Sanders is only the third Socialist elected to the House, and the first one elected since 1928. He remains the first truly independent member of the House since Henry Reams won a seat from Ohio in 1950.

One of the many advantages of being a newly arrived Democrat or Republican in Washington, D.C., is participating in the whirlwind of party-related social functions. When politicians come to the Capitol, they are greeted by fellow partisans who take them to dinner or ask them to play a hand of cards in the back rooms of the legislative office buildings. Much of what a new member learns during those first exciting days in office is over a cup of coffee, a glass of beer, or a plate of spaghetti. Sanders missed out on this socialization process, having no other Socialist or third-party member of Congress with whom to converse.

The formal organizations built by the two parties within Congress were formidable obstacles to Bernard Sanders's hopes of gaining influence. The **caucus,** or **conference** as it is called by Republicans, is a gathering of every elected partisan within their respective house (see Chapter 7). These organizations select the leaders of Congress—including the Speaker of the House, the majority and minority leaders, and whips. They also debate legislative policies, map out strategies on pending bills, provide valuable information to their members, and approve committee assignments. Without the aid of the caucus leaders, new members can count on undesirable committee assignments that are of little importance to voters back home. Noncaucus members accumulate no committee seniority—thus, dashing any hopes of one day becoming a committee or subcommittee chair. Recognizing this, Sanders's 1990 opponent—an incumbent House member—argued that the Vermont Socialist would inevitably be powerless, thereby hurting Vermont's interests. Sanders brusquely replied that he would petition the Democratic Caucus for admittance, believing that they would let him in despite his past criticisms of the Democratic Party.[1] But once Sanders landed in Washington, D.C., he discovered to his amazement that conservative Democrats saw him as a pariah. If he wanted to join the Democratic Caucus, they argued, let him formally become a Democrat. Even liberal Democrats thought that the presence of a Socialist in their party would harm their already tattered image. Sanders was denied admittance. Later, realizing that Sanders would side with them on most issues, Democratic leaders advised him that while he could not attend caucus meetings, he would receive favorable committee assignments.

After handsomely winning reelection in 1992, Democratic House leaders decided to consider Sanders as a "most junior second-term Democrat"—meaning that he would rank ahead of first-term Democrats. But the Democratic leadership avoided answering whether Sanders would someday become a committee chair. Two years later when the Democrats were relegated to minority status after forty years of controlling the House, they extended a heartier welcome, since they needed every vote they could muster to reclaim their majority. Moreover, Sanders predictably compiled a perfect liberal Democratic voting record, having garnered a 100 rating from the liberal group Americans for Democratic Action. Sanders also became an outspoken supporter of Bill Clinton. In 1996, Clinton advisor George Stephanopoulos spoke at a Sanders fund-raiser, ignoring the pleas of Sanders's nominal Democratic opponent not to come. Seven years after winning his House seat, the Democratic Caucus allowed him to accumulate enough seniority to make him the ranking minority member on the Governmental Affairs subcommittee. But whether Sanders can still become a committee chair should Democrats reclaim their majority is unclear. The Sanders example illustrates the difficult time third-parties have maneuvering their way through the two-party thicket.

THE THIRD-PARTY PARADOX

During the twentieth century, many nations have awakened to new forms of party competition. The British, whose Conservative Party is nearly as old as the Republican Party in the United States, saw a resurgent Labour Party emerge at the turn of the century to compete with the Conservatives. In western Europe, new forms of party competition emerged after World War II. But in the United States, the two-party Democratic-Republican battle has remained an enduring feature. Today, there are no survivors from the era when that famous 1854 meeting in Ripon, Wisconsin, created the Republican Party.

While the two-party system has endured, there have been times when one party or another has been effectively routed. From 1812 to 1824, the United States was a one-party country as the Jeffersonian-Republicans trounced what remained of the Federalists. Party competition virtually disappeared, and the near-unanimous election of James Monroe in 1820 ushered in the Era of Good Feelings. The violence of the Civil War created a different sort of one-partyism. From 1865 until the 1960s, a one-party system existed in the South. White southerners, who were embittered by the demise of slavery and their defeat by northern Yankees, created their own Democratic Party that became a repository for their anti-black racism and beliefs.

In the Information Age, there are many parties that compete with the Democrats and Republicans. Nearly every presidential election has several minor party candidates, and in recent years they have affected the outcomes of these all-important contests. But while minor parties proliferate, it is Democrats and Republicans who dominate. As political scientist Clinton Rossiter put it some years ago: "The most momentous fact about the pattern of American politics is that we live under a persistent, obdurate, one might almost say *tyrannical*, two-party system. We have the Republicans and we have the Democrats, and we have almost no one else, no other strictly political aggregate that amounts to a corporal's guard in the struggle for power."[2]

Third party or **minor party** (the terms can be used interchangeably) refer to entities that have formal organizational structures and procedures. Minor parties write platforms, nominate candidates for office, and have formal party positions (e.g., a state party chair). They persist for long periods of time—far longer than one election. **Splinter candidacies** differ from minor parties: they are "one moment wonders" when candidates who are particularly displeased with one of the two major parties, or who are unable to win a nomination from one of them, decide to go it alone. Recent splinter presidential candidates include Strom Thurmond in 1948, who strongly disagreed with Harry Truman's embrace of a pro–civil rights Democratic platform; George Wallace in 1968, who deplored Lyndon Johnson's support for civil rights; and John Anderson in 1980, who profoundly disagreed with the conservative direction of the Republican Party under Ronald Reagan. Each was a prominent Democrat and Republican prior to their independent bids for the White House.

There are signs that third parties might become more important players in the Information Age. The same year Vermont's Bernard Sanders won election to the House of Representatives as a Socialist, Connecticut voters opted for a third-party alternative, selecting former Republican and U.S. Senator Lowell Weicker to be their governor. Weicker, a liberal Republican, had become disillusioned with his party's conservative direction and formed "A Connecticut Party." In 1992, independent Ross Perot captured 19 percent of the vote in a hard-fought presidential contest. Perot's percentage was the largest since ex-president Theodore Roosevelt sought election as a third-party candidate in 1912. In 1994, Maine voters elected Angus King, a former Democrat, as an independent governor—this in a state where Ross Perot won his highest percentages in the nation in 1992 (30 percent) and 1996 (14 percent). In 1996, Ross Perot made his second foray into presidential politics as the candidate of the Reform Party. Although Perot posted only 8 percent of the vote—less than half of what he received in 1992—he still garnered the largest back-to-back votes given to a third-party candidate in this century. In 1998, the Reform Party scored a stunning victory when former professional wrestler Jesse ("The Body") Ventura scored an upset win in the Minnesota gubernatorial contest against Democratic Attorney General Hubert H. Humphrey III, son of the former vice president, and Republican Norm Coleman, the mayor of St. Paul. Also that year, Angus King, Maine's independent governor, won reelection. The Ventura and King wins brought the number of independent governors to two—a twentieth century record.

Despite these notable showings at the polls, third parties confront many difficulties in establishing themselves as viable alternatives. The dominance of America's two-party system is easy to understand. Institutional barriers, historical components, and the constraints of the political culture constitute major barriers to minor party growth. In this chapter, we pose several questions:

- Why have third parties generally failed at the polls?
- Which parties have captured the public's attention and why were they relatively successful?
- What is the state of the third-party movement in the Information Age?
- Have computers and the Internet altered the standing of third parties?
- How does our system's adherence to a two-party model square with the Jeffersonian and Hamiltonian views of democracy?
- Can we expect the two-party dominance to continue in the next millennium?

There is evidence to suggest the power of minor parties may be growing. In due time, politicians like Bernie Sanders may have more company in Washington, D.C., and at the fifty state capitals. For the moment, however, the Sanders, Kings, Perots, Venturas, and Weickers remain exceptions to the two-party hegemony.

Institutional Barriers

The American two-party system is supported by many institutional and legal barriers that limit minor party viability. This is not surprising since it is Democrats and Republicans who write the rules governing U.S. elections. Among their most important creations are single-member districts, the Electoral College, the use of the direct primary, and public funding of presidential elections. Our executive-centered system of governing is not a two-party creation, but it does give the two parties an important institutional lift.

In some democracies—including Austria, Germany, Japan, and Israel—a voting system known as **proportional representation** is used to elect legislative candidates. This system has two important components. First, more than one elected official is sent to the national or provincial assembly from each legislative district. Second, the number of representatives elected is directly proportional to the votes that the party receives on election day. If, for example, the Socialist Party of Austria receives 20 percent of the ballots and a district has five members, then the Socialists can expect to send one member to parliament from that district. The key element that fosters minor party activity is that there are benefits even when the party does not win a plurality of votes. Extremist or rigidly ideological parties are encouraged to participate, since this multimember proportional representation system all but guarantees that they will win a few seats.

This is in sharp contrast to the United States, which relies on a **winner-take-all single-member district** system for choosing most of its officeholders. No matter how hard a party might work, there is no payoff unless a candidate receives a plurality of votes on election day. Only one person is sent to the legislature. To better illustrate the contrast between the multimember proportional representation system and the winner-take-all single-member district method, imagine a situation in which four parties are competing for a single seat. Let's say that Party A is at the far left of the ideological spectrum (the most liberal); Party B, left-of-center; Party C, right-of-center; and Party D, the far right (the most conservative). In this hypothetical election, Party A won 20 percent of the votes; Party B, 30 percent; Party C, 27 percent; and Party D, 23 percent. Under the proportional system, each party has roughly the same number of legislators in the national assembly, with a small edge going to Party B. Under the winner-take-all single-member district system, only Party B would send legislators to the capitol. The British who use the winner-take-all method liken such electoral outcomes to horse races, and have characterized their system as being "first-past-the-post."

In a winner-take-all single-member district system, there are strong incentives for political parties located near each other on the ideological spectrum to merge. Using our previous example, operatives from Party C might say to Party D: "You know, we don't agree on everything, but we think alike. If we joined forces, we could surely overtake Party B. After all, they netted only 30 percent of the vote in the last election while together we grabbed 50 percent." Under these rules, Party C's operatives know that it does not matter whether there are four, fourteen, or forty parties vying for support. When the laws dictate a winner-take-all single-member district system, there is no payoff for coming in second.

Another institutional barrier limiting minor party success in the United States is the **Electoral College.** Recall that the Electoral College was designed by the Framers of the U.S. Constitution to nominate and elect a nonpartisan president (see Chapter 5). Electors were to be men of character who would rise above parochial interests and choose a statesman. The Electoral College still exists, though most Americans do not realize that on election day they are actually voting for electors instead of their favorite presidential candidate. Two aspects of the Electoral College hinder minor party success. First, each state is granted a number of electors equal to their total federal representatives in Congress, both House and Senate members combined. While the Constitution is silent on how each state should apportion these electors, most employ a winner-take-all scheme whereby the candidate who receives a plurality of votes receives *all* of that state's electors. Only Maine and Nebraska do not use the winner-take-all system; instead, they employ a congressional district winner-take-all process. Under the Electoral College rules, in order for any candidate to win the presidency, he or she must receive an absolute majority of the electoral votes cast—currently 270 out of 538. If this does not occur, the House of Representatives must choose the next president by having each state's delegation cast one vote. This happened only once in the disputed presidential election of 1824 when the House chose John Quincy Adams (see Chapter 2). Today, it is hard to imagine that a body almost entirely composed of Democrats and Republicans would select a third-party president—especially if that person did not garner more than 50 percent of the popular vote.

Election laws and constitutional arrangements make it highly unlikely that a third-party can capture the presidency. Two examples are illustrative. In 1912, Theodore Roosevelt was unable to wrest the GOP nomination from William Howard Taft, so he decided to head the Progressive (Bull Moose) Party (see Chapter 3). The ex-president finished an amazing second with 27 percent of the popular vote. But in the Electoral College he captured just 17 percent of the vote. Ross Perot met with a similar fate. Perot's 19 percent of the popular vote in 1992 was the third largest in American history—behind two ex-presidents, Theodore Roosevelt and Millard Fillmore, the 1856 candidate of the Know-Nothing Party who received 22 percent of the popular vote. Yet, for all of his money and hard work, Perot was unable to garner a single electoral vote.

In addition to the Electoral College, another reason for the persistence of the two-party system is that the American polity system is **executive-centered.** Voters willingly give considerable governing power to their executives—be they mayors, governors, or the president. Most citizens think of governing as an executive responsibility. When a great deal of power is given to one person and citizens accept this arrangement as legitimate, there are strong incentives for elites to form broad-based parties capable of winning the presidency. For their part, voters do not want to "waste their vote," since there is so much at stake. Norman Thomas, a six-time presidential candidate of the Socialist Party, attributed his failure to make a greater showing at the polls to the "wasted vote" phenomenon:

> The average American voter . . . may prefer a minor party candidate, but will cast his vote for one of the major party candidates. . . . Almost up to Election Day, he may think he will vote for his real preference, a minor-party candidate who managed to get on the ballot in his state, but then he will decide that he can't take a chance lest that [other] so-and-so-get in. How often I have been told just that![3]

Given the prevalence of these voter attitudes and the willingness of Democratic and Republican leaders to exploit them, the American two-party system has flourished.

Another legal mechanism that constricts minor party success are regulations that limit **ballot access.** As discussed in Chapter 3, one consolation party bosses received during the Progressive Era were election laws that made it difficult for minor parties to participate. Getting a new party on the ballot and keeping it there pose extraordinarily difficult legal challenges. The major parties have automatic ballot access by virtue of their prior success. For example, some states stipulate that the party whose gubernatorial candidate wins 10 percent of the vote is automatically listed on the next election ballot. Because Democrats and Republicans almost always garner that many votes, they have virtually automatic ballot access. One potential threat to this ironclad rule recently occurred in Maine. In 1998, both of that state's Democratic and Republican parties were in a frenzy. Independent Governor Angus King was so popular that many believed that neither the Democratic nor the Republican gubernatorial candidates might capture the 10 percent of the vote needed to remain on the ballot. A strong Green Party candidate added to the anxiety. On election day, both parties edged across the finish line with the Democrat winning 12 percent and the Republican garnering 19 percent. These were abysmally low totals, as independent Angus King won reelection with 59 percent of the vote. Still, both parties maintained their ballot access—for the time being.

For new parties, the struggle to get on the ballot often requires a costly petition-signing process. In most states, a single petition qualifies a new party for all ballot-listed offices. But in eleven states, a separate petition for each office is required. Table 10.1 notes the petition requirements for creating a new party and running its candidates for the U.S. Senate and the presidency. In Louisiana, for example, a minor party U.S. Senate candidate needs to collect 134,460 valid signatures from enrolled voters to qualify for the 2000 election. To run as a new party presidential candidate in North Carolina, more than 51,000 valid signatures are needed. The eleven states that have no procedure for a new party use candidate petitions whereby a petition signature drive must be undertaken for each candidate; they are Connecticut, Illinois, Indiana, Iowa, Kentucky, New Jersey, New York, Pennsylvania, Virginia, Washington, and West Virginia.

The case of Maine is especially telling. Given that Maine voters have thrice elected an independent governor (1974, 1994, and 1998), and Ross Perot's two excellent showings in that state—one would expect to find a viable multiparty system there. This is not the case. Maine has a stiff petition requirement for candidates wanting to be placed on the primary ballot. Two thousand signatures must be obtained from registered party members before one's name can appear on the ballot. While the Green Party of Maine has attracted a good deal of public support in recent elections, it has only three thousand registered members. Collecting two thousand signatures from three thousand voters widely scattered across the state is a difficult chore. Moreover, minor party primary voters cannot write-in candidates because these ballots count only if the total matches or exceeds the two thousand signatures required for a primary petition.[4] Thus, even though Maine appears to be fertile ground for the Green and Reform parties—the state's two largest minor parties—the best they could do was to sponsor a presidential candidate, Ross Perot, in 1996.

In 1997, the Supreme Court rendered a decision that buttressed the two-party model. *Timmons v. Twin Cities Area New Party* involved the Minnesota chapter of the New Party, which decided to nominate an incumbent for the state House of Representatives, who also happened to be the candidate of the Democratic-Farmer Labor (DFL) Party. In Minnesota, the two major parties are the Republicans and the DFL. Neither the New Party nor the Democrats objected to this cross-over endorsement, but the state election commission did—refusing to allow the same candidate to be nominated by more than one party. The New Party strongly opposed the state election commission's ruling, calling it a breach of their First Amendment rights to free association.

TABLE 10.1 ▪ 2000 Ballot Access for New Party Candidates

State	Qualified Party Signatures	Per-cent	Senate Signatures	Per-cent	President Signatures	Per-cent
Alabama	39,536	1.61	39,536	1.61	39,536	1.61
Alaska	6,596	1.45	2,217	0.49	2,410	0.53
Arizona	13,569	0.60	13,569	0.60	13,569	0.60
Arkansas	21,181	1.44	21,181	1.44	1,000	0.07
California	86,027	0.57	86,027	0.57	86,027	0.57
Colorado	1,000	0.04	1,000	0.04	0	0
Connecticut	no procedure		7,500	0.38	7,500	0.38
Delaware	235	0.05	235	0.05	235	0.05
Florida	0	0	0	0	0	0
Georgia	39,094	1.00	39,094	1.00	39,094	1.00
Hawaii	602	0.10	602	0.10	602	0.10
Idaho	9,835	1.49	9,835	1.49	9,835	.49
Illinois	no procedure		25,000	0.37	25,000	0.37
Indiana	no procedure		30,717	0.83	30,717	0.83
Iowa	no procedure		1,500	0.08	1,500	0.08
Kansas	14,854	0.98	14,854	0.98	14,854	0.98
Kentucky	no procedure		5,000	0.19	5,000	0.19
Louisiana	134,460	5.00	134,460	5.00	0	0
Maine	21,051	2.23	4,000	0.42	4,000	0.42
Maryland	10,000+25,694	1.39	10,000+25,694	1.39	10,000	0.39
Massachusetts	37,185	1.00	10,000	0.27	10,000	0.27
Michigan	30,272	0.44	30,272	0.44	30,272	0.44
Minnesota	105,268	3.02	2,000	0.06	2,000	0.06
Mississippi	0	0	0	0	0	0
Missouri	10,000	0.28	10,000	0.28	10,000	0.28
Montana	5,000	0.78	5,000	0.78	5,000	0.78
Nebraska	5,367	0.51	5,367	0.51	5,367	0.51
Nevada	4,099	0.46	4,099	0.46	4,099	0.46
New Hampshire	9,569	1.28	3,000	0.40	3,000	0.40
New Jersey	no procedure		800	0.02	800	0.02
New Mexico	2,494	0.27	4,988+2,494	0.82	2,494	0.27
New York	no procedure		15,000	0.14	15,000	0.14
North Carolina	51,324	1.08	51,324	1.08	51,324	1.08
North Dakota	7,000	1.47	7,000	1.47	7,000	1.47
Ohio	32,905	0.46	5,000	0.07	5,000	0.07
Oklahoma	43,680	2.13	43,680	2.13	36,202	1.77
Oregon	16,257	0.85	16,257	0.85	16,257	0.85
Pennsylvania	no procedure		25,000	0.34	25,000	0.34
Rhode Island	15,323	2.42	1,000	0.16	1,000	0.16
South Carolina	10,000	0.49	10,000	0.49	10,000	0.49
South Dakota	6,505	1.44	2,602	0.57	2,602	0.57
Tennessee	23,819	0.79	23,819	0.79	23,819	0.79
Texas	37,385	0.32	37,385	0.32	37,385	0.32

continued

TABLE 10.1 ▪ 2000 Ballot Access for New Party Candidates *(continued)*

State	Qualified Party Signatures	Per-cent	Senate Signatures	Per-cent	President Signatures	Per-cent
Utah	2,000	0.18	1,000	0.07	1,000	0.09
Vermont	20	0.0+	20	0	20	0.00+
Virginia	no procedure		10,000	0.27	10,000	0.27
Washington	no procedure		9,000+	0.29	200	0.01
West Virginia	no procedure		11,914	1.18	12,730	1.27
Wisconsin	10,000	0.26	2,000	0.06	2,000	0.06
Wyoming	3,485	1.47	3,485	1.47	3,485	1.47

Note: This table shows what a new party must do to obtain recognition as a "party" in time for the 2000 election. It also demonstrates the support necessary to place a new party senatorial or presidential candidate on the 2000 ballot. The percent represents the number of required signatures divided by the number of registered voters (as of fall 1998). In some states, there is no procedure for a new group to turn itself into a party within one election cycle. Such states are noted as "no procedure" above.

SOURCE: Richard Winger, ed., *Ballot Access News*, (San Francisco, Calif.), October 20, 1999.

The practice of multiparty nominations, also called **fusion balloting,** is allowed in eight states: Arkansas, Connecticut, New Hampshire, New York, South Carolina, South Dakota, Utah, and Vermont. A six-member majority of the Supreme Court upheld the Minnesota ban on fusion balloting. Writing for the majority, Chief Justice William H. Rehnquist noted that political parties have an unquestioned right to select their own candidates, but added that the "Constitution *also* allows states to protect political stability through a healthy *two-party* system [emphasis added]."[5] Considering that 99 percent of current state legislators are either Democrat or Republican, it is doubtful that many state legislatures will rescue third parties by making fusion legal.

Another strong institutional force limiting minor party success is the **direct primary system.** In most other political systems where nominations are controlled by party elites, intra-party dissidents often leave to form their own party. In the United States, the use of the direct primary system has the effect of channeling dissent into the two major parties.[6] Those frustrated with their party can support a maverick candidate in the primary—or become candidates themselves. There are many ways to change a party without leaving it. For example, after the disastrous showing of Democrat Walter F. Mondale in 1984, many Democrats were frustrated with the perception of their party as the protector of big government. Rather than abandon the party, they changed its direction by working to nominate a more middle-of-the-road presidential candidate. The Democratic Leadership Council (DLC) was formed in 1985. Designed to move the Democratic Party toward the political center, the DLC advocated ways for the federal government to remain an active player in policy development without creating new bureaucracies to administer any new programs. Arkansas Governor Bill Clinton chaired the DLC, and seven years after its formation, Clinton became the Democratic nominee for president.

The **presidential campaign finance system** is yet another institutional barrier to minor party success. The Federal Election Campaign Act (FECA) stipulates that a presidential candidate is eligible for public funds, provided that the party's nominee receives a given percentage of votes in the previous election. For "major parties," a 25 percent threshold is required. If this goal is met, then the nominee is entitled to full funding (approximately $75 million in 2000). For minor party candidates the threshold is only 5 percent, but the amount they receive from the federal government is far less than their Democratic or Republican counterparts. Ross Perot, who won 19 percent of the vote in 1992, was given $29 million in public funds in 1996—less than half of what Bill Clinton and Bob Dole received. This is a prime example of the old saying that those who write the rules, namely, Democrats and Republicans, do not want to change them to benefit someone else. For third parties, their real predicament is not how much money they might receive sometime in the future, but how much they can raise in the here and now. Minor party candidates can get postelection public money, but only if they appear on the ballot in ten states and receive 5 percent of the total vote.[7] Independent John Anderson campaigned feverishly during the waning weeks of his 1980 presidential bid not because he had a chance of winning, but because he had a real chance of garnering more than 5 percent of the vote. He won 6.6 percent. Thus, Anderson was granted $4.2 million in public monies, although he chose to forsake the 1984 presidential contest.

While money is a chief obstacle confronting minor party candidates, it is not the only one. In 1996, the Commission on Presidential Debates ruled that Ross Perot was not a serious contender and banned him from the televised debates featuring Bill Clinton and Bob Dole. Perot argued that he could not be a contender until he was allowed to debate the other candidates. But the commission, which was composed of Democrats and Republicans, lent an unsympathetic ear to Perot's complaint.

Overall, these legal and structural mechanisms stack the deck against minor parties. Many have argued that governing institutions cannot, by themselves, hinder minor party success if an electorate is inclined to support them.[8] Pundits cite the emergence of new multiparty systems in Canada and Great Britain—two nations that also use single-member legislative districts. The struggle third parties confront in the United States is much greater than overcoming the single-member district winner-take-all hurdle. The Electoral College, direct primary laws, and ballot access restrictions make third-party success exceedingly difficult. These laws serve to perpetuate the existence of the two-party model in the United States. But there is even more to the story than the legal superiority Democrats and Republicans have won over their potential competitors.

American Political Culture

A nation's **political culture** refers to the fundamental values and beliefs that influence society and within which political behavior and government policies are bound. It is the umbrella under which political activities take place and where public questions are resolved. Several core values of the American political culture help maintain a two-party system. These include (1) the adherence to peaceful resolutions of conflicts, (2) acceptance of compromise and incremental change, and (3) a strong endorsement of the nation's governing framework. The United States peacefully accepted the constitutional arrangements that the Framers instituted in 1787. Later, in 1801, the government of the United States peacefully changed hands from the Federalists to the Democratic-Republicans—a transfer of power that remains a rarity in the rest of the world. Americans extol their governing system as the best ever devised. During the depths of the Great Depression, pollsters asked: "Which one of the following most nearly represents your opinion of the American form of government? (a) Our form of government based on the Constitution is as near perfect as it can be and no important changes should be made in it; (b) the Constitution has served its purpose well, but it has not kept up with the times and should be thoroughly revised to make it fit present day needs; or (c) the systems of private capitalism and democracy are breaking down and we might as well accept the fact that sooner or later we will have to have a new form of government." Sixty-four percent said our political system is "as near perfect as it can be"—including 58 percent who were classified as being "poor."[9]

As the response to this survey question illustrates, Americans are decidedly centrist in their political outlook. It is often said that there is "not a dime's worth of difference between the Democratic and Republican parties." During the Cold War, for example, moderate thinking was strongly encouraged. Arthur Larson, an undersecretary of labor during the Eisenhower administration, wrote a book entitled *A Republican Looks at His Party*, in which he theorized that Americans had reached consensus on most fundamental issues. Larson attributed this formation of an "Authentic American Center" to the Cold War: "Principles that we have always taken for granted as the air we breathe are now flatly denounced and denied over a large part of the world—the principles, for example, of the preeminence and the freedom and the sovereignty of the individual person."[10] Dwight Eisenhower echoed Larson, telling his fellow Republicans in 1956 that they had become America's new "one-interest" party:

> The Republican party is again the rallying point of Americans of all callings, ages, races, and incomes. They see in its broad, forward-moving, straight-down-the-road, fighting program the best promise for their own steady progress toward a bright future. Some opponents have tried to call this a "one-interest party." Indeed it is a one-interest party; and that one interest is the interest of every man, woman, and child in America! And most surely, as long as the Republican party continues to be this kind of one-interest party—a one-universal-interest party—it will continue to be the Party of the Future.[11]

While the conformity of the 1950s has long since past, American political culture continues to reinforce moderate, centrist thinking. Republican 2000 presidential contender George W. Bush describes himself as a "compassionate conservative." Democrat Al Gore offers himself as a centrist who will not return to his party's old-style New Deal liberalism. Louis Hartz, a political theorist best-known for his commentary on the uniqueness of the American political culture, maintains that there exists a national consensus centered on individual freedoms. "It is a remarkable force," Hartz writes, "this fixed, dogmatic liberalism of a liberal way of life. It is the secret root from which have sprung many of the most puzzling aspects of American cultural phenomena."[12] So prevalent is the American ideology, that Alexis de Tocqueville warned that it stifled most political debate: "I know of no country in which there is so little independence of mind and real freedom of discussion as in America."[13] Indeed, the essence of the American polity is not in the maze of structures erected by the Founding Fathers in the Constitution; rather, it is located in the shared values of its citizens. Englishman G. K. Chesterton wrote in 1920 that the United States was founded on a "creed," elaborating: "That creed is set forth with dogmatic and even theological lucidity in the Declaration of Independence; perhaps the only piece of practical politics that is also theoretical politics and also great literature."[14]

This creed allows little tolerance for any diversity. Lewis Cass, the 1848 Democratic nominee for president, told a Tammany Hall audience that he was "opposed to all the isms of the day . . . to communism and socialism, and Mormonism; to polygamy and concubinage, and to all the humbugs that are now rising among us."[15] Abraham Lincoln warned that if the Declaration of Independence were amended to read that "all men are created equal, except Negroes, and foreigners, and Catholics," then "I should prefer emigrating to some country where they make no pretense of loving liberty—to Russia, for instance, where despotism can be taken pure, and without the base alloy of hypocracy."[16] Karl Marx acknowledged communism's failure in the United States blaming it on "the tenacity of the Yankees," citing their "theoretical backwardness" and their "Anglo-Saxon contempt for all theory."[17] The U.S. Communist Party has lots of company in the graveyard of failed political parties in the United States.

The media also plays a powerful role in perpetuating the two-party system. Minor party candidates are given scant attention, as the press protests that they have neither the time nor space to cover candidates with little chance of victory. Minor party candidates respond that without substantive press coverage they stand no chance of winning. When the media does pause to give minor party candidates their few seconds of fame, they are often portrayed as "fringe" candidates whose eccentricities become the story. Late in the summer of 1996, for example, the *Washington Post* ran an article entitled "There's the Ticket. . . . A Selection of Running Mates for Ross Perot." Included in the list were: Binti, a gorilla who had rescued a tot who had fallen into her cage; Prince Charles of Great Britain; and Jack Kervorkian, known as Doctor Death for his advocacy of physician-assisted suicides.[18] Prior to his upset victory in 1998, former pro-wrestler Jesse Ventura was given little coverage by the media, often ridiculed as a real-life cartoon character.

The entertainment industry has also played a role in constraining the party system. As noted earlier, one of the most remarkable things about the history of American politics is the relative void of economic-based parties. Following the economic deprivations of the Industrial Revolution at the turn of the century, several socialist organizations began to emerge. Their success at the ballot box was relatively limited, but these groups appeared in several cities. Fearing a growing threat to the nation's laissez-faire economic policies, a concerted effort was waged by the captains of industry to turn public sentiment against such "fringe" groups. Hollywood produced a series of movies that assailed socialists and "commies" as subversives bent on destroying the American way of life. A near identical attack was waged against left-leaning groups during the Cold War. Motion Picture Association of America chief Eric Johnston proclaimed his anticommunism, stating: "We'll have no more *Grapes of Wrath*, we'll have no more *Tobacco Road*s. We'll have no more films that show the seamy side of American life. We'll have no pictures that deal with labor strikes. We'll have no pictures that deal with the banker as villain." Johnston and Screen Actors Guild President Ronald Reagan distributed *A Screen Guide of Americans*, composed by the militant anticommunist Ayn Rand. The guide derided New Deal-era movie dialogue about the nobility of the "common man" as the "droolings of weaklings," and proposed a series of "don'ts":

- "Don't Smear the Free Enterprise System"
- "Don't Deify the Common Man"
- "Don't Show That Poverty Is a Virtue . . . and Failure Is Noble."[19]

Certainly, there is little doubt that the entertainment industry has played an important role in defining American political culture and in perpetuating our centrist, two-party model.[20]

The Momentum of History

A final set of forces helping to maintain the two-party dominance are the constraints of history and the power of momentum. Consider the words of V. O. Key on the connections between the formative years for political parties and the contemporary party system: "Human institutions have an impressive capacity to perpetuate themselves or at least to preserve their form. The circumstances that happened to mold the American party system into a dual form at its inception must bear a degree of responsibility for its present existence."[21] Human evolution and party evolution share one common trait: both have a strong instinct for survival.

In the United States, while there are numerous examples of violence that has created important social and political change (the Civil War comes readily to mind), there are several examples of evolutionary changes that have occurred with little or no violence. For example, although it is not generally recognized as the true party formation period, one of the most significant periods of American political history was the 1787 debate over ratification of the U.S. Constitution. As important as the outcome of this debate was, even more important was the fact that one form of government was scrapped in favor of another without a shot being fired. A similar evolution occurred in 1800 when Americans voted for a change in party control of the federal government from Alexander Hamilton's Federalists to Thomas Jefferson's Democratic-Republicans without violence. Many view these peaceful transitions and others that have taken place since as evidence of the genius of the American public. By contrast, in the years after World War II, there were numerous jokes about the coalition politics that produced ninety-day governments in France and Italy.

As noted in Chapters 1 and 2, the narrowness of American political argument has been attributed to its two most important party founders, Alexander Hamilton and Thomas Jefferson, each of whom had a distinct viewpoint about the proper role of government. The struggle between Hamiltonian Nationalism and Jeffersonian Localism that has been waged continuously throughout American history creates a sense of deja vu—issues change, but not the essential nature of the conflict. Journalist Walter Lippmann put it this way: "To be partisan . . . as between Jefferson and Hamilton is like arguing whether men or women are more necessary to the procreation of the race. Neither can live alone. Alone —that is, without the other—each is excessive and soon intolerable."[22] History is replete with periodic swings of its pendulum toward Hamiltonian Nationalism and back toward Jeffersonian Localism. With each tick of history's clock, Americans sense a return as old battle lines are redrawn on new, yet familiar, territory. Hamilton, for instance, would be astonished to learn that his concept of a national family is being used by Democrats to promote the interests of the have-nots, especially women and minorities. Likewise, Republican Ronald Reagan's espousal of his version of Jeffersonian Localism is premised on a welfare state established under Franklin D. Roosevelt's New Deal. The circumstances have changed, but the arguments carry a familiar ring.

As history reminds us, American politics is steeped in its dualist, two-party tradition. Throughout the American polity, change is the order of the day—especially as its governments reform themselves on the eve of the twenty-first century. Today's presidency is a vastly different institution than that conceived by the constitution's Framers. Likewise, the federal government has become the center of American politics—quite a change from the state and local dominance of the last century. The movement toward greater rights and protections for women and people of color represents another transformation of major proportions. Why, then, have Americans adhered to the two-party model?

Inertia and institutions provide the best clues. Accompanying the significant changes in the inner-workings of the U.S. government during this century have been numerous structural and legal adjustments. The presidency, for example, was transformed into something much bigger because Franklin Roosevelt's New Deal included scores of laws that placed the executive branch at the center of politics. Changing attitudes about people of color were spurred in part by congressional passage of the Civil Rights Act of 1964 and the 1965 Voting Rights Act.

Nevertheless, most of the legal mechanisms protecting the two-party system are still on the books, though some changes have occurred, of course—especially the use of open primary systems. Those who ran on third-party tickets often were unusual and distinctive characters who were determined to "educate" voters to their point of view. Political scientist Frank Smallwood interviewed all of the minor party candidates in the 1980 presidential election. His book, *The Other Candidates: Third Parties in Presidential Elections*, presents a colorful portrait of these individuals—ranging from the Prohibition Party to the Socialist Party, U.S. Communist Party, Libertarian Party, Right-to-Life Party, and John B. Anderson, who bolted from the

---

The Parties Speak: *Benjamin C. Bubar, 1976 and 1980 Prohibition Party Presidential Nominee*

Smallwood: Tell me a little about your background. When did you get started in politics?

Bubar: Let's see. It was back in 1938. I was living in the northern part [of Maine]. . . . I ran for the legislature as a Republican. It was during the [Great] Depression. Almost everybody up there was Republican in those days, since Maine and Vermont were the only two states that supported Alf Landon against [Franklin] Roosevelt in the '36 election. I was working part-time cutting pulpwood and part-time in a grocery store for twenty-five cents an hour, very proud of my big wages.

Smallwood: Why did you decide to run for the state legislature?

Bubar: We had a lot of good men in the legislature out of that area, but some of the young folk were dissatisfied, no different than they are today. When I look back on it, the only thing I can find wrong with the guy I ran against was that he was sixty years old. We thought he was over the hill and it was time to ditch him.

Four of us were discussing it at a soda fountain one night. The question was what we were going to do. You can stand outside, throw spitballs, and criticize. We said, well, why don't one of us run for the legislature and put that fellow away? Then the question was who was going to run. We drew straws. I got the short one, so I was the one who ran, even though I was only nineteen at the time and not even old enough to vote for myself in the primary.

Smallwood: What kind of campaign did you run?

Bubar: Well, it took three months for folks to take us serious. When we put in our nomination petition to go up and file, the folks laughed about it. It was a big joke in the area. The fellow I worked for in the grocery store came along one day and asked me if I was just kidding around about wanting to go to the legislature. I said, "No, I'm serious. I'm going to run, and these fellows are going to campaign for me. . . ." We campaigned. I spoke to my dad about it, and he thought it was great. I wasn't able to go to college—couldn't afford it. He thought this would be a good education for me. He told me that if I ran half a dozen times, someday I'd make it, because Abe Lincoln ran many times before he made it. The sad part of it was, I got elected the first time.

Smallwood: How long did you serve in the state legislature?

Bubar: I was elected in 1938, so I was in the House in 1939. I served for six years, until 1945. I'm still the youngest person ever to have served in the Maine legislature. . . .

Smallwood: You ran for the state legislature as a Republican. When did you get involved with the Prohibition Party?

Bubar: I've been interested in the Prohibition Party indirectly for as long as I can remember. You see, the Maine law back in 1856 was the first state law [mandating prohibition], and Maine was a prohibition state until 1933. My dad and my grandfather were both members of the party. My dad cast his first vote for a Prohibitionist when they used to run a full slate of officers in the state. So I've been interested in the party for a long time, although I didn't get actively involved until the 1950s.

Smallwood: The Prohibition Party has been around for more than a century. Where do you stand today? Are you a single-issue group, or are your concerns broader than the prohibition of alcohol?

Bubar: No, we're not a single-issue party. We've always had more than one string in our fiddle. We've been around a long time. Over the years we've initiated many major reforms. Way back in 1872, we were the first party to call for universal suffrage for all groups, including women's suffrage. We were the first to advocate civil service reforms and the direct election of senators. Although I hate to admit it, we were also the first to call for an income tax way back in 1896, but we're vehemently opposed to the rip-off we've got on our hands at the present time. . . .

Smallwood: What issues besides prohibition separate you from these other parties?

Bubar: We broke away from the Republican party after the Civil War, and they have tried for many years to hold themselves up as the party of morality, which is an awful sham. The only difference between the Republican party and the Democrats in the state of Maine is that, when they have conventions, the Republicans drink whiskey and vodka and the Democrats drink beer. They go to a hotel and have their convention, and it costs more to clean up after the Republicans than the Democrats. The Democrats make more noise, but the Republicans leave more of a mess.

Smallwood: One social issue that your party has always focused on is prohibition. Why has this always been so central to you?

Bubar: Actually, we support a state-by-state approach to this issue. We think the problem of drinking, which is the major drug problem in the nation, is way out of hand. Here in Maine, we have over 70,000 alcoholics, which is more than the population of our three smallest counties. We're not as bad on a per capita basis as some of the other states, but for the little state of Maine, with only one million people, this is pretty rough.

Smallwood: It's been argued that once the Eighteenth Amendment was adopted, this led to the decline and virtual demise of the Prohibition Party because your mission was completed. Is this one of the reasons you've experimented with new names, like the National Statesman Party, in an effort to resurrect your fortunes?

Bubar: I was one of the fellows who was pushing to change the name because I felt with a comprehensive platform like ours, prohibition was just one part of it. But it took several funerals before we were able to get it through. Some of the old-timers in the party wouldn't listen to it. There was only one plank in the platform as far as some of the old-timers were concerned. I started agitating for a name change back in the 1950s. In 1976, we finally decided to try it for three or four years to see what would happen.

Smallwood: What were the 1976 and 1980 [presidential] campaigns like? Did you go out and visit a lot of different states?

Bubar: Yes, we traveled quite a bit in 1976. We were on the ballot in fourteen states, and we visited every one of those states. In 1980, however, we were only on the ballot in eight states, and I didn't campaign much. We didn't have the money.

Smallwood: Was it difficult for you to get on the state ballots?

Bubar: You said it! The Democratic and Republican parties are fighting hard to keep the third parties off the ballot. They say they both support the free-enterprise system, but they sure don't want any competition in their own backyard. . . . We didn't even make it on the ballot in my home state. We listened to the Democratic attorney general and the Republican secretary of state, or just the reverse, and they botched everything up so we couldn't even run in Maine. Otherwise, we would have been on the ballot.

continued

The Parties Speak: *Benjamin C. Bubar, 1976 and 1980 Prohibition Party Presidential Nominee (continued)*

Smallwood: What about general media coverage? Did the press pay much attention to you?

Bubar: The press would ask me if I really planned to go to the White House. I looked back at them and replied, "Do I look that stupid?" Then they'd ask me why I was running. I told them we've got some issues that need to be discussed. It gave us a springboard. We have a political message that we think America needs. We're not going to the White House, and we may not win, but we're having an impact. . . .

Smallwood: Let me conclude with a question about personal motivation. What drives someone like you to run for president of the United States in the light of such overwhelming odds? Is it personal satisfaction? Some set of political ideals? A sense of duty to the party?

Bubar: My wife says I have a very perverted sense of humor, or I wouldn't stay involved. But actually we've got a message we think America needs to hear. We believe in a representative republic, but what we've got right now is a socialist democracy bordering on anarchy. This is bad. Everybody is doing his own thing. When America was growing, becoming great and having worldwide respect, we were a representative republic.

So we have a message we think America needs. We've lost our first love, which was honesty and integrity in government. We've lost pride in serving as public officials. Men of integrity don't want to run. There's no national pride in public office. It's even difficult to get people right here in Waterville [Maine] to run for local office. Why? Because the public has contempt for government.

If we don't turn this around, we are going to fall like Rome fell. We're rotting from within. Our public officials lack integrity. We raise their salaries, and the more they get, the poorer the quality of men and women who are willing to serve in public office. I think we have to turn this around. This is what keeps me going.

SOURCE: Frank Smallwood, *The Other Candidates: Third Parties in Presidential Elections* (Hanover, N.H.: University Press of New England, 1983), 33–34, 36–38, 39, 41, 43, 45.

Republican Party in 1980 to mount his third-party national unity campaign.[23] One of the most interesting of Smallwood's interviews was with Benjamin C. Bubar, a two-time Prohibition Party presidential nominee in 1976 and 1980 (see "The Parties Speak: Benjamin C. Bubar, 1976 and 1980 Prohibition Party Presidential Nominee").

SIGNIFICANT THIRD PARTIES IN AMERICAN HISTORY

Although the United States has held fast to its two-party model, minor parties have had their historical moments—tilting the outcome of an election, shifting the policy debate, or changing the direction of government. Following his impressive 1992 debut, Ross Perot undertook the hard task of forming a lasting political party. The

Reform Party is now organized in each of the fifty states. Its most impressive victory came in 1998 with Jesse Ventura's election as Minnesota's governor. Ventura was just one of hundreds of Reform Party candidates seeking election. While history has not been kind to minor parties, there are numerous examples when they have changed the direction of political debate and influenced the outcomes of elections.

The Anti-Mason Party

The first significant minor party emerged shortly after the Era of Good Feelings ended in 1824. For decades prior to the Revolution, nearly every large community in America had a Masonic Lodge, or what was called a Freemason organization. These secretive clubs were composed of middle- and upper-class white Protestant men, often the leading businessmen of their communities, who were interested in the political issues of the day, and had a strong belief in moral self-improvement. Prominent masons included George Washington, Henry Clay, and Andrew Jackson. According to historian Phyllis F. Field, "In a nation with high rates of geographic mobility, Masonry provided a convenient way for nomadic American middle-class men to integrate themselves quickly into a new community and feel at home there."[24]

But the elitism and secret masonic rites created a public backlash—especially among religious fundamentalists. Following the mysterious disappearance of New York Freemason William Morgan in 1826 after he had threatened to reveal the secret rituals of the group, the **anti-Mason** movement was born. Anti-Masons maintained that the secretive cliques were conspiring against the working class and, through their bizarre rituals like the frequent cross burnings, were a threat to Christianity. Within four years of their humble beginnings in 1826, the anti-Masons had become a powerful political force. In 1831, they held a presidential nominating convention—a novel idea for its day—and chose as their candidate former Attorney General William Wirt.

Wirt proved to be an ineffectual campaigner and the Anti-Mason Party finished a distant third in the 1832 presidential election with 100,000 votes (8 percent) behind Democrat Andrew Jackson and Whig Party candidate Henry Clay. However, Wirt finished first in Vermont, winning that state's seven electoral votes—the first time a third-party candidate had garnered any support in the Electoral College. The Anti-Masons fared better in state contests, winning the governorships of Vermont and Pennsylvania, and they won several congressional and state legislative seats in New York, Vermont, Pennsylvania, Rhode Island, and Connecticut. Even John Quincy Adams identified with the party for a short period. Looking back, their most significant policy achievement was the passage of a national law outlawing extrajudicial oaths of office.

By the mid-1830s, the Anti-Mason Party began to fade. Part of its demise was due to the fact that President Andrew Jackson endorsed policies that gave political leverage to working-class voters. More than anything else, the Anti-Mason Party disappeared because the Freemason movement was out-of-step with the democratic impulses of the 1830s. There was less public concern about elitism in the years after Jackson's election and his brand of Jacksonian Democracy.

The Free-Soil Party

Several anti-slavery groups nipped at the edges of the political system prior to the 1840s. The most notable of these were the Barnburners, the Conscience Whigs, and the Liberty Party. These groups were short-lived and relatively unpopular because they were controlled by extremists and religious fanatics who advocated such radical ideas as the abolition of slavery in the District of Columbia and an end to the interstate slave trade. Despite rising public opposition to slavery, the **Liberty Party**'s 1840 presidential candidate won approximately seven thousand votes. The party's greatest success came in 1842, when its Massachusetts gubernatorial candidate got 5 percent of the vote—enough to push the contest into the state legislature, which then determined the outcome in favor of another candidate.

The **Free Soil Party** had better luck. The initial impetus for this party's founding in 1848 was the debate over the Wilmot Proviso, which limited the extension of slavery into the new western territories (see Chapter 2). Operating on a platform of "free soil, free speech, free labor, and free men," the Free Soil Party combined opposition to slavery with a desire for cheap western land. As the Free Soil Party gained new followers, it became more pragmatic than its abolitionist predecessors. It advocated policies that would allow blacks to vote and attend school. At the same time, Free Soilers bowed to existing racial prejudices by arguing that the Wilmot Proviso would keep blacks hemmed in the South.[25] Free Soilers did not endorse the abolition of slavery, nor did they denounce the Fugitive Slave Act or the three-fifths clause of the U.S. Constitution (which counted blacks as "three-fifths" of a person for the purpose of determining how they would be represented in the House of Representatives). Other planks that broadened the Free Soil Party's appeal included cheaper postage, reduced federal spending, tariff reform, the election of all civil officers, and free homesteading in the West.[26]

In 1848, the Free Soil Party held a convention in Buffalo, New York, with nearly 20,000 delegates and spectators in attendance. Hopes were high and excitement was in the air when they nominated ex-President Martin Van Buren for president and Charles Francis Adams, son of John Quincy Adams and grandson of John Adams, for vice president. Despite the ticket's extraordinarily high name recognition, Van Buren and Adams won just 10 percent of the popular vote and failed to carry a single state. Congressional results were just as disappointing, as the party won a mere twelve seats. Shortly after the 1848 election, the Free Soil Party disappeared. Most Free Soilers returned to the parties they had previously supported, albeit with a renewed determination to change their party's respective stands on slavery-related issues. This movement back to the major parties caused considerable strife that led to today's current two-party system. Republicans replaced the Whigs and the Democrats became the party of the South.

The American (Know-Nothing) Party

It is a common misconception that the only controversial issue prior to the Civil War was slavery. For many Americans, particularly those in urban areas, immigration was a primary concern. A vast number of working-class, native-born Protestants were deeply concerned with the heavy influx of Irish Catholics beginning in the early 1840s. Jobs, cultural issues, and the transformation of the United States into an ethnic polyglot became contentious political issues.

Originally organized around two groups known as the Supreme Order of the Star Spangled Banner and the National Council of the United States of America, in 1854 this party became known as the **American Party.** They were dubbed the **Know-Nothings** after a reporter asked about their secret meetings only to be told that he "knew nothing." The party's core philosophy was simple: "Americans should rule America. . . . Foreigners have no right to dictate our laws, and therefore have no just ground to complain if Americans see proper to exclude them from offices of trust."[27] The Know-Nothing platform included planks mandating that immigrants live in the United States for twenty-one years before being allowed to vote; that they never hold public office; and that their children should have no rights unless they were educated in public schools. Taking aim at Catholics and their allegiance to the Pope, the Know-Nothings declared: "No person should be selected for political station (whether of native or foreign birth), who recognizes any alliance or obligation of any description to foreign prince, potentate or power."[28]

The popularity of the Know-Nothings—an openly bigoted, demagogic group—is one of the darker tales in American history. In 1854, the party achieved extraordinary success by capturing scores of congressional and state legislative seats mostly in the Northeast. In Massachusetts, where immigrants were pouring in at a rate of 100,000 per year, the Know-Nothings won an astounding 347 of 350 state house seats, and all of the state senate, congressional, and statewide contests, including the governorship. In New York, they elected forty members of the state legislature and took control of the governorship. The party also won the governorships of Rhode Island, New Hampshire, and Connecticut.

In 1856, the Know-Nothings became caught up in the politics of slavery. At the party's convention in Philadelphia, northern delegates wanted to nominate a presidential candidate who opposed the extension of slavery into the new western territories. Southerners blocked the move, and the northern delegates bolted out of the convention hall. The remaining southern delegates nominated former Whig President Millard Fillmore as their candidate for president and Andrew Jackson Dodelson of Tennessee for vice president. The ticket captured 875,000 votes, or 21 percent of the popular vote and eight Electoral College votes all from the state of Maryland.

After two stunning showings at the polls, the Know-Nothings faded fast. Passage of the 1854 Kansas-Nebraska Act accentuated the slavery issue and created deep sectional divisions. The Republicans—a Northern, anti-slavery party—burst on the scene and most of the northern Know-Nothings joined their ranks. In the South, the Know-Nothings were absorbed by the former Whigs. By 1860, the Know-Nothings were no more.

The Greenback and Populists (People's) Parties

After the Civil War, American politics settled into the now-familiar Republican-Democratic rivalry. During the 1860s, northern-based Republicans broadened their base of support. Laborers liked the high protective tariffs; entrepreneurs welcomed federal involvement in building a transcontinental railroad; and farmers strongly supported the land grants created by the Homestead Act. Republicans became the dominant party—a position they occupied for the next sixty years. This is not to say the GOP coalition persisted without internal strife. During the early 1870s, the nation entered hard times and Midwest farmers suffered from plummeting crop prices. Railroads were the only means to ship Midwest farm goods to major markets in the East, and privately-owned companies charged exorbitant rates. Adding to the farmers's plight was a deflation of the currency, which made it difficult for them to pay their high bills.

The first efforts to organize agricultural interests culminated in the formation of hundreds of local organizations called farmers' alliances or granges. Mixing political and social activities, the granges united farmers into a cohesive voting block. Many who belonged to the granges were attached to the idea of a third party, and after the economic panic of 1873, the **Greenback Party** was created. The party proposed an inflated currency based on cheap paper money known as "greenbacks" that were first introduced during the Civil War.[29] Their argument was simple: by making the greenback legal tender, there would be enough money in circulation to ease the burden of indebted farmers and laborers. The Greenback Party was also known as the Greenback-Labor Party.

In 1878, Greenback congressional candidates won more than 1 million votes and fourteen House races. Two years later they nominated General James Weaver of Iowa as their presidential candidate. By that time, however, the Greenback Party had lost its initial appeal, as the nation's economy had improved. Weaver won just 300,000 votes and the Greenbacks sent only eight members to Congress. In 1884, the Greenbacks found their presidential support almost cut in half. The party was disappearing, but it demonstrated the potential for an agrarian-centered political party.

Overproduction and increased world competition led to another agricultural crisis in the early 1890s. The remaining Greenbacks merged with a new party called the **Populists,** or **People's Party,** in 1891. Unlike the Greenbacks, the Populists' demands were more radical and far-reaching: "We meet in the midst of a nation brought to the verge of moral, political, and material ruin. . . . From the womb of governmental injustice, we breed the two great classes—tramps and millionaires."[30] Among other things, the Populist platform proposed public regulation of railroads and telegraphs; free coinage of silver and gold (as a means to increase currency in circulation); creation of postal savings banks; prohibition of alien ownership of land; a graduated federal income tax; direct election of U.S. senators; and a reduction of the workday to eight hours. The Populists readily won adherents in the Midwest, West, and even in the South. One historian summarized the new party's appeal this way: "The Populist Party was the embodiment of an attitude, a way of looking at life that had been prevalent for almost twenty years, and a general position taken against concentrated economic power."[31]

The Populists selected former Greenback James Weaver as its 1892 presidential nominee. Weaver won just 8 percent of the popular vote (about a million votes) and twenty-two Electoral College votes. Nearly all of his support came from Western states. In effect, the Populists split the Republican vote, giving Democrat Grover

Cleveland a chance to recapture the presidency. Democrats also won control of both houses of Congress—a rarity in this Republican-dominated era. Populist strength grew in 1894, when they won nearly 1.5 million votes and elected six U.S. senators and seven House members, all from the West.

Then, in 1896, something unusual happened: both the Populists and the Democrats nominated William Jennings Bryan for president. Bryan had endorsed many Populist planks—most notably, the elimination of the gold standard. At the Democratic National Convention Bryan gave one of the most famous speeches in the history of American oratory (see "The Parties Speak: William Jennings Bryan's 'Cross of Gold Speech'"). After the Democratic Convention, the Populists—also moved by Bryan's Cross of Gold speech—chose him for president. Curiously, the Populists refused to endorse the Democratic vice presidential candidate, Arthur Sewall, a banker from Maine. Although Bryan lost, many of the Populist Party's proposals were ultimately accepted by both parties and incorporated into law during the twentieth century. Political scientist Clinton Rossiter drew an important lesson from the Populist experience:

> Of all the scores of minor parties that have skipped fitfully across our political landscape, only one, the Populists, seems in retrospect to have mounted a serious challenge to the hegemony of the two major parties. . . . Yet, the nomination of Bryan in 1896 smashed their dreams with one blow of the hammer, and the Populists proved how complete the wreckage was by hastening to nominate Bryan themselves. . . . One of the persistent qualities of the American two-party system is the way in which one of the major parties moves almost instinctively to absorb (and thus be somewhat reshaped by) the most challenging third party of the time.[22]

The Progressives: 1912–1924

In Chapter 3, we outlined the rationale behind the Progressive movement, its numerous successes against machine-dominated locales, and the eventual coalescence into a third party in 1912. Since then, Progressive ideas have been a recurring force in American politics, although progressivism has assumed different meanings in different eras. Originally, its focus was centered in the religious belief that the human condition could be infinitely improved. By the end of the nineteenth century, progressivism meant ridding the political system of corrupt influences. At the turn of the twentieth century, Progressives wanted greater participation by average citizens in governmental affairs, and they believed that government could be improved by bringing scientific methods to bear on public problems. By the late twentieth century, progressivism became a collection of liberal ideas centered on greater government involvement in curing society's ills. Bernie Sanders recently formed the Progressive Caucus which attracted the support of fifty-eight liberal House members.

The Progressive Party of 1912 wanted to purge the American polity of rank corruption. Theodore Roosevelt led the Progressive Party after the Republican bosses shut him out. With a legion of backers, Roosevelt bolted the Republican Convention to form the **Progressive** (or **Bull Moose**) **Party.** Calling for a "new nationalism," Roosevelt ran on a platform that promised stricter regulation of corporations; downward revision of tariffs; popular election of U.S. senators; women's

The Parties Speak: *William Jennings Bryan's "Cross of Gold" Speech Presented to the Democratic National Convention, Chicago, Illinois, July 8, 1896*

I would be presumptuous, indeed, to present myself against the distinguished gentlemen to whom you have listened if this were a mere measuring of abilities; but this is not a contest between persons. The humblest citizen in all the land, when clad in the armor of a righteous cause, is stronger than all the hosts of error. I come to speak to you in defense of a cause as holy as the cause of liberty—the cause of humanity. . . .

Mr. Carlisle said in 1878 that this was a struggle between the "idle holders of idle capital" and "the struggling masses, who produce the wealth and pay the taxes of the country," and my friends, the question we are to decide is: Upon which side will the Democratic party fight; upon the side of "the idle holders of idle capital" or upon the side of "the struggling masses?" That is the question which the party must answer first, and then it must be answered by each individual hereafter. The sympathies of the Democratic party, as shown by the platform, are on the side of the struggling masses who have ever been the foundation of the Democratic party. There are two ideas of government. There are those who believe that if you will only legislate to make the well-to-do prosperous, their prosperity will find its way up through every class which rests upon them.

You come to us and tell us that the great cities are in favor of the gold standard; we reply that the great cities rest upon our broad and fertile prairies. Burn down your cities and leave our farms, and your cities will spring up again as if by magic; but destroy our farms and the grass will grow in the streets of every city in the country.

My friends, we declare that this nation is able to legislate for its own people on every question, without waiting for the aid or consent of any other nation on earth; and upon that issue we expect to carry every state in the Union. I shall not slander the inhabitants of the fair state of Massachusetts nor the inhabitants of the state of New York by saying that, when they are confronted with the proposition, they will declare that this nation is not able to attend to its own business. It is the issue of 1776 over again. Our ancestors, when but three million in number, had the courage to declare their political independence of every other nation; shall we, their descendants, when we have grown to seventy millions, declare that we are less independent than our forefathers?

No, my friends, that will never be the verdict of our people. Therefore, we care not upon what lines the battle is fought. If they say bimetallism is good, but that we cannot have it until other nations help us, we reply, that instead of having a gold standard because England has, we will restore bimetallism, and then let England have bimetallism because the United States has it. If they dare to come out in the open field and defend the gold standard as a good thing, we will fight them to the uttermost. Having behind us the producing masses of this nation and the world, supported by the commercial interests, the laboring interests and the toilers everywhere, we will answer their demand for a gold standard by saying to them: You shall not press down upon the brow of labor this crown of thorns, you shall not crucify mankind upon a cross of gold.

SOURCE: Henry Steele Commager, ed. *Documents of American History*, 6th ed. (New York: Appleton-Century-Crofts, 1958), 174–78.

suffrage; and support for the referendum, initiative, and recall. Winning 27 percent of the popular vote and eighty-eight Electoral College votes put Roosevelt in second place behind Democrat Woodrow Wilson. William Howard Taft, the Republican nominee, finished third—the first time that had happened to a GOP presidential candidate since the party's inception.

Certainly, the high point of the Progressive movement was Roosevelt's strong showing in the 1912 election. Afterward, President Wilson pursued a Progressive agenda including passage of new antitrust laws, banking regulations, and scores of business reforms. The Progressive Party did not die completely, however, especially in states with strong populist traditions. In 1924, Robert La Follette—a former U.S. representative, U.S. senator, and governor of Wisconsin—became the Progressive Party's presidential nominee. La Follette was an articulate champion of labor reform, business regulation, a graduated income tax, and a constitutional amendment providing for the direct election of judges to the federal courts. His party's platform proposed public ownership of the nation's water power, strict control and conservation of all natural resources, farmers' cooperatives, and legislation to make credit available to farmers and small businessmen. He drew support from Midwesterners, farmers, labors, and Socialists, who did not have a candidate of their own. La Follette won 17 percent of the popular vote (4.8 million ballots), but won only thirteen Electoral College votes, all from his home state of Wisconsin. With his death in 1925, La Follette's brand of progressivism went with him to the grave. Though his children and grandchildren became active in politics and continued to push the Progressive agenda, they did not attract much attention beyond the Wisconsin borders.

Henry Wallace and the Progressive Party of 1948

In 1948, the Progressive Party reemerged. That year, a group of left-wing ideologues led by former Vice President Henry A. Wallace, bolted from the Democratic Party. At issue was President Harry S Truman's "get tough" policy toward the Soviet Union which Wallace strongly opposed. In July 1948, the Progressive Citizens of America selected Wallace as its presidential candidate. The Progressive Convention with its 3,000 delegates—including an obscure Northwestern University graduate student named George McGovern—was characterized as being twenty years younger and thirty pounds lighter than its Democratic and Republican counterparts. The 1948 Progressive platform proposed new antilynching laws, scrapping the Electoral College in favor of a popular tally for president, price controls, and national health insurance.

But the Progressive Party's real focus was not on a liberal domestic agenda but foreign policy. Henry Wallace and the Progressive Party accused President Truman of being vociferously anticommunist which they said stemmed from "the dictates of monopoly and the military" and resulted in "preparing for war in the name of peace."[33] To the utopian-minded Progressives, peace was "the prerequisite of survival": "There is no American principle of public interest, and there is no Russian principle of public interest, which would have to be sacrificed to end the Cold War and open up the Century of Peace which the Century of the Common Man demands."[34] Most Progressives dismissed the Soviet Union as a serious national security threat. George McGovern remembered: "The Soviet Union was about 50 percent destroyed in World War II. Half the country was devastated. They were in no position to launch World War III. I always felt that our policy had a big streak of paranoia in that period after World War II, and that we greatly exaggerated the Soviet threat."[35] Given these views, the Progressive Party called for a wholesale reversal in how the U.S. government dealt with domestic communism. The party favored eliminating the House Un-American Activities Committee, claiming it had vilified and prosecuted citizens "in total disregard of the Bill of Rights." It also rejected any ban of the U.S. Communist Party or required registration of its members, likening such legislation to the Alien and Sedition Acts.

As the Progressive Party standard-bearer, Henry Wallace drew large crowds—including many young liberals, blue-collar workers, and blacks. His liberal listeners worried Truman, who attempted to link Wallace with the U.S. Communist Party. Wallace's public statements made Truman's task an easy one. Shortly after the Czechoslovakian coup when that country's leader was tossed out of a window into the street to his death by Soviet-minded communists, Wallace likened the communists to the early Christian martyrs—a comparison that appalled Truman.[36] Later, Wallace argued that the Berlin airlift (a response to the Soviet blockade of U.S. access to the western sectors of Berlin) was misguided, claiming the United States could afford to cede Berlin to the Soviets as a price for peace.[37] The U.S. Communist Party hailed Wallace, claiming he had forged a new alignment of the "people's coalition."[38] Wallace stubbornly refused to renounce communist backing of his candidacy, saying: "I will not repudiate any support which comes to me on the basis of interest in peace."[39]

Wallace's conciliatory statements helped Truman paint the Progressive Party and the communists as one in the public eye. At various whistle-stops, Truman vowed: "I do not want and I will not accept the political support of Henry Wallace and his communists."[40] A Gallup poll taken shortly before the Progressive convention found 51 percent agreeing that the Progressive Party was communist-dominated. Among those most likely to view Wallace as a communist dupe were Democrats, 57 percent; those sixty years of age or older, 56 percent; and Southerners, 62 percent.[41] Wallace-backer I. F. Stone conceded: "Turn off the white lights and lay off the hotfoot. I admit everything. The Communists are doing a major part of the work of the Wallace movement, from ringing doorbells to framing platforms. Okay if you want it that way, they 'dominate' the party. So what?"[42]

So what indeed, said Truman, who averred that Wallace was part of "the contemptible communist minority."[43] In a September speech at Gilmore Stadium in Los Angeles—surrounded by many Hollywood stars including Ronald Reagan— Truman urged liberals to "think again" and end their dalliance with Wallace: "This is the hour for the liberal forces of America to unite. We have hopes to fulfill and goals to attain. Together we can rout the forces of reaction once again."[44]

Despite Wallace's enormous political shortcomings, he influenced the election result. When the ballots were counted, Wallace received 1,157,172 votes (slightly more than 2 percent), and half of these were from liberal-dominated New York. This was enough to throw three states to GOP presidential nominee Thomas E. Dewey: New York, Maryland, and Michigan. If Wallace had done somewhat better in California, and had not been kept off the Illinois ballot, the 1948 contest could have been decided in the House of Representatives.

State's Rights Party (1948) and the American Independent Party (1968)

After the Civil War, the roots of the Democratic Party became deeply planted in the South. During the 1930s, Franklin Roosevelt transformed the Democratic Party from a minority into a majority by including labor, middle- and lower-class urban residents, Catholics, African Americans, and Jews it its ranks—along with the ever-loyal southerners. Relations between progressive northern Democrats and conservative southern Democrats became a "marriage of convenience." Northern Democrats controlled the White House thanks to their southern partners, and southern Democrats chaired important congressional committees thanks to their party's majority status and adherence to the seniority rule.

By the late 1940s, this marriage between northern and southern Democrats was in trouble. Civil rights split the two factions apart in 1948. That year, the Democratic Convention adopted a strong pro–civil rights plank. Many southern delegates walked out and reconvened in Birmingham, Alabama. The gathering adopted the name **States Rights Party** and quickly became known as the **Dixiecrat Party** given its overwhelming southern base of support. The convention reiterated a plank extracted from the 1840 Democratic Party platform: "Congress has no power under the Constitution to interfere with or control the domestic institutions of the several states, and that such states are the sole and proper judges of everything appertaining to their own affairs not prohibited by the Constitution."[45] This state's rights argument was designed to keep the existing racial segregation intact.

The delegates nominated J. Strom Thurmond, then governor of South Carolina, as their presidential candidate. On election day, Thurmond garnered 1.1 million votes (2.4 percent) and won thirty-eight Electoral College votes from five southern states. The party closed shop after the election while Thurmond went on to have a successful political career as a Republican. In 1954, Thurmond became the only U.S. senator ever to be elected in a write-in campaign after the state Democratic Party rejected him. By the early 1960s, Thurmond formally switched his party registration from Democratic to Republican. At the age of 94, Thurmond was reelected to the Senate in 1996. Already the oldest and longest serving U.S. senator in history, he is seriously considering another run in 2002.

The final blow to the post–Civil War Democratic coalition came in 1968. Once again, the breakdown centered around efforts to broaden legal protections for blacks. The **American Independent Party** was established in 1968 as the personal organization of Alabama Governor George C. Wallace. Wallace was elected governor in 1962 as a Democrat and ardent segregationist. In his inaugural address, Wallace professed his loyalty to the racial status quo that was under attack by northern liberal Democrats: "Segregation now, segregation tomorrow, segregation forever." A year later, Wallace entered the national spotlight when the federal government ordered the integration of public colleges. In a televised display of defiance, Wallace and several state troopers blocked access to the University of Alabama before stepping aside.

After an unsuccessful but impressive primary campaign against Democrat Lyndon B. Johnson in 1964, Wallace abandoned the Democratic Party in 1968 to form his own party which followed his get-tough, law-and-order, segregationist beliefs. With old-time populist themes and a powerful gift for oratory, Wallace won nearly 10 million ballots—13.5 percent of the total votes cast. His forty-six electoral votes from five southern states were more than Republican nominee Barry Goldwater received in 1964. Much of Wallace's southern strength came from former Democrats. These former yellow dog Democrats used the Wallace candidacy as a way station before entering the Republican Party. In 1972, Richard Nixon won over the vast majority of the 1968 Wallace backers, and during the 1980s the Wallace-ites began voting Republican for other offices such as governor, members of Congress, and the state legislature. Wallace, meanwhile, reentered Democratic presidential politics in 1972. At a rally in Laurel, Maryland, Wallace was shot and permanently paralyzed. Although he later won the Alabama governorship as a Democrat, Wallace's days in presidential politics were over. His American Independent Party and its offshoot, the American Party, continued to nominate candidates for a while before eventually disappearing altogether.

The Reform Party

The difference between minor parties and splinter candidacies is clearly evident when comparing Ross Perot's 1992 run for the presidency with his second try four years later. In his first effort, Perot did not field candidates for other offices, affirming his independence from all officeholders. Using his hefty pocketbook to finance his campaign, Perot ran on a platform that stressed the importance of a balanced federal budget and the need to enact major campaign finance reforms. His foremost strength was his charisma and can-do attitude. After winning an impressive 19 percent of the vote, Perot remained politically active by organizing a new political party centered on his core issues of a balanced budget and campaign finance reform. The Reform Party was born and by 1996 it qualified to run a slate of candidates in all fifty states. It had a national organization, developed formal rules, and even held a convention to nominate its presidential candidate who, not surprisingly, was Perot once more. This time, however, Perot accepted federal funds, thus saving him from once again having to finance his own campaign. Although Perot was relatively unsuccessful, this time winning just 8 percent of the vote, the Reform Party persisted. In many states, the organization has foundered without Perot's leadership and financial backing; but in others it is growing. The Reform Party's greatest success came in 1998 with the election of Jesse Ventura as Governor of Minnesota.

THIRD PARTIES IN THE INFORMATION AGE

One theme that has been repeated throughout the pages of this book is that Information Age technologies are transforming political parties. Third parties are not immune from the technological innovations spawned by the Information Age. This section charts the explosion of minor parties vying for office; explores changing voter attitudes toward minor party candidates; and examines how the World Wide Web has bolstered the prospects of a viable multiparty system.

An Explosion of Minor Parties

Despite the numerous barriers they confront, there has been an explosion of minor parties during the 1990s in the United States. Table 10.2 highlights the number of campaigns that involved at least one minor party candidate from 1968 to 1994. During the three decades prior to the 1990s, less than half of U.S. House and

TABLE 10.2 ▪ Minor Parties and Candidates in the United States, 1968–1994								
	1968	*1972*	*1976*	*1980*	*1984*	*1988*	*1992*	*1994*
Number of parties	28	31	33	38	34	33	69	51
Number of candidates for governor	11	19	26	11	9	7	18	79
Number of candidates for U.S. Senate	22	40	65	54	39	42	72	49
Number of candidates for U.S. House	180	190	335	264	190	189	440	252
Number of candidates for State Legislature	664	756	820	902	702	764	1,195	876
Number of races with three candidates*	122	106	129	128	134	99	141	141
Number of races with four candidates	30	45	58	48	26	36	75	55
Number of races with five+ candidates	8	13	45	26	9	13	58	32

*The measure combines the candidacies for Governor, U.S. Senate, and House of Representatives; state legislative races are excluded.

SOURCE: Christian Collet and Jerrold Hansen, "Minor Party Candidates in Subpresidential Elections," in John C. Green and Daniel M. Shea, eds. *The State of the Parties: The Changing Role of Contemporary American Parties*, 2nd ed. (Lanham, Md.: Rowman and Littlefield, 1997), 242.

Senate contest had minor party candidates. By the 1990s, that number had grown by some 50 percent. The same trend is evident in state legislative races. In 1968, 664 contests had more than two candidates vying for office; by 1992, that figure had nearly doubled.[46] Especially significant is the fact that the number of races at all levels with two, three, and four minor party candidates slugging it out has also greatly increased. Thus, while few minor party candidates have been elected, there is little doubt that more political activists are willing to create and maintain a minor political party.

Who are these minor party candidates and why are there so many more of them in the 1990s? The most comprehensive answers come from two graduate students at the University of California at Irvine, Christian Collet and Jerrold Hansen.[47] Interviewing nearly six hundred minor party candidates, they made several important discoveries. First, the vast majority belonged to one of the major parties before striking out on their own. In fact, 14 percent had actually belonged to both parties at one time in the past. Most cited the failure of two-party politics—claiming that the Democrats and Republicans were ineffective, elitist, committed to the status quo, and corrupt. Second, although they were disillusioned with the two parties, nearly all believed in the party system. Few agreed with the statement that, "The truth is, we probably don't need political parties anymore." Third, most minor party candidates were lukewarm toward other members of their party's ticket. Just slightly more than one-half (56 percent) supported their own party's candidate for president in 1992. Fourth, most minor party candidates were well-educated and affluent: 77 percent had personal incomes over $40,000 per year, and 33 percent made over $60,000 annually.

Similar research projects have been conducted to better understand the motivations of Ross Perot's supporters. The most extensive one was undertaken by a team of scholars at the University of Colorado.[48] Random-sampling of 450,000 people who called Ross Perot's toll-free telephone number in the summer of 1992, has provided much information about who might support minor party candidates. These findings mirror those of the Collet and Hansen study. Perot activists tended to be better-educated and had high incomes; most had been affiliated with either the Democratic or Republican party; and the principal reason for abandoning the two major parties was their considerable cynicism toward them. As the authors of the study concluded: "Perot attacked 'politics as usual' and our evidence shows that he was successful in attracting a constituency of the discontented."[49]

Perhaps the most significant finding from these scholarly studies is that, like their nineteenth and twentieth century predecessors, Information Age third parties emerge because neither party is addressing the concerns of the ordinary voter. Abolitionist parties emerged because of slavery, the Populists and Greenbacks because of economic issues, the Progressives because of corruption, and the segregationist parties in response to pending civil rights legislation. This does not appear to be the case in the 1990s. Third parties are being born because consumers of party politics are increasingly discouraged by the status quo. Contemporary third-party activists may have faith in the usefulness of political parties—perhaps unlike the average voter—but it is certainly not the two-party system.

Changes in Voter Attitudes toward Minor Parties

Throughout our history, political parties have fallen in and out of favor with their American consumers. Table 10.3 depicts the strong public sentiment for discarding the status quo-oriented two-party system. In 1938, the Roper Center for Public Opinion Research asked voters if they believed the two-party system was best for America or whether a strong third party should join the act. Only 13 percent

---

TABLE 10.3 ▪ **Changing Support for a Viable Third Party, 1938 and 1995**

Item 1: The following question was asked by the Roper Center for Public Opinion in 1938, and a very similar query by CNN/*USA Today* in 1995: "What parties would you like to see competing in the next presidential race . . . Republican and Democrat, Republican, Democrat and a new strong third-party . . . or two new parties with all conservatives and liberals voting together?"

Respondent	Roper 5/38	CNN/USA Today 9/95
Republican and Democrat/continuing two-party system	65%	26%
Republican, Democrat, and a strong new third party that would exist along with other parties	13%	53%
Two new parties with all conservatives and liberals voting together	6%	12%
Don't know/Other/Refused	16%	9%
Sample Size (N)	5,151	640

Item 2: The following question, or one quite similar, was asked by different polling firms between 1944 and 1994: "On the whole, how do you feel about the present set-up of the political parties here in the United States—Do you find that you are usually satisfied with the stands taken by one or the other present big parties, or would you like to see a strong new party entirely different from either of the present parties?"

Respondent	Roper 8/44	Gallup 9/68	USORC 11/81	CNN/USA Today 10/94
Usually satisfied, two parties are adequate	78%	67%	53%	40%
Like to see a strong new party	14%	27%	43%	53%
Other/Don't know/ No opinion	8%	6%	4%	4%
Sample size (N)	5,131	1,500	1,005	1,007

SOURCE: Christian Collet, "Third Parties and the Two-Party System." *Public Opinion Quarterly,* 60 (1996): 431–49.

wanted a viable third party. Fifty-seven years later, CNN and *USA Today* asked a similar question. This time the results were quite different: 53 percent wanted a new third party, while 26 percent preferred the existing two-party system. Trend data gathered since 1944 also point toward a weakening of traditional two-party politics. When respondents were asked whether they were "usually satisfied" with the positions taken by the two major parties, 78 percent answered "yes." By 1994, those calling themselves satisfied had fallen to just 40 percent; 53 percent preferred a strong, new party.

Other polling data also point toward a weakening of traditional two-party politics. When the *Los Angeles Times* asked in 1995 whether the "two-party system in this country is basically sound or unsound," 49 percent replied "unsound." Polls conducted by CBS News and the *New York Times* in 1996 found 57 percent saying that the United States needs a new political party to compete with the two major parties. The desire for a new party seems strongest among younger voters, which suggests the movement toward a multiparty system could gain steam.

But analysis of the data reveals less disenchantment with the two-party system in general than with the Democratic and Republican parties in particular. Information Age voters want more choices at the polling places, yet they have serious doubts about whether a third party can govern successfully. Ross Perot aside, there have been very few big third-party vote-getters in the 1990s. Bernie Sanders, Jesse Ventura, Angus King, and Lowell Weicker remain exceptions to the two-party hegemony. Failures are more commonplace. The Libertarian Party, for example, fielded and supported 166 House candidates in 1998, but not one got 10 percent of the vote. Of the 7,621 state legislative seats nationally, only 29 are filled by politicians who are not Democrats or Republicans—less than one-tenth of one percent. Despite some encouraging trends in the public opinion polls, third parties have a long way to go in American politics.

Minor Parties and the Internet

Although dissatisfaction with the two major parties is a primary cause for increased third-party activism, it is certainly not the only reason. Minor party activists are better able to communicate with voters. The World Wide Web has vastly simplified the job of creating, maintaining, and broadening the reach of third parties. The type of person who might be interested in third-party activities is likely to own a personal computer and have access to the Internet. Table 10.4 lists the Web site addresses of several third parties.

Of the larger third parties, the Reform Party has the most extensive Web site. This is not surprising since the party's founder, Ross Perot, made his mark using computer technology during the early 1960s. The site has an extensive biography of Perot and a link to his personal homepage. In addition to promoting Perot, the Web site informs Reform Party members of upcoming events; publishes a newsletter; promotes the party's radio show; uses a "postcard Friday" program to mobilize legislative support for its initiatives; solicits campaign volunteers and donations; contains a list of places where Reform Party candidates can buy campaign materials;

TABLE 10.4 ▪ Minor Parties on the Web: Web Site Addresses of Prominent Contemporary Third Parties

Party	World Wide Web Address
American Conservative Union	http://www.conservative.org/
American Reform Party	http://www.americanreform.org/
Communist Party	http://www.hartford-hwp.com/cp-usa/
Constitution Action Party	http://www2.ari.net/home/CAP/
Creator's Rights Party	http://www.christiangallery.com/creator.html/platform/ppp02_o.htm
Democratic Socialists of America	http://www.dsausa.org/pc/pc.html
Green Party	http://www.environlink.org/greens/cgi-bin/HyperNews/get/10k.html
Libertarian Party	http://www.lp.org/
National Party	http://www.cyberg8t.com/natlprty/onissues.htm
Natural Law Party	http://www.natural-law.org/nlpusa/
New Liberty Party	http://expage.com/ page/newlibertyparty
Patriot Party	http://205.232.76.174/patriot/patriot.html
Peace Party	http://www.neosoft.com/~eris/PPP
Prohibition Party	http://pages.whowhere.com/politics/clgammon/index.html
Reform Party	http://www.reformparty.org/
Royalist Party of America	http://www.prairienet.org/~cwolf/r-index.html
Social Democrats	http://www.socialdemocrats.org/sdusa/Pansexual Unites
States Taxpayers Party	http://www.usataxpayers.org/

and provides several direct e-mail links to Reform Party leaders. During the fall of 1998, those who clicked on the Reform Party homepage were invited to respond to a survey seeking opinions about the impeachment of Bill Clinton. By December, there were more than 460,000 responses. While the results of this survey are not an accurate barometer of public opinion, the overwhelming response suggests the enormous potential of minor party Web sites to recruit new supporters.

The Green Party of North America also boasts an especially effective site. This homepage informs browsers about Green Party candidates; describes the party's mission; charts the growth of new members; lists state and local leaders; and enlists volunteers. The site lists the ten key values to unite Greens worldwide: social justice, community-based economics, nonviolence, decentralization, future focus/ sustainability, feminism, personal and global responsibility, respect for diversity, grassroots democracy and ecological wisdom.

Even the smallest third-party Web sites contain vast amounts of information. The United States Taxpayers Party, for instance, describes their overall goals; posts position papers on a host of issues; lists the addresses and phone numbers of their headquarters; and has information on how to become a member. With 172,768 hits in a four-month period in 1998, the site has been extremely cost-effective. Several pro-labor third-party organizations are also located on the Information Superhighway. The Social Democrats' page proclaims: "We are not conservatives, who say that there have always been and will always be the weak and the strong, and the role of civilized people is to vitiate only the most vicious aspects of that reality. Nor are we liberals, who say that the role of civilized people is to protect the weak from the strong. That chivalric impulse ultimately weakens those protected, making them dependent on the good will of the powerful." The Democratic Socialists of America Party has a Web site that allows browsers to learn more about the party and its mission. It encourages programs that build economic security, reverse entrenched discrimination, achieve a sustainable use of both human and environmental resources, and build a society that values and embraces all its members. The site introduces surfers to the party's think tank, the Progressive Challenge.

At the opposite end of the ideological spectrum, the American Conservative Union's (ACU) Web page reads, "We believe that collectivism and capitalism are incompatible, and that when government competes with capitalism, it jeopardizes the natural economic growth of our society and the well-being and freedom of the citizenry." The party's Web site invites visitors to read pro-ACU columnists, become members, and view the ACU congressional ratings. The Libertarian Party has a sophisticated Web site that has quick access to directories and lists of candidates, official documents, information about the party in any state, the organization's history, and news announcements. One notable feature is a list of the party's current activities. For instance, each year on April 15—tax day—the Libertarian Party sponsors a nationwide antitax rally at local post offices. The site gives information about rally sites and how to sponsor a local protest. The party communicates via an e-mail bulletin that can be obtained through the Web site.

What good does a sophisticated Web site do for a candidate? Does it actually attract new members? Is there a payoff on election day? While the jury is still out on these questions, many commentators and analysts believe the Internet may be the key that unlocks the door for a multiparty system. One illustration of the potential that the World Wide Web has for minor party candidates is the case of Jesse Ventura. Ventura's use of the Internet—grassroots democracy via cyberspac—allowed him to keep costs down, spread the word, target high voter areas like Minneapolis, and get feedback from chat rooms (see "The Parties Speak: Ventura Win Marks Dawn of New Era").

JEFFERSON, HAMILTON, AND THE FUTURE OF THIRD PARTIES IN AMERICA

A review of the history of American third parties underscores several conflicting themes. On the one hand, the chips are clearly stacked against third parties. Scores of institutional barriers—including the winner-take-all system, Electoral College, difficult ballot access, and a host of historical and cultural forces—push the American polity toward a two-party model. Yet minor parties have played a critical role at

---

The Parties Speak: *Ventura Win Marks Dawn of New Era:*
Age of Digital Politics

Reform Party candidate Jesse Ventura's use of the Internet proved to be an invaluable tool in his stunning 1998 victory over two established Democratic and Republican party opponents. This excerpt describes how Ventura did it.

In January, nobody believed an outside-the-Beltway political consultant who predicted the Internet would be the key to a major election victory in November. In March, nobody really believed a third-party candidate who said he'd be the next governor of Minnesota. Today, the Reform Party's Jesse "The Body" Ventura, a former wrestler, is more than the governor-elect of Minnesota. He's the first candidate to win a major race because of the Internet. And his use of the Internet in the 1998 elections will be the hottest topic of discussion among political consultants, gurus, and Webheads. Consider the following:

Exhibit 1: Ventura truly represents the grassroots democratic nature of the Internet. He had only two paid staff members, a glitterless Web site <www. jesseventura.org> and content that could have been better written. But his Internet presence—lots of digital pictures, flurries of e-mail to supporters and use of the medium to coordinate research on issues—reflected the type of candidate he was and the kind of campaign he ran.

Exhibit 2: The Governor-elect used the Internet to build, expand, and promote his campaign. His database volunteer team, or D-Team, input data, uploaded digital pictures from the campaign trail, posted messages on a bulletin board, arranged chats and followed him on a 72–hour statewide campaign tour on election eve. By integrating the Web into a living, physical campaign tool, Ventura's supporters were able to keep in touch and spread his message.

Exhibit 3: He built on the Perot/Reform Technology Base. Ross Perot left a legacy of using the Internet in campaigning to the third parties. The Reform Party, and Ventura in Minnesota, adopted the Net as a significant tool for their campaigns. His campaign essentially built an Intranet of supporters and volunteers to motivate the electorate.

Exhibit 4: The Net delivered. Steve Clift of Minnesota E-Democracy, the state's foremost nonpartisan, citizen-based Internet project, said Ventura's campaign got an extra bump because of the effective use it made of the Internet. "I'd even go as far to say that Ventura received 2 to 3 percentage points based on what they did on the Net, which happens to be his margin of victory," Clift said. Phil Madsen, Ventura's Webmaster, agreed: "There is no way on Earth that we could have organized the tour without the Internet. And without the tour, we might not have had those votes to win. If you removed the Internet, we would not have won."

Exhibit 5: Minnesota has high Internet usage. To use the Internet effectively in elections, you've got to have Internet users who can access the online campaign. Yahoo! Internet Life ranks Minneapolis as the sixth most-wired city in America. While nominees from the Democratic and Republican Parties maintained good Web sites, they could have underestimated the effect and usage of the medium in Minnesota. Ventura, on the other hand, tapped into a virtual army of hundreds of online volunteers to organize support, get out his message, build rallies, and garner publicity.

continued

The Parties Speak: *Ventura Win Marks Dawn of New Era:*
Age of Digital Politics (continued)

Exhibit 6: Ventura reached new, young, and motivated Internet voters. The campaign's use of the Internet apparently had an impact on the civic participation of Generation X. Ventura's campaign provided Gen X voters with a way to participate and get involved through his Internet site. "Throughout the campaign, Ventura supporters said they either hadn't voted in years or had never voted at all," according to the *Minneapolis Star Tribune*.

Ventura is the first CyberGovernor. While some may view the Reform candidate as a yahoo, Ventura was the mayor of the sixth largest city in Minnesota (Brooklyn Park). His campaign represented a true grassroots democratic use of the Internet because it used the medium to provide more than information. It organized, motivated, and prodded voters to the polls.

Whenever there is a new technology, a political figure masters and uses that technology to his advantage. For example, John F. Kennedy defined and created the era of television politics. In Minnesota, Jesse Ventura might not be the Kennedy of the Internet, but he fundamentally understood how to use the new medium of the Internet to win an election. His victory marks the dawn of a new era—the age of digital politics. Members of Congress should take note and adjust their future campaign strategies accordingly.

SOURCE: Excerpted from Phil Noble, "Ventura Win Marks Dawn of New Era: Age of Digital Politics," *Roll Call*, December 7, 1998.

---

key moments before fading into the history books. Thus, to ignore minor parties is to overlook a key factor in shaping the evolution of the American party system.

One way to conceptualize the role of minor parties is to return to the models of party politics: Hamiltonian Nationalism and Jeffersonian Localism. American parties rest on a Hamiltonian foundation—meaning that party elites at the state and national levels control the inner-workings of their respective party. For these folks, community-based party organizations and grassroots activism is directed toward winning elections. Policy innovation is usually sluggish, as party operatives retreat to proven themes that win at the polls. Yet the desire for a Jeffersonian-style party system centered around deep-seated policy concerns is a powerful and recurring counterforce. When a sizable segment of the electorate feels that issues important to them are not being adequately addressed by the Hamiltonian-style parties, minor parties burst on the scene. Third parties become a manifestation of voter desire for a policy-driven politics. The party system may be shaken, but the two-party Hamiltonian-style party system reasserts itself.

The theme that minor parties help introduce a profoundly different party system has been explored by several scholars. Theodore J. Lowi, a former president of the American Political Science Association, writes: "New ideas and issues develop or redevelop parties, but parties, particularly established ones, rarely develop ideas or present new issues on their own. . . . Once a system of parties is established, the range and scope of policy discussion is set, until and unless some disturbance arises from other quarters."[50] The "disturbance" Lowi speaks of is the development of aggressive third parties. Lowi notes there have been four historical eras when Democrats and Republicans have been especially innovative: (1) 1856–1860; (2) 1890–1900; (3) 1912–1914; and (4) 1933–1935. In these years, party leaders became more susceptible to mass opinion as a result of third-party competition. Once policy innovations were achieved, the third parties withered away. Using the Hamilton-Jefferson model, third parties have periodically shaken the system and have temporally shifted it toward Jeffersonian Localism.

How will third parties fare in the Information Age? Third-party advocates have much to cheer about. For one thing, many Americans appear ready to scrap the two-party model. Though the success of third-party candidates has been limited, more are jumping into the political fray. The major hurdle they face is convincing voters that their ballots will not be wasted. Perhaps as more minor party candidates like Jesse Ventura, Angus King, Bernard Sanders, and Lowell Weicker overcome the odds, more voters will act upon their pro-third-party proclivities. There are also some institutional changes underway that may aid minor party efforts. Certainly, Information Age technologies have made it easier for minor party leaders to connect with potential supporters at a greatly reduced cost, and the World Wide Web should become even more important in the years ahead. In short, it seems entirely likely that minor parties will find the political environment in the next millennium more hospitable than during the past one hundred years.

Nonetheless, the prospects for developing a viable multiparty system remain daunting. Over the past three decades we have witnessed a centralization and professionalization of electoral politics with a profound shift toward Hamiltonian Nationalism. Candidates realize that the best way to win elections is to amass huge war chests and implement high-technology voter communication techniques. The level of funding and campaign technologies needed to become competitive are beyond their reach of most third parties. Given the increased professionalization of American politics, it is likely that minor parties will remain the orphans of American politics.

FURTHER READING

Bibby, John F. and L. Sandy Maisel. *Two Parties—Or More? The American Party System.* Boulder, Colo.: Westview Press, 1998.

Herrnson, Paul S. and John C. Green. *Multiparty Politics in America.* Lanham, Md.: Rowman and Littlefield, 1997.

Kruschke, Earl R. *Encyclopedia of Third Parties in the United States.* Santa Barbara, Calif.: ABC-CLIO, 1991.

Sanders, Bernie. *Outsider in the House.* New York: Verso Press, 1997.

Smallwood, Frank. *The Other Candidates: Third Parties in Presidential Elections.* Hanover, N.H.: University Press of New England, 1983.

NOTES

1. Bernie Sanders, *Outsider in the House* (New York: Verso Press, 1997), 94.

2. Clinton Rossiter, *Parties and Politics in America* (Ithaca: Cornell University Press, 1960), 3.

3. Quoted in Frank Smallwood, *The Other Candidates: Third Parties in Presidential Elections* (Hanover, N.H.: University Press of New England, 1983), 9.

4. Richard Winger, "Institutional Obstacles to a Multiparty System." In Paul S. Herrnson and John C. Green, eds. *Multiparty Politics in America* (Lanham, Md.: Rowman and Littlefield, 1997), 167.

5. Ibid.

6. This argument is made in John F. Bibby and L. Sandy Maisel, *Two Parties-Or More? The American Party System* (Boulder, Colo.: Westview Press, 1998), 58.

7. Herbert B. Asher, *Presidential Elections and American Politics* (Pacific Grove, Calif.: Brooks/Cole, 1992), 215.

8. See, for instance, Bibby and Maisel, *Two Parties or More*, 63-4; and Paul R. Abramson, John H. Aldrich, Phil Paolino, and David W. Rhode, "Third-Party and Independent Candidates: Wallace, Anderson, and Perot," *Political Science Quarterly* 110, 349–68.

9. Survey conducted by the Roper Organization, December 1939. The results are taken among "whites only." There are no dollar definitions as to what constitutes "poor" in this survey.

10. Arthur Larson, *A Republican Looks at His Party* (New York: Harper, 1956), ix, 14, 15.

11. Dwight D. Eisenhower, "Acceptance Speech," Republican National Convention, August 23, 1956.

12. Louis Hartz, *The Liberal Tradition in America: An Interpretation of American Political Thought Since the Revolution* (New York: Harcourt Brace, 1955), 7.

13. Alexis de Tocqueville, *Democracy in America*, ed. Richard D. Heffner (New York: New American Library, 1956), 117–18.

14. Quoted in Everett Carll Ladd, *The American Ideology: An Exploration of the Origins, Meaning, and Role of American Political Ideas* (Storrs, Conn.: Roper Center for Public Opinion Research, 1994), 32.

15. Quoted in John Gerring, "A Chapter in the History of American Party Ideology: The Nineteenth Century Democratic Party, 1828–1892" (paper presented at the Northeastern Political Science Association; Newark, N.J., November 11–13, 1993), 36–37. Cass made these remarks on September 2, 1852.

16. See Roy P. Basler, ed., *The Collected Works of Abraham Lincoln* (New Brunswick, N.J.: Rutgers University Press, 1953), 323.

17. Cited in Seymour Martin Lipset, "Why No Socialism in the United States?," in Seweryn Bailer and Sophia Sluzar, eds., *Radicalism in the Contemporary Age* (Boulder, Colo.: Westview Press, 1977), 40.

18. "There's the Ticket . . . A Selection of Running Mates for Ross Perot," *Washington Post*, September 7, 1996. Cited in Herrnson and Green, eds., *Multiparty Politics in America*, 20.

19. Lary May, "Movie Star Politics: The Screen Actors' Guild, Cultural Convention, and the Hollywood Red Scare," in Lary May, ed., *Recasting America: Culture and Politics in the Age of the Cold War* (Chicago: University of Chicago Press, 1988), 145.

20. For an interesting work on the connection between popular culture and political culture, see Daniel M. Shea, *Mass Politics: The Politics of Popular Culture* (New York: St. Martin's Press, 1999). For more information on the impact of the Cold War on American politics see John Kenneth White, *Still Seeing Red: How the Cold War Shapes the New American Politics* (Boulder, Colo.: Westview Press, 1998).

21. Shea, *Mass Politics*, 207.

22. Quoted in James Reston, "Liberty and Authority," *New York Times*, June 29, 1986, E23.

23. Smallwood, *The Other Candidates*.

24. Phyllis F. Field, "Masons," in L. Sandy Maisel, ed., *Political Parties and Elections in the United States: An Encyclopedia* (New York: Garland, 1991), 641–42.

25. Robert J. Spitzer, "Free Soil Party," in Maisel, *Political Parties and Elections in the United States: An Encyclopedia*, 409–10.

26. Edward W. Chester, *A Guide to Political Platforms* (New York: Archon Books, 1977), 58.

27. See Elinor C. Hartshorn, "Know-Nothings," in Maisel, *Political Parties and Elections in the United States: An Encyclopedia*, 549–50.

28. See Edward W. Chester, *A Guide to Political Platforms*, 70.

29. Earl R. Kruschke, *Encyclopedia of Third Parties in the United States* (Santa Barbara, Calif.: ABC-CLIO, 1991), 71.

30. Edward W. Chester, *A Guide to Political Platforms*, 121–35.

31. Frederick J. Augustyn, Jr., "Populists (People's) Party," in Maisel, *Political Parties and Elections in the United States: An Encyclopedia*, 849–50.

32. Rossiter, *Parties and Politics in America*, 73.

33. "Progressive Party Platform, 1948," in Kirk H. Porter and Donald Brace Johnson, *National Party Platforms: 1840–1968* (Urbana: University of Illinois Press, 1970), 437.

34. Ibid., 439.

35. John Kenneth White, interview with George S. McGovern, Washington, D.C., January 4, 1996.

36. Clark Clifford with Richard Holbrooke, *Counsel to the President: A Memoir* (New York: Anchor Books, 1991), 234.

37. David McCullough, *Truman* (New York: Simon & Schuster, 1992), 646.

38. Quoted in V. O. Key, Jr., *Politics, Parties, and Pressure Groups*, 5th ed. (New York: Crowell, 1964), 272.

39. Quoted in Clifford, *Counsel to the President*, 224.

40. Quoted in A. James Reichley, *The Life of the Parties* (New York: Free Press, 1992), 297.

41. Gallup poll, June 16–23, 1948. Text of question: "Do you think that the Henry Wallace third party is run by Communists?"

42. I. F. Stone, *The Truman Era* (New York: Random House, 1973), 67–68.

43. Quoted in Richard Norton Smith, *Thomas E. Dewey and His Times* (New York: Simon & Schuster, 1982), 509.

44. Harry S Truman, "Address at the Gilmore Stadium in Los Angeles," September 23, 1948, in *Public Papers of the Presidents of the United States: Harry S Truman* (Washington, D.C.: Government Printing Office, 1949), 559, 610.

45. Kruschke, *Encyclopedia of Third Parties in the United States*, 183.

46. Christian Collet and Jerrold Hansen, "Minor Party Candidates in Subpresidential Elections," in John C. Green and Daniel M. Shea, eds. *The State of the Parties: The Changing Role of Contemporary American Parties*, 2nd ed. (Lanham, Md.: Rowman and Littlefield, 1997), table 15.1.

47. Ibid.

48. Several studies have been conducted by Walter J. Stone, Loir M. Weber, Randall Partin, and Patricia Jaramillo of the University of Colorado and Ronald B. Rapoport of the College of William and Mary. Three of these studies appear in the subsequent editions of John C. Green and Daniel M. Shea, eds., *The State of the Parties: The Changing Role of Contemporary Party Organizations*. (Lanham, Md.: Rowman and Littlefield, 1994, 1997, and 1999).

49. Randall Partin, Lori M. Weber, Ronald Rapoport, and Walter J. Stone, "Perot Activists in 1992–1994: Sources of Activism," in Green and Shea, *The State of the Parties: The Changing Role of Contemporary American Parties*, 2nd ed., 236.

50. Theodore J. Lowi. "Toward a Responsible Three-Party System," in John C. Green and Daniel M. Shea, eds., *The State of the Parties: The Changing Role of Contemporary Party Organizations*. (Lanham, Md.: Rowman and Littlefield, 1994), 47.

Hamilton's Triumph and the Advent of the "Base-Less" Party System

As noted in Chapter 1, Alexander Hamilton and Thomas Jefferson passionately dis-agreed about the proper course for governing their new nation, leading them to confront each other "like two cocks in a pen" during George Washington's cabinet meetings. By 1800, each had established a political party, and carried their battle of ideas from behind closed doors into the electoral arena. The origins of the U.S. party system can be traced to their heated debate. Yet, the two men remained civil, honorable adversaries. After all, they had worked closely on a deal placing the nation's capital on banks of the Potomac River as Jefferson had hoped, while Hamilton won Jefferson's backing for a tax and spending plan designed to boost the fortunes of the business class. In fact, Jefferson so admired Hamilton that he had a bust of his erstwhile opponent placed in the front hall of his home, Monticello; the two busts faced each other, since Jefferson admitted both had been opposites in life.

If we could resurrect these two important figures from our past, they would no doubt marvel at the changes that have taken place in their native land. Among the things that might surprise them would be the omnipotence of the federal gov-ernment, the relative equality afforded blacks and women (including the right of both groups to vote, as now enshrined in the U.S. Constitution), the rise of near-instantaneous communications, and the high-technology techniques used by Infor-mation Age political parties to acquire political office. Still, some things would be familiar—especially the broad outlines of the federal government that each helped fashion more than two hundred years ago. Especially heartening to them would be the public's steadfast commitment to the ideas of liberty, individualism, hard work, self-reliance, and self-governance. Alexis de Tocqueville's observation that the American voters' penchant for "standing alone,"[1] believing that the future lies in one's individual efforts, endures. Continued faith in the American Dream—the idea that individual effort and hard work are the only requirements needed to get ahead—also remains strong, though it was buffeted during the twentieth century by two world wars, a cold war, and a great depression. On the eve of the twenty-first century, freedom and liberty—the two ideals that make America great—are on the march around the globe. The fall of the Berlin Wall, the collapse of the Soviet Union and the relegation of communism to history's dustbin, and the rise of demo-cratic regimes in former dictatorships (especially in Latin America and South Africa) are signs that the American Century—said to have reached its zenith in the years following World War II—is far from over.

While both Hamilton and Jefferson would take solace in the public's contin-ued commitment to a robust form of classical liberalism, it is Hamilton who would have the most to gloat about. As we enter the new millennium, it is Hamilton's vision of America that has triumphed. Out of the Framers' original vision of a constitution with numerous checks and balances, has come a strong governing enterprise that gives the president primacy for taking action. Hamiltonian Nation-alism—the idea that the United States is best viewed as one family with a concen-tration of power at the federal level—has won widespread acceptance. Even though this proposition is not endorsed by the public in principle—Americans like the idea of a smaller government—it is endorsed in practice whenever serious attempts are made to shrink the size of government, as the 1994 Republican congressional class learned to its regret.

When it comes to the extra-constitutional device known as political parties, Hamilton's triumph is even more complete. Just as the federal government has become more powerful, so too has the American party system with its hierarchal structure and professional politicians overseeing aggressive party organizations. Referring to the business firm analogy outlined in Chapter 1, Hamiltonian Nation-alism has created a top-down party system, where elites manage the business firm.

Thomas Jefferson's idea of a community-based politics is on the wane. Recall that Jeffersonian Localism refers to the idea that given the size and diversity of the United States, it is impossible to view the United States in terms other than a series of relatively independent communities. In this view, power is vested at the local level and great trust is placed in the hands of ordinary citizens. Party politics is best undertaken by amateurs, whose virtue and commitment are to ideas benefitting the local citizenry. Jeffersonian Localism places a premium on policy coherence and intraparty democracy. It is a bottoms-up political system where individuals are at the center of politics of ideas designed to reorient the government in a particular direction.

The victory of Hamiltonian Nationalism over Jeffersonian Localism came only after two centuries of struggle. Throughout this period, the two surviving major parties, Democrats and Republicans, experienced a change of heart—each taking a turn as guardians of the Hamiltonian or Jeffersonian approach. During the Civil War and Industrial Revolution, the newly formed Republican Party became closely identified with Hamiltonian Nationalism as it sought to give the federal government the necessary tools to fight the Civil War, end slavery, and transform an agricultural society into an industrial one. Democrats, largely dominated by their southern wing, emphasized state's rights—code words for continuance of the separation between blacks and whites. Franklin D. Roosevelt's New Deal, Harry S Truman's Fair Deal, John F. Kennedy's New Frontier, and Lyndon B. Johnson's Great Society aligned the Democratic Party with the Hamiltonian idea that the national government must overcome the Great Depression and be strong enough to lead the nation through World War II and the Cold War. From the 1930s to the 1960s, Americans believed in a simple proposition that big government worked. When pollster George Gallup asked in 1936, "Which theory of government do you favor: concentration of power in the federal government or concentration of power in the state government?" respondents chose the federal government by a 56 percent to 44 percent margin.[2]

At first glance, Jeffersonian Localism today appears to have gained the upper hand. When Americans were asked in 1987 which theory of government they favored, 63 percent picked their state government, while 34 percent preferred the federal government have more power.[3] Rampant inflation coupled with high unemployment, the capture of U.S. hostages in Iran, the defeat suffered by the U.S. military during the Vietnam War, the Watergate scandal, and a series of failed presidencies from John F. Kennedy's interrupted tenure to Jimmy Carter's uninspired one, left many with a profound sense of disillusionment. The idea that big government worked was no longer in vogue. Faith in the American Dream was temporarily shaken, and Jefferson's vision of a downsized federal government held great appeal. Like Jefferson, Ronald Reagan won the presidency by promising to reduce the size and scope of the "puzzle palaces" scattered along the Potomac. In his first speech before Congress, Reagan told the legislators that "spending . . . must be limited to those functions which are the proper province of government. We can no longer afford things simply because we think of them."[4]

Of course, neither Jefferson nor Reagan delivered on their promises. Jefferson vastly expanded the power of the presidency by deciding on his own initiative to make the Louisiana Purchase, an area covering more than 800,000 square miles, for $15 million. Reagan, too, failed to deliver on his promise to trim the federal government. The Energy and Education departments that he promised to abolish remain standing. The best Reagan could do was slow the rate of government growth. Reagan's successors in the Newt Gingrich-led 104th Congress experienced a similar fate. Although they pledged to close the Education and Commerce departments and eliminate the National Endowment for the Arts, these agencies endure. The Republican-led government shutdown of November–December 1995 proved disastrous for their party. Despite lingering public doubts about government's ability to act effectively, this is still Hamilton's America.

Looking at the American party system from the perspective of Hamiltonian Nationalism versus Jeffersonian Localism, Hamilton's triumph is even more complete. During the heyday of party politics, stretching from the Jacksonian Democracy of the 1830s to the Industrial Revolution of the early 1900s, Jeffersonian Localism dominated. Party politics was local politics. What job one had, who one socialized with, and how one viewed the issues and candidates of the day were matters of party choice. Parties were the key mechanisms for integrating whole groups of immigrants into the culture and mores of American life—and were celebrated by political scientists for the job they did. In his 1942 book *Party Government*, E. E. Schattschneider wrote: "Modern democracy is unthinkable save in terms of parties."[5]

As this text has documented, the party machines of the late nineteenth and early twentieth centuries were not models of democracy. Progressives wanted to clean up the machines, but in so doing they reduced the impact of amateur activists. Progressive reforms transformed political parties into regulated public utilities controlled by federal, state, and local laws. In effect, the Progressives legalized the two-party system of Democrats versus Republicans, thus making it difficult (but not impossible) for grassroots minor parties to become viable players. Still, by attacking the party machines and focusing on how politics could be better managed, the Progressive reformers further isolated the people from politics—even as they threw open the once-closed doors to smoke-filled party back rooms.

The nationalization of party politics during the New Deal era solidified Hamilton's triumph. As government shifted to the national sphere, so did the party system. By the 1970s, local party committees were in crisis as fewer citizens saw them as effective means for constructive change. Interest groups dominated the policy process and campaign consultants sold their wares to candidates. These trends were denounced by the Committee for Party Renewal, a group of several hundred political scientists committed to revitalizing U.S. political parties. In their 1977 "Statement of Principles," the committee declared that voter dissatisfaction with traditional party politics had created a new style of politics characterized by "excessive media influence, political fad-of-the month clubs, massive private financing by various 'fat cats' of state and congressional campaigns, gun-for-hire campaign managers, lowered concern for policy, and maneuvering and management by self-chosen political elites."[6] The resultant clanking of the engines of government, they claimed, resulted from the parties' inability to supply the oil.

Operating behind the scenes, national party organizations began looking inward even as they expanded their operations. They provided more cutting-edge services and trunk loads of money to always-needy candidates. Having become professional, centralized organizations, political parties were the new kids on the election block. Only one ingredient was missing: the voters. Just when party organizations were reviving and party ties were becoming more important within the halls of government, an increasingly larger number of citizens were eschewing partisan politics. By the time the U.S. Senate had voted to acquit Bill Clinton in the winter of 1999, most Americans saw the Clinton-Lewinsky scandal as another episode of partisan politics at its worst. Just prior to the "not guilty" verdict, 51 percent told pollsters they wanted the whole matter dropped without a final vote.[7]

Hamilton's hollow victory has not ended the battle between the descendants of Alexander Hamilton and Thomas Jefferson. Rather, his triumph leaves many with a sense of unease, and raises anew questions about the role parties should play in the American polity:

- Are parties a desirable feature in a democratic system or do they detract from allowing the will of the people to prevail?
- Should parties be more concerned with winning elections or implementing policies, and can both objectives be realized?
- Is American-style democracy best served by having nationally centered party organizations where elites rule or with a diverse Jeffersonian-like system of community-level organizations dominated by amateurs?
- Should elected officials use party affiliation as a guide to voting or should they be independent operators hired to represent their local constituencies?
- Is intraparty democracy necessary or a hindrance to electoral efficiency?

- Why is the United States one of the few democracies that relies on a two-party model, and is this something we might wish to change?
- What role should parties play in the presidential nominating process, and can they continue to help presidents to govern?
- How have court decisions and state and national regulations reshaped the party system?
- How might we conceptualize the complex, changing relationship between party organizations and voters?

Answers to these and other questions are needed as a new millennium approaches. Clearly, many old notions about how the American party system should work have become inoperative. As noted at the beginning of this text, the party-in-the-electorate (PIE), party organization (PO), and party-in-government (PIG) tripod has become a rickety mechanism for viewing politics in the Information Age. The business firm analogy offers a superior way of understanding contemporary politics (see Chapter 1), where voters are likened to consumers that the firms (i.e., party organizations) attempt to attract each election. The goal of the party organizations is to instill party brand loyalty in order to expand their market share. Candidates are the products offered by the firm at each election cycle, and elected officials are the "reluctant sales force" that the firm hopes to control.

Hamilton's triumph has removed both voters and elected officials from the old PIE, PO, PIG trilogy. Party organizations and the party-in-government have been reinvigorated, but increasingly removed from the voters. To be sure, the Information Age makes the party loyalty that the old urban machines once inspired a thing of the past. Constant change is a primary characteristic of the Information Age, leaving astute politicians like Bill Clinton virtually breathless:

> As we move from the Industrial Age to the Information Age, from the Cold War to the global village, the pace and scope of change is immense. Information, money, and services can and do move around the world in the blink of an eye. There's more computing power in a Ford Taurus than there was in Apollo 11 when Neil Armstrong took it to the moon. By the time a child born today is old enough to read, over 100 million people will be on the Internet.[8]

Nowhere are the personal changes Americans experience more evident than in the college classrooms and what happens to students after they graduate. In the Information Age, education has become the union card for employment, accounting for the extraordinary number of Americans aged eighteen to twenty-four who sit in college classrooms. Indeed, as many liberal arts undergraduates are aware, the B.A. or B.S. is no longer sufficient to ensure secure employment, and many students undertake graduate education on a full- or part-time basis. Moreover, Americans are less likely than ever before to work for a single employer most of their adult lives. During the twenty-first century, it is estimated that many Americans will change employers half a dozen times during their careers—sometimes having to undertake significant retraining in the process.

These changes affect our politics since a sophisticated, more educated, and more credentialed electorate is likely to resist party-based appeals. In fact, the idea of a party-based mandate is no longer a reality in an era when voters prefer to size up individual candidates. For some time now, television has allowed candidates to pose their own questions that voters must answer. In 1980, for example, Ronald Reagan asked voters: "Are you better off than you were four years ago?" Eight years later, candidate George Bush wondered whether voters agreed with his proposition of "no new taxes." In 1992, Clinton reduced the election to a single phrase, "It's the economy stupid!" The multitude of questions/statements and the various answers voters give often results in an electoral muddle of divided-party government with Congress and the president stymied by pitched partisan battles. But the emergence of strong national parties portends an even greater danger than government grid-lock. It marks the beginning of a period when the parties themselves are driving voters away from politics. Voters who once formed the "mainsprings" of American politics[9] now seem totally disengaged from the process. This new party system is base-less, and its effects were readily apparent in the 1998 midterm elections.

THE 1998 ELECTION AND THE "BASE-LESS" PARTY SYSTEM

Much has been made of the historic nature of the 1998 election—the last of the twentieth century. For the first time since 1934, the president's party added seats in a midterm contest; not since 1822 has any political party won seats while control-ling the presidency for six years. But this election was historic for an even more important reason: it heralded the advent of a new **base-less** party system—a change that extends far beyond the pundits' predictions about who will win the 2000 presi-dential contest.

Both parties were at the top of their game in 1998. After decades of decline, the Democratic and Republican party organizations were again key players in the election process. Money, polls, and strategic advice now stream out of party head-quarters in Washington, D.C., to the hinterlands. Yet, at the same time, fewer vot-ers identify with a political party, participate in party-related activities, or even bother to vote. The last point is especially important. After much ballyhoo about long lines at the polls, voter turnout in 1998 was a mere 36.06 percent—the lowest figure since 1942.[10] What is especially startling is that this trend has accelerated at precisely the moment when party organizations are stronger than ever. Is it possible that the Democratic and Republican organizational powerhouses have done what no one ever envisioned—push voters away?

Earlier, we described how the Democratic and Republican national commit-tees, and their congressional counterparts, once seemed headed for the junkyard. But after Barry M. Goldwater's disastrous loss to Lyndon B. Johnson in 1964, Republican National Chairman Ray C. Bliss set his sights on improving candidate services. A decade later his successor, Bill Brock, initiated a direct mail campaign that paid handsome dividends in GOP coffers. Caught unaware, Democrats scram-bled to play catch-up. National Chairman Charles Manatt began direct mail solici-tations, and his successors sought to provide candidates with more services.

Democrats even built a spanking brand new party headquarters in Washington, D.C., to rival the handsome digs of their Republican counterparts. By 1998, both parties had arrived. The phoenix had risen from the ashes.

But what about the voters? Defenders of Jeffersonian Localism claim that the rationale for having parties is to invite voters into the public dialogue so they may become part of the process. Yet, the fastest growing segment of the electorate are those who reject party labels. A vast array of polling data suggest one-third of the voters call themselves independents—a figure three times greater than that during the 1950s. In a CBS News/*New York Times* survey taken just days before the 1998 balloting, fewer than half chose either party as best able to keep the nation prosperous, uphold family values, or reduce crime. When asked which characterization best applied to the two parties, a majority withheld support from both as being the party that "cares about people like yourself," "has higher ethical standards," is "more likely to reduce taxes," or "has the better ideas for leading the nation into the twenty-first century."[11]

Traditional party loyalties have been replaced by neutral or negative feelings toward both parties. *Newsweek* magazine conducted a postelection poll that contained bad news for Democrats and Republicans: 54 percent said the two-party system reflects "the isolated agenda of the establishment"; 30 percent said the system "offers a good range of views and candidates"; 36 percent said Reform Party candidate Jesse Ventura's victory in Minnesota was "evidence of a serious trend in the country away from major parties."[12] Regarding the last point, the survey respondents may be right. Four times in the past three decades, a third-party candidate has played a major role in presidential contests: George Wallace (1968), John Anderson (1980), Ross Perot (1992 and 1996). Moreover, 1996 had the largest number of third-, fourth-, and fifth-party candidates competing in House, Senate, and governors races since the 1960s. Shortly after the Senate acquitted Bill Clinton in February 1999, only 23 percent said the Republican Party was addressing important issues, while 35 percent thought that was true of the Democrats. A stunning 48 percent of respondents in a December 1999 national survey commented that it would make little difference if a Democrat or a Republican won the presidential election. A full 40 percent suggested that they would consider supporting a third party in the 2000 election.[13] These trends signal just how "base-less" the American party system has become.

We noted in Chapter 3 that a leading explanation for the movement away from party politics during the 1960s and 1970s was the disillusionment that resulted from the U.S. defeat in Vietnam and the Watergate scandal that followed. In his famous 1979 "malaise speech," Jimmy Carter captured the prevailing sentiments of his fellow Americans—both then and now:

> What you see too often in Washington and elsewhere around the country is a system of government that seems incapable of action. You see a Congress twisted and pulled in every direction by hundreds of well-financed and powerful special interests. You see every extreme position defended to the last breath by one unyielding group or another. You see a balanced and fair approach that demands sacrifice, a little sacrifice from everyone, abandoned like an orphan without support and without friends.[14]

The failures of the 1960s and the malaise of the 1970s created the conditions for a generation of Americans to become social nonpartisans. A series of failed presidencies helped reinforce the view that politics does not matter. John F. Kennedy, the youngest president ever to die in office, had his term shortened by his assassination in 1963. Lyndon B. Johnson became mired in the Vietnam War, which ultimately consumed both him and his presidency. Richard M. Nixon fell victim to his own extreme form of partisanship with the Watergate scandal abuses of wiretapping his enemies (and, famously, himself), opening mail received by private citizens, and authorized break-ins at the Democratic National Committee (DNC). Gerald Ford's brief tenure was marked by an extraordinary number of presidential vetoes (sixty-six). Ford was defeated by Jimmy Carter in 1976, who, in turn, was unable to cope with the twin crises of inflation and loss of faith in government. Four years later he lost to Ronald Reagan. Reagan turned out to be a much-beloved president, and the most successful of his era. But Reagan's successor, George Bush, lasted only one term before succumbing to Bill Clinton in 1992. Clinton managed to survive two terms, but his second administration was marred by media coverage of his dalliance with White House intern Monica Lewinsky and his subsequent impeachment for misleading courtroom testimony and obstructing justice about the affair.

However, to blame these presidential failings on social nonpartisanship misses the point. To borrow a quote from former Texas Governor Ann Richards, "That dog don't hunt." Hamiltonian parties do little to cultivate party-backers and sometimes even discourage them from joining. Like a crack addict, party elites perpetually seek the next fix—i.e., the "election box-score"—that puts them on top for the time being. As Richard Nixon said after eking out a narrow victory over Democrat Hubert H. Humphrey in 1968, "Winning's a lot more fun."[15] Today, winning is not only fun; it's the only thing that matters. Not surprisingly, both parties have erected substantial campaign organizations aimed at securing wins in presidential and congressional races. The Democratic and Republican national committees, and their House and Senate campaign counterparts, use all the tools of the Information Age and employ topnotch professionals to get their clients elected. But they rarely transfer money, share information, or conduct joint activities with other party members running for different offices. Sometimes they even jettison candidates when things aren't going well. On election night 1996, Republican strategists cobbled together a television advertisement for West Coast viewing that all but abandoned their presidential candidate Bob Dole: "Remember the last time Democrats ran everything? The largest tax increase in history. Government-run health care. More wasteful spending. Who wants that again? Don't let the media stop you from voting. And don't hand Bill Clinton a blank check. The polls close at eight."[16] In 1998, House Democrats berated the DNC for hoarding money in anticipation of Al Gore's 2000 presidential candidacy. Charles Rangel, a Democratic Congressional Campaign Committee official, was so peeved that he told Democratic National Committee General Chairman Roy Romer, "Keep your money and shut your mouth." Indeed, why should anyone vote the party line, when the parties themselves use these lines?

Service-oriented parties have adapted to the hard-hitting, shrill campaign tactics that win elections, yet alienate voters. This was particularly true in 1998 when party operatives conceived, produced, and sponsored profoundly negative spots. In New York and Ohio, voters showed a distaste for such highly partisan, negative campaigns. New Yorkers cast fewer ballots in the hotly contested U.S. Senate race between Democrat Charles Schumer and Republican Alfonse D'Amato than in the gubernatorial contest which Democrats left largely uncontested to Republican Governor George Pataki. The reverse happened in Ohio. There, a negative gubernatorial campaign between Republican Bob Taft and Democrat Lee Fisher turned off voters, while the U.S. Senate contest remained a more genteel affair and got more voters interested in it.[17] Nationally, negative campaigning hurt both parties but the Republicans were punished more than the Democrats. During the last days of the midterm election, Republicans spent $10 million on a now infamous advertisement focusing on the Monica Lewinsky affair. They did so despite reams of polling data strongly indicating that Americans were tired of the scandal, did not want to hear any more about it, and were more concerned with other issues like saving Social Security. Pollster Dick Morris commented that these ads were "incredibly stupid," adding, "Whoever thought that up had $10 million too much money to play with and didn't know what to do with it."[18] Still, the temptation to attack Clinton proved too great—especially when many Republicans believed that voters would punish Clinton for his dalliance with a White House intern.

Indeed, the 1998 election was the most expensive midterm campaign in history. Some estimates put the cost at $2 billion. One reason is the degree to which parties are able to raise large sums of soft-money, the unlimited sums of cash individuals can give to political parties (see Chapter 8). Soft money made headlines in 1996, as the Clinton-Gore campaign used Democratic Party funds from questionable sources to purchase $85 million in campaign advertisements. In 1998, both parties perfected issue advocacy television commercials that derided the opposition candidate. The money needed for such advertisements is astronomical, and most voters do not like it. According to a June 1998 CBS News/*New York Times* poll, 49 percent are worried about the way money is raised for political campaigns. What bothered them most were the attention given to lobbyists and special interests, the presence of foreign money in campaigns, the cover-ups, and "just how they do it."[19]

It should be noted that characterizing the party system as "base-less" does not imply a lack of policy concerns. We noted in Chapter 9, the current system has a strong policy element and much of the financial brawn comes from committed ideologues. Still it remains elite-centered. Contributors and activists (including state and local party officials and delegates to the national conventions) worry about scores of issues, but little of what party organizations actually do affect voters. The gap between what activists desire and what the voters care about is growing. This ideological component is further muted by party operatives who measure success by the number of victories on election night.

So what's the big deal? Why are we concerned about the repercussions of our new Hamiltonian-like party system? For one thing, a base-less party system is likely to produce "do-nothing" Congresses, since neither party can mobilize anything like a majority behind their cause. For another, campaigns are often reduced to pitched battles between unattractive personalities. Clinton strategist James Carville has admitted as much. Just when the Clinton-Lewinsky scandal erupted, Carville appeared on NBC's *Meet the Press* and announced a declaration of war on Independent Counsel Kenneth Starr: "The reason this happened is because there's this concentrated effort to 'get the president.'"[20] First Lady Hillary Rodham Clinton agreed. Appearing on NBC's *Today* show, she told host Matt Lauer that "a vast right-wing conspiracy" was to blame for the Lewinsky affair.[21] Just as it had on numerous occasions before, the White House established a "war room" to deal with the latest scandal.

The Clinton-Lewinsky affair and Clinton's subsequent impeachment point to a coarsening of the public dialogue that is an inevitable outcome of the jihads ambitious politicians pursue in an era where party loyalties are weak and voters long for issue-based discussions. Suzanne Garment of the conservative-based American Enterprise Institute writes that a "self-enforcing scandal machine" has come into existence involving the parties, courts, and news media: "Prosecutors use journalists to publicize criminal cases [involving members of the administration] while journalists, through their news stories, put pressure on prosecutors for still more action."[22] Reflecting on the Clinton-Lewinsky scandal and the numerous inquiries it spawned, a female Republican schoolteacher in upstate New York said: "I don't think the investigation is going to end anytime soon. They'll find something else to draw it out a little longer. I've lost all faith in the process. It's like a circus."[23] Scandal politics has transformed our once firmly-based party politics into a new form of media entertainment. Presidents are now just as likely to appear on *Entertainment Tonight* or *Inside Hollywood* as they are on the evening newscasts.

In this new era where entertainment values prevail over issue-based discussions, civility has become rare. Longtime members of the Washington establishment say that the most important change in the last three decades has been the erosion of comity that permitted ideological opposites to form long-lasting friendships. Senate Majority Leader Bob Dole, for example, introduced legislation to name the Health and Human Services building for former Vice President Hubert H. Humphrey, and lauded Democrats Ted Kennedy and George McGovern in his farewell address to the Senate. Now instead of listening and deliberating, Republicans and Democrats alike are busily declaring war on each other—either by negative campaigning while seeking office, or by charges of ethical violations against each other while in office. The most recent example is Bill Clinton's impeachment and the year-long domination of the Clinton-Lewinsky scandal in the media—especially on the cable news networks and Sunday talk shows. Although history has yet to render its judgment on Clinton and the Republican-controlled Congress, it is a fair guess that future historians will examine the highly partisan congressional votes and conclude that Clinton was a victim of both his own misdeeds and the intense hatred his opponents reserved for him.

Base-less parties that love to declare war on each other leave many Americans confused, frustrated, and cynical—emotions not associated with a vibrant party system. But the most pernicious outcome of party resurgence is what happens to the American spirit. While party organizations give candidates fistfuls of cash and cutting-edge services, little of what they do fosters an affinity for the political process. In the new base-less party system more is less.

PARTY POLITICS IN THE NEXT MILLENNIUM

Realizing the dangers of predicting trends in politics, especially in an era of fast-paced change that characterizes the Information Age, we remain undaunted and make some informed judgements about what lies ahead. We have collapsed our projections into five areas: voter trends, organizational developments, legislative politics, new laws, and the role of minor parties.

Voter Trends

It is likely that party organizations will continue to grow in power and influence. Party operatives realize that the only way to remain players in electoral politics is aggressively to raise money, provide cutting-edge services to candidates, and stay abreast of the technological changes made possible by the Information Age. The political environment is increasingly competitive with a volatile electorate and many new-style campaign consultants anxious to sell their wares. This accentuates the importance of centralized, professional party organizations. Once again, Alexander Hamilton has won the day in American party politics. The days of community-centered, volunteer-oriented local party politics will gradually fade away.

Organizational Developments

We can only imagine that the consumers of party politics will continue to shun any sort of rigid party brand loyalty. Throughout American history, there have been times when voters have moved away from parties only to be reconnected through an economic crisis or war. Realignment elections reestablished the party connection (see Chapter 6). Some have suggested that party brand loyalty may again swell under similar conditions. But Information Age politics is vastly different from the past—especially given the array of media outlets, special interest groups, and parties that bombard voters with political cues via cable television, e-mail, talk radio, and the Internet. Parties no longer have the political playing field to themselves. Indeed, no generation of Americans has ever been exposed to more campaign information. With all this data, voters are inclined to eschew party brand loyalty and take one election at a time. Instead of party-based mandates envisioned by the responsible party advocates, the orders given by the voters for action are much more personal in nature. Nearly fifty years ago, President-elect Dwight D. Eisenhower declared his intention "to redeem the pledges of the [Republican] platform and the campaign." When he informed Republican congressional leaders of his intentions, Eisenhower described their response: "More than once I was to hear this view derided by 'practical politicians' who laughed off platforms as traps to catch voters.

But whenever they expressed these cynical conclusions to me, they invariably encountered a rebuff that left them a bit embarrassed."[24]

Today, Eisenhower's words seem quaint. Presidents run for office selling themselves and not their party. We may again see "party periods," but they are likely to be short-lived aberrations, not the long thirty-year realignment cycles of the past. The overall trend will be toward greater split-ticket voting, with control of both the federal and state governments alternating from one party to another. The Information Age is changing what Americans do for a living, how we spend our free time, and how we communicate with one another. Thus, the nearly religious connection voters had to parties only a few decades ago will not return.

Legislative Politics

We believe that the ideological polarization within Congress and the state legislatures will continue. Declarations of war by individual candidates are likely to contribute to continued declines in voter turnout, leaving self-recruited ideologues with the loudest voices and nastiest campaigns. Elected officials will be especially responsive to the small activist wing of their party, because Information Age style campaigning is aggressive, targeted, and negative. Such candidates and their campaigns will continue to alienate middle-of-the-road voters, making them less likely to cast a ballot. The outcome of this self-perpetuating cycle will be a shrinking pool of voters and an even more extreme group of elected officials unwilling to communicate with each other.

New Laws

As the public becomes increasingly discouraged with the partisan bickering in legislatures and distant party organizations in state capitals and in Washington, laws will be passed to further open the party system. Most of these adjustments will center around ballot access and the nominating process. The recent shift in California to an open primary system where everyone regardless of partisan affiliation participates (see Chapter 7) will be mirrored across the country. Some states will remain closed—meaning that only registered party members can vote—but they will be the exception rather than the rule. Given that many state legislatures will be highly partisan and not especially anxious to unlock the system, many of these changes will come through ballot initiatives and referenda.

Minor Parties

Finally, the crack in the armor surrounding the two-party system may widen in the next millennium. Voters are poised for new choices and they will find outlets in minor party candidates. This will be especially true for middle-of-the-road voters who are increasingly alienated from the choices offered by Democrats and Republicans. Jesse Ventura's upset victory in Minnesota may be the tip of the iceberg. As noted in Chapter 10, the Information Age has afforded minor parties a greater opportunity than ever before to communicate with a large pool of voters at minimal cost. We do not suggest that the next century will witness an end to the two-party model, only that a significant change ushered in by the Information Age will be the growing role of third parties.

◆   ◆   ◆

At the end of this millennium Americans are prosperous and relatively happy. The desire of the Framers as expressed in our Constitution to form a "more perfect Union, establish Justice, insure domestic Tranquility, provide for the common defense, promote the general Welfare, and secure the Blessings of Liberty" seems to have been realized. In our personal lives, we are more inclined to view the traditional family with greater reverence. The rate of divorce has fallen, a new baby boom is underway, the American Dream of owning one's home is a reality for the largest number of citizens in our history. Yet, Americans are beset with a public life that is marked by the failure of parties to reestablish their connection with the voters. Some have even said that both the Democratic and Republican parties are "brain dead."[25] In its place has come a plethora of special interest groups that dominate the public discourse with demands that their rights be respected. As we enter the twenty-first century, the American polity is presented with a paradox: the unrivaled success of the American ideals of individualism, freedom, equality of opportunity, and a politics and party system that continues to fail us.

NOTES

1. Alexis de Tocqueville, *Democracy in America* (New York: New American Library, 1956), 194.

2. George Gallup, survey, 1936. Text of question: "Which theory of government do you favor: concentration of power in the federal government or concentration of power in the state government?" Federal government, 56 percent; state government, 44 percent.

3. Decision/Making/Information, survey for the Republican National Committee, April 21–23, 1987.

4. Ronald Reagan, "Address to Congress," Washington, D.C., February 18, 1981.

5. E. E. Schattschneider, *Party Government* (New York: Rinehart, 1942), 1.

6. "Declaration of Principles," Committee for Party Renewal, September 1977.

7. See Richard L. Berke with Janet Elder, "Damaged by Clinton Trial, Senate Sinks in Public's Eye; GOP Is Hurt More," *New York Times*, February 3, 1999, A1.

8. Bill Clinton, *Between Hope and History* (New York: Times Books, 1996), 10–11.

9. See especially Walter Dean Burnham, *Critical Elections and the Mainsprings of American Politics* (New York: Norton, 1970).

10. Will Lester, "Voter Turnout Lowest Since 1942," Associated Press, February 9, 1999.

11. CBS News/*New York Times*, poll, October 26–28, 1998. Text of questions: "Regardless of how you usually vote, do you think the Republican Party or the Democratic Party is more likely to make sure the country is prosperous?" Republican, 36 percent; Democratic, 42 percent. Upholding traditional family values: Republican, 47 percent; Democratic, 31 percent. Reduce crime: Republican, 38 percent; Democratic, 31 percent. Cares about people like yourself: Republican, 25 percent; Democratic, 46 percent. Has higher ethical standards: Republican, 41 percent; Democratic, 24 percent. Is more likely to reduce taxes: Republican, 40 percent; Democratic, 40 percent. Has better ideas for leading the country into the twenty-first century: Republican, 33 percent; Democratic, 44 percent. Has more honesty and integrity: Republican, 31 percent; Democratic, 27 percent.

12. *Newsweek* magazine, postelection poll, November 5–6, 1998. Text of questions: "Do you think the two-party system as we know it offers a good range of views and candidates or does it reflect the isolated agenda of the establishment?" Good range of views, 30 percent; reflects establishment, 54 percent. "As you may know, former pro-wrestler Jesse Ventura was elected governor of Minnesota on Tuesday. Do you think Ventura's election is evidence of a serious trend in the country away from major parties or a fluke that the media is playing up for entertainment purposes?" Evidence of a serious trend, 36 percent; a fluke, 43 percent; don't know, 21 percent.

13. Associated Press, "Poll: We Want Honest Office Seekers," *Meadville Tribune*, December 1, 1999, A1.

14. Jimmy Carter, "Address to the Nation," Washington, D.C., July 15, 1979. Carter never actually used the term "malaise." It was a moniker placed on the speech first by his Democratic challenger, Massachusetts Senator Edward M. Kennedy, and later by Ronald Reagan.

15. See Stephen C. Shadegg, *Winning's a Lot More Fun* (New York: Macmillan, 1969).

16. Warren P. Strobel, "President Improves on His 1992 Showing," *Washington Times*, November 6, 1996, A1.

17. See Lester, "Voter Turnout Lowest Since 1942."

18. Quoted in "National Briefing—Ad Blitz '98: Democrats 'Scramble,' and Respond," *Hotline*, October 29, 1998.

19. CBS News/*New York Times*, poll, June 7–9, 1998. Text of questions: "Is there anything in particular that bothers you about the way money is raised to pay for political campaigns?" Yes, 49 percent; no, 38 percent. "What bothers you the most?" Lobbyist/special interest, 16 percent; fix system, 11 percent; foreign/China, 7 percent; illegal money, 3 percent; cover-up/lying/unethical, 2 percent; selling the White House, 2 percent; just how they do it, 2 percent; both parties do it, 2 percent; nothing bothers, 38 percent.

20. James Carville, interview, *Meet the Press*, January 25, 1998.

21. Hillary Clinton, interview, *Today*, January 27, 1998.

22. Quoted in Paul Johnson, *A History of the American People* (New York: HarperCollins, 1997), 937.

23. Quoted in Berke with Elder, "Damaged by Clinton Trial," A1.

24. Dwight D. Eisenhower, *Mandate for Change, 1953–1956* (Garden City, N.Y.: Doubleday, 1963), 194–95.

25. See Theodore J. Lowi, "Toward a Responsible Three-Party System," in Theodore J. Lowi and Joseph Romance, *A Republic of Parties: Debating the Two-Party System* (Lanham, Md.: Rowman and Littlefield, 1998), 3.

Table 5.4 "Issue Comparison of Public to 1996 Democratic and Republican Delegates." Adapted from the Washington Post. Copyright © 1996 The *Washington Post*. Reprinted with permission.

Figure 6.1 "The Funnel of Causality Predicting Vote Choice ('Michigan Model')." Adapted from data on p. 178 in *Citizen Politics in Western Democracies* by Russell J. Dalton. Copyright © 1988 by Russell J. Dalton. Reprinted by permission of Chatham House.

Table 6.2 "The Un-Anchored American Electorate, 1996." Adapted from data on p. 190 in *America at the Polls, 1996* by Regina Dougherty, Everett C. Ladd, David Wilber, and Lynn Zayachkiwsky, eds. (1997). Reprinted by permission of Roper Center for Public Opinion Research, Storrs, CT.

Table 6.3 "Voter Attitudes toward the Major Parties by Issue, 1998." Adapted from *ABC News/Washington Post* survey, January 15–19, 1998. Copyright © 1998 The Washington Post. Reprinted with permission.

Table 7.3 "Elazar's Typologies of Political Subcultures." Adapted from data in *The American Mosaic: The Impact of Space, Time, and Culture on American Politics* by Daniel J. Elazar. Copyright © 1994 by Daniel J. Elazar. Reprinted by permission of Westview Press.

Table 7.4 "State Parties and the Internet." Adapted from "The New Party Machine Information Technology in State Political Parties" in *The State of the Parties* by John C. Green and Daniel M. Shea. Copyright © 1999 by John C. Green and Daniel M. Shea. Reprinted with permission of Rowman and Littlefield.

"The Parties Speak: Ten Myths about Money in Politics." Excerpted from *Ten Myths about Money in Politics*. Copyright © 1995 Center for Responsive Politics. Reprinted by permission.

Table 8.3 "When A Campaign Ad Is Not a Campaign Ad: Issue Advocacy Spots from the 1996 Election." Adapted from "Financing the 1996 Campaign: The Law of the Jungle," by Brooks Jackson, p. 237, in *Toward the Millennium: The Elections of 1996* by Larry J. Sabato, editor. Copyright © 1997 by Allyn & Bacon. Reprinted by permission of Addison-Wesley Educational Publishers, Inc.

Table 8.6 "Top Ten Soft Money Donors to the National Party Committees for the 1996 Election Cycle." Adapted from "Financing the 1996 Campaign: The Law of the Jungle," by Brooks Jackson, p. 245, in *Toward the Millennium: The Elections of 1996* by Larry J. Sabato, editor. Copyright © 1997 by Allyn & Bacon. Reprinted by permission of Addison-Wesley Educational Publishers, Inc.

"The Parties Speak: The House Judiciary Committee and the Question of Impeachment." From "We Stand Poised on the Edge of a Constitutional Cliff" in the *Washington Post*, December 11, 1998, p. A-28. Reprinted with permission.

Table 9.2 "Party Unity Average Scores in Both Chambers of Congress, 1963–1998." From "Party Unity Background" in *Congressional Quarterly Weekly Report*, January 9, 1999, p. 92. Reprinted by permission.

Table 10.1 "2000 Ballot Access for New Party Candidates." Adapted from chart in *Ballot Access News*, Richard Winger, editor, Box 470296, San Francisco, CA 94147. Reprinted by permission.

"The Parties Speak: Benjamin C. Babar, 1976 and 1980 Prohibition Party Presidential Nominee." Excerpts from Q&A between Frank Smallwood and Benjamin C. Bubar in *The Other Candidates: Third Parties in Presidential Elections* by Frank Smallwood. Copyright © 1983 by Frank Smallwood, Wesleyan University Press. Reprinted by permission of University Press of New England.

Table 10.2 "Minor Parties and Candidates in the United States, 1968–1994." Adapted from "Minor Party Candidates in Subpresidential Elections," by Christian Collet and Jerrold Hansen, p. 242 in *The State of the Parties: The Changing Role of Contemporary American Parties*, second edition, by John C. Green and Daniel M. Shea, eds. Reprinted by permission of Rowman & Littlefield.

Table 10.3 "Changing Support for a Viable Third-Party, 1938 and 1995." From "Third Parties and the Two-Party System" by Christian Collet in *Public Opinion Quarterly*, 1996, vol. 60, pp. 431-449. Reprinted by permission.

"The Parties Speak: Ventura Win Marks Dawn of New Era: Age of Digital Politics." Excerpted from Phil Noble, *Roll Call*, December 7, 1998. Copyright © 1999, Roll Call, Inc. Reprinted by permission.

Index

ABC, 146, 172 n. 23
abolitionist parties, 292
Abramson, Paul R., 300 n. 8
ACU. *See* American Conservative Union (ACU)
Adams, Abigail, 15
Adams, Charles Francis, 282
Adams, John, 15, 34, 35, 39–40
Adams, John Quincy, 42, 53 n. 17, 54 n. 18, 269, 281
Advisory Commission on Intergovernmental Affairs, 176
AFDC. *See* Aid to Families with Dependent Children (AFDC)
AFL-CIO, 129
agency agreements, 229
Agnew, Spiro, 109, 242
Aid to Families with Dependent Children (AFDC), 238
Albert, Carl, 254
Albright, Madeleine, 73
Aldrich, John H., 24, 32 n. 31, 86, 106 n. 7, 262 n. 20, 262 n. 27, 262 n. 28, 300 n. 8
Alexander, Herbert, 235 n. 5, 235 n. 17, 236 n. 29
Alexander, Lamar, 2, 110
Alien Acts, 40
AllPolitics, 146
Amalgamated Clothing Workers of America, 181
The Amateur Democrat: Club Politics in Three Cities (Wilson), 193–194
American Association of Retired Persons, 18, 19
American Civil Liberties Union, 75
The American Commonwealth (Bryce), 16, 52
American Conservative Union (ACU), 296
American Dream Restoration Act, 238
American Enterprise Institute, 311
American Exceptionalism, 27
American Family Association, 75
American Independent Party, 289
American Medical Association, 75
American Medical PAC, 220
American Nurses Association, 75
American Party, 47, 282–283
American Political Science Association (APSA), 10, 69, 71, 244, 245, 298
American Railway Union, 57
Americans for Tax Reform, 181
The American Voter (Campbell, Converse, Miller, and Stokes), 143–144, 147
Amway Corporation, 231, 233

Anderson, Jane, 51–52
Anderson, John B., 136, 266, 273, 277–278, 308
Andrew, Joe, 2–4
Ansolabehere, Stephen, 249–250, 262 n. 26
Anti-Federalists, 36
Anti-Mason Party, 43, 118, 281
APSA. *See* American Political Science Association (APSA)
Aristotle, 13
Armey, Richard, 156, 254
Arnold, Laurence, 11 n. 3
Arthur, Chester, 121
Articles of Confederation, collapse of, 35
Asher, Herbert B., 300 n. 7
AT&T, 22, 233
Augustyn, Frederick J., Jr., 300 n. 31
Australian ballot, 58–59, 68

Bailer, Seweryn, 300 n. 17
Bailey, John M., 126
Baker, James, 73
Baker, Peter, 262 n. 52
ballot access, 269–270
ballot initiative, 62–63
Bank of the United States, 37
Barbour, Haley, 239
Barnburners, 282
Barone, Michael, 207 n. 9, 207 n. 30, 262 n. 30, 262 n. 31, 262 n. 32
Barr, Bob, 243, 250
Barry, Dan, 207 n. 29, 207 n. 31, 207 n. 32
baseless party system, 307–312
Basler, Roy P., 300 n. 16
Basnight, Mark, 200
Batt, Phil, 202
Bayard, Ferdinand, 210
Bayh, Birch, 11 n. 20
Beck, Paul Allen, 206 n. 4
Beer-Lovers Party (Russia), 5
Bell, Daniel, 21, 31 n. 24
Bement, Howard, 53 n. 4
Berelson, Bernard R., 142, 171 n. 11, 171 n. 12
Berke, Richard L., 262 n. 51, 314 n. 7, 315 n. 23
Beschloss, Michael R., 51, 262 n. 18
Bibby, John F., 106 n. 12, 107 n. 25, 107 n. 26, 300 n. 6, 300 n. 8
Bill of Rights, adoption of, 36
Binning, William C., 206 n. 1
Blair, Tony, 239

blanket primaries, 6, 187
Bliley, Thomas, 248
Bliss, Ray C., 307
Block, Kenan, 254
Blumberg, Melanie J., 206 n. 1
Blumenthal, Fred, 137 n. 1
Boehner, John, 255
Bonior, David, 255
Bono, Mary, 250
Bono, Sonny, 237
Boorstin, Daniel, 32 n. 36
Boston Junta, 35
Boston Tea Party, 35
Boucher, Rich, 250
Boxer, Barbara, 187
Bradley, Bill, 4–5, 110, 233
Brady, James, 168
Brady Bill, 19, 168
Bread-Lovers Party (Poland), 5
Brennan, William, 7
Breslau, Karen, 137 n. 9, 172 n. 33
Brewer, Daniel Chauncey, 54 n. 27
Brinkley, Alan, 172 n. 25
Brinkley, David, 141
Brock, William, 87, 88, 94, 221
Broder, David S., 85, 106 n. 3, 106 n. 4
Brooklyn Women's Martial Arts, 75
Brown, Harold, 73
Brown, Jerry, 177, 190
Bryan, William Jennings, 67, 129, 211, 285, 286
Bryce, James, 16, 52, 115, 138 n. 14
Bubar, Benjamin C., 278–280
Buchanan, James, 47, 119, 148
Buchanan, Patrick J., 2, 132, 133, 190
Buckley, James, 218
Buckley v. Valeo, 218–220, 226–227, 228, 236 n. 30
Bucktails, 42
Bull Moose Party. *See* Progressive Party
bundling, 232
Burgchardt, Carl R., 62
Burke, Edmund, 24, 35
Burnham, Walter Dean, 12 n. 34, 32 n. 37, 98–99, 107 n. 24, 150, 152, 155, 157, 172 n. 31, 172 n. 41, 314 n. 9
Burns, James MacGregor, 31 n. 3, 31 n. 4, 53 n. 6, 54 n. 19, 138 n. 22, 171 n. 1
Burr, Aaron, 38, 40
Busch, Andrew E., 139 n. 45
Bush, George, 73, 78, 109, 110, 116, 132, 133, 136, 141, 142, 155, 190, 231, 234
Bush, George W., 2, 208, 233, 274
business firm analogy, 22–23, 170
Business-Industry PAC, 220

Caldwell, Christopher, 11 n. 27
Calhoun, John C., 42, 43, 118
Campaign 2000, use of Internet in, 2–5
campaign finance, 208–234
    agency agreements, 229
    Buckley v. Valeo and, 218–220

bundling, 232
    contributions, 224
    coordinated expenditures, 229
    efforts to regulate, 214–222
    funding nominating conventions, 233
    future of, 233–234
    hard money, 229–231
    history of money in elections, 210–214
    independent expenditures, 227–229
    in Information Age, 222–233
    issue advocacy and, 209, 223, 227
    media-centered elections, 213–214
    money as supplement to party activities, 210–211
    PACs and, 220–222
    private financing, 225
    professional campaign consultants, 213
    public financing, 226
    rise of corporate politics and, 211–212
    role of parties in, 219–220
    skyrocketing election costs, 213
    soft money, 209, 222–223, 229–231
    transfers of large contributions, 231–232
    Watergate and, 216–217
Campbell, Angus, 143, 171 n. 14, 171 n. 15
Campbell, Anne, 106 n. 13
Campbell, Colin, 172 n. 41
Campbell, Tom, 187
Canady, Charles T., 252
candidate-centered politics
    concepts of, 76
    party activist versus professional consultant, 76–77
    party affiliation versus voting choice, 79
    party identification and, 144–145
    party member versus nonpartisan candidate, 77, 79
    rise of, 76–80
Capuano, Michael, 167
Caro, Robert A., 83 n. 18, 171 n. 8
Carr, Billie, 109
Carter, Jimmy, 11 n. 20, 16, 87, 108–109, 129, 134, 141, 151, 164, 240, 309, 315 n. 14
Carville, James, 311, 315 n. 20
Casey, Robert P., 8
Cass, Lewis, 46, 275
caucuses, 126, 128–130, 264–265
CBS News, 82 n. 1, 146, 157, 171 n .16, 172 n. 44, 173 n. 52, 308, 310, 314 n. 11, 315 n. 19
CCC. *See* Civilian Conservation Corps (CCC)
Ceaser, James W., 138 n. 23, 139 n. 45
Center for Responsive Politics, 224, 235 n. 1, 235 n. 7, 235 n. 8, 235 n. 10, 235 n. 12, 235 n. 22
Chafee, John, 258
Chafee, Lincoln, 243
chair of the policy committees, 242
Chamber of Commerce (United States), 181
Chambers, Whitaker, 72
Chambers, William Nisbet, 32 n. 37

The Changing American Voter (Nie, Verba, and Petrocik), 144–145
Chavez, Cesar, 122
Chenoweth, Helen, 201–202
Chester, Edward W., 300 n. 26, 300 n. 28, 300 n. 30
Chesterton, G. K., 275
Christian Coalition, 8, 181, 183, 184
Christopher, Warren, 73
CIO. *See* Congress of Industrial Organizations (CIO)
Citizen Legislature Act, 238
Citizens for Eisenhower, 77
Civilian Conservation Corps (CCC), 70
Civil Rights Act of 1964, 277
Civil Service Commission, 60
Civil Service Reform Act, 215
Civil War, 45–48, 148, 156
Clark, Champ, 119
Clarke, James W., 207 n. 25
Clay, Henry, 42, 43, 46, 281
Clean Politics Act. *See* Hatch Act of 1939
Cleveland, Grover, 48, 57, 166, 284–285
Clifford, Clark, 301 n. 36, 301 n. 39
Clift, Steve, 297
Clinton, Bill, 1–2, 9, 15, 16, 20, 22, 27, 32 n. 34, 73, 74, 79, 84, 85, 109, 110, 115, 116, 133, 136, 141, 143–144, 156, 160–161, 164, 168, 169, 173 n. 57, 190, 209, 215, 223, 227, 241, 247, 251–252, 257–258, 262 n. 50, 272, 295, 305, 306, 309, 314 n. 8
Clinton, Dewitt, 42
Clinton, George, 38, 40
Clinton, Hillary Rodham, 311, 315 n. 21
closed primaries, 126
    completely closed, 185
    partially closed, 185, 187
Clymer, Adam, 173 n. 58
CNN, 11 n. 18, 11 n. 19, 137 n. 13, 146, 172 n. 28, 173 n. 45, 173 n. 47, 262 n. 50, 294
Coelho, Tony, 94, 96
Cohen, Adam, 262 n. 29, 262 n. 33
Cohen, Richard E., 207 n. 9, 207 n. 30
Cohn, Mary W., 236 n. 27, 236 n. 28
Cold War, 72–73, 81
Coleman, John J., 103–104, 106 n. 3, 107 n. 30
Coleman, Norm, 267
Collet, Christian, 292, 301 n. 46, 301 n. 47
Collins, Susan, 258
Colorado Republican Federal Campaign Committee v. Federal Election Commission, 227–228
Colson, Chuck, 73
Commager, Henry Steele, 53 n. 5
Commission on Delegate Selection and Party Structure. *See* Mikulski Commission
Commission on Presidential Debates, 273
Commission on the Role and Future of Presidential Primaries. *See* Winograd Commission
Committee for Party Renewal, 16, 31 n. 18, 31 n. 19, 305

Committee on Party Structure and Delegate Selection, 124
Committee on Political Parties, 12 n. 32, 71, 83 n. 20, 245, 261 n. 12, 261 n. 13
Committee to Reelect the President (CREEP), 217
Common Cause, 217
Commonsense (journal), 88
Common Sense Legal Reforms Act, 238
Common Sense (Paine), 35
communication, between politicians and citizens, 104
Communist Party (United States), 72, 275, 277, 288
Concord Conferences, 88
conference, 264–265
Congress
    delegates view of themselves, 259–260
    members as trustees, 259–260
    parties in, 241–247
    Speaker of the House, 242
Congressional Caucus, 42, 117, 135
Congressional Quarterly, 9, 146, 147, 251
Congress of Industrial Organizations (CIO), 181
Conlan, Timothy, 206 n. 4
Conscience Whigs, 46, 282
Consequences of Party Reform (Polsby), 136
Conservative Party (Great Britain), 265
Constitution (United States)
    adoption of, 36
    organizing elections and, 13–14
contextual approach, 86
Contract with America, 9, 155, 237–238, 247–251, 255–256
convention system
    rise of, 117–120
    two-thirds rule, 118–119
    unit rule, 118–119
    as vital party instrument, 118
Converse, Philip E., 143, 171 n. 14, 171 n. 15
Conway, M. Margaret, 207 n. 20
Conyers, John, Jr., 251, 252
Cook Political Report, 95
Coolidge, Calvin, 70
coordinated expenditures, 95, 229
Corrado, Anthony, 107 n. 29, 235 n. 4, 236 n. 31, 236 n. 36
Corrupt Practices Act, 215–216
Costain, Anne N., 207 n. 25
Cotter, Cornelius P., 107 n. 25, 107 n. 26
Cotton Whigs, 46
Country Party. *See* Whig Party
Court Party. *See* Tories
Cousins v. Wigoda, 125, 138 n. 34
Cox, George, 66
Crawford, William, 42, 117
CREEP. *See* Committee to Reelect the President (CREEP)
critical elections, 148, 149

Critical Elections and the Mainsprings of American Politics (Burnham), 150
Croker, Richard, 48
Cronin, Thomas E., 83 n. 11
Crotty, William, 171 n. 5, 207 n. 23
C-SPAN, 136
Cuomo, Mario M., 29, 32 n. 44, 110, 142, 184
Curley, James Michael, 166
cyber-volunteer, 202

Daley, Richard J., 50, 51, 124, 126, 133, 140, 174, 240
D'Amato, Alfonse, 197, 310
Daniels, Josephus, 120
Dare County Democratic Committee, 200
Davis, John W., 120
Davis, Reed, 198–199, 207 n. 36
DCCC. *See* Democratic Congressional Campaign Committee (DCCC)
dealignment, 152, 170
Debs, Eugene, 57
Declaration of Independence, 275
The Decline of American Political Parties (Wattenberg), 85
declinists, 103–105
Defense of Marriage Act, 250
DeFrank, Tom, 78, 83 n. 27
DeLay, Tom, 156, 181
Delegate-Organization (DO) Committee, 131–132
Democracy Place, 146
Democratic Congressional Campaign Committee (DCCC), 93, 94
Democratic-Farmer Labor (DFL) Party, 270
Democratic Leadership Council (DLC), 183, 272
Democratic National Committee (DNC), 20, 71, 84–85, 89, 90, 92, 175, 208
Democratic Party
  immigration and, 119–120
  Internet use, 2–5, 7
  nominating conventions, 118
  origin of, 43
  PACs and, 221
  party finances in Information Age, 222–233
  shifts in coalitions, 162
  unofficial party organizations and, 183
  voting blocs, 162–163
Democratic-Republican Party, 43, 241, 276
Democratic Senatorial Campaign Committee (DSCC), 93, 94
Democratic Socialists of America Party, 296
Dennis, Jack, 11 n. 15, 11 n. 16
Department of Education, creation of, 129
DeSapio, Carmine, 126
Deukmejian, George, 32 n. 44
Dewey, Thomas E., 289
Dickerson, J. E., 31 n. 25
Dilger, Robert, 206 n. 4
Diller, J. R., 45
DiMeo, Steve, 80

Dinkin, Robert J., 235 n. 6, 235 n. 9
Dionne, E. J., Jr., 11 n. 17, 31 n. 14, 54 n. 33
direct mail, 88, 204
direct primary system, 59–60, 68, 272
DiSalle, Mike, 126
Disraeli, Benjamin, 10
divided government, 21, 33, 166–169
Dixiecrat Party, 243–244, 246–247, 289–290
DLC. *See* Democratic Leadership Council (DLC)
DNC. *See* Democratic National Committee (DNC)
Dodd, Christopher, 158, 308
Dole, Bob, 79, 84, 85, 110, 133, 136, 156, 164, 169, 208, 209, 273, 309, 311
Dole, Elizabeth, 181
Donald, David Herbert, 31 n. 13, 54 n. 21, 54 n. 26
Dougherty, Regina, 11 n. 26, 173 n. 56
Downs, Anthony, 145, 172 n. 19
Drew, Elizabeth, 207 n. 12
DSCC. *See* Democratic Senatorial Campaign Committee (DSCC)
Dukakis, Michael, 110, 116, 133, 142
Duke, David, 188
Duncan, Philip D., 235 n. 21
Dwyre, Diana, 227, 236 n. 37

Earle, Edward Meade, 31 n. 7, 31 n. 8, 31 n. 9, 53 n. 9
e-blocks, 2
An Economic Theory of Democracy (Downs), 145
Edsall, Thomas B., 139 n. 43, 173 n. 50
Edwards, Edwin, 188
Ehrenhalt, Allen, 80
Ehrlichman, John, 73
Eisenhower, Dwight D., 73, 77, 121, 143, 166, 274, 300 n. 11, 313, 315 n. 24
Eisenhower, Julie Nixon, 171 n. 3
Elazar, Daniel, 192
Elder, Janet, 262 n. 51, 314 n. 7, 315 n. 23
Eldersveld, Samuel J., 177, 207 n. 8, 207 n. 21
Electoral College, 113, 135, 268–269
Elefante, Rufus P., 80
e-mail, 1, 2, 22, 204
The Emerging Republican Majority (Phillips), 151
Empower America, 183–184, 207 n. 15
e-national committees, 2
Endangered Species Act, 19
e-neighborhoods, 2
England, roots of American political parties in, 33–34
entertainment industry, party system and, 275–276
Environmental Defense Fund, 18, 19
Epstein, Leon D., 24, 31 n. 17, 32 n. 30
Era of Good Feelings, 41, 117, 266, 281
Erdly, Wendy, 207 n. 36
Estrich, Susan, 116
executive-centered government, 71, 269

Executive Office of the President, creation of, 71
Executive Reorganization Act, 71
exit polls, 140–141

Fair Deal, 303
Family Reinforcement Act, 238
Farquhar, Michael, 53 n. 16
FECA. *See* Federal Election Campaign Act (FECA)
FECA Amendments of 1974, 217–218
Federal Election Acts, 76
Federal Election Campaign Act (FECA), 209, 217–218, 273
Federalist Papers, 36, 113, 114, 239, 259
Federalist Party, 36, 276
  death of, 117
  versus Republicans, 37–40
  support of Jay Treaty, 241
Federal Republican, 41
Federal Reserve Board, 240
Federal Trade Commission, 240
Federation of Labor, 57
Feigert, Frank B., 207 n. 20
Feingold, Russell, 7, 215
Fenno, John Ward, 38
Ferraro, Mark V., 107 n. 28
Field, Phyllis F., 281, 300 n. 24
Fillmore, Millard, 47, 269
fire-house primary, 199
Fiscal Responsibility Act, 238
Fisher, Lee, 310
Flemming, Gregory, 107 n. 27
Flexner, James Thomas, 31 n. 10, 53 n. 12
Flowers, Gennifer, 116
Flynt, Larry, 255
Foley, Tom, 254
Fong, Matt, 187
Forbes, Malcolm, 2
Forbes, Steve, 2, 5, 115
Ford, Betty, 248
Ford, Gerald R., 15–16, 109, 132, 218, 242, 248, 309
Ford Motor Company, 177
Formisano, Ronald P., 12 n. 35
Fortune (magazine), 157
4 Politics, 146
Fourteenth Amendment, 93
Fowler, Linda L., 106 n. 18
Frank, Barney, 94, 243, 251, 252
franking privilege, 167
Franklin, Grace A., 262 n. 17
Fraser, Don, 124
Freedman, Anne, 207 n. 33, 207 n. 35
Freedman, Dan, 206 n. 5
Freedmen's Bureau, 93
Free Soil Party, 282
Fremont, John C., 47
French Revolution, 38–39
Frendries, John, 31 n. 28, 99, 107 n. 27, 207 n. 28
Freneau, Philip, 38, 210

Frisch, Morton J., 32 n. 39
Fugitive Slave Act, 282
functionalist model, 86
funnel of causality, 143–144. *See also* The American Voter
Fusaro, Roberta, 11 n. 4
fusion balloting, 272

Gallup, George, Jr., 82 n. 2, 115, 138 n. 16, 303, 314 n. 2
Gallup Organization, 173 n. 47, 173 n. 48, 173 n. 49
Gamache, Murielle, 214, 235 n. 18, 235 n. 19, 235 n. 20
Gardner, John, 217
Garfield, James, 60, 148
Garin, Geoffrey, 147, 172 n. 24
Garment, Suzanne, 311
Gaspee (ship), 35
Gaudet, Hazel, 171 n. 11
Gay Men's Health Crisis, 75
Gazette of the United States, 38, 210
Gejdenson, Sam, 17
gender gap, 163–165
Gephardt, Richard, 249, 255, 259, 262 n. 48
German Republican Society, 38
Gerring, John, 300 n. 15
Gibson, James L., 107 n. 25, 107 n. 26, 207 n. 28
Gienapp, William E., 54 n. 25
Gierzynski, Anthony, 106 n. 20
Gingrich, Marianne, 237
Gingrich, Newt, 85, 151, 155, 156, 168, 169, 237–239, 248–249, 252, 254–255, 260, 261 n. 1, 263 n. 55
Ginsberg, Benjamin, 173 n. 51
Gitelson, Alan R., 99, 107 n. 27
Glendening, Parris, 165
Going Negative: How Political Advertisement Shrink and Polarize the Electorate (Ansolabehere and Iyengar), 249–250
Goldman, Ralph M., 31 n. 22
Gold-Plated Politics (Morris and Gamache), 214
Goldwater, Barry, 72, 83 n. 21, 87, 144, 164, 214, 225, 290
Gompers, Samuel, 235 n. 15
Goodgame, Dan, 32 n. 46
Goodhart, Noah J., 207 n. 38
Gore, Al, 3–4, 84, 109, 110, 129, 156, 157, 233, 247, 274
Governing Team Day, 237
Graham, Lindsay, 243, 250, 251, 255
Gramm, Phil, 243
Great Depression, 30, 70, 148
Great Society, 9, 75, 249, 303
Green, John C., 31 n. 28, 83 n. 16, 107 n. 29, 107 n. 30, 206 n. 1, 207 n. 38, 236 n. 37, 262 n. 19, 300 n. 4, 300 n. 18, 301 n. 46, 301 n. 47, 301 n. 48, 301 n. 50
Greenback-Labor Party, 284
Greenback Party, 283–285, 292

Greenblatt, Alan, 11 n. 29, 262 n. 46
Green Party, 270, 295
Greenpeace, 74
Gwynne, S. C., 31 n. 25

Hadley, Charles D., 31 n. 22, 207 n. 23
Haig, Alexander, 73
Haldeman, H. R., 73
Hall, Ralph, 243
Hamilton, Alexander, 13, 53 n. 9, 86, 133, 137 n.
    10, 138 n. 17, 138 n. 39, 210, 241, 261 n. 4,
    263 n. 53
    beliefs about political parties, 14
    on choosing presidents, 113, 114, 115
    on Congress members as trustees, 259–260
    disagreement with Jefferson, 27–30, 37, 38–39,
        116
    disagreement with Madison, 37–38
    economic plan, 37–38
    on Electoral College, 239
    on Shays's Rebellion, 36
Hamiltonian Nationalism, 27–30, 104
    defined, 27–28
    difference from Jeffersonian Localism, 28
    history of, 29–30
    party structure and, 178, 180
    presidential nominations and, 116–120
    rise of, 120–135
    shifts to and from, 29–30
    third parties, 276–277, 298–299
    triumph of, 302–314
Handgun Control, Inc., 224
Hanna, Mark, 211
Hanni, Don, 174–175
Hansen, Jerrold, 292, 301 n. 46, 301 n. 47
Harding, Warren, 70
hard money, 35, 229–231
Hardy, Chris, 200
Harlan, John Marshall, 56
Harris, Douglas B., 262 n. 36, 262 n. 37, 262 n.
    38, 262 n. 39, 262 n. 40, 262 n. 41, 262 n. 42
Harris, Fred, 6, 11 n. 20
Harris, Lou, 74
Hart, Gary, 134
Hart, Peter, 172 n. 26
Hartshorn, Elinor C., 54 n. 24, 300 n. 27
Hartz, Louis, 274–275, 300 n. 12
Hastert, J. Dennis, 252, 255, 260
Hatch Act of 1939, 216
Hatfield, Mark, 207 n. 13
Hayworth, J. D., 237
heads of the campaign committees, 242
Heinemann, Fred, 96
Helms, Jesse, 77, 243
Henschen, Beth, 11 n. 2, 171 n. 6
Heritage Foundation, 183
Herrnson, Paul S., 106 n. 14, 106 n. 15, 107 n. 23,
    221–222, 227, 236 n. 32, 236 n. 37, 300 n. 4,
    300 n. 18
Herschensohn, Bruce, 187

Hertzberg, Hedrick, 171 n. 10
hill committees, 93–95. *See also* legislative cam-
    paign committees
    brokerage role, 95
    campaign managers/strategists, 94
    coordinated expenditures, 95
    event coordinators, 94–95
    fund-raising, 94
Hillman, Sidney, 181
Hiss, Alger, 72
Hoadley, John F., 241, 261 n. 9
Hoebeke, C. H., 83 n. 13
Hoffman, Paul, 77
Hofstadter, Richard, 211, 235 n. 13
Holbrooke, Richard, 301 n. 36
Hollings, Ernest, 243
hollow realignment, 153
Homestead Act, 48, 284
homosexuals, in military, 165, 168
Hoover, Herbert, 70, 240–241
Horton, Willie, 116
House Committee on Un-American Activities,
    72
Huckshorn, Robert J., 107 n. 25, 107 n. 26
Hughes, Richard, 121
Hugick, Larry, 137 n. 11, 137 n. 13
Human Events, 218
Human Rights Campaign, 183
Humphrey, Hubert H., 109, 122, 133, 138 n. 31,
    140, 150, 178, 188, 309, 311
Humphrey, Hubert H., III, 267
Hunt, James, 134, 200
Hunt Commission, 134
Hussein, Saddam, 165
Hyde, Henry, 248, 249, 251, 259

IBM, 22, 177
immigration
    effect on Democratic Party, 119–120
    expansion of electorate through, 212
    political machine and, 48, 50
    political parties and, 46–47
incomplete realignment, 153
independent primaries, 126
Independent Republicans, 178
Individual Retirement Accounts (IRAs), 238
Industrial Revolution, 48
Information Age
    communication with voters in, 6–7
    creative party finances in, 222–233
    developments affecting American life, 21–22
    family life, 1
    local parties, 175–184
    state parties, 175–184
    technology, 2–5, 89–90
    work habits, 1
instant parties, 79
interest groups, 7
    differences from political parties, 18–19
    rise of, 74–76

Internet, 1–2, 90, 146–147, 170, 180, 201–203, 204, 233–234, 255, 294–296
IRAs. *See* Individual Retirement Accounts (IRAs)
Issa, Darrell, 187
issue advocacy, 209, 223, 227. *See also* campaign finance
ITT, 177
Iyengar, Shanto, 249–250, 262 n. 26

Jackson, Andrew, 42–44, 118, 150, 281
Jackson, Brooks, 233, 236 n. 39
Jackson, Jesse, 110, 132, 134, 135
Jacksonian Democracy, 44
Jaramillo, Patricia, 301 n. 48
Jay, John, 39, 53 n. 9, 261 n. 4
Jay Treaty, 39, 241
Jefferson, Thomas, 86, 210, 241, 303
  beliefs about political parties, 14
  on Congress members as delegates, 260
  disagreement with Hamilton, 27–30, 37, 38–39, 116, 302
  election of 1800, 40
  opposition to Jay Treaty, 39
  support for Hamilton's economic plan, 38
Jeffersonian Localism, 27–30, 72, 104, 303–304
  defined, 27
  difference from Hamiltonian Nationalism, 28
  history of, 29–30
  party structure and, 178–180
  presidential nominations and, 116–120
  shifts to and from, 29–30
  third parties, 276–277, 298–299
Jeffords, James, 243, 258
Job Creation and Wage Enhancement Act, 238
Johnson, Andrew, 93
Johnson, Donald Brace, 83 n. 8, 83 n. 9, 301 n. 33, 301 n. 34
Johnson, Hiram, 63
Johnson, Lyndon B., 9, 20, 50, 51, 72, 77, 87, 109, 116, 121, 138 n. 16, 138 n. 18, 138 n. 29, 138 n. 31, 141, 164, 243, 248, 249, 266, 290, 303, 309
Johnson, Paul, 315 n. 22
Johnson, Sam, 141
Johnston, Eric, 276
Jordan, Hamilton, 78
judicial review, 41
Judiciary Act, 41
The Jungle (Sinclair), 66

Kansas-Nebraska Act, 46, 283
Kaufman, Leslie, 137 n. 9, 172 n. 33
Kayden, Xandra, 106 n. 5, 203, 207 n. 40
Keith, Bruce E., 172 n. 20
Kelley, Stanley, Jr., 261 n. 8
Kennedy, Edward M., 202, 243, 311, 315 n. 14
Kennedy, John F., 13–14, 31 n. 5, 47, 50, 77, 108, 113, 115, 126, 135, 138 n. 16, 140, 160, 166, 243, 244, 303, 309
Kennedy, Joseph P., II, 166–167

Kennedy, Michael, 167
Kennedy, Robert F., 32 n. 42, 50, 122–123, 124, 138 n. 31, 166, 207 n. 24, 263 n. 54
Kerry, John F., 2, 202
Key, V. O., Jr., 12 n. 34, 31 n. 21, 148–152, 157, 172 n. 29, 172 n. 30, 172 n. 38, 207 n. 7, 276, 301 n. 38
Killian, Linda, 261 n. 2, 261 n. 3, 262 n. 24, 262 n. 45
King, Angus, 266, 267, 270, 294, 299
Kings County Republican Committee, 198–199
Kirk, Paul, 1
Kirkpatrick, Evron, 12 n. 33
Kirkpatrick, Jeane J., 88, 129, 138 n. 36
Kissinger, Henry, 73
Klein, Joe, 262 n. 47
Klinkner, Philip A., 106 n. 9, 106 n. 10, 106 n. 13, 106 n. 16, 207 n. 10
Knights of Columbus, 75
Knights of Labor, 57
Know-Nothing Party. *See* American Party
Koch, Edward I., 184
Koppel, Ted, 136
Korean War, 143
Kruschke, Earl R., 300 n. 29, 301 n. 45

labor unions, 57
Labour Party (Great Britain), 265
Ladd, Everett Carll, 11 n. 26, 31 n. 22, 79, 83 n. 28, 138 n. 40, 152–153, 154–155, 157, 172 n. 34, 172 n. 36, 172 n. 37, 172 n. 42, 173 n. 56, 300 n. 14
LaFollette, Robert M., Sr., 60, 61–62, 68, 287
Landon, Alf, 278
LaPolla, Louis, 79, 80
Larson, Arthur, 274, 300 n. 10
Lasswell, Harold D., 170, 173 n. 59
Lauer, Matt, 310
Lawrence, Christine C., 235 n. 21
Lawrence, David, 126
Lawson, Kay, 12 n. 36
Layzell, Anne, 107 n. 27
Lazarsfeld, Paul F., 142, 143, 171 n. 11, 171 n. 12
LCCs. *See* legislative campaign committees (LCCs)
League of Conservation Voters, 181
legislative campaign committees (LCCs)
  emergence of, 93–99
  hill committees, 93–95
  state level, 97–99
Lehmann, Christopher, 235 n. 3
Lester, Will, 314 n. 10, 315 n. 17
Leuchtenberg, William, 53 n. 5
Levine, Mel, 225
Lewinsky, Monica, 2, 251, 309, 310
Libertarian Party, 277, 294, 296
Liberty Party, 282
Lincoln, Abraham, 13, 15, 30, 31 n. 2, 148, 150, 156, 208, 247, 275
Lincoln, Mary Todd, 47

Lippmann, Walter, 277
Lipset, Seymour Martin, 32 n. 35, 54 n. 33, 106 n.
   6, 300 n. 17
Livingston, Robert, 38, 40, 156, 248, 255, 259,
   260, 262 n. 49, 263 n. 55
local parties, 99–103. *See also* political parties;
   state parties
   activists, 191
   activities, 195–201
   committee persons, 189–190
   computer use and, 201
   county organizations, 190
   evidence of decline, 102
   evidence of renewal, 99
   in Information Age, 175–184
   manifest party functions, 195–197
   membership, 184–192
   officials in, 189–190
   precinct captains, 189
   primary voters, 184–189
   structure, 177–180
local political culture, 192–195
   individualistic, 192, 195
   moralistic, 192, 195
   traditionalistic, 192, 195
Lochner v. New York, 56, 82 n. 5, 82 n. 6
Locke, John, 13
Lodge, Henry Cabot, 138 n. 16
Lorch, Robert S., 207 n. 22
Los Angeles Times, 53 n. 2, 173 n. 56, 294
Lott, Trent, 20, 29, 77, 169
Loudoun County Democrats, 199–200
Louis Harris and Associates, 115, 138 n. 15,
   261 n. 6
Lowi, Theodore J., 69, 83 n. 16, 173 n. 51,
   298–299, 301 n. 50, 315 n. 25
loyalists, 35
Luntz, Frank, 152

Mackie, Thomas T., 12 n. 36
MacNeil/Lehrer's NewsHour (television program),
   254
Madison, James, 14, 31 n. 7, 31 n. 8, 31 n. 9,
   37–38, 40, 53 n. 9, 55, 117, 261 n. 4
Madsen, Phil, 297
Magleby, David B., 172 n. 20
Mahe, Eddie, Jr., 106 n. 5, 203, 207 n. 40
Mahoning County Democratic Committee,
   174–175
Maine, 270
Maisel, L. Sandy, 54 n. 24, 106 n. 5, 171 n. 5, 300
   n. 6, 300 n. 8, 300 n. 24, 300 n. 25
majority leader, 242, 243
Malbin, Michael J., 12 n. 30, 173 n. 53, 173 n. 54,
   236 n. 33, 236 n. 35
Manatt, Charles, 89, 307
manifest party functions, 195–197
   aiding candidates, 196
   allocating patronage, 196
   educating voters, 196
      getting out the vote, 196
      nominating candidates, 195
      overseeing election process, 196
      promoting patriotism, 196
      providing a social outlet, 196
      providing information to media, 196
      raising/distributing money, 196
      recruiting public servants, 195
      registering new voters, 196
      slating, 196
      uniting diverse interests, 196
Mann, Thomas E., 12 n. 30, 173 n. 53, 173 n. 54,
   235 n. 33, 235 n. 35
Mansfield, Mike, 9
Mao Zedong, 72
Maraniss, David, 109, 137 n. 6, 137 n. 7
Marbury, William, 40–41
Marbury v. Madison, 40–41, 53 n. 15
Marcy, William, 54 n. 20
Marshall, John, 40–41
Martin, D. G., 96
Martino, Ann, 206 n. 4
Marx, Karl, 275
Massachusetts' Eighth Congressional District,
   166–167
May, Lary, 300 n. 19
Mayer, William G., 139 n. 45
McAuliffe, Terrence, 115
McCain, John, 7, 215, 234
McCarthy, Eugene, 121, 122, 124, 138 n. 31, 218
McCarthy, Joseph R., 72
McClure, Robert D., 106 n. 18
McClure's (magazine), 65, 66
McCollum, Bill, 251, 252
McConnell, Mitch, 215
McCormack, John, 254
McCulloch v. Maryland, 37
McCullough, David, 301 n. 37
McGerr, Michael E., 171 n. 7
McGinniss, Joe, 77
McGovern, George S., 79, 120, 124–125, 129,
   132, 133, 138 n. 31, 138 n. 33, 138 n. 38,
   144, 188, 214, 287, 288, 301 n. 35, 311
McGovern-Fraser Commission, 121–122,
   124–127
   agenda behind reforms of, 125
   consequences of, 126, 132–133
   creation of, 121
   delegate selection changes, 125–126
   recommendations adopted by, 124
   Republicans and, 130–132
McGreevey, James, 164
McHugh, John, 167
McKinley, William, 67, 150, 211–212
McLaughlin Group, 147
McNamara, Robert, 73
McPhee, William N., 171 n. 12
Media Studies Center, 83 n. 17
Medicare, 9, 71
Meredith, James, 29

merit system, 60, 62, 68
Merkl, Peter H., 12 n. 36
Merton, Robert, 86, 106 n. 7
Michel, Bob, 250
Microsoft, 233
Mikulski, Barbara, 133
Mikulski Commission, 133–134
Milbank, Dana, 11 n. 5, 11. n. 7, 11. n. 8, 11 n. 9, 11 n. 10
Mileur, Jerome M., 32 n. 43, 83 n. 19, 83 n. 20, 139 n. 47
Milkis, Sidney M., 83 n. 19, 139 n. 47
Miller, James, 184
Miller, Warren E., 143, 171 n. 14, 171 n. 15
minimalist model. *See* rational-efficient model
Minnesota Reform Party, 239
minority leader, 242, 243
minor parties. *See* third parties
Mitchell, Greg, 83 n. 15
Molyneux, Guy, 11 n. 28
Mondale, Walter, 108, 109, 129, 134, 151, 272
Mondello, Joseph, 197–198
Monroe, James, 15, 39, 41, 266
Montesqieu, 13
Morehead, Carlos, 248
Morella, Constance, 243
Morgan, J. P., 56
Morgan, Ted, 32 n. 40
Morgan, William, 281
Morin, Richard, 31 n. 14
Morley, Michael, 174–175
Morris, Dick, 7, 11 n. 23, 74, 77, 83 n. 25, 106 n. 1, 115, 137 n. 12, 310
Morris, Dwight, 214, 235 n. 18, 235 n. 19, 235 n. 20
Morrison, Samuel E., 53 n. 5
Morse, Walter F., 139 n. 46
Motion Picture Association of America, 276
Mrs. O'Reilly, Irish American tale, 52
MSNBC, 146
muckrakers, 65–66, 81
mugwumps, 57, 60
Murr, Andrew, 137 n. 9, 172 n. 33
Muskie, Edmund S., 188
Myers, Lisa, 254

Nadler, Jerrold, 252
NAFTA. *See* North American Free Trade Agreement (NAFTA)
Nassau County Republicans, 197–198
National Abortion Rights League, 181
National Association of Evangelicals, 75
National Association of Manufacturers, 18
National Beer Wholesalers Association, 181, 182–183
National Council of the United States of America, 283
National Education Association, 129, 181
National Election Study, 191
National Endowment for the Arts, 304

National Federation of Independent Businesses, 181, 182
National Gazette, 38, 210
National Intelligencer, 41
National Journal, 9, 146
National Opinion Research Center, 15, 31 n. 15
National Organization for Women, 74, 129, 181
national presidential primary, 119
National Recovery Administration (NRA), 70
National Republican Coalition for Choice, 183
National Republican Congressional Committee (NRCC), 85, 93, 94
National Republican Senatorial Committee (NRSC), 93, 94, 215, 229
National Rifle Association, 168, 181, 224
National Right-to-Life Committee, 75
National Security Restoration Act, 238
National Union, 15
Natsios, Andrew, 6
Nelson, Candice J., 172 n. 20
New Deal, 9, 29, 30, 70–72, 75, 81, 148, 152, 155, 157, 162, 175, 239, 277, 303
New Frontier, 303
New Party, 270
New Politics Democrats, 125
newspapers, 210–211
Newsweek, 308, 315 n. 12
New York Civil Liberties Union, 218
New York Times, 82 n. 1, 134, 157, 171 n. 16, 172 n. 44, 173 n. 52, 197, 294, 308, 310, 314 n. 11, 315 n. 19
Nie, Norman H., 144, 172 n. 18
Niemi, Richard G., 172 n. 21
Nineteenth Amendment, 65, 163
Nixon, Richard, 15, 25, 72, 73, 77, 83 n. 23, 87, 109, 115, 125, 126, 136, 138 n. 16, 140, 141–142, 150, 151, 171 n. 9, 188, 242, 290, 309
Noble, Phil, 298
nonpartisan municipal elections, 63–64
nonpartisan primaries, 188
North, Oliver, 185
North American Free Trade Agreement (NAFTA), 9, 249
NRA. *See* National Recovery Administration (NRA)
NRCC. *See* National Republican Congressional Committee (NRCC)
NRSC. *See* National Republican Senatorial Committee (NRSC)

Oakland Technology Exchange, 183
O'Neill, Thomas P. "Tip," 99, 166, 254
open primaries, 126
  completely open, 187
  partially open, 187
Ornstein, Norman J., 12 n. 30, 173 n. 53, 173 n. 54, 236 n. 33, 236 n. 35
Orr, Elizabeth, 172 n. 20
Ostrogorski, M. I., 261 n. 14

*The Other Candidates: Third Parties in Presidential
    Elections* (Smallwood), 277
Overtaker, Louise, 235 n. 16
Owens, John E., 262 n. 21

Packard, David, 187
PAC kits, 95
Packwood, Bob, 181
Paddock, Joel, 195, 207 n. 26, 207 n. 27
Paine, Thomas, 35, 38
Paolino, Phil, 300 n. 8
parliamentary prerogative, 35
parliamentary systems, 239
The Parties Respond (Maisel), 86
Partin, Randall, 301 n. 48, 301 n. 49
party affiliation, 18, 45, 79. *See also* party brand
    loyalty; party identification
party brand loyalty, 22, 160, 308. *See also* party
    affiliation; party identification
    American voter and, 140–170
    decline of, 213
    parental party identification, 141–142
party coalitions, 160–169
    divided government, 166–169
    gender gap, 163–165
Party Decline in America (Coleman), 85
The Party Goes On (Kayden and Mahe), 86
party government, 243
Party Government (Schattschneider), 5, 304
party identification. *See also* party affiliation; party
    brand loyalty
    candidate-centered politics and, 144–145
    decline of, 147
    importance of, 142–147
    issues and, 144
    measuring, 145–147
    parental, 141–142
    rational-actor model, 145
    rational-choice model, 145
    rational voter model, 144–145
    sociological model, 142–143
    sociological-psychological model, 143–144
    variables affecting, 146
party-in-government (PIG), 20, 21, 104, 306
party-in-the-campaign, 104
party-in-the-electorate (PIE), 20, 21, 104, 306
party-line voting, 21
party organization (PO), 20, 104, 306
party realignment, 148–157. *See also* realignment
    theory
    conditions of ideal-typical, 150
    critical elections, 148, 149
    dealignment and, 152
    hollow, 153, 170
    incomplete, 153
    Key and, 148–152
    realigning elections, 148
    rolling, 153, 170
    secular realignments, 148, 153
    stages of, 153, 155

Party Renewal in America (Pomper), 86
The Party's Just Begun (Sabato), 86
The Party's Over (Broder), 85
party structure
    chair of the policy committees, 242
    heads of the campaign committees, 242
    majority leader, 242, 243
    minority leader, 242, 243
    Speaker, 242
    vice president, 242–243
    whip, 242
Party Transformation Study (PTS), 99
Pataki, George, 158, 233, 308, 310
patriots, 35
Patterson, Thomas E., 11 n. 22, 53 n. 12
Paul, Mark, 207 n. 17
Pawlinga, Stephen J., 80
Penrose, Boies, 235 n. 15
The People's Choice (Lazarsfeld, Berelson, and
    Gaudet), 142
People's Party. *See* Populists
Perot, Ross, 10, 77, 78, 84, 115, 136, 151, 266,
    269, 273, 280, 290, 292, 294–295, 308
Personal Responsibility Act, 238
Petrocik, John R., 144, 172 n. 18
Pew Center for Civic Journalism, 146, 173 n. 56
Philadelphia Inquirer, 141
Philip Morris (tobacco manufacturer), 231, 233
Phillips, Kevin P., 151, 172 n. 32
PIE. *See* party-in-the-electorate (PIE)
Pierce, Franklin, 115, 119, 148
PIG. *See* party-in-government (PIG)
Pika, Joseph A., 138 n. 37
Pinckney, Thomas, 40
Platt, Thomas C., 67
Platt machine, 50
plebiscitary presidents, 73
Plunkitt, George Washington, 42, 48–51, 52,
    55–56, 57
PO. *See* party organization (PO)
Polakoff, Keith Ian, 235 n. 14
Political Action Committee (PAC), 15, 76, 181,
    220–222, 224
political culture
    American, 273–276
    local, 192–195
political machine, 48–52
    corruption in, 50–52
    immigration and, 48, 50
    local election laws and, 50
political parties. *See also* local parties; state parties
    academicians on, 16
    accomplishments sought by, 23–27
    allied party groups, 180–184
    American attitudes toward, 5–6, 14–18,
        159–160
    in American setting, 13–30, 52–53
    anti-Catholic sentiment, 47
    anti-immigrant sentiment, 46–47
    ascendance of party politics, 33–52

Bill of Rights and, 36
business firm analogy, 22–23, 170
Civil War and, 45–48
Cold War and, 72–73
Colonial Era, 34–36
coming of political machine, 48–52
components of, 19–21
computer use, 201–204
in Congress, 241–247
consequence of fragmentation, 170
contextual approach, 86
continuing role of, 30
decline of party politics, 55–82
differences from interest groups, 18–19
elected officials as sales force for, 237–261
entertainment industry and, 275–276
Federalists versus Republicans, 37–40
functionalist model, 86
history of, 33–53
as indicators of democratic development, 5
intermediary functions, 8–10
Internet and, 2–5
legislative politics and, 313
local level, 99–103
minimalist perspective of, 23–27
minor parties, 314
new laws and, 313
organizational adjustment/growth, 86–93,
   312–313
origins of, 33–34
party finances, 222–233
partyless age, 81–82
party organization in twenty-first century,
   84–105
party politics in next millenium, 312–314
party rule, 1824-1912, 40–52
politics without, 16–18
pre-party era, 33–34
president as party leader, 240–241
Progressive movement, 56–69
rational-efficient perspective of, 23–27
responsible party model, 24–27
rethinking, 1–11
revivalists versus declinists, 103–105
role in American polity, 305–306
role in campaign finance, 219–220
role in media-centered elections, 214
as service organizations, 169–170
service-oriented, 310
slavery and, 45–46
stages of development, 241–242
structure, 177–180, 242
third parties, 314
as tripod, 19–23
voter trends and, 312
Polk, James K., 115
Polsby, Nelson, 136, 138 n. 41, 139 n. 48, 256
Pomper, Gerald, 106 n. 5, 106 n. 12, 107 n. 24,
   144, 171 n. 17, 235 n. 4, 262 n. 19
Pope, Charles, 262 n. 43

Populists, 283–285, 292
Porter, Kirk H., 83 n .8, 83 n. 9, 301 n. 33,
   301 n. 34
post-materialist perspective, 75
Powell, Colin, 110
Power, Pasta, and Politics (D'Amato), 197
president, as party leader, 240–241
President Ford Committee, 31 n. 16
presidential campaign finance system, 273
presidential elections, 2–5, 39, 41–42, 84–86, 157,
   211–212
presidential nominations, 108–137
   dilemma of choosing presidents, 113–116
   future of, 135–137
   Hamiltonian Nationalism versus Jeffersonian
      Localism, 116–120
   ideas for fixing system of, 116
   lack of qualified candidates, 110
   McGovern-Fraser Commission, 121–127,
      130–133
   Mikulski Commission, 133–134
   national presidential primary, 119
   rise of nominating conventions, 117–120
   selection process, 108–116
   two-thirds rule, 118–119
   unit rule, 118–119
   Winograd Commission, 133–134
presidential primaries, 59–60, 68, 126–127
presidential system, 239–240
Pressler, Larry, 168
Price, David E., 96, 261 n. 16
primaries
   blanket, 6, 187
   closed, 126, 185, 187
   direct, 59–60, 68, 272
   independent, 126
   nonpartisan, 188
   open, 126, 187
   presidential, 59–60, 126–127
   representative, nature of, 128–130
primary voters, 184–189
Princeton Survey Research Associates, 82 n. 3
Profiles in Courage (Kennedy), 14
Progressive Citizens of America, 287
Progressive Party, 56–69, 81, 269, 304–305
   1912-1914, 62–63
   1948, 287–289
   Australian ballot, 58–59, 68
   ballot initiative, 62–63
   direct election of U. S. senators, 64–65, 68
   direct primary, 59–60, 68
   entrance of, 57–65
   merit system, 60, 62, 68
   municipal ownership of utilities, 62, 68
   nonpartisan municipal elections, 63–64
   reasons for success of, 65–68
   recall, 62–63
   referendum, 62–63
   reform methods evolved from, 69
   women's suffrage, 64–65, 68

Prohibition Party, 277–280
Project Vote Smart, 146
proportional representation, 267–268
Proxmire, William, 225
PTS. *See* Party Transformation Study (PTS)
Public Works Administration (PWA), 70
Publius, 36
Pullman Car Strike, 57
PWA. *See* Public Works Administration (PWA)

Quayle, Dan, 2, 109
Quay Machine, 48, 50

Radical Republicans, 93
Rae, Nicol C., 262 n. 22, 262 n. 23, 262 n. 25
Rand, Ayn, 276
Rangel, Charles, 310
Ranney, Austin, 261 n. 15
Rapoport, Ronald B., 301 n. 48, 301 n. 49
rational-actor model, 145
rational-choice model, 145
rational-efficient model, 23–27
    definitions of party, 23–24
    Information Age and, 26
    organizational structure, 25
    party functions, 24–25
    role in government, 26
rational voter model, 144–145
Rayburn, Sam, 20, 250, 253–254
Reagan, Ronald, 29, 30, 32 n. 45, 71, 73, 78, 79,
    109, 132, 134, 141, 147, 151, 155, 160, 164,
    172 n. 40, 178, 237, 240, 249, 266, 276, 277,
    309, 314 n. 4, 315 n. 14
realigning elections, 148
realignment theory, 142. *See also* party realign-
    ment
Reams, Henry, 264
recall, 62–63
reciprocal deference, 44
Reeves, Richard, 32 n. 41, 135, 139 n. 44
referendum, 62–63
Reform Party, 239, 266–267, 281, 290, 294–295,
    298–299
Rehnquist, William, 206 n. 6, 272
Rehr, David, 182
Reich, Robert, 22
Reichley, A. James, 31 n. 12, 32 n. 38, 32 n. 43, 53
    n. 3, 53 n. 10, 53 n. 13, 53 n. 14, 54 n. 20, 54
    n. 22, 54 n. 32, 83 n. 12, 106 n. 11, 106 n. 17,
    138 n. 24, 138 n. 25, 138 n. 26, 236 n. 34,
    301 n. 40
A Republican Looks at His Party (Larson), 274
Republican Mainstream Committee, 183
Republican National Committee (RNC), 20, 22,
    71, 85, 239
    candidate recruitment, 88
    fund-raising, 87–88
    image repair, 88–89
    organizational improvements, 88
    rebirth of, 87–89

technology and, 90, 91
Republican Party
    conference, 264–265
    creation of, 46
    Delegate-Organization (DO) Committee,
        131–132
    election of 1824, 41–42
    versus Federalists, 37–40
    Internet use, 2, 7
    majority in Congress, 237
    McGovern-Fraser Commission and, 130–132
    National Beer Wholesalers Association and,
        181
    nominating conventions, 118
    PACs and, 221
    party finances in Information Age, 222–233
    popularity of, 48
    rise of, 46
    shifts in coalitions, 162
    unofficial party organizations and, 183–184
    voting blocs, 162–163
responsible party government, 24–27, 244, 246
    definitions of party, 24
    Information Age and, 26
    organizational structure, 25–26
    party functions, 25
    role in government, 26
Reston, James, 300 n. 22
Revenue Act, 217
revivalists, 103–105
Revolutionary War, 34
Rhode, David W., 262 n. 20, 262 n. 27, 262 n. 28,
    300 n. 8
Richards, Ann, 309
Richmond Enquirer, 117
Ridge, Tom, 233
Right Side of the Web, 146
Right-to-Life Party, 277
Riordan, William, 49, 54 n. 30, 54 n. 31, 82 n. 4,
    82 n. 7
Ripley, Randall B., 262 n. 17
Rising Tide, 90
Ritchie, Thomas, 117–118
RNC. *See* Republican National Committee
    (RNC)
Robb, Chuck, 184
Robertson, Pat, 129, 132, 135
Roch, Don, 87, 106 n. 8
Rockefeller, Jay, 110
Rockefeller, John D., 56
Rockefeller, Nelson, 109
Rockman, Bert A., 172 n. 41
Roe v. Wade, 19
Rokkan, Stein, 106 n. 6
rolling realignment, 153
Rollins, Ed, 77, 78, 83 n. 27
Romance, Joseph, 315 n. 25
Romer, Roy, 310
Roosevelt, Eleanor, 70

Roosevelt, Franklin D., 9, 19, 30, 70–72, 81, 83 n. 19, 83 n. 22, 120–121, 136, 140, 147, 152, 175, 239, 240, 277, 303
Roosevelt, Theodore, 62, 65, 66–68, 119, 215, 269, 285
Roper Center for Public Opinion Research, 83 n. 17, 235 n. 2, 293, 300 n. 9
Rose, Gary L., 137 n. 8
Rose, Richard, 12 n. 36
Rosenbaum, David E., 12 n. 31, 263 n. 56
Rosenberg, Debra, 137 n. 9, 172 n. 33
Rossiter, Clinton, 5, 7, 11 n. 12, 285, 300 n. 2, 300 n. 32
Rothenberg Political Report, 95
Rothman, Steve, 2
Rove, Karl, 233–234
Rowland, John, 158, 308
Rule 14C, 132
Runkel, David R., 138 n. 19
Rusk, Dean, 73
Rutan v. Republican Party of Illinois, 7, 11 n. 24, 11 n. 25

Sabato, Larry J., 106 n. 5, 236 n. 39
Salmon, Matt, 250
Sanders, Bernard, 264–265, 266, 294, 299, 300 n. 1
Sarbanes, Paul, 1
Saturday Evening Post, 66
Sauerbrey, Ellen, 165
Scalia, Antonin, 7, 188–189
Scammon, Richard, 138 n. 31, 173 n. 55
Schattschneider, E. E., 5, 7, 11 n. 11, 33, 53 n. 1, 138 n. 27, 304, 314 n. 5
Schlesinger, Joseph A., 24, 31 n. 28, 32 n. 29
Schneider, William, 83 n. 26
Schumer, Charles, 158, 308
Scott, Wilson, 236 n. 38
A Screen Guide for Americans, 276
scrip, 57
Sears, 22
secret ballot. *See* Australian ballot
secular realignments, 148, 153
Sedition Act, 39–40
Segal, Rick, 2
The Selling of the President, 1968 (McGinniss), 77
senators, direct election of, 64–65, 68
Senior Citizens Equity Act, 238
Sensenbrenner, F. James, 252
Seventeenth Amendment, 65, 94
Sewall, Arthur, 285
Shadegg, John, 250
Shadegg, Stephen C., 315 n. 15
Shafritz, Jay M., 24, 32 n. 32
The Shame of the Cities (Steffens), 66
Shays, Christopher, 243
Shays, Daniel, 36
Shays's Rebellion, 36
Shea, Daniel M., 5, 11 n. 14, 31 n. 28, 83 n. 16, 97–98, 106 n. 19, 107 n. 21, 107 n. 22,

107 n. 29, 107 n. 30, 206 n. 1, 207 n. 36, 207 n. 38, 236 n. 37, 262 n. 19, 300 n. 20, 300 n. 21, 301 n. 46, 301 n. 47, 301 n. 48, 301 n. 50
Sherman, Roger, 109
Shriver, Sargent, 11 n. 20
Sidlow, Edward, 11 n. 2, 171 n. 6
Sierra Club, 74, 181, 184
silent majority, 168
Simpson, O. J., 19
Sinclair, Upton, 66
Skelly, Yankelovich, 172 n. 35
slavery, 45–46
Sluzar, Sophia, 300 n. 17
Smallwood, Frank, 277, 300 n. 3, 300 n. 23
Smith, Alfred E., 119–120, 148
Smith, Gordon, 181
Smith, Howard, 243–244
Smith, Richard Norton, 301 n. 43
Smith v. Allwright, 176, 206 n. 2, 206 n. 3
Snowe, Olympia, 258
Social Democrats, 296
Socialist Party, 269, 277
Social Security, 9, 70, 71
sociological model, 142–143
sociological-psychological model, 143–144
soft money, 7, 180, 209, 222–223, 229–231, 310
Sons of Liberty, 35
Sorauf, Frank, 211, 216, 235 n. 11, 235 n. 16, 235 n. 23, 235 n. 24, 236 n. 25, 236 n. 26
Soule, John W., 207 n. 25
South (United States region), 156–157
Speaker, 242, 252–255
specie, 35
Specter, Arlen, 258
Spitzer, Robert J., 300 n. 25
splinter candidates, 266
spoils system, 44–45, 57
Squier and Associates, 214
Stanley, Harold W., 207 n. 23
Starr, Kenneth, 2, 143–144, 251, 311
state legislative campaign committees, 97–99
state parties. *See also* local parties; political parties
   activities, 195–201
   chair, 190
   committees, 190
   computer use and, 201
   in Information Age, 175–184
   on the Internet, 201–203
   manifest party functions, 195–197
   membership, 184–192
   officials in, 189–190
   primary voters, 184–189
   regulating, 176–177
   structure, 177–180
State's Rights Party, 289–290
stay laws, 36
Steffens, Lincoln, 66, 83 n. 14
Stephanopoulos, George, 265
Stevenson, Adlai E., 121, 136, 143
Stokes, Donald E., 143, 171 n. 14, 171 n. 15

Stone, Clement, 217
Stone, I. F., 301 n. 42
Stone, Walter J., 301 n. 48, 301 n. 49
Storing, Herbert J., 53 n. 7, 53 n. 8
stratarchy, 177
Strauss, Robert, 133, 221
Strobel, Warren P., 106 n. 2, 315 n. 16
Subcommittee Bill of Rights, 247
Sun Oil Company (SunPAC), 220
SunPAC. *See* Sun Oil Company (SunPAC)
superdelegates, 134–135
Supreme Order of the Star Spangled Banner, 283

Taft, Bob, 310
Taft, William Howard, 67, 119, 269, 287
Taking Back Our Streets Act, 238
Tammany Hall, 48, 52, 55, 57
Tashjian v. Republican Party of Connecticut,
    188–189, 207 n. 18, 207 n. 19
Tate, Randy, 8
Taylor, Gene, 243
Taylor, Morry, 115
Taylor, Zachary, 45, 46
Team 100, 231
television, 6–7, 90, 134–135, 136, 151, 170, 241
tender laws, 36
Ten Myths About Money in Politics (Center for
    Responsive Politics), 224–226
Tennessee Valley Authority (TVA), 70
Terror of 1793, 39
Thayer, George, 235 n. 15
third parties, 55
    American political culture and, 273–276
    defined, 266
    explosion of, 291–292
    future of, 296–299
    Hamiltonian Nationalism and, 276–277,
        298– 299
    history and, 276–277, 280
    information age and, 264–299
    institutional barriers to growth of, 267–273
    Internet and, 294–296
    Jeffersonian Localism and, 276–277, 298–299
    paradox, 265–280
    significant examples of, 280–290
    voter attitudes toward, 293–294
Thomas, Evan, 137 n. 9, 172 n. 33
Thomas, Norman, 269
Thurmond, J. Strom, 168, 243, 266, 289
ticket-splitting, 157–160, 169
Tillman Act of 1907, 215
Time (magazine), 11 n. 18, 30, 72, 173 n. 45,
    262 n. 50
Time Warner, 233
Timex candidates, 135
Timmons v. Twin Cities Area New Party, 270
Tocqueville, Alexis de, 27, 32 n. 33, 116, 138 n.
    21, 275, 300 n. 13, 302, 314 n. 1
Tories, 34

Toward a More Responsible Two-Party System
    (American Political Science Association), 10,
    244–246
*Transforming Democracy: Legislative Campaign
    Committees and Political Parties* (Shea), 98
treating, 210
triangulation, 160–161
Truman, Harry S, 85, 244, 266, 287, 288–289,
    301 n. 44, 303
Tsongas, Paul, 190
Turner, Julius, 12 n. 33
Turn Left, 147
TVA. *See* Tennessee Valley Authority (TVA)
Tweed, William Marcy, 116
Twelfth Amendment, 113
two-thirds rule, 118–119

Ujifusa, Grant, 207 n. 9, 207 n. 30, 262 n. 30, 262
    n. 31, 262 n. 32
United Electrical, Radio, and Machine Workers
    of America, 75
The United States of Ambition (Ehrenhalt), 80
United States Taxpayers Party, 295–296
unit rule, 118–119, 121
unofficial party organizations, 183–184
Unruh, Jesse, 95
USA Today, 90, 137 n. 13, 172 n. 28, 173 n. 47,
    294
utilities, municipal ownership of, 62, 68

Valeo, Francis R., 218
Van Buren, Martin, 29, 42–44, 117, 118, 282
Vance, Cyrus, 73
Vanderbilt, Cornelius, 56
Ventura, Jesse, 239–240, 241, 261 n. 5, 267, 281,
    290, 294, 296, 299, 308
Verba, Sidney, 144, 172 n. 18
Vertz, Laura L., 207 n. 28
vice president, 109, 242–243
Vietnam War, 75, 116, 121, 124, 144, 304
Vinyard, Dale, 261 n. 11
voting
    gender gap, 163–165
    party brand loyalty and, 140–170
    in South, 156–157
    ticket-splitting, 157–160
Voting (Berelson, Lazarsfeld, and McPhee), 142
Voting Rights Act, 277

Wallace, George C., 151, 188, 214, 266, 289–290,
    308
Wallace, Henry A., 287–289
war, gender gap and, 165
Warner, John, 185
War of 1812, 41
Washington, George, 13, 14–15, 31 n. 1, 31 n. 11,
    36, 37, 113, 210, 281, 302
Washington Post, 85, 146, 172 n. 23, 275
Watergate babies, 87

Watergate scandal, 75, 87, 151, 178, 216–217, 304, 309
Waters, Maxine, 243, 250
Watson, Richard A., 138 n. 37
Wattenberg, Ben J., 138 n. 31, 173 n. 55
Wattenberg, Martin P., 31 n. 6, 106 n. 3, 135, 172 n. 22, 173 n.46
Weaver, James, 284
Weber, Lori M., 301 n. 48, 301 n. 49
Weber, Vin, 182
Web sites, 2–5
  AllPolitics, 146
  Congressional Quarterly, 147
  Democracy Place, 146
  Democratic State Committees, 205–206
  election-oriented, 146–147
  4 Politics, 146
  McLaughlin Group, 147
  politically oriented, 7
  for possible Bush running mates, 234
  Republican State Committees, 204–205
  Right Side of the Web, 146
  state parties, 201–203
  Turn Left, 147
Webster v. Reproductive Health Services, 75
Weicker, Lowell, 266, 294, 299
Weinberger, Caspar, 73
Weir, Margaret, 173 n. 51
Weisberg, Herbert F., 146, 172 n. 21
Welles, Gideon, 47
Wellstone, Paul, 243
Westlye, Mark C., 172 n. 20
Whig Party, 34, 43, 44–45, 177, 281
whip, 242
Whiskey Insurrection, 37
Whiskey Tax, 37
White, John Kenneth, 5, 6, 11 n. 1, 11 n. 13, 11 n. 21, 17, 32 n. 43, 54 n. 23, 83 n. 19, 83 n. 20, 83 n. 24, 87, 106 n. 8, 137 n. 8, 139 n. 47, 153, 155, 171 n. 4, 172 n. 35, 172 n. 39, 179, 207 n. 11, 300 n. 20, 301 n. 35

White, Leonard D., 83 n. 10
White, Theodore H., 124, 138 n. 30, 140, 171 n. 2
Whitman, Christine Todd, 164, 233
Whitmer, David, 199–200, 207 n. 37
Wicker, Tom, 134, 139 n. 42, 261 n. 10
Wilber, David, 11 n. 26, 173 n. 56
Williams, Walter, 77
Wilmot, David, 46
Wilmot Proviso, 45–46, 282
Wilson, James Q., 193–194
Wilson, Woodrow, 48, 63, 67–68, 70, 119, 240, 246, 261 n. 7, 261 n. 15, 287
Winger, Richard, 300 n. 4, 300 n. 5
winner-take-all single-member district, 268
Winograd, Morley, 134
Winograd Commission, 133–134
Wirt, William, 281
Wirth, Tim, 227–228
Wirthlin, Richard B., 141, 147, 153, 155, 171 n. 4, 172 n. 26
Wisconsin, 60
Witcover, Jules, 11 n. 20
Wolfinger, Raymond E., 172 n. 20
women's suffrage, 64–65, 68, 212
Woodburn, James Albert, 54 n. 29
Wooten, James, 137 n. 2, 137 n. 3, 137 n. 4, 137 n. 5
Workmen's Compensation Act, 56
Works Progress Administration (WPA), 70
World Wide Web. *See* Internet
WPA. *See* Works Progress Administration (WPA)
Wright, Jim, 254
Wyden, Ron, 181
Wyoming, 65

yellow dog Democrats, 79, 141
YWCA of the U. S. A., 75

Zayachkiwsky, Lynn, 11 n. 26, 173 n. 56